THE
STORY
of
ISLAMIC
ARCHITECTURE

The Story of Islamic Architecture

of

Islamic Architecture

Richard Yeomans

Garnet
PUBLISHING

CONTENTS

The Story of Islamic Architecture

Published by
Garnet Publishing Ltd
8 Southern Court, South Street
Reading RG1 4QS, UK

First edition 1999

ISBN 1 85964 108 3

British Library Cataloguing-in-Publication Data
A catalogue record for this book is available from the
British Library.

House Editor: *Emma Hawker*
Production Controller: *Nick Holroyd*
Senior Designer: *David Rose*
Designers: *Michael Hinks, Neil Collier*
Printed in Lebanon

FACING TITLE PAGE
Minarets in Cairo

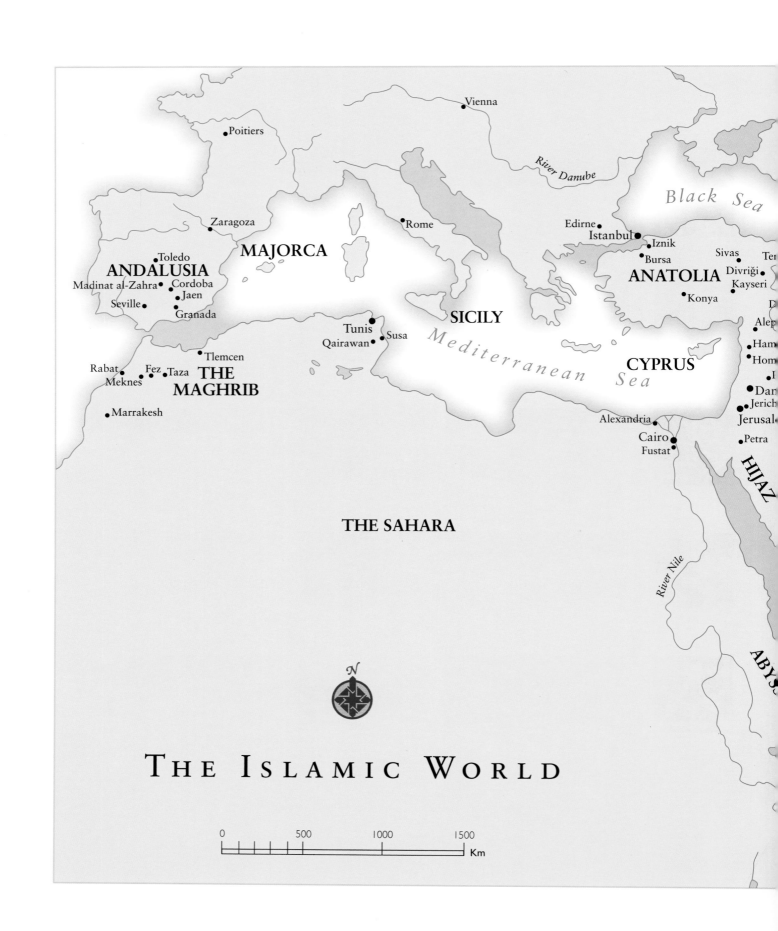

Vienna

Poitiers

River Danube

Black Sea

Rome

Zaragoza

Edirne
Istanbul
Iznik

Sivas
Ter

MAJORCA

Toledo
ANDALUSIA
Madinat al-Zahra · Cordoba
· Jaen
Seville ·
Granada

Bursa
Divriği
ANATOLIA
Kayseri
Konya

D

Alep

Ham

Tunis
Qairawan · Susa

SICILY

Mediterranean

Hom

Tlemcen
Rabat · Fez · Taza **THE**
Meknes **MAGHRIB**

CYPRUS
Sea

Dan
Jericho
Jerusal

Marrakesh

Alexandria

Petra

Cairo
Fustat

HIJAZ

THE SAHARA

River Nile

ABYS

N

THE ISLAMIC WORLD

0   500   1000   1500
|____|____|____|____|____|____|
                                    Km

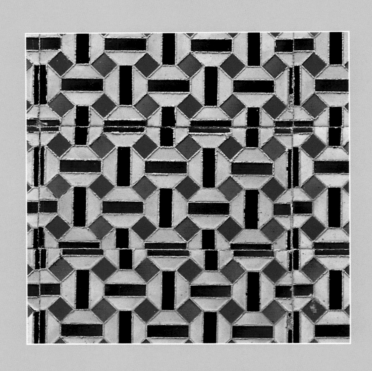

PREFACE

For the last twenty-five years I have been painting and drawing the architecture of the Middle East, but in the summer of 1995 I decided to give the paintbrush a rest and start writing. Hence this book which I have been thinking about but diffidently postponing for almost as long as I have been painting.

My purpose is to address the educated layman, the kind of person I had been teaching in the sphere of adult education, as well as my students at graduate and under-graduate level. This book is therefore the outcome of teaching, rather than of research, bringing together the notes and observations which have been the substance of my lectures and study tours. It is also a product of my painting, because it is driven by the same impulse – a desire to share and give permanent form to those pleasures and experiences the Muslim world has yielded over many years.

Until quite recently the subject of Islamic architec-ture was regarded as arcane, and experiencing it at first hand was a remote possibility for many people. There is now a growing interest in the subject across a wide spectrum of the public, and I have no difficulty in attract-ing students to extramural classes. This is mainly because travel opportunities to countries like Tunisia, Morocco, Egypt and Turkey are so much greater, and people have become more curious about the world of Islam. The architecture is far more accessible than it was, but informa-tion is still patchy. For the most part books are either too specialised – the province of archaeological reports – or too superficial. Many sources read like manuals, dryly dispensing information on size, dimension and building technology, without explaining architectural meaning or context. They ignore the aesthetic dimension and are frequently devoid of stylistic analysis. Equally there are those books that dwell exclusively on metaphysical interpretations and show scant regard for the mundane, functional and pragmatic nature of much architectural development. Such books are strong on mysticism but misrepresent both the spirit of the faith and the architec-ture by isolating them from their social base.

It is the aim of this book to address the middle ground, to explain the architecture within an historical framework and, where appropriate, to relate it to the wider religious, social and cultural context. In the process of writing I quickly discovered that it was history that provided me with the nuts and bolts of the narrative. Beginning with Muhammad's ministry, a sustaining narrative seemed to emerge, which finally persuaded me to borrow from E. H. Gombrich the word 'story' for my title – *The Story of Islamic Architecture*. As each chapter emerged, I felt I was episodically telling a story which lasts, more or less, until the end of the seventeenth century. It made sense to end geographically at the farthest point east and chronologically with the best of Mughal architecture. Thereafter the story is one of decline. It is a fascinating story, and compared to western architecture it is a remarkably coherent one, noted for its continuity, breadth and diversity. Of necessity it covers unfamiliar ground for the western reader, and for this reason I have provided two chapters of an introductory nature. The first gives a brief outline of the Muslim faith, and the second explains the theological attitudes that determine the form and function of Islamic art and archi-tecture. Thereafter the chapters form a straight historical narrative, looking at the genesis of Islamic architecture and then taking the reader chronologically through the various changes and regional developments. Points raised as generalities at the beginning are qualified and explained more fully in relation to specific buildings in subsequent chapters.

This book draws attention to the best-known monuments and the mainstream of Islamic achievement. It ignores the present and deals principally with the medieval world. I have had to be geographically selective, excluding Africa (except the North), South-East Asia and most of those countries where Islam today is making its greatest impact. Except for the discussion on the Prophet's mosque, Saudi Arabia receives scant attention, and countries like Yemen, which have evolved distinctive regional styles, have also been excluded. My selection has been conditioned by a number of factors. To begin with, I concentrated on those regions of the Muslim world I know – those that I have painted. Accessibility was another factor, so attention has been given to those countries that now attract western visitors. I have tried, however, not to allow these factors to upset the balance or override the quality of selection.

The relevance of a given argument has also determined the selection of material. For example, the chapters on Persia deal principally with tombs and mosques, with no mention of caravansarais. I chose to exclude them because my priority was to reveal the special religious climate of that country. In a number of instances, I have subordinated technical and structural analysis to political, religious and social considerations, because I felt these were of more interest to the general reader. Some buildings have been singled out for greater attention because of their point in the narrative and their chronological significance. Far more space has been devoted to the Great Mosque at Damascus than to the Taj Mahal, because there was so much to explain about the nature and evolution of the congregational mosque in the opening chapters. The Alhambra receives more attention than the Topkapı, because it presented the first opportunity of looking at a Muslim palace in detail. The contextual information and generalities established in earlier chapters are not repeated for similar building types in later chapters. For these reasons some of the more spectacular buildings, which arrive later on the scene, appear to have relatively less consideration than their more austere predecessors. Finally, publishing limitations make it impossible to illustrate all of the material I discuss in the text.

Although I was determined to avoid specialised vocabulary, I quickly concluded that an informed vocabulary is both necessary and desirable. Without a precise nomenclature one is forced to resort to long-winded, cumbersome and repetitious descriptions. In addition to architectural terms there are Islamic words that have to be accepted as a fact of life in this field of study. Familiarity with these words at an introductory stage is essential if the reader wishes to explore further. Finally, there is the problem of spelling. The transliteration of Arabic, Turkish and Persian words into English has not yet achieved a standard form. More pedantic conventions offer accuracy, but they involve a multiplicity of hyphens and apostrophes which add density to the text and impede the flow of the reader. For this reason I have avoided using too many diacritical marks and have sacrificed accuracy for simplicity. The spelling of so many place and proper names across a complex linguistic field has been tedious and difficult; I have done my best to ensure accuracy.

The writing of this book has been an intense retrospective exercise. It embodies a long-term accumulation of field-work, reading and observation, and the main task over the last two years has simply been writing the material up. In that time I have returned to Syria, Egypt, Turkey and Jerusalem, visited a number of museums and worked in the isolation of my studio, relying for the most part on my personal library, slide collection and lecture notes. It has essentially been a solitary affair without dialogue, discussion and feedback from other academics in the field. There has been no lengthy correspondence or recent access to specialised libraries and archives. For this reason my acknowledgements do not involve the usual list of researchers, academics, librarians and archivists. However I would like to acknowledge my long-term indebtedness to those individuals and institutions that have made this book possible.

I must first thank my immediate family, my wife, Ann, and sons, Jonathan and Thomas, whose holidays have frequently been blighted by visiting one mosque too far. Also, in the writing of this book, they have suffered my reclusive behaviour and irritability with patience and fortitude. Four institutions have been significant in providing me with the short, medium and long-term wherewithal for this undertaking. I am grateful to the University of Warwick for giving me moral support, as well as time and money through sabbatical leave and the resources of their Research and Innovations Fund. I feel indebted to the University of London, School of Oriental and African Studies. It was the teacher-fellowship they offered me in the mid-1970s, and the exposure to such a wide body of scholars, including Geza Fehervari, that provided me with the academic foundation for much of this work. In a more indirect way, the University of Newcastle-on-Tyne provided me with an excellent liberal art education, which encouraged imaginative exploration beyond the confines of art. Finally my thanks to Messrs J. P. M. Jones, R. Johnstone, P. N. Lees, G. Metcalfe, J. W. Taylor and F. Williamson, formerly of

Leamington College for Boys, who nurtured my interests across the arts and provided the basic disciplinary skills.

In many ways this is an eclectic work, and I have drawn liberally from a number of leading scholars who are acknowledged in the text and whose works I include in my bibliography. Of these I would particularly like to single out D. Behrens-Abouseif, S. S. Blair, J. M. Bloom, K. A. C. Creswell, Richard Ettinghausen, Godfrey Goodwin, Oleg Grabar, Robert Hillenbrand, John D. Hoag, R. A. Jairazbhoy and G. H. R. Tillotson. On a personal level I am particularly grateful for the kindness and interest of the late Richard Ettinghausen, whom I encountered at the Freer Gallery, Washington, when I

was a student. His act of hospitality was the first of many which I have received during the course of numerous journeys investigating the art and architecture of Islam. My travels in the Muslim world have been marked at every stage with courtesy and countless offers of hospitality by ordinary people, often in the most stricken circumstances. Some I vividly recall, like the proprietor of the Palestine Hotel in Ma'an, and Mehmet the Istanbul fisherman, but the rest are those anonymous individuals who offer you accommodation, pay for your meal, fuss over your children or stand you a cup of tea from some distant corner of the tea house.

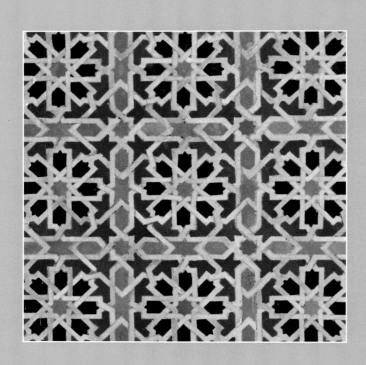

INTRODUCTION

THE PROPHET'S MINISTRY AND THE MUSLIM FAITH

THE MOSQUE

There is probably no better place to observe how a living faith like Islam functions in its architectural setting than in the courtyard and prayer hall of the Great Mosque at Damascus. It is also the most appropriate place to begin a history of architecture, because it was built in 715 by the Caliph al-Walid and is the oldest congregational mosque in the Muslim world. Despite its antiquity, what can be observed in the mosque today is of great significance, because it sustains an extraordinary continuity of worship and social behaviour reaching back nearly 1,400 years to the Prophet Muhammad's own mosque in Medina. Islam's past and present are vividly affirmed in this building, not so much in the monumental mass and space of its architecture but in the devotion of its congregation and the diverse social activities which mark its day-to-day use. The Damascus Mosque reflects many of Islam's core values and functions, and for this reason it is perhaps appropriate to begin as an observer and then consider the historical events that explain it.

As we enter the courtyard of the Great Mosque we encounter informal gatherings of families passing the time of day in conversation and taking part in various forms of social intercourse. Occasionally the tranquillity of this space is agitated by the activity of excited children who use sections of it as a playground, oblivious to its ancient solemnity and grandeur. Parts of the mosque courtyard are transformed into a crèche in order that mothers can shop in the nearby bazaars, leaving their children under the protective eye of family friends. The mosque is set in the traditional commercial heart of the city, and with the exception of children and criss-crossing pedestrian traffic, it generally provides a spacious oasis of peace and calm, in marked contrast to the frenetic activity of the noisy, narrow streets of the bazaars, which crowd in near its

RIGHT
Damascus, the Great Mosque

OPPOSITE
Damascus, the prayer hall
of the Great Mosque

perimeter walls. Away from family groups, worshippers perform their preparatory ablutions at the courtyard fountain, while others seek rest and seclusion in the shade of the arcades, and students do their homework or find solace for examination revision.

Inside the prayer hall of the mosque learning activity is more structured and directed as children attend Qur'an classes, and elsewhere adults sitting crossed-legged on the floor gather themselves less formally around a number of religious teachers. The peace of the mosque prompts some to lie full length on the floor and sleep, while others find an isolated space for private prayer and meditation. Some pray with due veneration at the domed shrine near the transept, which houses the relic of John the Baptist's head. Just off the courtyard is another shrine containing the relic of the head of Husain (the grandson of the Prophet), and Shi'ite pilgrims gather here to make their lamentations. At the set prayers, five times daily, the congregation will form into long rows looking towards the *qibla* wall, which is aligned on the side facing Mecca, and say the prescribed prayers made up of recitations

accompanied by the ritual postures of standing, bending and prostration. The prayer leader, or *imam*, will chant the liturgy in front of an architectural feature forming a semicircular niche in the *qibla* wall known as the *mihrab*. Flanking the *mihrab* is the *minbar*, a domed triangular pulpit, reached by a flight of steps, from which traditionally the sermon, or *khutbar*, is preached at the larger congregational gathering for the Friday noonday prayers.

During the prayers the mood is serene and elevating, but at other times the Damascus Mosque, despite its architectural grandeur, has a casual workaday atmosphere. Unlike many Christian churches, this mosque is constantly in daily use on both a formal and informal level and is very close to, and embroiled in, the daily lives of ordinary people. There is little that is remote, awesome or intimidating about this building which has served the Muslim population for centuries. The mosque principally addresses the spiritual and educational needs of the community, but it is also a meeting place which makes possible those wider social actions and responsibilities that characterise Islam's collective identity. In Islam the

Damascus, the *mihrab* and the *minbar* of the Great Mosque

religious and secular domains are not separated, and it is here, in its routine functioning, that one can observe the warp and weft of religious and secular life woven into one complex composite fabric. The Great Mosque in Damascus bears witness to a fundamental religious and social continuum which is also manifest in Islam's architecture. In order to understand this, it is necessary to go back to the beginning and look at the roots of religion through a brief account of the Prophet's ministry, the sacred scripture, pillars of faith, law and mysticism.

THE MINISTRY

The Prophet Muhammad, son of Abdallah and Amina of the Quraysh tribe, was born in Mecca in approximately 570. Mecca was a thriving city and commercial centre, being the hub of the Arabian caravan business, which nurtured those vital trade routes linking the Byzantine Empire to the north, with South Asia and Africa. In matters of trade, the Meccans were extremely sophisticated, and their mercantile economy touched all classes of society. Mecca was also an important religious centre, where pilgrims would gather and worship at a large sanctuary containing numerous stone idols and a cubic structure known as the Ka'ba, famed for its sacred stone. Pre-Islamic Arabia had a polytheist religion, involving a complex mixture of animism and litholatry, in which idol worship played a major role, and trees and stones were venerated and invested with supernatural powers. The Ka'ba itself was said to have contained three hundred and sixty idols, including images of the patriarchs Abraham and Ishmael. Arabia also had settled Jewish communities, and many heterodox Christians of the Nestorian and Monophysite persuasion. Commerce and religion coalesced in Mecca, and the annual pilgrimage, which at times resembled a trade fair, provided plenty of opportunity for commercial transaction. It was Muhammad's destiny to challenge this lucrative alliance between the pagan gods and mammon.

Muhammad's family were respected members of the Banu Hashim clan, and a number of his predecessors had held religious office, serving the sanctuary by dispensing food and water to pilgrims. His father died before he was born, and a few years later his mother died leaving Muhammad an orphan at the age of six. He was thus among the weakest in Arabian society, and for this reason he was taken under the protection of his clan by his uncle Abu Talib. Little is known about his childhood, except one legend that describes a visit to Bosra, in Syria, where the young Muhammad encountered the Nestorian monk Bahira who identified the mark of prophecy between the boy's shoulders and predicted his future greatness. Early experience travelling with the caravans to Syria, gave him the necessary background to pursue his own career as a merchant, and he advanced his position when, at the age of twenty-five, he married and formed a business partnership with a wealthy widow called Khadija. For the next fifteen years Muhammad ran a successful business and was generally regarded as a respected citizen whose sound judgement and mediation were often sought. He would frequently take time out to seek refuge in the hills and caves around Mecca, where he would pray and meditate. It was on Mount Hira in 610 that Muhammad received the first messages from God through the intermediary of the Angel Gabriel, and it was the advent of these revelations which marked the beginning of his ministry.

These revelations, which he received throughout his life, form the substance of the Qur'an, Islam's holiest scripture. At first Muhammad doubted the authenticity of these messages, but further revelation, and the support of Khadija, helped him come to terms with the situation. Thus began his ministry, and from a small core of converts within his own family circle and friends the Muslim community gradually expanded to include many young people from influential families, as well as other supporters who were socially weaker and fell outside the protection of the Quraysh clans. The revelations which Muhammad passed on to his followers proclaimed God's goodness, power and providence, and the Prophet's emerging message was clearly monotheist. The revelations also called upon individuals to demonstrate their gratitude for God's providence through acts of faith and worship, as well as to show generosity and charity by giving support to the poorer and weaker members of the community.

This message was not well received by those who occupied the most wealthy and powerful positions in Arab society, because they feared Muhammad's increasing political power, which grew with his prophetic status. Although nothing in his revelation weakened the religious status of Mecca as such, his message seemed to attack the fundamental beliefs, traditions and commercial values by which the people lived. They did not like being told that material values had corrupted their religious practices, and greed had led to indifference towards the plight of women, the widowed, the poor, orphaned and outcast. Muhammad's monotheist preaching was also seen as an attack on the numerous cults and shrines outside Mecca and had a knock-on effect on pilgrimage and trade networks. So Muhammad and his followers encountered growing hostility and persecution, until he was obliged to leave Mecca with his followers and settle in the northern oasis of Yathrib (later to be known as Medina).

When the Prophet migrated with his followers from Mecca to Medina in the year 622, he found that it was no longer sufficient to be a charismatic and visionary preacher. His ministry changed dramatically, and circumstances obliged him to take on the political leadership of the community, defend it, establish a new political and social order and find ways for his followers to be economically self-sufficient in a strange environment. With the migration (the *hijra*), the Muslims had been transplanted from the relative security of a mercantile economy in Mecca to the uncertainties of an agrarian economy in the oasis of Medina, where they had no land and little experience of agricultural life. In Mecca Muhammad had been the leader of a persecuted minority, but in Medina he had to add to his religious authority the roles of statesman, diplomat, economist, law-giver, arbitrator, teacher and military commander. He was compelled to become a man of action, and he quickly had to deal with the pressing daily needs of a complex and insecure society. It is for this reason that Islam, from the outset, became a religion concerned not only with the spiritual life but also with the material welfare of the community. This duality of spiritual and practical values defines and characterises much of the ethos of Islam that is so vividly manifest in the Great Mosque at Damascus.

The Prophet's political role changed and expanded as he began to take responsibility not only for his own Muslim emigrants but also for the other Arab clans in the Medinan confederation. He had been invited a year earlier by the Medinan chiefs who wanted him to act as a mediator among warring factions within the oasis, as a religious authority and arbitrator, although his position as head of the Muslim emigrants was clearly recognised and accepted. His role very quickly involved political management, for it was obvious that the social and political discord in Medina could only be remedied by the unifying power and vision of the new religious faith and social order that he was forging. Before long, all of the disparate Arab factions, except the Jews, united under Islam, and this gathering of the clans under one banner established the genesis of the Muslim nation which, after his death, was to extend far beyond the confines of the Arabian Peninsula.

In addition to political responsibility, Muhammad assumed military leadership, because he not only had to defend his community but also to take a long-term view of his relationship with Mecca. Conflict with Mecca was inevitable: the migrant Muslims were landless in a community that lived off the land, so they indulged in time-honoured *razzias*, or raids on the Meccan caravans. Meccan retaliation caused a number of skirmishes, which eventually led to the set battle of Badr, in which a small Muslim force routed a larger Meccan army. The psychological impact of the battle was enormous; Mecca was humiliated, and God had delivered the Muslims from the enemy. In the next major battle, that of Uhud, the Muslims did not fare so well, and could have suffered a serious defeat had the Meccans not failed to follow up their advantage. The battle ended in a stalemate, with the Muslims taking the bulk of the casualties. The final conflict was the siege of Medina, in which the Meccans' attempt to capture the city with an overwhelming force was thwarted by the device of a defensive ditch, which was an innovation in Arab warfare and something that the Meccans failed to come to terms with. After much rhetoric and several assaults on the ditch, the Meccans abandoned the siege after two weeks. Muhammad's position gradually became unassailable, as numerous tribes from the region joined him and converted to Islam, and it was only a matter of time before Muhammad moved on Mecca itself.

As a diplomat, Muhammad aimed in the long term to win over, rather than to conquer, the Meccans and the rest of the Arabian tribes. His only diplomatic failure was with the Jews of Medina, who rejected conversion and took a neutral stance during his most bitter conflicts with Mecca. When it was suspected that the Jews had played a less than neutral role during the siege of Medina, many were executed and the rest expelled from the oasis. Despite hostilities, Muhammad had established diplomatic ties with Mecca and soon became involved in negotiations which culminated in the treaty of al-Hudabiyah in 628. This allowed the Muslims to make the pilgrimage to Mecca the following year, and when an incident subsequently broke the terms of that treaty, Muhammad marched on Mecca in 630 and entered the city, meeting hardly any resistance. He cleansed the sanctuary of its idols and dedicated it and the Ka'ba to Islam. The Meccans were finally won over, and quickly all the south Arabian tribes rallied to his cause. Muhammad returned to Medina, and by the time of his death in 632 he had more or less united the whole of the Arabian Peninsula under Islam.

Muhammad's political, military and diplomatic skills gave birth to the Muslim nation, but what secured its enduring success was the religious and social code that underpinned it. Muhammad had created and consolidated not just a political entity but a community with a religious and social code which provided those core beliefs and values that guaranteed its cohesion and identity. Through God's will and commands, Muhammad had established a structure of belief and morality which ultimately became enshrined in the religious law of Islam (the *sharia*). The *sharia* is God's all-embracing law, reaching into every aspect of life, determining codes of religious practice, criminal law, commercial law, family law and even rules concerning manners and personal hygiene. In Islam, law and morality are indivisible, and it was through the legal regulation of the community that Muhammad engineered a social revolution which offered protection to those who had been exploited and marginalised under the old regime. The status of women was raised, divorce laws reformed, rules of inheritance established, infanticide abolished and alms-giving was instituted to ensure provision for the poor and weak. It is law, rather than theology, that has dominated the intellectual life of Islam, and it is law that has shaped the community, reflecting those very practical concerns that characterised the Prophet's ministry. It is this that explains that complex warp and weft of religious and secular life described in the Great Mosque at Damascus.[1]

SECTARIANISM

When Muhammad died in 632 he had succeeded in uniting the whole of Arabian society under one religious faith. With his death there was a crisis, and every likelihood that the Muslim community (the *umma*) would disintegrate and fragment into the old tribal confederations. It was immediately decided to elect a successor, a *khalifa*, or caliph, who would take up the leadership of the *umma*. Abu Bakr, one of Islam's first converts and one of Muhammad's most loyal companions, was chosen as first caliph because he was regarded as the most able. He was elected as a paid public servant, and his role was essentially political, although it was also his duty as caliph to uphold and defend the faith. From the outset, Abu Bakr made it clear that he claimed no divine power, that Muhammad was the last of the Prophets and the Qur'an the final revelation. The era of revelation and prophecy was over, and the light of faith was henceforth to be guided by the Qur'an and those best qualified for religious office. The election of Abu Bakr was, however, contentious, and a significant faction (the Shiat Ali) championed Ali, Muhammad's cousin and son-in-law, as the rightful successor. This group, better known as the Shi'ites, believed that spiritual leadership was of the essence, and that only Ali and his successors (the Imams) could inherit the religious authority and divine wisdom (*nas*) of the Prophet. In so doing, they initiated the notion of divine leadership and the subsequent doctrine of the Imamate.

Ali eventually became the fourth caliph, but he was assassinated, and instead of the caliphate passing on to his sons, Hassan or Husain, as the Shi'ites demanded, it went to Mu'awiya, the founder of the Umayyad dynasty. Thus it was that Sunni Islam became the official religion of state, and Shi'ite Islam a focus of opposition challenging the legitimacy of the caliphate. Sunni Islam is the faith of the majority which regards Shi'ites as heterodox. The Shi'ites nevertheless represent a significant minority, and in some areas of the Muslim world, like Iran, Shi'ism has become the state religion. Shi'ism, perhaps influenced by Christian and Jewish thought, believes in a messianic figure, called the Mahdi, emerging from the Imamate. This belief is expressed in several branches of Shi'ism, of which the Twelvers is the largest. Their adherents believe that the twelfth Imam, Muhammad al-Muntazar, who disappeared in Samarra in 880, will reappear as the Mahdi and rule the world in peace and justice. The other main sect, the Severners, known as the Ishma'ilis, believe that Ishmail, the elder son of the sixth Imam, Jafar al-Sadiq, was the legitimate Imam who will return as the Mahdi. Although Shi'ism has spawned a number of Islam's more extreme sects, at a popular level it does have something in common with Christianity. There is an intense veneration of the holy family: Muhammad, his daughter, Fatima, her sons, Hassan and Husain, as well as their descendants, the holy Imams. They believe in the second coming, and the remembrance of the martyrdom of Husain, in its emotional expression, bears strong parallels to the Christian Passion.

THE FIVE PILLARS OF ISLAM

The first pillar of Islam is belief (*iman*), and each Muslim must profess the *shahada*: 'There is no God but God, and Muhammad is the Prophet of God'. (The Shi'ite *shahada* is slightly different '[I bear witness that] There is one God; Muhammad is his Prophet and Ali is the friend of God'.) There is only one God and He is the transcendent creator, sustainer and judge. He is omnipotent, and omniscient, and has ninety-nine names. One of the most beautiful expressions of God's being is contained in the 'Throne' verse of Chapter (*Sura*) two ('The Cow') in the Qur'an:

> God – there is no god but He, the Living, the Self-subsistent. Slumber seizeth Him not, neither sleep. To Him belongeth whatsoever is in the Heavens and whatsoever is in the Earth. Who is there who should intercede with Him save by His will? He knoweth what is present with men and what shall befall them, and nought of His knowledge do they comprehend, save what He willeth. His Throne is wide as the Heavens and the Earth, and the keeping of them wearieth Him not. And He is the High, the Mighty One (Sura 2:255).

God is both transcendent and immanent, and alongside those attributes that convey His awesome, omnipotent and judgemental personality must be balanced those of providence, compassion and mercy. God's nearness to humanity is vividly expressed in the following Qur'anic verse beloved by Sufi mystics:

> We created man. We know the promptings of his soul, and we are closer to him than the vein of his neck (*Sura* 50:16).

Another striking passage from the Qur'an dealing with God's being is the magnificent 'Light' verse which inspires mystic contemplation, as well as underpinning much of the metaphysical content of the visual arts.

> God is the Light of the Heavens and of the Earth. The similitude of His Light is as it were a niche wherein is a lamp, the lamp within a glass, the glass as though it were a pearly star. It is lit from a blessed Tree, an olive-tree neither of the East nor West, the oil whereof were like to shine even though no fire were applied to it; Light upon Light; God guideth to His Light whom He will (*Sura* 24:36).

In addition to belief in God, Muslims must accept the prophetic tradition. It is a common misapprehension among many that Muhammad founded a new religion. Muslim belief denies this and asserts that Islam is the original, and true religion, in which God revealed his purpose to humanity through the angels to the prophets, beginning with Adam and ending with Muhammad. It was Muhammad's role to reinstate and reaffirm this, as well as receive the final revelation. This was the great supernatural event in his life, and he worked no miracles and possessed no divine power. All the Old Testament prophets are venerated by Muslims, and twenty-eight are mentioned in the Qur'an. Among those venerated are Jesus, Zachariah and John the Baptist and the Virgin Mary. The Holy Family occupies a place of honour within the faith, and there are more references to the Virgin Mary in the Qur'an than in the New Testament. The Old and New Testaments are recognised as holy scripture, but it is believed that these are now abrogated and superseded by God's final revelation in the Qur'an. Muslims respect the Jews and Christians as People of the Book, and they have traditionally held a protected position within Muslim society, but nevertheless Muslims assert that they have transgressed from the true path of faith.

It was the Angel Gabriel who transmitted the Qur'an to Muhammad, and angels were used as messengers to convey God's word to the earlier prophets. Angels occupy a significant supernatural plane within traditional Muslim belief, as do devils, or *jinn*, who lead humanity astray. Belief in Heaven, Hell and the Last Judgement is fundamental, and many of the most powerful Meccan Suras, such as 'The Cataclysm', deal with this.

The second pillar of Islam is prayer (*salat*), which is said five times daily: at daybreak, noon, afternoon, sunset and in the early night. The prayer is recited with set movements and postures, known as *rak'ah*, facing Mecca, and normally performed congregationally in the mosque. On Friday, the Muslim equivalent to the Sabbath, the major congregational prayers take place at noon, and all the faithful are expected to attend. Before any of the prayers

take place, ritual ablutions are necessary, washing the hands, face, arms and feet. 'Cleanliness,' as the Prophet said, 'is half the faith'. If it is not possible to attend the mosque, then the prayers can be performed anywhere. Women usually pray at home, and travellers will pray on the road, or wherever they can put down their prayer mats and determine the direction of Mecca. It is suggested that the invention of the astrolabe, and the development of astronomical and navigational knowledge by the Arabs, was prompted by the necessity to establish the direction of prayer through the observation of the stars.

The third pillar of Islam is fasting, which takes place from sunrise to sunset during the lunar month of Ramadan. During these hours it is forbidden to eat, drink

The Ka'ba at Mecca

or indulge in sexual intercourse. Not everyone is expected to fast, and exemptions are made for the sick, pregnant and nursing mothers, young children and travellers. With the exception of children, those exempted on such conditions are expected to make up the fast at some other time. The fourth pillar of Islam is alms-giving, or *zakat*, where it is expected that one-fortieth of one's income should be given to the poor and needy.

The fifth pillar of Islam is the pilgrimage to Mecca (*hajj*), which is expected of every adult once in a lifetime (excepting the disabled and those without the means). The pilgrimage rites, performed in Mecca and other locations in the neighbourhood, were established by Muhammad during his Farewell Pilgrimage in 632, when he received a premonition of his impending death. Before entering Mecca, pilgrims must sever their worldly connections and renounce their identity, class, nationality and all those outward signs that divide humanity. They perform the ablutions and men enter a state of purity (*ihram*) by shaving their heads and wearing the seamless pilgrimage robes (women cover their hair and their faces are unveiled). The pilgrimage in Mecca involves the circumambulation of the Ka'ba (the house built by Abraham) and running seven times between the two nearby small hills of Safa and Marwa, to commemorate Hagar's search for water in the desert for her son, Ishmael. The climax is the massing of all pilgrims for the congregational prayers, and the contemplation of God at Mount Arafat, which are said until sunset. The pilgrims then spend the night at Muzdalifah and proceed to Mina for three nights, where the ritual stoning of the devils takes place, and the pilgrimage formally ends with the sacrifice of sheep and camels. The sacrifice at Mina, in memory of Abraham's intended sacrifice of Ishmael (not Isaac in the Arab tradition), is celebrated across the whole Muslim world as the festival of Eid al-Adha.[2]

SACRED SCRIPTURE: THE QUR'AN AND HADITH

The Muslim faith asserts that the Qur'an is God's uncreated word conveyed through the Angel Gabriel to the Prophet Muhammad, who is the last of the prophets. Muhammad received revelations throughout his life,

and they were initially committed to memory and then written down and arranged according to their length, rather than chronology. The final canonical form of the Qur'an was completed during the caliphate of Othman in approximately 650. This arrangement of the Qur'an, according to chapter (*sura*) length, beginning with the longest, bears no relation to the sequence of the revelation, because the longer *suras* tend to reflect his later ministry, where the content is more complex and legalistic. It is generally acknowledged, for instance, that the first revelation is 'The Blood Clots', which appears as *sura* ninety-six out of a total of one hundred and fourteen. The distribution of the *suras* therefore falls broadly in reverse of their chronological order of revelation. The revelations closely address the changing patterns and circumstances of Muhammad's ministry. At the beginning he was very much the outsider and preacher, appealing to the Quraysh to abandon their polytheism and fulfil their traditional patriarchal duties. The early revelations frequently warn of God's wrath to come and have a rhetorical grandeur which is unsurpassed in their visionary, awesome and apocalyptic expression.

> When the sun ceases to shine; when the stars fall down and the mountains are blown away; when camels big with young are left untended and the wild beasts are brought together; when the seas are set alight and men's souls are re-united; when the infant girl, buried alive, is asked for which crime she was thus slain; when the records of men's deeds are laid open and the heaven is stripped bare; when Hell burns fiercely and Paradise is brought near: then each soul shall know what it has done (*Sura* 81:1–14).

Poetic, transcendental and visionary passages like this provide the keynote for much of the content of Islamic art. The celestial imagery in this, and other Qur'anic verses, establishes a cosmic vision that ultimately finds its expression in the infinitely complex visual geometry of Islamic art. Unlike the Old and New Testaments, the Qur'an contains little in the way of a sustained narrative or history and does not lend itself to illustration, only to illumination. Nevertheless, much of its striking poetic imagery runs deep in Islamic art, despite Islam's rejection of figurative imagery. For example, the

Qur'anic vision of Paradise, expressed so vividly in such *suras* as 'The Merciful', provides a fundamental theme in Islamic art which underpins the floral patterns of arabesque, woven carpets, mosaic decoration and the layout of gardens.

The transformation of the Muslim community in Medina is clearly reflected in the Qur'an, where the sublime and poetic aspects of the Meccan *suras* give way to the longer, prosaic Medinan *suras* dealing with mundane, social and legal matters. These *suras* are not susceptible to visual interpretation or illustration. They emphatically demonstrate the necessity to establish solid, practical ground rules for religious, political and social conduct. The Medinan revelations therefore become correspondingly legalistic, with large sections, like the following, concerned with marriage and family law:

> You are forbidden to take in marriage your mothers, your daughters, your sisters, your paternal and maternal aunts, the daughters of your brothers and sisters, your foster-mothers, your foster sisters, the mothers of your wives, your step-daughters who are in your charge, born of the wives with whom you have lain (it is no offence for you to marry your step-daughters if you have not consummated your marriage with their mothers), and the wives of your own begotten sons. Henceforth you are also forbidden to take in marriage two sisters at one and the same time (*Sura* 4:23).

The Qur'an establishes the theological groundplan of faith as well as its social and legal basis. It reveals an extraordinary manifold of metaphysical and mundane values and meanings, correspondingly expressed in poetic and prosaic language and, like the religious practice observed in the Damascus Mosque, presents us with a fluid continuum between the spiritual and practical domains. A corresponding visual continuum also exists in the architecture of Islam, where the distinction between religious and secular form and function is frequently interchangeable and indeterminate.

The *hadith*, meaning tradition, is the other source of sacred scripture and is comparable to the Christian gospels in so far that its content presents detailed accounts of the Prophet's life, ministry, example, wisdom and words. The *hadith* gives accumulated accounts of the Prophet's life transmitted through his family, companions and followers, and the quality and reliability of this transmission, known as *isnad*, has been a major preoccupation of Muslim scholarship. As the Prophet's life and example provides a model for the community, and the subsequent basis for the religious law of Islam (*sharia*), there was an absolute necessity to guarantee the accuracy and authenticity of this material. Unlike the Qur'an, *hadith* material has never been assembled into one universal, canonical form. Consensus has not prevailed, and each law school has its own preferences. *Hadith* transmissions are broadly categorised as 'genuine', 'good' or 'weak', although other finer subdivisions have proliferated over centuries of scholarship.

The *hadith* provides explanation, elaboration and detail, which is often lacking in the Qur'an. For example, the Qur'an establishes general guidelines, such as the necessity to pray five times daily, but how you pray, the ritual of prayer, and the necessary acts of preparatory ablution, are set out at some length in the *hadith*, as the following passage illustrates:

> Abu Hurairah reported that a man entered the mosque, and the Messenger of Allah (peace and blessings of Allah be on him) was sitting in the corner of the mosque; . . . he said, 'teach me Oh Messenger of Allah!' He said: 'When thou risest for the prayer, then perform the ablution in a right manner, then turn thy face towards the *Qibla*, then say *Allahu Akba*, then recite what thou canst afford of the Qur'an, then bow down until thou art at rest in bowing down (*ruku*'), then rise thyself up until thou art firm in the standing posture, then fall down in prostration until thou art at rest in prostration, then rise thyself up until thou art at rest in sitting; and according to one report, then rise thyself up until thou art firm in the standing posture; then do this in the whole of thy prayer' (Bukhari 4:10).[3]

It is principally through these accounts that we can reconstruct in some detail the daily life of the community and those actions of the Prophet that established the precedence for the *sharia*.[4]

THE SHARIA

The *sharia*, rather than theology, has always dominated much of the intellectual life of Islam, and this reflects not just the practical features of the Prophet's ministry but the nature of Qur'anic revelation. The content of the *sharia* covers, among other things, religious duty, marriage and family law, contracts, inheritance, criminal law and judicial procedure and evidence. The Qur'an is the primary source of the *sharia* because it reveals God's will, and His commands are immutable and unquestionable. In its general precepts and injunctions, the Qur'an establishes the principles of the *sharia* but, as in the case of prayer, not always in sufficient detail to deliver its practical implementation. Supplementary material in the *hadith* is invariably necessary to do this, and if this proves insufficient then reasoning and consensus also have to be employed. The *sharia* is therefore based on revelation and reason and formulated on the four-fold basis of the Qur'an, *hadith*, consensus (*ijma*) and analogical reasoning (*qiyas*). For example, the Qur'an explicitly forbids wine drinking but says nothing about whisky. In order to formulate a view on whisky drinking, a jurist would then consult *hadith*, and although no mention of whisky can be found here there is sufficient condemnation of intoxication to form a consensus that whisky, like wine, should be forbidden.

> Jabir said, 'The messenger of Allah (peace and blessings be upon him), said, "Of whatever thing a large quantity intoxicates, even a small quantity is prohibited" ' (Abu Dawud 25:5).

If, on any given point of law, there is no established view in the Qur'an or *hadith*, then jurists must form a judgement on the basis of consensus arrived at by analogical reasoning. One saying of the Prophet, 'My community will never make a judgement in error', is sufficient to embody *ijma*, formulated by the learned authorities (*ulama*), as one of the pillars of the *sharia*. The development of the *sharia* was the main preoccupation of jurists during the first centuries of Islam, and by the tenth century the *sharia* became fixed and immutable. The exercise of free reasoning (*ijtihad*) was forbidden, and the 'gates of *ijtihad* were closed'. Nevertheless, the *sharia* is

not monolithic, and four separate schools emerged, which are all regarded within Sunni Islam as orthodox. These schools (*madhahib*), named after their founders, are the *Maliki, Hanbali, Shafi'i* and *Hanafi*.[5]

SUFISM

The dogmatic image of Islam, which the West frequently perceives, is due usually to the excessive emphasis placed on the *sharia* by vociferous clerics of a conservative persuasion. Islam cannot be presented or propagated in terms of the regulatory nature of the *sharia*, and attempts to do so lead to a partial and misleading view of the faith. Islam has a long and deep mystical tradition, which is expressed through the doctrine of the Sufis. The *sharia* represents what the Sufis call the *exoteric*, or easily accessible, path of Islam, and many believe that following this alone cannot guarantee salvation. Obeying an externally imposed discipline, and observing the letter of the law, frequently ignores the heart and spirit of the faith. The *esoteric* path is that of the Sufi, who would claim that the love of God, and the soul's ultimate mystical union with God, transcends the *sharia*. Sufism has its origins in the early asceticism practised by those Muslims who had come into contact with and been influenced by Christian anchorites. Asceticism is regarded by Sufis as just one stage on a long spiritual journey in which the individual self is lost and the universal self found. Such views are close to Neo-Platonism – and Buddhism – and Sufism acknowledges its common mystical ground with other faiths. There is a strong ecumenical aspect to Sufism, which accepts that all faiths are like the spokes of a wheel pointing to one common centre.

Many Sufis have a pantheistic view of God and believe that He reveals Himself principally through His creation. This view is expressed in one frequently quoted *hadith*: 'I was a hidden treasure and I desired to be known; therefore I created the creation in order that I might be known'. Above all, they believe that it is only within the human heart that God can be fully known and apprehended, and they invoke the following *hadith* to support this: 'Consult thy heart, and thou wilt hear the secret ordinance of God proclaimed by the heart's inward knowledge, which is the real faith and divinity'. The famous 'Light' verse in the Qur'an, in which God is compared to a mosque lamp hanging in the niche, uses the niche as a metaphor of the human heart illuminated by God's divine light. Such expressions of God's indwelling nature within the heart, and nearer than the jugular vein, bring God closer to humanity and explain the popular following of much Sufi doctrine, because it ameliorates the remote and awesome aspect of a transcendental God conveyed in more orthodox circles.

A number of Sufis have identified the contradiction between the exoteric and esoteric paths, represented by the *sharia* on the one hand and the promptings of inner experience on the other. Niffari, a tenth-century mystic, writes that, 'My exoteric revelation does not support my esoteric revelation'. For many initiates the *sharia* represents a lower order of religious experience, conditioned by blind reason and the manacles of tradition, which obstruct the path of true enlightenment. For this reason there has always been some tension between Sufism and conservative Islam, and in order to counter the rigidity of many orthodox zealots Sufis have occasionally been moved deliberately to flout the *sharia*. This antinomian response has led to some of the so-called lawless dervish orders. However, it has been the task of the greatest Sufi teachers to reconcile these contradictions. Hujwiri, a Persian mystic writing in the eleventh century, says that 'The Law without Truth is ostentation, and the Truth without Law is hypocrisy. Their mutual relation may be compared to body and spirit.' The greatest of all the great reconcilers was the theologian and philosopher al-Ghazali (1058–1111), who abandoned his pre-eminent position as professor of theology and law at the Nizamiya *madrasa* (theological college) in Baghdad and devoted himself to the study of mysticism. His great work, *The Revival of the Religious Sciences*, to paraphrase R. A. Nicholson, made orthodoxy mystical and mysticism orthodox.[6]

Sufism accepts that the language of theology has its limitations and cannot match the majesty of its concepts. When expressing the higher states of mystical awareness and experience only the language of poetry and art can suffice. Mystical notions of divine love have to be expressed symbolically, ambiguously and metaphorically through poetry. The great Sufi poets, such as Omar Khayyam, Rumi, Sadi, Attar and Nizami, communicate mystical experience through the vehicle of love poetry, in which erotic love and wine drinking become metaphors for divine love and ecstasy. The following verse from Omar Khayyam's *Rubaiyat* expresses metaphorically the soul's yearning for the 'inebriate' state of ecstasy:

> I cannot live without wine,
> Without the cup's draught I cannot carry my body.
> I am the slave of that breath in which the saki says
> 'Take one more cup' – and I cannot do so.

There are no such vivid, figurative metaphors and symbols of divine love and ecstasy in the visual arts, although love poetry finds its parallel in Arab and Persian manuscripts illustrating such love stories as Bayad and Riyad, or Majnun and Laila. In the visual arts, Sufi metaphysical values find a more appropriate expression through the language of abstraction. Here such notions and feelings of transcendence, unity and harmony are expressed, as well as induced, through a complex manipulation of those defining formal elements which make up the language of Islamic art – geometry, arabesque and calligraphy. It is the purpose of the next chapter to explain those distinctly Islamic attitudes which made this formal language possible.[7]

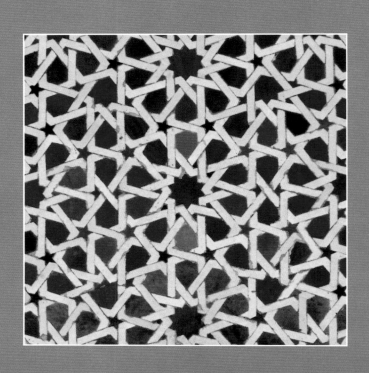

THE RELIGIOUS BASIS OF FORM AND FUNCTION IN ISLAMIC ARCHITECTURE

FORM

What is remarkable about the religious art of Islam, unlike that of any other religion, is that it expresses the sacred and the divine in a uniquely abstract and formal way and emphatically rejects the representation of the human figure. It is this uncompromising abstract order of Islamic art and architecture which makes possible the expression of those transcendental and metaphysical values that unite the sacred and secular domains in Islamic architecture. In marked contrast to the arts of Islam, Christian, Hindu and Buddhist art have evolved a complex vocabulary of representational art which is mainly symbolic and narrative in character. Christian figurative images, such as icons, altarpieces and narrative paintings dealing with biblical subjects, function in a specific devotional, liturgical or didactic way. Such usage in the Christian world was established at the outset in Byzantium and was later endorsed by the Catholic Church where images of Christ, the Virgin Mary and saints were sanctioned to stimulate veneration, while narrative paintings were used to instruct, remind and hold in mind the articles of faith.[1] In the case of Islamic art, as Titus Burckhardt argues, there is no representational symbol system or narrative which can be *read*; it expresses notions of the divine, not through devotional images but through the totality of its form, and it is this totality of form that unites and characterises all the visual arts of Islam.[2]

To understand why Islam rejected figurative imagery and took this iconoclastic path it is necessary to examine theological attitudes towards the arts through the sources in the Qur'an and *hadith*, as well as further exegesis in Muslim law. Attitudes regarding the use of images in the religious sphere were loosely formed in the early eighth century, but little detailed commentary on this matter became available until much later. As Oleg Grabar suggests, these later legal commentaries are retrospective in character, and attitudes towards the arts were more likely to have been formed at an early stage on the basis of custom, taste and pragmatism, rather than on rigorous theological reasoning.[3] Nevertheless, by the thirteenth century religious laws were formed on this matter, and legists, like Nawawi, were prepared to pronounce on such matters as artistic representation with some precision and detail.

The learned authorities of our school (Shafi'i) and others, hold that the painting of a picture of any living thing is strictly forbidden and is one of the great sins, because it is treatened with the above grievous punishment as mentioned in Traditions, whether it is intended for common domestic use or not. So the making of it is forbidden under every circumstance, because it implies a likeness to the creative activity of God... On the other hand, the painting of a tree or of camel saddles and other things that have no life are not forbidden.[4]

For such a view to reach canonical form, it would have to be based on revelation and reason, revelation through the primary sources of the Qur'an and *hadith* and reason based on the consensus of learned authorities.

So what does the Qur'an and *hadith* have to say about art and architecture? The Qur'an has nothing to say about art and architecture, although it is uncompromising with regard to idolatry: 'Believers, wine and games of chance, idols and divining arrows are abominations devised by Satan. Avoid them, so that you may prosper' (*Sura* 5:95); and 'Tell of Abraham, who said to Azar, his father: "Will you worship idols as your gods? Surely you and all your people are in palpable error"' (*Sura* 6:75).

That the Qur'an should reveal this opposition to idolatry comes as no surprise, because Muhammad's Meccan ministry was primarily concerned with preaching monotheism and denouncing polytheist idolatry. He aroused so much hostility among the ruling Quraysh tribe because of his attack on their paganism and the idolatrous use of the sanctuary and the Ka'ba, a rectangular structure built by Abraham, in which was incorporated a sacred black cornerstone. The sanctuary in pre-Islamic times was initially the shrine of the god Hubal, an oracular divinity who was consulted by means of divining arrows. Several other idols were introduced into the precincts, including Manaf, Quzah, Nasr and Wadd, as well as the gods who featured in the episode of the Satanic Verses, al-Lat, al-Uzza and Manat (when Satan caused Muhammad to unwittingly sanction their worship). The annual pilgrimage was also a time of festivity and fairs, at which much drinking and gambling took place. In the passage quoted above, the Qur'an clearly condemns this idolatrous and bacchanalian behaviour, and when Muhammad conquered Mecca in 630 his first act was to cleanse the sanctuary of idols and throw out those from inside the Ka'ba. It is also significant that during this operation he preserved paintings of Abraham, Jesus and Mary, which he found inside the Ka'ba. While he was consolidating his position in Mecca he also ordered the destruction of the idols of al-Lat and al-Uzza at their shrine in nearby Ta'if. Muhammad reconstituted the pilgrimage in 632, and opposition to idolatry is still symbolically expressed today with the stoning of the idols at the town of Mina during the closing stages of the annual pilgrimage.

Apart from idolatry, there is nothing in the Qur'an that mentions works of art, although one passage dealing with one of the miracles of Jesus is regarded as significant. In this passage Jesus fashions the image of a bird out of clay and, by God's will, the bird is animated and flies away.

He replied: "Such is the will of Allah. He creates whom He will. When He decrees a thing He need only say: 'Be', and it is . . . He will say, 'I bring you a sign from your Lord. From clay I will make for you the likeness of a bird. I shall breathe into it and, by Allah's leave, it shall become a living bird. By Allah's leave I shall give sight to the blind man, heal the leper and raise the dead to life' (*Sura* 3:43).

This story, also recounted in the apocryphal Christian Gospel of Saint Thomas, is used to suggest that only God has the power to create, and that the artist who makes images is guilty of usurping God's creative prerogative. It explains that sentence in Nawawi where he states that image-making 'implies a likeness to the creative activity of God'. The Arabic word for painter is *musawwir*, which means fashioner and modeller, and is a word used in the Qur'an to describe one of God's attributes:

'He is Allah, the Creator, the Originator, the Modeller' (*Sura* 59:24).

While the Qur'an's revelation is clear on matters of idolatry, elsewhere it is ambiguous, and for this reason the *hadith* must be consulted for more definitive answers. Here the material is uncompromising in its condemnation of the artist, and in a number of passages

the artist is ranked with the lowest of criminals and condemned to Hell.

Those who will be most severely punished on the Day of Judgement are the murderer of a Prophet, one who has been put to death by a Prophet, one who leads men astray without knowledge, and makers of images and pictures.[5]

However, as Sir Thomas Arnold points out, these passages are at variance with the more ambivalent attitude of Muhammad, and he suggests that these iconoclastic assertions might be interpolations added by later writers.[6] Muhammad did show a degree of toleration when he preserved the paintings of Abraham, Jesus and Mary in the Ka'ba, and he did discuss accounts of paintings seen by his companions in the churches of Abyssinia. Nevertheless, those *hadith* that refer to images in the domain of the mosque are quite clear and unambiguous: 'Umar said, "We do not enter your churches on account of the statues on which are figures"' (Bukhari 8:54). Again: 'Anas said "A'ishah had a figured curtain of red wool, with which she covered a side of her apartment. The Prophet (peace and blessings of Allah be on him) said: "Remove from us thy curtain, for its figures come before me in my prayers"' (Bukhari 8:15).

Another tradition suggests that A'ishah (the Prophet's youngest wife) cut up the curtain and made cushion covers, which explains why Nawawi goes on to say that figurative designs are acceptable if they are 'on a carpet trampled underfoot, or on a pillow, or cushion, or any similar object of domestic use'.[7]

What the Qur'an and *hadith* have to say about art is ambiguous and inconclusive, and therefore in order that jurists can formulate a clearer view on this matter, reason must be employed, calling on learned consensus and analogical reasoning. Revealed sources in the Qur'an and *hadith* normally have to be supplemented by such reasoning, but there are no documentary sources that give us any insight into the arguments used to explain the decisions of thirteenth-century jurists like Nawawi, whose verdict, and that of others, came retrospectively, several centuries after a clear iconoclastic attitude was manifest in Islam's first buildings of the seventh and early eighth centuries. With the exception of Caliph Yazid's edict in 721, there is a documentary vacuum between the visual evidence of those early buildings and the legal directives of the thirteenth century. In order to fill this vacuum and understand how those early Muslim iconoclastic attitudes developed, it is useful to consider them in relation to contemporary iconoclast controversies within the Byzantine world.

Islam was forged in a more pragmatic environment than Christianity and was not afflicted by the theological problems which divided early Christianity. Its divisions were prompted by political rather than theological concerns. As Oleg Grabar has suggested, Muslim iconoclasm was essentially an attitude, whereas Byzantine iconoclasm was an event and an issue.

The debate between the iconoclasts and the iconodulists within Byzantium followed in the wake of controversies about the nature of Jesus, his substance and his relationship with the Father. These were the profound issues that divided Christianity between orthodoxy and various heterodox groups. The iconoclasts believed that an image was of the same nature as the subject represented and therefore devotion to it was idolatrous. The iconodulists argued that the image, while connected to its subject, was of a distinct and separate nature. Christological issues concerned the question of whether Christ's divine nature was susceptible to representation, and the matter was resolved for the time being at the Iconoclast Council of Hiereia.

No such dilemmas faced the early Muslim world with regard to Muhammad, because he was human, with no divine attributes, and the Islamic transcendent God was uncircumscribable. The only record we have of an official Muslim position on images is the so-called edict of the Caliph Yazid of 721. There is no mention of this in early Muslim sources, and we encounter it in St John of Damascus's submission to the Seventh Ecumenical Council of the Christian Church at Nicaea of 787 which restored the veneration but not worship of icons. The account of Yazid's edict that all pictorial representation in Christian churches should be destroyed, was presented by St John in order to discredit early iconoclasm, suggesting that its origins came from Muslims and Jews, and for this reason it needs to be looked at sceptically as a political statement within the highly charged climate of the Council.

In Byzantium the iconoclast controversy was a political issue bound up, to some extent, with the conflict between Islam and Christianity. The Emperor Leo III, who issued his iconoclast edict in 730, was denigrated by his enemies who claimed that he was influenced by Yazid's example, but it is more likely that the emperor's action was prompted by his belief that the Christian defeats at the hands of the Muslims were an expression of God's displeasure over the corrupt and superstitious use of icons.

There is some archaeological evidence that Yazid's edict may have taken place, but Muslim resistance to figurative representation was already clearly manifest in buildings like the Dome of the Rock (690) and the Great Mosque in Damascus (715), both built well before Yazid's edict. It is also interesting to note that mosaics in the Church of the Nativity in Bethlehem confirm that there was also an absence of figurative imagery in contemporary Christian art during this period, and as Oleg Grabar has suggested, the Christians may have been conforming to a prevailing taste before iconoclasm became an issue.[8] When the Muslims initially occupied the Byzantine territories aesthetic issues were a low priority, and it is unlikely that they had a decisive view on these matters. It has been suggested that they may have been influenced by the Jewish and heterodox Christian communities they encountered. There was almost certainly a deep-rooted Semitic resistance to graven images, and this may have been strengthened by the influence of Judaism and the presence of a number of Jewish converts to Islam. It is unlikely that either side of the Christian iconoclast debate had a decisive influence on Muslim attitudes. With such notable exceptions as Yazid's edict, Muslim rule allowed a degree of tolerance for Christian iconoclasts and iconodulists alike, and it was only under Muslim protection that St John of Damascus found it possible to challenge Byzantine orthodoxy by writing his celebrated defence of icons.

When the Muslims encountered Christian culture their reactions were mixed, because on the one hand they were profoundly impressed by the magnificence of Christian art, but on the other they felt a degree of distaste and resentment towards a superior artistic culture which so effectively flaunted its visual imagery for religious and state purposes. The political use of statues as symbols of imperial power goes back to Roman times, and the Byzantine emperors, who assumed the title of Vicar of Christ, followed their pagan predecessors by expecting their statues and portraits to be venerated. The cross surmounting the orb and sceptre became an imperial symbol, and the monogram of Christ, the Chi-Rho, replaced the old Roman insignia on battle standards. The superstitious use of portable and domestic icons was rampant (they stood in as godparents at baptisms), and it is small wonder that this corrupt, idolatrous and blatant political use of sacred images and relics repelled Muslim sensibilities. Along with this went an Arab distaste for the *objet d'art* and its association with the extravagance, luxury and display of the Byzantine court. The first generation of Arab conquerors were warriors conditioned by the discipline of desert warfare and the abstemiousness of bedouin attitudes.

So what was the nature of Islamic art that rejected figurative iconography, and how did it differ from Christian art during this period of iconoclasm? To begin with, Arab rulers relied on Christian architects and craftsmen and employed existing decorative and architectural forms with a new synthesis and orientation. Calligraphy established its presence in the inscriptions of the Dome of the Rock, and it is here that we begin to see a distinctly Islamic aesthetic emerging. Islam was able to reject much of the ethos of Byzantine art because it had its own unique revelation in the form of the Qur'an, and from the outset it was the word that established the Muslim identity and dominated its mode of worship. The Prophet had stated that pictures were a distraction (Bukhari 8:15). In Islamic art it is the manifestation of God's word in calligraphic form which, alongside architecture, represents the highest and most respected expression of Islamic art. The art of calligraphy is honoured and held in the highest esteem, and its practice is encouraged at all levels of society as an act of religious piety and merit.

In contrast to *hadith* statements regarding the painter, the fourteenth-century writer Muhammad ibn Mahud al-Amuli has this to say about calligraphy in an encyclopaedic work entitled *Nafa'is al-funun*:

> The art of writing is an honourable one and a soul nourishing accomplishment; as a manual of attain-

ment it is always very elegant, and enjoys general approval; it is respected in every land; it rises to eminence and wins the confidence of every class; being always to be held in high rank and dignity . . . The Prophet (peace and blessings be upon him) said: 'Beauty of handwriting is incumbent upon you, for it is one of the keys of daily bread'. A wise man said: 'Writing is a spiritual geometry, wrought by a material instrument'.[9]

The key phrase here is 'spiritual geometry', as this aptly describes not only the structure of Islamic calligraphy, but the whole essence and spirit of Islamic art. As the language of Islamic art began to develop and mature, three defining elements emerge: calligraphy, arabesque and geometry. Of these three, it is geometry that functions as the unifying ground, uniting and extending a complex repertoire of abstract forms on both two-dimensional and three-dimensional planes. Islam's visionary aspect finds no expression through figurative art, but transcendental and mystical values are manifest in its geometry, calligraphy and arabesque. Those writers of a Sufi persuasion, such as Martin Lings and Titus Burckhardt, argue that these abstractions function as analogues to the harmony, totality and unity of God's creation. Those ineffable feelings of God's presence and purpose in His creation, that awareness of wholeness and infinitude, manifest in the natural world, and in those patterns and rhythms which govern it, are exemplified in iconic form in the art of calligraphy and illumination,

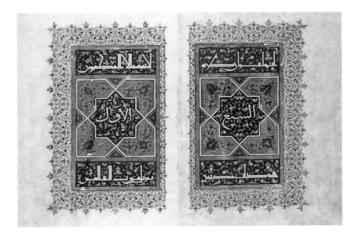

Mamluk Qur'an written by Muhammad ibn al-Wahid and illuminated by Muhammad ibn Mubadir and Aydughdi ibn 'Abd Allah al-Badri, 1304

as well as in the abstract disposition of mass, space and surface in architecture.

An example of these qualities, in their most refined and developed form, is demonstrated in the frontispiece of an early fourteenth-century Mamluk Qur'an in the British Library written by Muhammad ibn al-Wahid and illuminated by Muhammad ibn Mubadir and Aydughdi ibn 'Abd Allah al-Badri for Rukn ad-Din Baibars. The geometric base of this design is a series of interlacing circles which function as a hidden trellis supporting a delicate tracery of arabesque, as well as the rectangular and stellar panels which contain calligraphic inscriptions. Two forms of calligraphy are used, the cursive flourish of the Thuluth script in the central panel, and the older hieratic forms of the Kufic in the upper and lower panels. The composition is a harmonic resolution of static and dynamic patterns, in which the whole page presents a sensation of shifting and pulsating rhythms, in which boundless arabesques are contained within the finely proportioned geometry of the enclosing panels. It functions principally as an object for contemplation in which the mind becomes unfocused, thus rendering it susceptible to meditation.

The contemplative function of this illuminated manuscript finds its counterpart in the spatial organisation of the mosque interior, where the same geometries are expressed through architectural mass, volume, plane, colour and surface decoration. There are no distracting pictures, and the spatial domain is uncluttered by seating, furniture, tombs, and all those accretions of Christian churches. In the mosque we are confronted with a geometry which establishes the generality and totality of form, and invariably its cold linearities are enlivened by colour, which also animates those complementary interlocking patterns of intricate vegetal and floral arabesque. Colour, in later architecture, is autonomous and has been liberated in the Muslim world and allowed an expressive function unparalleled in any other world art. It is the crowning glory of Islamic art, and in the mosque it resonates in the variegated pattern of carpets, stained glass, tiles and sumptuous mosaic. This enfolding totality presents us with a complex visual interplay which unites all the arts and renders the interior space conducive for concentrated prayer and meditation.

FUNCTION

Those metaphysical values of totality and unity are correspondingly found in more practical, concrete and functional terms, because architecture must reflect the needs and structure of the society it serves. Unity and indivisibility are defining characteristics of Islam, and in Islamic architecture religious and secular functions are rarely separable. The Damascus Mosque, with its courtyard plan and adjacent prayer hall, characteristic of so many congregational mosques, has its antecedent in the crude makeshift structure which served as the Prophet's original mosque and house in Medina. This consisted of a simple rectangular gravel courtyard surrounded by a wall of sun-dried brick and stone measuring about 50 metres square and just over 3 metres high. The bricks were arranged in alternating courses of verticals and horizontals, and initially three entrances pierced the east, west and southern walls. To begin with, prayers were said facing the north, towards Jerusalem, but then the direction of prayer, the *qibla*, was changed to face south towards Mecca, and subsequently the southern entrance was bricked up. There were two sheltered areas of palm trunks supporting a thatched roof of palm fronds plastered with mud ('like Moses' cradle', as Muhammad described it). The sheltered area inside the south *qibla* wall was known as the *zulla*, and it functioned as a prayer hall. Opposite was another shaded structure (the *suffah*) built to accommodate the poorest in the community, the 'People of the *suffah*'. According to *hadith*, seventy people could be housed here, including students who received instruction. On the outer side of the eastern wall were nine rooms with access to the courtyard, private residential quarters for the Prophet, his wives and children. These simple buildings were separate from, and adjacent to the courtyard, which functioned principally as a mosque where the main religious and social activities took place.

The religious and social life of the Damascus Mosque also has its origins in the Prophet's mosque. The courtyard functioned as a meeting point for the whole community and served a variety of religious and secular purposes. It was here that the format and orientation of the communal prayers was established. It was also the seat of government, and the Prophet would hold council here as well as act as judge and arbitrator. *Hadith* sources also reveal less formal uses for the courtyard – hospice, sanctuary and refuge. The sick and wounded were cared for, as testified in one *hadith*, where Sa'd, one of Muhammad's injured companions, had a tent erected for him so that he could be visited by the Prophet and receive medical attention. Women were given sanctuary in the mosque and A'ishah (the Prophet's youngest wife) describes in one *hadith* how a black slave girl, who had recently been manumitted and converted to Islam, was given tented accommodation in the mosque. Prisoners were sometimes held here, and occasionally the atmosphere could be more rumbustious, when for example Abyssinian tribesmen sported and practised their martial arts with spears. Noisy behaviour, however, was not generally tolerated, and another *hadith* states that Omar had a separate courtyard (the *butaiha*) built to one side of the mosque in order that people could talk more freely and recite poetry. The mosque was also used as a treasury, but the Prophet strictly forbade any commercial activity inside its precincts.

This wide spectrum of activity within the Prophet's mosque has broadly determined the development of religious and secular building throughout the Muslim world. Its primitive architectural form and space provided a loose sketch for subsequent designs, based on variations of the prayer hall and courtyard plan, which have effectively served the liturgy of Islam for centuries. Its other diverse functions have evolved and fanned out into a variety of specialised structures, which can most appropriately be demonstrated in the architectural monuments of Ottoman Turkey, where they are accommodated on a grand scale. Around the great imperial mosques in Istanbul are complexes of ancillary buildings known as *külliya* (meaning 'totality' or 'universality'), which provide purpose-built accommodation for the general education and welfare of the community. Süleyman the Magnificent's *külliya* in Istanbul, designed by the great architect Sinan, is a small conurbation containing the mosque, several *madrasas* (theological colleges), an advanced law school, a Qur'an school, hospital, asylum, soup kitchen, hospice, baths, mausoleum and shops. Under the umbrella of the *külliya* most of Ottoman Turkey's principal building types are found, and following similar models it is from the religious

centre that the various categories of Islamic architecture as a whole radiate.

In Istanbul successive sultans fulfilled their religious duty and made their mark on the city by adding numerous *külliya*. The multiplication of these complexes, however, failed to meet the demands of the whole community, and we see in Istanbul the proliferation of smaller satellite mosques and other purpose-built units, like baths, developing separately from the *külliya*. Other parts of the Muslim world made similar provision but did not develop the idea of the *külliya* on such a grand scale or in such a comprehensive way. Elsewhere specialised buildings evolved less systematically within or outside the mosque precincts in various combined or separate units. One such building type is the *madrasa* which owes its origin to the educational role of the *suffah* for the poorest people in the Prophet's mosque. Education is central to Muslim culture and early mosques generally accommodated educational activity within the prayer hall, or in the arcaded porticos (*riwaqs*) surrounding the courtyard. Later, particularly in the tenth century, purpose-built *madrasas* multiplied rapidly in order to combat the successful religious propaganda of the Shi'ites of Fatimid Egypt. The *madrasa* emerged as an important instrument of religious instruction and regulation, playing a major role in defending and consolidating the teaching of the *sharia* within the orthodox Sunni tradition.

A number of *madrasas* became independent residential institutions outside the precincts of the mosque. Some functioned as separate buildings within mosque complexes (as in the Ottoman *külliyas*), while others, like the Masjid i Shah in Isfahan, were integrated into a unified architectural whole with the prayer hall and court (*sahn*). Many distinguished buildings in Cairo, like the Sultan Hasan Mosque, or funerary complexes, such as the Qa'it Bay, integrate a number of building functions, including prayer hall, *madrasa*, mausoleum and *sabil kuttab*, into one architectural scheme. Some of the Cairo complexes incorporate accommodation for Sufi dervishes (*khanqahs*), which are both functionally and formally indistinct from *madrasas*, thus creating architectural ambiguities which are typical of much Islamic architecture. The Cairo mosque complexes frequently combine space in such a way as to allow for activities to overlap, so that congregational prayers, for instance, might extend into the teaching space of the *madrasa* and vice versa. Such a multipurpose use of space finds its parallel in secular architecture, and both domains show an open-ended architectural interpenetration of form and function which expresses in concrete terms that fundamental continuum of religious and secular life.

Like *madrasas*, a number of other buildings which were closely associated with the mosque have assumed an independent identity without entirely relinquishing their religious roots. According to one *hadith*, the Prophet said that 'cleanliness was half the faith', and fountains and washing facilities are an essential feature in every mosque. These amenities are sufficient for the daily prayer ablutions, but cannot meet the full demands of a society in which cleanliness is so deeply ingrained (the Mongols were slow to adopt Islam because their nomadic way of life in the Asian steppes did not encourage habitual washing). Consequently public fountains (*sabils*), often given as charitable endowments, dispense water on street corners. One distinctive building which characterises the architecture of Egypt is the *sabil kuttab*, a Qur'an school built over a public fountain. Following the legacy of ancient Rome, public and private baths are an important architectural feature of many Muslim cities and palaces. The city of Cordoba in the tenth century boasted three hundred public baths, and some of the finest Ottoman buildings in Istanbul today are still fully operational baths dating from the sixteenth century.[10]

When the Prophet died in 632, he was buried beneath the floor of one of the private rooms adjacent to the courtyard of his mosque. Despite his disapproval of funerary monuments, his own tomb in Medina set a precedent for the construction of subsequent mausolea in the precincts of mosques. It was after Caliph al-Walid rebuilt the Medina mosque in 709 that the Prophet's tomb became a monumental feature and focus for veneration and pilgrimage. The Prophet was emphatically against any form of ostentation and there are various *hadith* which discourage tomb building.

To begin with modest graves and orthodoxy prevailed, but by the ninth century a distinctive tomb architecture began to emerge at Samarra in Iraq. Robert Hillenbrand suggests that the origins of the Islamic mausoleum may be found in Syria, where the building of tombs and honorific monuments had been well established since classical times.[11] Martyria, built to house relics or honour sacred sites and events, were common within the Christian world, and despite the strictures of orthodoxy the Muslims readily absorbed these traditions, as their first great building, the Dome of the Rock, so spectacularly demonstrates. Later, tombs assumed a religious significance if the deceased had a particular reputation for holiness, such as martyrs and the founders of Sufi orders. Tombs like these became a focus for pilgrimage, and the sanctity of a martyr's or sheikh's tomb could transmit *baraka*, or blessing, so that it became common practice for other tombs to be built in its vicinity in order that *baraka* could be absorbed and shared. Prayers of supplication are made in tombs, and the deceased are often called upon through prayer to act as spiritual intermediaries, guides and mentors (*pirs*). Tombs punctuate the landscape and townscape of the Muslim world, and wayside travellers pay their respects in order to receive *baraka*. It is thought that the great traveller, Ibn Battuta (1304–68), was motivated by a search for *baraka* when he visited so many tombs on his extraordinary travels which took him 75,000 miles across West and North Africa, Spain, India, China and the Middle East. The political significance of tombs should not be underestimated, and both Sunni and Shi'ite dynasties exploited the potent symbolism of tomb architecture. In the Shi'ite world the tombs of the Prophet's descendants, the Imams, became an important focus for their religious and political aspirations.

Muhammad forbade mercantile activity within the precincts of his mosque, but mosques have invariably been located near the commercial centres of the city, and it has been common practice in countries like Turkey for the rents of shops to contribute to the upkeep of the mosque. This practice prevailed in the Süleymaniya Külliya in Istanbul, and a similar arrangement occurs in the great *külliya* of Sultan Selim at Edirne, where the mosque is built over and structurally incorporates a covered bazaar. On a smaller scale, Sinan's Rüstem Paşa mosque is built on a raised platform containing storerooms for the local bazaar in the heart of the tinsmiths' quarter of Istanbul. Elsewhere, commercial buildings like bazaars, caravansarais and *khans* have developed their own architectural forms outside the mosque, but these buildings are frequently multipurpose and the division between the secular and religious sphere remains open ended. Caravansarais were built as fortified wayside buildings along caravan and pilgrimage routes. They consisted of walls and bastions enclosing a courtyard for the loading, unloading and tethering of animals. Surrounding the courtyard were arcaded porticos (*riwaqs*) containing rooms for storage, accommodation and stabling. Some of the larger caravansarais would include a mosque, kitchens, baths, coffee rooms and workshops. The *khan*, *wakala* or *han* fulfils the same function within the urban context, usually in or adjacent to a bazaar.

The plan of many of these buildings probably originated in pre-Islamic military camps or houses. In frontier territory during the early years of conquest this format was adapted for fortified *ribats*, which provided accommodation for soldiers. Some *ribats* were like monasteries, with individual cells arranged around the upper tier of the courtyard next to a prayer hall. During settled times *ribats* were easily adapted to more peaceful purposes and later served as caravansarais. Early Muslim palaces demonstrate a further adaptation of this basic fortified courtyard plan on a grander and more complex scale. Many of these early buildings lack differentiation, and palaces like Qasr al-Hair East, Syria, contain structural elements that are formally indistinguishable from caravansarais. Such buildings suggest dual function and it seems that much Islamic architecture evolved to be flexible and adaptable. Early *ribats* were quasi-monastic institutions for soldiers who formed a militant religious caste, like the Knights Templar, but such forms of monasticism did not develop in the Muslim world. The nearest equivalent to a monastery is a *khanqah* accommodating the Sufi or dervish orders, with buildings originally closely related to the *ribat*. *Khanqahs* were independent institutions providing alternative religious tutelage to that of the official *madrasa*, but later they were occasionally incorporated into the fabric of the mosque (in order to ensure a degree of regulation), and in Ottoman times purpose-built rooms (*tabhane*) adjacent to the prayer hall were frequently set aside for dervishes. What has emerged therefore are clusters of buildings – caravansarais, *khans*, *ribats*, palaces and *khanqahs* – which have grown organically from a common centre, so creating a fluid interchange of function that accounts for the essential unity and diversity of Islamic architecture.

All those activities described in the Prophet's mosque have broadly remained within the domain of the mosque, with the major exceptions of government and defence. These functions were quickly transferred to the citadel and palace, and it is the development of palace architecture, along with ostentatious tombs, which most transgresses the modest spirit of the Prophet's foundation in Medina. Such a change was unavoidable because the early expansion of Islam created a dramatic new set of circumstances in which the Arabs found themselves ruling an expanding empire. This initially involved the relocation of political power from Medina to Damascus, and after the assassination of three of the early caliphs the need to protect and isolate political leaders. The sheer scale of administration, bureaucracy and diplomatic and military activity necessitated a radical change and a more secure environment. Palaces became lavish, but they were not generally built to last, and with one or two exceptions they did not become solid monuments of dynastic power. Materials were not very durable, and to some extent the monuments became disposable, as successive rulers built their own palaces.

Because of the use of impermanent building materials, surviving palace architecture is flimsy and patchy. Lack of reliable documents makes it particularly difficult to identify the varied functions of many palace complexes. The archaeological evidence of early palaces, like Qasr al-Hair East in the Syrian desert, reveals architectural ambiguities and unresolved questions, which have been a continuous problem in the study of palace architecture. Even in well-preserved fourteenth-century palaces, like the Alhambra, and in seventeenth century Mughal architecture, the purpose of its many buildings remains a mystery. Multipurpose units, like palace pavilions, changed and rotated in use. They could serve as dining rooms, sleeping quarters or more frequently as reception and entertainment areas. In some palaces, receptions and banquets were held in bath houses, and the nearby residential and ceremonial areas could create formal and informal juxtapositions, such as in the Alhambra Palace, where the sultan's bed and sitting-room is next to the throne room. This adaptability and interchangeability of parts is central to much Islamic architecture, and this, along with its formal geometry, brings it close to the spirit of modern architecture.

CHAPTER 2

UMAYYAD ARCHITECTURE

Following the death of the Prophet, the Arabs emerged from the Arabian Peninsula and began an extraordinary campaign of conquest which within a century established their rule from Spain in the west to the borders of China. They brought in the wake of their brilliant military successes their religion and their political and mercantile acumen. Artistically they were renowned for their oral poetry, but they had no significant building traditions or knowledge of architecture. Art emerges from somewhere, and architecture cannot spring from a void, or creativity flourish in a cultural vacuum, so initially the Arabs had to rely on and absorb the skills and building expertise of the people brought under their rule. The early monuments of Islam represent and reflect a new cultural synthesis, and the story of Islamic architecture is one of continuing adaptation, change and innovation in response to the complex cultural and racial diversity which makes up the Muslim nation.

The first four caliphs, Abu Bakr, Omar, Othman and Ali, are known as the *rashidin*, or 'rightly guided' caliphs. Under their leadership the Arab people conquered the two great empires of Byzantium and Sasanian Persia, which were exhausted after many years of warfare. The war between Byzantium and Persia began in 603. By 617 the Persians had captured land near Constantinople, Antioch, Damascus and Egypt, and after the siege of Jerusalem carried off the holy relics of the True Cross, Lance and Sponge to the Persian capital of Ctesiphon. The emperor Heraclius led the Byzantine counter-attack and after a long military campaign, which ended in 628, the new Persian king, Kavadh-Siroes, agreed to a peace treaty fully restoring Byzantine territory and returning the sacred relics. After this long and debilitating conflict, the exhausted Byzantines and Persians were unable to resist the invading Arabs who were inspired by a new faith and sense of purpose.

The Arab conquests began in 633 when Khalid ibn al-Walid, the chief general of the first caliph, Abu Bakr, led an expedition to Palestine and Syria. By 638 most of Syria, including Jerusalem, was in Arab hands and Khalid then moved on to Persia and captured the capital of Ctesiphon which fell in 637. General Amr ibn al-As invaded Egypt in 639 and established his military base at the Roman fortress of Babylon at Fustat, a location which now contains the Coptic quarter of modern Cairo. This choice of Fustat established the foundation of Cairo as Egypt's capital, rather than Alexandria which had been the capital since Ptolemaic times. The great Arab conquests continued westward with the occupation of Spain, and exactly one hundred years after the Prophet's death in 732, Islam reached the limit of its penetration into western Europe when Charles Martel repulsed Abd al-Rahman al-Ghafiqi's army between Poitiers and Tours, just south of Paris. Muslim armies, however, continued eastwards bringing Khurasan under Arab rule, and by 771 Arab raiders had crossed the Jaxartes and engaged in a number of skirmishes with Chinese forces.

The years of the first four caliphs were turbulent. Three of them were murdered as a consequence of rivalries between the older ruling families of Mecca. Omar was murdered in 644, and the election of Othman, a member of the aristocratic Ummaya family, precipitated a power struggle. Othman was a weak ruler, and he in turn was murdered during the siege of Medina in 656. Ali succeeded to the caliphate and the Shi'ite party at last had the leader they wanted. Ali was generally respected as a devout religious leader, and the fact that he was the Prophet's son-in-law gave him special authority, but he proved to be weak and indecisive as a political leader. He succeeded in putting down a rebellion at the battle of the Camel, but failed to persuade Mu'awiya, his powerful Syrian governor, to give his support and allegiance. Mu'awiya was the nephew of the murdered Othman and he demanded vengeance and questioned Ali's entitlement to the caliphate. After further battles, a truce and convoluted negotiations, Ali's authority was weakened, and his support gradually ebbed away. During this stalemate Ali was stabbed to death in the mosque at Kufa in 661. After Ali's murder, his son Hasan surrendered authority to Mu'awiya who was elected caliph. He established Damascus as the centre of Muslim power and founded the Umayyad dynasty, which ruled until 750.

It has been a popular assumption in the West that the Arab conquests were an expression of a militant faith which indulged in a programme of forcible mass conversion to Islam. But, as Bernard Lewis explains, the conquests were more an 'expansion not of Islam, but of the Arab nation'.[1] One explanation for the remarkable success of the conquests is that the Arabs were viewed by others, such as Jewish and heterodox Christian minorities, as liberators from Byzantine oppression.

Those non-Muslims (*dhimmis*), who had a sacred scripture, such as the Christians and Jews, were designated 'People of the Book', and were tolerated and protected under Islamic law. As the Muslim empire spread this protection was extended to the Zoroastrians of Persia, as well as to Buddhists and Hindus in India. *Dhimmis* were not equal citizens – they paid higher taxes and were subject to some discriminatory laws such as those regarding marriage (a *dhimmi* man cannot marry a Muslim woman). Nevertheless, they were exempt from military service, were able to reach the highest offices of state and, more significantly, able freely to practise their religion. Under Islam many Jewish and Christian minorities generally flourished, and with one or two exceptions they were only to experience persecution again when the Crusaders occupied Syria and Palestine in the eleventh century. The success of the early Arab conquests was partly due to the collusion and support of a number of dissident minority communities which had an interest in the overthrow of Byzantine and Persian rule.

The Umayyad dynasty had to come to terms with a population, the majority of which was non-Muslim and culturally superior in terms of its machinery of government, institutions, art and architecture. Mu'awiya in Damascus retained and improved many existing structures of government and administration and appointed a Syrian Christian as his chief secretary. In addition, he added a council of sheikhs (the Shura), which drew on the political traditions of the Arabs. The conversions to Islam, the adoption of Arabic as the official language and the general Arabisation of the regions was very slow and gradual. In a similar way, a distinctly Islamic form of art and architecture took years to evolve, and initially the Arabs, who brought no architectural skills or knowledge with them, were totally dependent on the art, craft and building skills of the indigenous populations. Just as the Arabs sustained existing structures of government, so they absorbed Byzantine building forms but amended and adapted them.

When the Persians invaded Jerusalem with Jewish help in 614 they plundered the city, destroyed churches and took the Christian survivors into captivity. As a reward for their support, the Persians handed the city over to the Jews, but when Heraclius recaptured the city in 621 they were expelled. Byzantine sovereignty was

short lived, and Jerusalem fell to the Arabs led by the second caliph, Omar, in 637. Omar met the Patriarch Sophronius on the Mount of Olives and gave assurances that the lives of the population would be secure, religious toleration upheld, Christian churches respected and the Jews allowed to return. He asked to be taken to the location of the Temple of Solomon which had associations for the Arabs with Muhammad's visionary ascension to heaven in his 'night journey'. Every trace of the Temple had been destroyed by the Romans in 70 AD, and all that remained was the huge platform built by Herod the Great. The Christians had desecrated the site by using it as a refuse dump to avenge the Jews for their part in the Persian invasion, but Omar ordered its clearance and the sacred rock of Mount Moriah was eventually exposed. Besides being the place where Muhammad left the earth on his mystical journey, Mount Moriah has many sacred associations for both Muslims and Jews, being the place where Abraham attempted his sacrific of Isaac, Araunah's threshing floor, the rock anointed by Jacob, the omphalos or centre of the earth, the well of souls, as well as the place where the Ark of the Covenant is concealed. Omar built a wooden mosque over the sacred rock, which remained there until Abd al-Malik commenced the building of the Dome of the Rock in 687.

The Dome of the Rock is Islam's oldest building, and with its gold dome, brilliant tiles and polychrome marble, still stands like a sumptuous jewelled reliquary and as one of the architectural masterpieces of the world. For Islam's first architectural monument, dominating the city of Jerusalem on the great Herodian platform, there is nothing cautious or formative about it, and what is remarkable is the confidence, coherence and unity of its conception, despite the later external decoration of the Turks. In one sense the explanation for its mature form is obvious, because it represents the outcome of a long architectural tradition which had its origins in the Roman mausoleum. Its centralised and octagonal plan is characteristic of many notable Byzantine churches as far as the fourth-century church of Sta Costanza in Rome. The architectural conformation of the Dome of the Rock is essentially Byzantine, and the debt to Byzantium is even more obvious inside, where the use of decorative mosaic and polychrome marble panelling clearly indicates Islam's early dependence on the skills of Greek builders and craftsmen.

Jerusalem, the Dome of the Rock

Over a natural rock outcrop, like a monumental ciborium, is placed a gilded elliptical dome on a high drum supported on a circular arcade made up of twelve columns and four piers. The architectural plan is essentially a circle within an octagon, and around this central circle are two ambulatories enclosed by the octagonal perimeter walls. Between the perimeter walls and the inner circular arcade is an intermediate octagon, made up of an arcade of sixteen columns and eight piers. The earliest centralised plans of this type can be seen in Roman temples and mausolea which the early Christians adapted as a basis for their baptistries. The Church of Sta Costanza, originally built as a tomb by Constantine in 330, has a central dome, drum and arcade, identical in concept to the Dome of the Rock, although the perimeter wall is circular and not octagonal. The Baptistry of Constantine (440) has a dome supported by circular columns inside an octagon, and the best-known building using this type of plan is the church of San Vitale in Ravenna (546). Opposite the Dome of the Rock on the Mount of Olives is the small Chapel of the Ascension (375) in which the original building consisted of a sacred rock, open to the sky (according to the pilgrim Arculf's description of 680), surrounded by sixteen columns inside an octagon. The purpose and proximity of this chapel suggests that it may have provided the model for the Dome of the Rock.

With such ancient architectural roots, what is original or Islamic about the Dome of the Rock? Oleg Grabar[2] has suggested that the building has complex religious and political meanings and associations which may ultimately symbolise Islam's ascendancy over Christianity and Judaism. First, the Dome of the Rock is not a congregational mosque but a shrine designed for pilgrims honouring

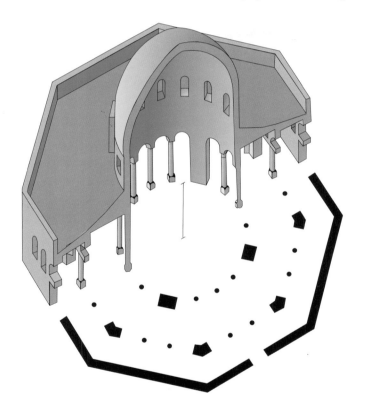

ABOVE
Jerusalem, perspective of the Dome of the Rock

ABOVE LEFT
Jerusalem, the Dome of the Rock: exterior

LEFT
Jerusalem, the Dome of the Rock: interior

the sacred ground where Muhammad was believed to have ascended into heaven in his 'night journey' visions. But Grabar suggests that at the time of building, the older association with Mount Moriah and Abraham's attempted sacrifice of Isaac in Genesis 22 (or Ishmael according to Arab tradition) may have been of some significance. He suggests that the Abrahamic association was valued at this early period in Islamic history, because Abraham was revered by Muslims, Christians and Jews alike, and in venerating this sacred spot the Muslims were symbolically celebrating a common religious heritage.

Grabar also draws attention to Abd al-Malik's possible desire to promote the pre-eminence of Jerusalem as a centre of pilgrimage. This explanation follows an allegation by the Shi'ite historian and geographer Ya'qubi, writing in the ninth century, stating that Abd al-Malik attempted to relocate Muhammad's pilgrimage (*hajj*) from Mecca to Jerusalem. Ya'qubi, however, was a partisan historian with anti-Umayyad views, and such an assertion amounts to a charge of heresy because pilgrimage to Mecca is one of the pillars of faith. Nevertheless, the Dome of the Rock was built at a time of civil war between Abd al-Malik and a rival caliph, Ibn al-Zubayr of Mecca, and this may have been enough cause for the two centres of pilgrimage to be rivals. The Ka'ba in Mecca, according to Qur'anic revelation, was built by Abraham and Ishmael: 'Abraham and Ishmael built the House and dedicated it saying: "Accept this from us, Lord. You hear all and You know all"' (*Sura* 2:127).

The Meccan sanctuary and surrounding areas, as well as the pilgrimage rites themselves, are intimately bound up with associations of Abraham, Hagar and Ishmael. Most significant is the sacrificial rite on the last day of the *hajj*, where animals are slaughtered in the main street of Mina at a point near the '*aqaba* (one of the stone idols), which is also reputed to be the site where Abraham prepared his sacrifice of Ishmael. On the face of it, there appear to be strong conflicting claims between Mecca and Jerusalem if Grabar is right in his contention that the Dome of the Rock originally enshrined the place of Abraham's intended sacrifice, rather than of Muhammad's 'night journey'.

Whatever the hypothesis, the Dome is placed over a sacred rock and appears to suggest that Islam was staking out its own sacred territory. The Christians had sanctified

their holy places, most notably the Church of the Holy Sepulchre, which enshrines the sites of Golgotha and the Tomb of Christ. After Queen Helena's discovery of the Tomb, Constantine encircled the site with twelve columns, and erected a domed rotunda (or *anastasis*) over the natural rock containing the Tomb. This description of the original construction is strikingly similar to the form of the Dome of the Rock today. After the destruction of the Church of the Holy Sepulchre by the Persians, Abbot Modestus restored the church and the dome was replaced by a conical wooden roof similar in diameter to that of the Dome of the Rock. Another sacred rock in Jerusalem is marked by the Chapel of the Ascension, an octagon surrounding the rock that bears the footprint of Christ where he ascended into heaven. It seems obvious that following the Christian model the Muslims were determined to honour their own holy ground and astutely chose the lofty site of the Temple Mount where the Dome of the Rock manifests and asserts Islam's presence in a most beautiful and spectacular way.

Jerusalem, the Chapel of the Ascension

The Dome of the Rock's interior scheme of decoration consists of mosaics and marble panelling in the Byzantine style. What is new and distinctly Islamic in the design is the use of Qur'anic inscriptions, and the message of these, as Grabar points out, is uncompromisingly Islamic. Like the following, these inscriptions frequently assert the unity of God:

'Say: he is God, the One, God the Eternal; He has not begotten nor was he begotten; and there is none comparable to Him' (*Sura* 112).

Occasionally the inscriptions point a warning finger to the 'People of the Book', and Christians in particular, where Trinitarianism is roundly condemned.

'O ye People of the Book. overstep not bounds in your religion; and of God speak only truth. The Messiah, Jesus, son of Mary, is an apostle of God, and His word which he conveyed unto Mary, and the Spirit proceeding from Him. Believe therefore in God and His apostles and, say not 'Three'. It will be better for you. God is only one God. Far be it from His glory that He should have a son . . . The Messiah does not disdain being a servant of God, nor do the Angels who are near Him' (*Sura* 4:171).

The message reminds Muslims of the fundamentals of their faith and points out to Jews and Christians the error of their ways.

Another distinctly Islamic attitude is manifest in the mosaics, where no figurative images are present at this stage in the genesis of Islamic art despite the cultural debt to Byzantium and Persia. Not one human figure appears among this lush representation of acanthus scrolls, fruits, plants, vases and cornucopias – all classical motifs which vividly demonstrate the continuity of the Hellenistic tradition within Byzantium. This repertoire of classical forms can also be seen in the inner ambulatory where gilded Corinthian capitals support tie-beams festooned with vine-scrolls, bunches of grapes, palmettes and pine-cones picked out in elegant gold relief, all adding lustre and opulence to the general iconic theme of God's providence. The gilded capitals recall the more extravagant

TOP AND ABOVE
Jerusalem, the Dome of the Rock: details of mosaics and inscriptions

expressions of Hellenistic art, such as the gilded bronze capitals that once adorned the peristyle of the Temple of Bel at Palmyra. A new affiliation between east and west is apparent too in the hybrid devices growing from the mosaic acanthus scrolls: stylised plants, which have been identified as Sasanian in origin, and emblematic palms, which may have more ancient roots in Archaemenid Persia and Assyria. There is a dazzling display of gems, breast-plates, diadems and crowns, which are a mixture of Byzantine and Sasanian motifs. Springing from jewelled vases are acanthus scrolls framing the double-winged crowns of the Sasanian monarchy. Grabar suggests that these royal insignia may symbolically represent the ancient practice of enriching a holy shrine with the trophies of war, as well as function as a metaphor for Islam's new triumphal pre-eminence.[3] Political symbolism in mosaic art at this time is not unique to Islam, for there are contemporary mosaics in the Church of the Holy Nativity at Bethlehem (694) containing decorative motifs similar to those in the Dome of the Rock, but in Bethlehem the political and doctrinal content is quite explicit, proclaiming in some detail the decisions of the Six General Ecumenical Councils of the Church, following the supplementary Quinisextine Council of Constantinople in 692.

Like any great work of art the Dome of the Rock adds up to more than the sum of its parts, and the meaning of detail should not be allowed to obscure the building's overall significance and impact. This is a masterpiece, and what impresses is the precision of its geometry, its fine proportions and its clarity, symmetry and unity of form. The sanctity of its interior is expressed through a marriage of natural and man-made forms. The natural, informal beauty of the consecrated rock, with its awesome and sublime associations, is complemented by the precision and formality of the architectural space which encloses and crowns it. The Dome of the Rock has been spared the fate of many ancient buildings, like the Church of the Holy Sepulchre, where accretions of building activity and restoration have destroyed the original architectural concept. The strict absence of monuments, tombs, icons and altarpieces ensures that in Muslim architecture clarity and integrity of purpose is usually retained. The simple geometry of the Dome of the Rock enforces a classical rigour whereby nothing can be added or subtracted without destroying its essential form. Where changes have occurred they have generally respected and complemented the character of the building. The opulence of the gold, green and mother-of-pearl mosaics is crowned by the rich red and gilded arabesques of the Mamluk inner dome built by Sultan an Nasir Muhammad in 1319. The exterior has changed much since Abd al-Malik's time, and in 1552–54 tiles replaced the original mosaics on the upper octagon and drum. The tilework of Süleyman the Magnificent has in turn been replaced by modern copies installed between 1958 and 1962. The craftsmen who produced the original work for Süleyman were from Tabriz and led by Abdalah Tabrizi, which explains the Persian rather than Iznik flavour of contemporary Ottoman tilework. Nevertheless, the orchestration of pattern and colour and the abstract organisation of the drum and windows work in perfect concord with the horizontal courses of calligraphy and panels of arabesque.

Perhaps the most distinctive feature of its external architectural composition is the gilded dome. How innovative this imposing form was is a matter of speculation. The original construction was made up of two domes, a wooden inner and an outer one covered in lead and plates of copper gilt. It is likely that the original dome was the same as that we see today (which is now substantially based on the reconstruction of 1022), but how common this type of dome construction was in seventh-century Palestine is uncertain. Most Byzantine domes, like those on the Haghia Sophia in Constantinople, appear shallow and saucer shaped on the outside, and double-dome construction was generally uncommon. They occur in later Byzantine buildings such as St Mark's, Venice, but here the original brick inner domes are like that at the Haghia Sophia, and the outer wooden domes were added much later in the thirteenth century. Of Palestinian and Syrian examples, we know that the rotunda of the Holy Sepulchre consisted of a conical wooden roof, which is consistent with many early Christian and Byzantine buildings of that period. K. A. C. Creswell claims that there was a wooden dome on the fifth-century Syrian church of St Simeon Stylites, and there is evidence that there may have been a similar structure on the cathedral of Bosra.[4] The Dome of the Rock's elliptical form is one feature that makes it distinctively Islamic, and it established a model for subsequent developments in dome construction.

The Arabs, as the new ruling class, were aware of the political necessity to make a visual statement in Jerusalem which would monumentally assert Islam's presence. Culturally they felt inferior, and they recognised the propaganda value of imposing architecture. The tenth-century historian Muqaddasi confirms that al-Walid

> . . . sought to build for the Muslims a mosque that would be unique and a wonder to the world. And in like manner is it not evident that Abd al-Malik, seeing the greatness of the Martyrium of the Holy Sepulchre and its magnificence was moved lest it should dazzle the minds of the Muslims and hence erected above the Rock the Dome which is now seen there.[5]

Adjacent to the Dome of the Rock, on the Temple Mount, is the Aqsa Mosque, which is the main

Jerusalem, the Aqsa Mosque

congregational mosque of Jerusalem. The first mosque on this site was a wooden construction built by Omar, accommodating up to 3,000 people according to Arculf, a French pilgrim who visited Palestine in the seventh century and who wrote a description of the holy places entitled *De Locis Sanctus*. This mosque was rebuilt by Caliph al-Walid about the year 715, but was destroyed by earthquake in 748. In approximately 774 Caliph al-Mahdi built a fifteen-aisled mosque with a wide central aisle and narrower side aisles arranged perpendicular to the *qibla* wall. Muqaddasi in the tenth century described a mighty gabled roof over the centre aisle of the sanctuary with a beautiful dome. This mosque in turn was destroyed by earthquake in 1033 and a smaller one was built in the reign of the Fatimid Caliph az Zahir in 1035. A substantial part of the mosque we see today, including the central aisle arcades, the four arches supporting the dome, and the drum of the dome, dates from this period. The most striking decorative feature of the mosque is the gold and green Fatimid mosaic covering the spandrels of the north face of the north dome-bearing arch, consisting

Jerusalem, the Aqsa Mosque: detail of mosaics

of a Kufic inscription and spreading acanthus scrolls, similar to those on the inner face of the drum of the Dome of the Rock. The inspiration for this decoration is Umayyad, rather than Fatimid, and this stylistic revival might be explained by the fact that az Zahir employed the same craftsmen who had restored the mosaics in the Dome of the Rock eight years earlier. The mosaics in the drum and dome of the Aqsa Mosque depicting vases, trees and rosettes are also derived from Umayyad designs.

This wooden double dome is sheathed in dark, dull, opaque grey lead, making a striking contrast and complement to the gold lustre on the Dome of the Rock.

In 1099, after the Crusader conquest, Godfrey de Bouillon took possession of the mosque and it became his headquarters and a palace for his successor, Baldwin I. It was later converted into a church, and with the foundation of the Order of the Knights Templar in 1118, it became their spiritual and temporal home. The additional ancillary buildings, which now form the Women's Mosque and the Museum of Islamic Art, originally housed the Templar Hall and other facilities. The main north façade of the Aqsa Mosque consists of a portico pierced by a large central pointed arch with Romanesque chevron moulding, flanked on each side by three smaller pointed arches. The three central arches and bays of the portico represent the work of the Crusaders, but the rest of the façade has additions from the thirteenth and fourteenth centuries. When Salah al-Din restored the city to Muslim rule in 1187, he rededicated the mosque and refurbished it, restoring the mosaics and adding his own *mihrab* and *minbar*.

The interior of the present mosque consists of a wide central aisle flanked on either side by three narrower aisles arranged perpendicular to the *qibla* wall. The dome of the penultimate bay establishes a form of transept to its right and left running parallel to the *qibla* wall, thus establishing a T-plan which became a feature of many North African mosques. The mosque we see today has been restored numerous times after many natural disasters, including the recent fire of 1969. Much of the restoration is twentieth century, including the columns, which were replaced in the late 1930s, and the coffered roofing in the side aisles, as well as the central nave roof which was restored by King Farouk in 1943. The Dome of the Rock and the Aqsa Mosque complement each other, and the difference between them could not be more striking as you leave the concentrated atmosphere of the former, with its glittering, sumptuous and pulsing colours, and enter the light, spacious and dignified simplicity of the latter. The Temple Mount or Haram al-Sharif ('Noble Sanctuary') provides a vast and majestic space for these two buildings. It is a huge precinct relieved by landscaping and the disposition of arcades, steps, terraces, outdoor *minbars*, fountains and a multiplicity of

smaller domed structures, which, like the Dome of the Chain, appear as if maquettes for the Dome of the Rock.

Hardly anything of the Umayyad period survives in the Aqsa Mosque, and we have to look to Damascus to find the the oldest congregational mosque in the Muslim world, built in 715 by Abd al-Malik's son, Caliph al-Walid. Like the Dome of the Rock, it was executed by Greek craftsmen. The historian al-Tabari (839–923) said that al-Walid sought help from the Byzantine emperor for his building projects: the emperor sent one hundred workmen and forty loads of mosaic tesserai, so despite periodic Arab attacks on Constantinople good diplomatic and cultural contact was maintained. In practical terms the Great Mosque at Damascus is architecturally more significant than the Dome of the Rock because it established the basic format of the congregational mosque. This consists of a covered prayer hall adjacent to a large courtyard (*sahn*) following the precedent of the Prophet's mosque in Medina. Like the Dome of the Rock it demonstrates how Islam absorbed and adapted not just local building and craft methods but also something of the older religious traditions of the region.

The mosque occupies an ancient religious site which previously housed the Roman Temple of Jupiter and the Church of St John. The Temple of Jupiter was situated in a large sacred enclosure known as the *temenos*, and the outer *temenos*, dating from the first century AD, still forms much of the mosque enclosure today. The masonry of the *temenos* forms a substantial part of the south, east and west walls, and remains of a Roman colonnade can still be seen near two of the mosque entrances. Under Theodosius, the pagan temple was transformed into a church, and it is assumed that he later destroyed the temple and built a new church in its place. Some Arab sources suggest that when Damascus was conquered, the Christians and Muslims shared the Church of St John for a time, and when al-Walid became caliph in 705, he evicted the Christians, demolished the church and commenced the building of the Great Mosque. It has also been asserted by some scholars that the prayer hall of al-Walid's mosque, aligned against the south wall of the *temenos*, is the original Church of St John simply adapted to Muslim usage. This theory is emphatically rejected by Creswell who argues that the Church of St John was in the centre of the *temenos* over the site of the original temple, and that the Muslims shared the *temenos* enclosure with the Christians, rather than their church, praying towards the south *temenos* wall where the mosque prayer hall was subsequently built.[6]

In refuting the notion that any of al-Walid's mosque is substantially the original Church of St John, Creswell states that there were no churches in Syria at that time which resembled, in terms of proportion and spatial division, al-Walid's building. The plan of the prayer hall of the Damascus mosque is superficially like a Christian basilica with its interior space divided by central nave, side aisles and transept. However, there are major differences between this and Christian basilicas. The internal spatial division of any church would ensure that the nave was at least taller and twice the width of the side aisles, whereas in the Damascus mosque there are, in effect, three 'naves' of equal height and width. The central placing of a transept, or crossing, which forms such a distinctive feature of al-Walid's mosque, is unprecedented in Christian basilican plans of this period. Above all, the Damascus mosque, unlike any Christian building, has a *lateral* orientation towards Mecca reflecting the horizontal spread of Muslim prayer.

The plan is that of the classic congregational mosque with a prayer hall and rectangular *sahn* surrounded on three sides by the *riwaqs* (cloistered arcades) which form a double-tiered arcade. The arch openings in both tiers are the same size and proportion as those on the façade of the prayer hall on the south side, so that the architectural rhythm of all four sides of the *sahn* is unbroken. The arches of the lower arcade on the north *riwaq* are placed on piers broadly echoing those on the prayer hall opposite, whereas the arches on the east and west sides rest on paired columns alternating with piers. Little remains of the original marble lining in the *riwaqs*, but some splendid examples of richly veined marble panels, similar in quality to those in the Haghia Sophia in Constantinople, can be found in the east vestibule. There are some surviving original marble window grills which superbly demonstrate the emerging geometric language of Islamic art. The use of geometry in Roman mosaic and architectural ornament was well established, but the lightness and elegance of these interlacing marble filigree window panels announces a significant innovation and change of direction. These window grills also provide

Damascus, the courtyard of the Great Mosque

evidence of what the original windows in the Dome of the Rock looked like.

The prayer hall is divided into three equal 'naves' by arcades that run parallel to the south *qibla* wall. Below three gabled roofs, the arcades support long horizontal beams that span the whole width of the building. The interior arcades echo those of the *sahn*, with the lower arches springing from Corinthian columns supporting a second tier of smaller paired arches like a lightly constructed Roman aqueduct. Unlike a Christian basilica where the central nave axis, higher and wider, centralises and directs our attention towards the east end of the church, the Damascus mosque presents a greater sense of spatial equilibrium. The light, open, double arcades act as space markers outlining a series of voids through which we perceive a continuity of space. The wall opening on to the *sahn* is pierced with clear upper windows and the lower arches filled with wooden latticed screens that admit a stream of light that floods over the variegated brilliance of multicoloured carpets. The impact of an uncluttered, continuous floor plane, enlivened by densely patterned carpets, is one of the most distinctive and striking features of the interior spatial organisation of this and any mosque – it is one of the keynotes of Islamic architecture. The transept, which supports the dome, clears a wider and taller space in the centre of the prayer

TOP
Ravenna, St Apollinare Nuovo: mosaic showing Theodoric's palace

ABOVE
Damascus, the Great Mosque: *sahn* mosaics

hall and functions like a Christian nave in providing the central axis leading to the marble *mihrab* and *minbar* in the *qibla* wall.

From the outside, the Damascus prayer hall presents a lofty edifice of substantial mass which dominates the *sahn*. The dome, transept and crossing endow the prayer hall with an architectural authority of some magnitude unlike other early congregational mosques, like Qairawan in Tunisia, where the prayer hall is simply a deeper extension of the eastern *sahn riwaq*, modestly articulated by a larger central arch surmounted by a dome. From the *sahn* the Damascus prayer hall resembles the Byzantine palace of Theodoric, rather than any known Christian church.[7] A remarkable mosaic in the church of St Apollinare Nuovo in Ravenna shows a detailed and accurate picture of Theodoric's palace which was

supposed to have been inspired by, and copied from, the imperial palace of Constantinople. The Ravenna mosaic shows an open arcaded façade, the two wings of which are double arcaded and divided by a triple-arched gabled transept. Curtains hang in the open arcades just as they did at the time of al-Walid, and the façade is covered with rich mosaics as at the Great Mosque at Damascus. The Damascus Mosque retains (with the help of much over-restoration) extensive exterior mosaics, and here in the *sahn* is perhaps the nearest surviving architectural relative to the great imperial Byzantine palaces.

This architectural and palatial theme is extended to the façade and *sahn* mosaics in the Damascus Mosque, where we find some of the most extensive and extraordinary mosaics of the eighth century. The pictorial scheme is of architectural panoramas and vistas set along the banks of a flowing river among verdant trees. The tradition of architectural representation goes back to the Roman wall paintings of Pompei and Herculaneum and splendid Byzantine examples of this genre can be seen in the fourth-century mosaics of Hagios Georgios in Salonica. In Damascus there are representations of shell niches with curtain drapes similar to those in the sixth-century mosaics of St Apollinare in Classe and St Apollinare Nuovo in Ravenna. The acanthus scroll-work in the soffits of a number of arches in the Damascus Mosque is similar to eighth-century iconoclast decoration in the Haghia Sophia in Constantinople. Unlike the Dome of the Rock, the decorative scheme at Damascus is entirely western in its inspiration, and this supports al-Tabari's account that the work was carried out by craftsmen from Constantinople. Richard Ettinghausen distinguishes three types of building, the two-storied palace pavilion, the domestic house and open roofed gateways.[8] The palatial buildings, with their pilasters, niches, balustrades and scrolls, are flat, decorative and emblematic in treatment, whereas other buildings are integrated into rocky landscapes and rendered in light and shade with a quirky perspective reminiscent of the early Cubist paintings of Picasso and Braque.

As at the Dome of the Rock, there are no human and animal forms and the meaning of these mosaics is still open to much speculation. Some believe that they represent a paradisial image of the city of God, but Ettinghausen suggests that they may represent the known world in a state of peace and harmony under Muslim rule.[9] He points out that architectural imagery in contemporary Christian art invariably includes figures and realistic detail showing the defensive aspect of towns with walls and battlements, whereas the Damascus mosaics present an idyllic vision of a golden age, in which palaces, pavilions and villas luxuriate in a lush landscape set among flowing streams. For the Arab people arriving from the arid landscape of Arabia this is a bountiful vision of paradise, and the Damascus mosaics show freshness and energy, and these must be ranked among the best examples of eighth-century iconoclast art.

Soon after these mosaics were completed, the Byzantine world followed Muslim iconoclasm, but the remains of Christian iconoclast art are patchy, and John Beckwith suggests that to arrive at any estimation of what it was like you have to look at the Umayyad monuments of Palestine and Syria.[10] The whole iconoclast controversy reflects the symbiotic relationship between Islam and Christianity at this time. Islam provided a haven for heterodox Christianity, and some of the most outspoken Christian iconodulists, like the anathemised St John of Damascus (c. 675–749), were able to challenge the new orthodoxy under the security of Muslim jurisdiction. St John, like his father and grandfather, held high political office in Damascus. He served as a high-ranking financial officer to the caliph and was free to indulge in Christian and Muslim polemic within the tolerant atmosphere of Damascus. His great theological work, *The Fount of Knowledge*, written during his retirement in the Palestinian monastery of Mar Saba, not only argues the iconodulist case but also gives the first Christian critique of Islam which he perceived as another manifestation of Christian heresy. In Syria, Palestine and Egypt there was a fluid relationship between Islam and Christianity, and the differences between them were not initially perceived as insurmountable. Many Byzantine theologians regarded Islam as an expression of the Arian heresy which denied the divinity of Christ, maintaining that he was not of the same substance as the Father. This view is proclaimed in the Qur'anic inscriptions on the Dome of the Rock, and it is clear that Islam made its own voice felt in the wider Christological controversies. Islam did not claim to be a new faith, but stressed the prophetic tradition which Muslims, Jews and Christians have in common. That is

why Abraham, Ishmael and John the Baptist are venerated in Damascus and Jerusalem and why Muslims believe Jesus will appear in the Damascus Mosque on the Madinet 'Isa ('Jesus minaret') on the Day of Judgement. Evidence of the close and complex relationship between Islam and Christianity is clearly manifested in its most creative and visible form, in the architecture of the Dome of the Rock and the Great Mosque at Damascus.

Islam's skilful absorption and adaptation of existing cultural traditions can also be seen in secular architecture, although here the picture is more fragmented and ambiguous. Umayyad secular architecture is represented by a number of ruined palaces, but the meanings we can ascribe to them have to be provisional, because archaeological evidence is patchy and incomplete. In one sense the Umayyads left an impressive legacy of palace architecture because they built in reasonably permanent materials. But whole epochs of Muslim history reveal no architectural evidence of court life whatsoever. Our knowledge is largely supplied by literature, and much of this, like the *Arabian Nights*, is fed on romance and mystique and belongs to the realm of the imagination. We have to wait for the fourteenth-century palace of the Alhambra, in Granada, to see a complete architectural expression of Muslim courtly splendour, but this also has been distorted and romanticised by the arts and literature – this time by western writers and composers like Washington Irving and Francisco Tarrega. Nothing has survived of the great Umayyad imperial court at Damascus, and ruins of palace architecture consist of desert palaces or country retreats.

These buildings were unlikely to have been used by the caliphs; they probably served the needs of an aristocratic elite who may have exercised here devolved powers of government. They are described by Oleg Grabar as typologically related to the Roman villa, or villa rustica.[11] Many contain features, like bath-houses, which appear to be straight adaptations of Roman domestic architecture, but their fortified aspect suggests other influences, such as Roman frontier garrisons and military camps. As previously stated, the genesis of secular architecture is characterised by ambiguity – certain categories of building, such as caravansarais, *ribats* and palaces, share a common architectural language.[12] Function cannot necessarily be deduced from form, because they evolved and diverged from flexible multi-purpose structures which lack clear differentiation. Robert Hillenbrand points out, for instance, that the Syrian palaces of Qasr al-Hair West and Qasr al-Hair East may also have served as caravansarais.[13] Most palaces share with caravansarais and *ribats* a square plan with curtain walls, bastions, a main gate and two-tiered arrangements of rooms around an inner court. Later palaces evolved more elaborate complexes of buildings within the curtain wall, forming a city within a palace, and such configurations derive in equal measure from Roman and Sasanian prototypes.

The notion of a desert palace has been revised, since archaeology has revealed that they occupied cultivated ground and relied on sophisticated systems of irrigation. Qasr al-Hair East (728–29), now isolated in the desert 200 kilometres east of Palmyra, was supplied by a water course which flowed from a nearby dam. The palace formed two enclosures and occupied what may have been an oasis garden as well as a cultivated estate. The smaller enclosure almost certainly was a caravansarai, suggesting a degree of commercial development. The best preserved is the smaller enclosure, square in plan, with a curtain wall in which are engaged twelve semicircular towers at regular intervals, forming bastions at the corners and flanking the entrance gate. The towers bestriding the gate are capped by brick domes under which are decorative bands of brickwork, panels and stucco. The gate has a horizontal lintel, surmounted by a semicircular relieving arch flanked by blind niches with fluted hoods. Between the entrance towers is an early manifestation of a machicolation (a projecting parapet supported on corbels from which projectiles and boiling oil could be disgorged), a device which was commonplace during the Crusader period.

The use of decorative stucco, an aggregate of plaster with cement or concrete, is widespread in the east, suggesting Parthian and Sasanian influence. A fine example can be seen on the gate of Qasr al-Hair West (727), which has now been reconstructed and moved to the National Museum in Damascus. The composition of the gate is broadly similar to that at Qasr al-Hair East, with two semicircular towers flanking a rectangular door with a horizontal lintel surmounted by a semicircular relieving arch. There is no machicolation between these towers; instead a blind arcade is surmounted by two windows.

The towers are ringed at the top with stepped crenellations (merlons) containing arrow slits. However, this fortified aspect is completely contradicted by the fragile, lace-like stucco covering the whole façade. The towers are decorated with alternating lozenge and square panels, bands of rosettes and trellises arranged in oblique and trefoil patterns containing beautifully incised sprays of acanthus leaves. Other decorative features suggest Roman influence and include blind arcading made up of alternating triangular and semicircular niches and pediments.

In addition to surface decoration, figurative sculpture adorned both the façade and the interior of the palace, showing that iconoclasm did not apply here. During the steady decline of Byzantine rule, figurative sculpture took on a new lease of life in Muslim secular art. While the Umayyads rejected the religious imagery that so vividly expressed Byzantine cultural identity, it appears they wilfully felt free in the secular domain to create what the Byzantines neglected. The revival of sculpture in the round was facilitated by the use of stucco,

Syria, the gate of Qasr al-Hair West reconstructed in the National Museum of Damascus

a significant import from Persia and Central Asia, which proved flexible and easy to manipulate. It was used liberally in many Umayyad palaces, producing remarkably rich and exuberant programmes of figurative sculpture, but it was short lived. Figurative art was to flourish in secular painting, but sculpture in the round, both human and animal, did not develop in any significant form after the fall of the Umayyad dynasty.[14]

The decoration and sculpture of Qasr al-Hair West provide further evidence of the cultural appropriation and synthesis of the Dome of the Rock and the Great Mosque at Damascus. The relief decoration of the façade is hybrid, but Grabar has identified clear Palmyrene imitation in the reclining and draped figures, as well as Byzantine and Sasanian borrowings in others.[15] Similar loans from eastern and western sources are confirmed in two contrasting fragments of floor fresco at Qasr al-Hair West. They are painted imitations of mosaic, and Ettinghausen points out the classical tradition of one, featuring two centaurs above a roundel containing the earth goddess Gaea, and the Sasanian style of the other, depicting two musicians and a huntsman on horseback.[16] Further examples of cultural synthesis can be seen in other palaces, such as Mshatta in Jordan (744). Its

Syria, Qasr al-Hair West: early eighth century fresco of two musicians and mounted horseman

limestone façade, now preserved in Berlin, contains some of the most celebrated decorative stone carving in early Muslim art. It consists of large, upright and inverted triangular panels, set in zigzag moulding, enclosing large rosettes formed in octagonal and lobed hexagons. The main field of the design consists of finely carved interlacing vine-stalks enlivened by winged palmettes, grapes, heraldic animals, birds, cupids and human-headed lions. Creswell points out that some of the mythic animals are Sasanian in origin, and the vine, grape and rosette motifs can be traced to Coptic ivories and wood carving.[17] There is also a revealing insight into decorative propriety, in that animal and figurative emblems on the left hand façade give way to non-figurative arabesques on the right, where they adorn the outer wall of the mosque.

One of the richest and most complex of palace structures was Khirbet al-Mafjar, built by Caliph Hisham just outside Jericho in Palestine (724–43). Here is an enigmatic sculptural art in the palace entrance and dome canopy, where repeated stucco busts project from medallions wreathed with beaded interlaced ribbons. Oleg Grabar suggests that these figures may derive from Coptic textiles, but their stark frontality, enlarged almond shaped eyes and stylised hair call to mind Palmyrene funerary busts. Grabar observes other cultural influences on the sculpture in the bath-house, where a prince in the Sasanian style and other figures may possibly have a Central Asian origin.[18] Perhaps the most striking feature of this palace is the use of mosaic, which decorates the floor of the bath-house. The scheme is essentially geometric, but the geometry belongs to Roman and Byzantine tradition and the distinctive dynamic of Islamic geometry is not yet discernible. The patterns are arranged in rectangular and circular panels and borders, like the pavements at Ephesus, and many of the motifs can be identified as Roman.[19] In Qasr al-Hair West, fresco imitated mosaic, but at Khirbet al-Mafjar discrete panels of mosaic give the impression of individually patterned rugs, and for all of its richness the overall design lacks coherence. The textile comparison is confirmed by one masterpiece of mosaic design presented like a tapestry bordered by tassels. On a raised platform in an apsidal audience room off the main hall, it depicts an apple tree sheltering three grazing gazelles. The tranquillity of the scene is broken by the leap of a lion, which attacks one of the creatures. According to Ettinghausen this subject has long traditions associated with royalty in the ancient Near East.[20]

The central dome and cross-vaults of the bath-house are supported on sixteen piers, and in structural terms it owes much to Byzantium. So do the clusters of apses on all sides of the main hall, but the shape of the piers, which are square in plan with engaged corner columns, foreshadows Abbasid architecture; similar piers were used in the Great Mosque at Samarra, Iraq (847) and in Ibn Tulun's Mosque in Cairo (879). The sculptural richness of the interior, with its atlas figures, bare-breasted women, loin-clothed men, kaftanned caliph and density of stucco

decoration gave it an oriental flavour which complemented the western-style mosaics below. This was a prestigious and sumptuous building, probably more than just a bath-house. Oleg Grabar suggests that it served as a supplementary reception hall for pleasure, entertainment and banquets, and supports this hypothesis with evidence from sources describing the lavish ceremonies of the Umayyad court.[21] The heirs to the Roman Empire adopted the life-styles as well as the architectural, decorative and pictorial language of their predecessors.

This pleasure-loving and worldly aspect of the Umayyad character is further revealed in the palace at Qusair Amr in Jordan (712–15). The audience hall and

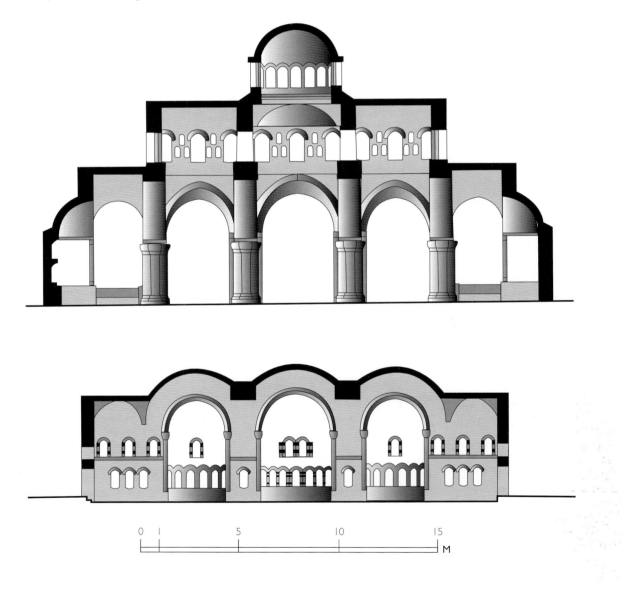

Palestine, perspective of Khirbet al-Mafjar

baths, which are in a remarkable state of preservation, survive, unlike at Khirbet al-Mafjar, which we can only envisage in its totality through R. W. Hamilton's reconstructions. The audience hall of Qusair Amr is like a basilica divided by pointed transverse arches and roofed by three parallel barrel vaults. The central aisle terminates with a throne recess giving access to, and flanked by two rooms with apsidal ends. To the left of the hall a door leads to the baths which consist of a barrel-vaulted changing room, a cross-vaulted *tepidarium* and a domed *calidarium* with half-domed recesses. Structurally, this modest building, like Khirbet al-Mafjar, owes much to Byzantium, but such innovations as the pointed transverse arches are among the earliest in Islamic architecture. The most interesting and revealing features are the painted frescoes which adorned all the rooms above wainscot level. These, like the building itself, have their roots in Roman and Byzantine art, but they also reveal other cultural traditions and values.

Due to habitation by bedouins, the frescoes have deteriorated considerably since Alois Musil discovered the palace in 1898. Much of our knowledge relies on copies made at the time by the Austrian artist Mielich who accompanied Musil, but as Creswell points out most of these were painted retrospectively in the studio rather than in situ, and they are an unreliable record of the originals.[22] The subject-matter includes scenes of hunting and building, athletics, gymnastics, nudes, monarchs, mythological personifications, stars and astral symbols. Greek tradition accounts for the hunting, athletics and wrestling, as well as the personifications of Poetry, History and Philosophy. The *calidarium* is depicted as a heavenly vault showing the constellations and signs of the zodiac. Female nudes occur in the *tepidarium*, and while such figures are common in classical art they are extremely rare in the art of Islam and only appear subsequently in the private setting of the harem. Ettinghausen points out that while the painting technique is essentially Roman, the expression of female beauty is very unclassical and conforms more to the ideals of the East (possibly India), as well as descriptions in bedouin erotic poetry.[23]

In the audience hall are two frescoes deriving from Byzantine and Persian iconography symbolising Islamic conquest and supremacy. In the throne recess is a seated and haloed figure, in the Byzantine style, placed under a baldachin and surrounded by birds and sea monsters; it is thought that he represents the caliph. The fresco on the west wall depicts six monarchs with hands raised in a gesture which has been variously interpreted as deference or greeting.[24] Four of the figures are identified by Greek and Arabic inscriptions: they are the emperor of Byzantium, the Shah of Persia, the Negus of Ethiopia and Roderick, the last of the Visigothic kings of Spain. The monarchs are arranged in geographical order, west to east, with the great empires represented in front and the lesser behind. The emperors of Byzantium and Persia stand in front of Roderick and the Negus, and it has been deduced that the unidentified figures are the emperor of China and the Khan of the Turks. Some, but not all of the figures, represent vanquished nations, but there is no sense of triumphalism in the presentation, and they appear to be acknowledging the caliph in the throne recess with dignified respect. Oleg Grabar has interpreted the scene as a representation of a family of kings paying homage to the caliph whom they accept as their superior and successor.[25]

Like the mosaics and inscriptions of the Dome of the Rock, these frescoes are a manifestation of Islamic supremacy, and the Umayyads skilfully manipulated pre-Islamic symbol systems to assert and proclaim their inheritance of and entitlement to the lands, crowns and governance of their expanding empire. The Qusair Amr frescoes also draw attention to the wider political geography of the Muslim world and its relationship with neighbouring empires in China and Africa.

Because Syria was the geographical centre of the Umayyad Empire, its art and architecture were bound to draw initially on the cultural legacy of Byzantium. However, the evidence of secular architecture reveals the growing impact of eastern influences from Persia and Central Asia, and in a number of palaces, like Mshatta, in Jordan, and Khirbet al-Mafjar, just outside Jericho, new decorative and structural combinations appeared. This emerging synthesis mirrors the growing importance of the peoples of the eastern empire who were soon to challenge the Umayyad status quo and dramatically change the course of Islamic history. The relationship between Muslim and *dhimmi* culture became less of an issue as the expanding Muslim nation came to terms with the pluralism of its own society and struggled to accommodate and express this with new ways of architectural thinking.

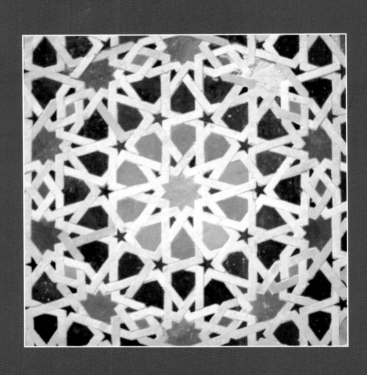

CHAPTER 3

AN EMERGING
ISLAMIC IDENTITY

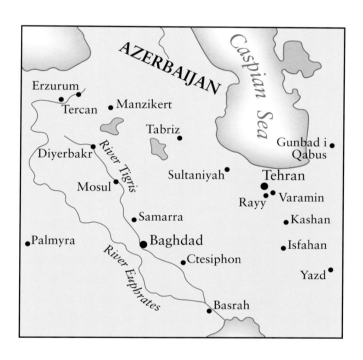

Like Christianity, Islam has never been monolithic, and from the outset the Muslim community was diverse and complex, and that complexity was compounded by vast territorial gains. Arab migration outside the Arabian Peninsula did not begin with the first wave of conquest. There had been substantial Arab settlement, particularly in Palestine and Syria, in pre-Islamic times. There were numerous scattered bedouin groups, and the populations of the great cities of Palmyra and Petra were principally Arab. Those older Arab communities were not, of course, Muslim at the time of the Arab conquests. The new ruling class of Muslim Arabs who established centralised government from Damascus was very much an aristocratic elite unwilling to extend its social and economic privileges to Muslims outside its own Arab caste. They paid no taxes on their newly acquired estates, while relying on substantial tax revenues from *dhimmis* and non-Arab converts to Islam known as the *mawali*. The *mawali* were mainly native Persians, Egyptians, Berbers and other non-Arabs who had converted to Islam but found themselves, like the *dhimmi*, second-class citizens, despite the notion that they were equal in the faith. These inequalities fostered resentments which ultimately brought down the Umayyad dynasty.

As Bernard Lewis explains, discontent among many Muslim converts attracted them to Shi'ite rather than Sunni Islam.[1] Zoroastrian conversion to Islam in Persia was far more widespread than Christian and Jewish conversion in the west, and Shi'ism became a focus for political dissent because it challenged the *status quo* and questioned the legitimacy of the Umayyad caliphate. The Shi'ites only recognised the descendants of the Prophet through Ali and Fatima as legitimate successors, and their notion of the Imamate, embodying divine knowledge and authority, is in marked contrast to the more pragmatic and secular concept of the caliphate in Sunni Islam. The worldly life-styles of some Umayyad caliphs prompted a demand in some quarters for a spiritual revival expressed in a belief in a leadership embodying infallibility and divine right. It is also significant that this desire for divine leadership sprang from and took root in those parts of the empire, such as southern Arabia and Persia, where there was an ancient history of divine monarchy in the form of priest kings. Shi'ism represented a serious threat to the Umayyad caliphate, which explains why the revolt of

Ali's son, Husain, was put down so ruthlessly at the battle of Karbala in 681.

A broad alliance of various discontented factions, both Arab and *mawali*, brought down the Umayyad dynasty. Many Arab communities had always maintained a traditional resistance to any form of centralised control, and like the *mawali*, they also felt marginalised and excluded by the ruling elite of Damascus. The wars of conquest had subsided, and according to Bernard Lewis, the ruling Arab class was losing its role and purpose in the new order, which demanded the skills of bankers, merchants, artisans and those most effectively able to contribute towards a peacetime economy.[2] Opposition to the Umayyads started in Kufa, where Muhammad ibn Ali ibn al-Abbas, a descendant of the Prophet's uncle Abbas, took over the leadership of the rebel Hashimiya faction, which also had strong support in Khurasan. After Muhammad's death, his son Ibrahim took over, and with the help of Abu Muslim, who rallied the forces in the east, the Umayyad dynasty was overthrown at the battle of the Great Zab in 750. Ibrahim was succeeded by his brother Abu al-Abbas, who established the Abbasid dynasty, which lasted for five centuries.

The second caliph, al-Mansur, established the new city of Baghdad as the capital of the empire in 762, a move that inaugurated a radical change between the old and new Arab dynasties. The Umayyad dynasty, constructed on Byzantine foundations, had been ruled by an Arab aristocracy in its own interests, whereas the Abbasid Empire was an Islamic empire with a much broader, more cosmopolitan outlook. The new dynasty assumed the autocratic style of the old Sasanian monarchy with all its courtly magnificence, and al-Mansur established a basis for government that secured a degree of stability until the end of the reign of Harun al-Rashid (d. 809). Something of this centralisation of power and autocratic style of government is reflected in the city of Baghdad itself where the palace, government buildings and mosque form a kind of omphalos, a nucleus, dominating the centre of a circular city. It was like a huge fortified palace in a circular enclosure 2,300 metres in diameter. Perimeter walls were divided into quadrants by four equidistant gates surmounted by gilded domes, and the whole city was encircled by a ditch. The walls were strengthened by intermediate towers with

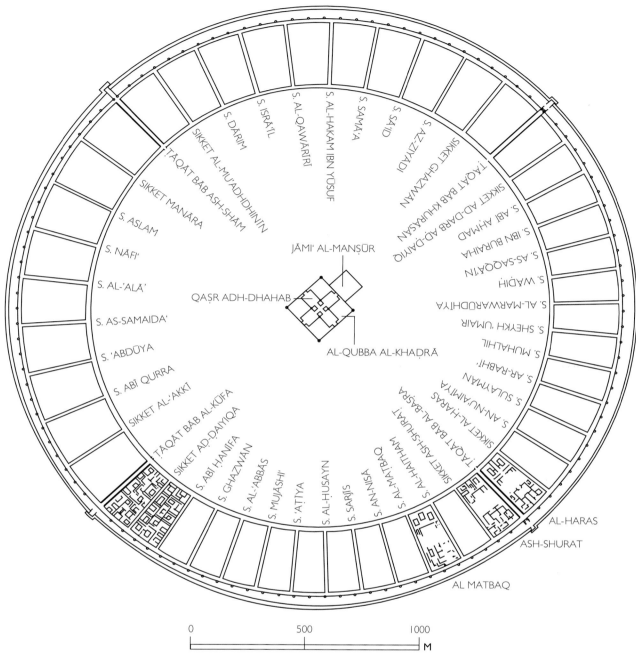

Plan of Baghdad. (After Creswell)

ramparts wide enough to allow patrols of equestrian soldiers. Ringed inside the perimeter walls were the guards' quarters, arcades of shops and residential districts divided, like the spokes of a wheel, by eight to twelve streets in each quadrant. The hub of the city contained the palace; little is known about its form, but there are descriptions of a reception *iwan* (a vaulted hall open at one end) behind which stood a domed audience chamber surmounted by a second chamber covered by the famous

green dome with a weather vane on top in the form of a horseman holding a lance.

In its time Baghdad's circular form was regarded as unique, but this defensive plan has ancient roots which can be traced back to Assyrian military camps, and Creswell has identified at least twelve pre-Islamic cities that were similarly round or oval in this fashion.[3] Antecedents to Baghdad's city plan can be seen in the ruins of Hatra and the Sasanian city of Takht i Sulaiman, where royal and sacred precincts are set at the heart of circular fortifications. Very quickly the city expanded, and could not be contained within the original radius of the city walls, which eventually collapsed in the siege of 813 when al-Mamun became caliph after seizing the throne from his brother al-Amin. Nothing has survived of the age of al-Mansur, or of Harun al-Rashid, and the oldest buildings in Baghdad today are late Abbasid. These include the Tomb of Sitt Zubaida (1179–1225), the Minaret of Jami' al-Qumriyya (1228), the Mustansiriya (1233) and the Bishiriya Madrasa (1255), now known as the 'Abbasid Palace'. The Mongol sack of the city in 1258 effectively destroyed most of the city along with the Abbasid caliphate. Nevertheless, something of the imperial splendour of early Abbasid palatial architecture can be reconstructed in the desert palace of Ukhaidir 192 kilometres south of Baghdad.

Iraq, the Great Hall of Ukhaidir

Ukhaidir was unlikely to have housed the caliph, and according to Creswell it was probably built in 778 by Isa ibn Musa after he was forced to relinquish his claims to the throne and settled for a more reclusive life.[4] It remains one of the most impressive and awesome of desert ruins, and its state of preservation owes much to the permanence of its building material and its defensive character. Unlike most Umayyad palaces, this was a genuine fortified structure with strong curtain walls, corner and intermediary towers, machicolations, arrowslits and portcullises. The curtain wall is pierced on the south, east and west sides by gates, flanked by semicircular towers, with portcullises opening into vaulted vestibules, through which missiles, molten lead and boiling oil could be ejected. Ukhaidir was a palace fortress that occupied a

fertile tract of land; it stands as a self-contained unit set in the walls of an outer enclosure. In plan it resembles a number of its Umayyad predecessors, like Mshatta in Jordan, but the symmetrical and axial plan owes much to Sasanian architecture. It resembles the palaces of Qasr i Shirin in Iraq and Firuzabad, in southern Persia, with a formal layout suggesting a ceremonial way from the gate-house to the reception *iwan* and audience hall.

Two square towers in the centre of the north side form the main entrance to a vaulted room which leads to a second room covered with a fluted dome. From this domed chamber, two vaulted transverse corridors branch off left and right connecting the palace proper to the outer enclosure. The presence of horse-troughs in these passages suggests that they were used for tethering and stabling animals. The right wing of the corridor gives access to the mosque, which had an open *sahn* with

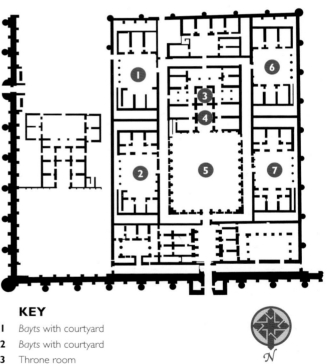

KEY
1 *Bayts* with courtyard
2 *Bayts* with courtyard
3 Throne room
4 Reception Hall
5 Court of Honour
6 *Bayts* with courtyard
7 *Bayts* with courtyard

Iraq, plan of Ukhaidir. (After Creswell)

Iraq, the palace of Ukhaidir

arcaded *riwaqs* on three sides, the widest forming a lateral barrel-vault over the *qibla* end. The position of the mosque to the right of the main entrance follows the example of Mshatta, and established a precedent for a number of subsequent *madrasas* and caravansarais. Returning to the main central axis of the building, the most impressive surviving feature today is the great hall, flanked with arched recesses and covered with a pointed vault over 10 metres high. This leads to the open Court of Honour surrounded by blind arcades, overlooked on the north side by an impressive three-storied façade and on the south by a vaulted *iwan* in the Persian style. The arch of the *iwan*, built higher than the flanking walls, was probably set in a rectangular frame, thus forming an early example of a monumental portal, or *pishtaq*.

Flanking the *iwan* were four rooms with decorative vaults, which probably supplemented the rear throne room as public and private audience chambers. A passageway encircled the whole of the central section, separating this official area from the *bayts*, or self-contained living apartments. This passage also provided the only access to the *bayts*, which formed four separate

units, each with its own central court. Two sets of triple barrel-vaulted rooms faced opposite sides of the court, and the central room of each, with its wider arched entrance, served as a reception room. The purpose of the space created by the outer enclosure is unknown. It may have provided additional defence, functioned as a corral or served to emulate the spatial ethos of the royal precincts of Baghdad.[5] Ukhaidir lacks the decorative refinement of earlier Umayyad palaces but impresses through its scale, mass and structural organisation. It carries imperial gravitas and stands as a forbidding monument, expressing in its formal layout and unyielding structure something of the autocratic power of the Abbasid regime. The rigidity of plan which characterises this and a number of early Muslim palaces was relatively short lived, and a distinguishing feature of later palace architecture is the asymmetrical, informal and often fortuitous patterns of organisation.

The Abbasid Empire reached its peak of political, economic and cultural power under Harun al-Rashid, and his reign is associated with great cultural and intellectual pursuits, as well as the vivid accounts of courtly splendour recalled in the *Arabian Nights*. His death, however, precipitated a war of succession between his sons, the first of many political and religious insurrections which gradually weakened the authority of the caliphate. In order to control an increasingly divided and fragmented military, the caliphs began to rely increasingly on Turkish slave troops from the Caucasus and Transoxiana. These slave troops, who were independent of the various warring factions, and who were loyal, gradually replaced regular Persian and Arab forces. They formed a *corps d'élite*, and Turkish slaves were used to fill the highest civilian offices of state. Gradually the caliphs surrendered their control to this emerging meritocracy and eventually became subordinate to their own viziers, bureaucrats, bodyguards and generals. The Turkish military became a law unto itself, and Baghdad's religious divisions between Sunni and Shia became so aggravated by Turkish policing that the city became ungovernable. Caliph al-Mu'tasim decided to abandon Baghdad, and in 836 he founded a new capital at Samarra, ninety-six kilometres to the north.

The building of Samarra was a major enterprise, and Mu'tasim brought in builders from all over the empire, including Egypt, where a number of churches were pillaged to provide suitable marble and columns. Samarra, and the neighbouring district of Ja'fariya, flourished as the seat of the empire for nearly thirty years before they were abandoned and the capital restored to Baghdad in 892. Today Samarra is a vast unexcavated archaeological site with few remains above ground. However, the monumental scale of the ruins of the Great Mosque provides one of the most impressive sights in the Muslim world. This haunting and evocative desert location outside the new town allows the distance, space and isolation necessary to appreciate the ruin's rugged weight and mass. Built by al-Mutawakkil in 852, this hypostyle mosque accommodated 100,000 people, making it the largest mosque in the world. All that remains are the bulk of the perimeter walls and the minaret. The walls, 3.65 metres in width, are made of brick and form a huge rectangle measuring 240 metres by 156. The east and west walls contain twelve semicircular bastions, the north and south walls, eight, and the whole architectural composition is rounded off and stabilised by the weight and projection of four circular corner towers. Sixteen doorways perforate the walls at regular intervals and between the bastions at the top of the curtain wall is a frieze of recessed squares and roundels. On the south side below the frieze the wall is pierced by twenty-four windows, which on the inside are set in recessed frames and crowned with five-lobed scallops.

Nothing remains of the interior of the mosque, and the only place to gain any visual impression of its plan and interior is from the minaret, where faint traces of the original piers can be seen. The prayer hall had twenty-five aisles perpendicular to the *qibla* wall, and the *sahn* was surrounded by *riwaqs* four aisles in width. The piers were brick-built octagons finished in stucco, on square bases, with marble columns at each corner. It was generally assumed that the roof rested on these piers in trabeated form, because there is no archaeological evidence of any arch springing. However, this assumption has been questioned by Robert Hillenbrand who suggests that probably arches did surround the *sahn*.[6] Traces of gold mosaic have been found in the spandrels of the *mihrab*, and contemporary descriptions say that Samarra rivalled Damascus in the splendour of its mosaics. Ernst Herzfeld's excavations at the beginning of the twentieth century found scattered remains of glass mosaic.

The most extraordinary feature of the mosque is its spiral minaret (the *malwiya*), probably the most intriguing architectural form in the Muslim world. This is freestanding and consists of a five-tiered solid brick helicoidal tower 53 metres high, set on a square base punctuated by nine arched recesses. A ramp of just over 2 metres in width spirals up the outside of the minaret, making five turns until it terminates at a cylindrical arcaded tower on the top. According to one source, al-Mutawakkil could ride up the ramp on a donkey.[7] This is such a singular construction that scholars have searched for explanations and sources in pre-Islamic architecture. Hillenbrand suggests two possible origins in the Zoroastrian fire towers of Persia and the Mesopotamian ziggurat. While most ziggurats had squared stepped elevations, like the step-pyramid at Saqqara, Hillenbrand identifies two at Khorsabad and Babylon that had cylindrical cores with encircling ramps similar to the Samarra minaret. Of the two possible sources, fire towers or ziggurats, for political reasons Hillenbrand is persuaded by the Persian fire tower. Persian influence, allied with anti-Syrian feeling, would have persuaded the Abbasid court to adopt a more

Iraq, the minaret of the Great Mosque at Samarra

Iraq, Samarra: the gate of Jausaq al-Khaqani

eastern architectural identity, and the ancient fire towers represented a continuity of religious usage that could appropriately be adapted to the new faith. Whatever may be the precise origin of this minaret, it was natural that long-standing local building styles and methods would be absorbed, and one major feature of the Samarra mosque is the use of brick, which is the ancient building material of Mesopotamia and Persia. The creative use of this material under subsequent Muslim patrons was to achieve spectacular results and fundamentally determine the course of Islamic architecture in Persia.

Al-Mutawakkil proved to be one of the stronger Abbasid caliphs, adopting a more autocratic style of government and dispensing with the services of his vizir. His attempt to sort out the religious divisions between Sunni and Shia led to less religious toleration and a more conservative affirmation of Sunni Islam. Free discussion of the traditional articles of faith was forbidden, restrictions were placed on the Shi'ites and further discriminatory laws were introduced against Christians and Jews. His despotism was matched by his passion for building, and after completing the Great Mosque he set about building

a new palace complex and mosque north of Samarra at Ja'fariya. Here stand the ruins of the Abu Dulaf Mosque, which has a plan and minaret similar to the Great Mosque at Samarra, but is much smaller in scale. Here the internal structure is well preserved, while the perimeter walls have collapsed. Mutawakkil's building activity, energetic as it was, represented a continuity of those ambitious programmes initiated by the caliphs Mu'tasim and al-Wathiq. Each caliph felt compelled to build his own palace, and Hillenbrand describes Samarra as a city of palaces, listing Istabulat, al-Huwaisilat, Ashnas, al-Quwait, Balkuwara, Qasr al-Jiss, Zanqur and Jausaq al-Khaqani, to name but a few.[8]

All that remains of most of the palaces are unexcavated traces; only a few fragments stand above ground. One of the best preserved standing buildings is the Bab al-Amma, the gate of the Jausaq al-Khaqani, or palace of al-Mu'tasim. A flight of marble steps led up to this gate with its imposing triple arched façade overlooking the Tigris. Its central recessed arch, 11.1 metres high and 17.5 metres deep, formed a substantial *iwan* in the Mesopotamian tradition. It marked the only formal entrance to a huge palace complex, and the central *iwan*, an audience hall, was originally decorated like the rest of the palace in richly patterned stucco. This decoration, consisting of large upright and inverted triangular panels, enclosing octagonal and lobed hexagons, is strikingly similar to the façade of Mshatta in Jordan. The scale of the *iwan* is significant because it demonstrates the growing use of the monumental gate as a symbol of royal authority, which has its antecedents in Roman, Parthian and Sasanian architecture. The flanking arched recesses, 4.1 metres deep, led into tunnel-vaulted rooms which accommodated the guards.

Behind the central *iwan* there were six antechambers leading to a court with a fountain. Beyond this was a Court of Honour and to the north of this main axis were private rooms belonging to the caliph arranged around three courts. The harem, on the south side of the throne room, contained a number of rooms with well-connected

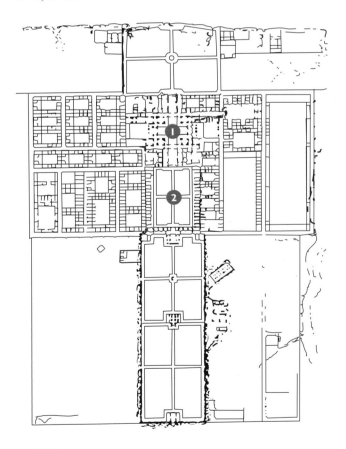

KEY

1 Throne Room
2 Court of Honour

Samarra, plan of the Palace of Balkuwara

water supplies, arranged around a court. The throne room itself had a domed square chamber in the centre, from which radiated four arms of a cross made up of triple-aisled basilican halls. The only clear antecedent for such a cruciform plan of basilica is the fifth-century church of St Simeon Stylites in northern Syria. From the eastern side of the throne room a wide hall opened on to a huge open esplanade measuring 350 by 180 metres. In the centre of the eastern side of this space is the small square *serdab*, consisting of parallel rows of stables enclosing an underground room with grottoes and a water basin. Beyond this another courtyard opened on to the polo ground, which was overlooked on the east side by a pavilion for spectators, who also had a view of the race-track behind. Other buildings within the palace complex included the great *serdab*, with its flooded basin, a treasury and barracks.

The palace of Balkuwara (849–59), built for al-Mutawakkil's son, has an enormous enclosure which also backs on to the Tigris. Unlike Jausaq al-Khaqani the plan of Balkuwara is much tighter and formally controlled. Within the rectangular enclosure, which is more than half empty, the buildings form a T-plan, the main axis being a processional way through three successive courts to the cruciform throne room. A series of monumental gates marked the progress through each court to the triple *iwan* entrance leading from the Court of Honour to the throne room. The right arm of the throne room led to a courtyard, in the north-west of the palace, and a number of *bayts*, probably the harem. Nearby were two open spaces forming a polo ground and a square lined with shops and more *bayts*. The left arm of the throne room led to a labyrinthine concentration of residential accommodation made up of clustered *bayts* around courtyards surrounded by up to twenty-one rooms.

Our knowledge of the Samarran palaces is fragmentary. They were constructed very quickly in mud brick and seem to have disappeared as rapidly when they were abandoned and their materials plundered for other building purposes. What has survived in some quantity is the stucco decoration, which was less useful for recycling. The use of stucco was extensive, as it was cheap, malleable and ideally suited for covering coarse surfaces of mud brick and rubble. It may have been that the necessity to cover large surfaces of this nature fostered the occasional tendency in subsequent Islamic architecture for surface decoration to take precedence over structure. Little stucco decoration remains *in situ*, but there is sufficient to indicate the extent of design innovation. Creswell has identified three styles. Style A relates to the Dome of the Rock and Mshatta in Jordan, and consists of vine patterns with five-lobed leaves, stalks, grapes and palmettes. Style B is less naturalistic and made up of more compact, centralised rosette forms arranged in squares, octagons and lozenges. Style C relied on the use of moulds to produce repeat patterns in shallow bevelled relief. What emerges is a new decorative language of unbounded arabesques, in which vegetal forms are locked into a repeat system in such a way that no individual element dominates, but functions in one tightly organised unit. Such decorative innovations were brought to maturity when they were exported to the mosque of Ibn Tulun in Cairo and regulated within a more rigorous geometric framework.

Samarra was built because the capital was ungovernable, but the caliphs faced even greater difficulties maintaining authority over the empire. Only Mutawakkil was successful, but after his death anarchy returned, and the caliphs became puppets in the hands of their Turkish *amirs*. When al-Mu'tamid became caliph in 870 he returned to Baghdad, but in his weak reign the empire disintegrated further. In the east the Tahirid, Saffarid and Samanid sultanates broke away in Khurasan, Transoxiana and Sijistan. From 882 the governor of Egypt, Ahmad ibn Tulun, ruled independently of Baghdad and established a dynasty that lasted until 905. Spain had broken away at the birth of the Abbasid caliphate when a surviving member of the Umayyad family, Abd al-Rahmin, escaped to the West and founded a new Umayyad dynasty in Cordoba in 756. Tunisia became independent in 800, and it is here that an architecture of monumental simplicity developed in a way that expresses a grandeur born of the austerity, piety and discipline that governed the empire's expanding frontier.

The first successful invasion of Tunisia was in 647 when Arab forces routed an army of 120,000 men led by the Patrician Gregory at Sbeitla. However, it was the third Muslim invasion, led by Oqba ibn Nafi, that permanently established Arab rule in Tunisia and secured the foundation of the city of Qairawan in 670. The most significant

ruling dynasty were the Aghlabids, founded by Ibrahim ibn Aghlab, governor of Tunis, in 800. The Aghlabids were Arabs who served as governors ruling in the name of the Abbasids, but Baghdad had no control over their affairs and they were to all intents and purposes independent rulers. The native population was Berber, and although they frequently resisted Arab rule they did convert to Islam, join Arab armies and as co-religionists felt generally less alienated under the new regime than they had under Byzantine, Vandal and Roman occupation. Where disaffection occurred, the Berbers expressed their resistance, like groups in the East, by embracing Shi'ism, thus sowing the seeds of the future Fatimid dynasty. Among the Arabs themselves there was fragmentation into a number of sects, and Qairawan for a time became a centre for religious puritanism. Nevertheless, the Aghlabid dynasty ruled for over a century and presided over a golden age in which its political and cultural strengths were manifested in an architecture of strength and integrity.

Tunisia, Qairawan: the exterior of the Great Mosque

The Great Mosque of Qairawan in Tunisia was founded by Oqba ibn Nafi in 670 and was rebuilt several times before the present building was constructed in 836 by Ziyadat Allah. The minaret survives from an earlier period, possibly from 724, but the *mihrab* and the dome in front of it were added by Abu Ibrahim Ahmad in 862, and two aisles were built to the north of the sanctuary by Ibrahim II after 875. The building today is, nevertheless, substantially the original work of Ziyadat Allah, and it presents a remarkable unity of design and form for a mosque of this antiquity. It is a hypostyle congregational mosque, essentially Muslim in its architectural concept and owing little to Rome, Byzantium or any pre-Islamic building tradition. There are plenty of recycled pre-Islamic Roman and Byzantine parts, in the form of masonry fragments and columns, but the general plan and layout, which was repeated across much of North Africa and Spain, is new and characteristically Arab.

Unlike the Damascus Great Mosque, the Qairawan Mosque is in the *medina* within the city walls in a residential area away from the main shopping streets. It is in complete harmony with the surrounding flat-roofed traditional buildings and the wider landscape beyond. The perimeter walls are massive, broken only by irregular heavy buttresses and gates which give the building a strong fortified aspect. These buttress reinforcements have been added piecemeal over the centuries and they abound in all shapes, sizes and varieties of form. Some are sturdy

Tunisia, Qairawan: the *qibla riwaq*

Tunisia, Qairawan: the prayer hall of the Great Mosque

Tunisia, Qairawan: Bab Lala Rejana at the Great Mosque

rectangular piers of differing width, others are flat topped, while the majority have sloping tops which angle back at various levels. This pattern is periodically broken on the east and west sides by eight arched doorways flanked by columns. The most striking of these is the domed porch on the east side known as the Bab Lala Rejana, built in 1294 when the mosque was restored under the Hafsid Dynasty. Creswell describes the exterior irregularities as unsatisfactory and laments the use of whitewash, but the whitewash has gone today and it is the fortuitous accumulation of these buttresses and excrescences that give the walls their sculptural complexity and interest. These walls, with their variety of shape, angle, disposition and massing, create a rich and complex visual interplay of solid, void, shadow and interval, which invite the spectator to explore the textures, planes and surfaces like a good piece of sculpture.

There is a *sahn* and prayer hall, but the plan is very different from that at Damascus in several respects. In Damascus the arcading of the prayer hall runs parallel to the *qibla* wall. Here the prayer hall is divided by a central nave, with eight flanking aisles, sixteen in total, which

step seven arches deep towards the *mihrab* and terminate at a transverse arcade 6 metres short of the *qibla* wall. This space between the arcade and *qibla* wall forms a transverse aisle which, combined with the perpendicular central nave, forms a T-shape plan which is a common feature of a number of early mosques, including the Aqsa Mosque in Jerusalem. The sense of space in the prayer hall is very different from that in Damascus, where the double-tiered arcades produce a lofty grandeur with an airy feeling of light and colour. The grandeur of this interior is of a different order. It is simple and dignified, with a lower ceiling giving more weight and prominence to the arcades, which articulate a stronger horizontal movement across an expansive floor space of simple rush matting. Compared to Damascus this is a densely packed hypostyle hall of columns, arches and bays, creating a more intimate interior, with the light entering laterally from the *sahn*, illuminating the columns and highlighting the rhythmic springing of the arches.

Perhaps the most significant feature of the prayer hall is the beautiful *mihrab*, which was the earliest to have received substantial decorative elaboration. This consists of a semicircular niche flanked by rich red marble columns with Corinthian capitals. Inside the recess are twenty-seven marble panels carved with arabesques, rosette motifs and openwork filigree. The hood has a delicate gilded arabesque of vine scrolls and grapes against a dark background. The *mihrab* arch forms a pointed horseshoe, and around the arch and surrounding it are monochrome and polychrome lustre tiles. These tiles, arranged in lozenge formation, contain Sasanian winged palmettes, peacock eyes and floral emblems, as well as geometric star patterns and calligraphic forms; these motifs are similar to contemporary wood and stucco decoration at Samarra. According to Creswell, these tiles appear not to have been designed specifically for this *mihrab*, and he quotes one documentary source that states that the Emir originally imported the tiles for a reception hall, as well as teak and marble panels from Iraq.[9] It is likely that these reception hall tiles were used for the *mihrab*, and Creswell mentions that their body clay was made of fine yellowish white clay which is characteristic of Samarra ware. Imports of porcelain from T'ang China, as well as the demands of the Abbasid court for luxury goods, considerably increased ceramic production in Iraq at this time. Lustre ware in particular became popular as a substitute for gold plate, and the tiles in Qairawan are the earliest dated lustre tiles of this period.

There is a degree of austerity in the early North African mosques, possibly reflecting something of the prevailing religious pietism. Here at Qairawan the only decorative feature is the *mihrab*, and this is the earliest use of one as a focal point of a mosque (the ones at Damascus are much later). The origin and meanings of the *mihrab* are essentially unknown. The first *mihrab* was installed in the Prophet's mosque at Medina by Umar ibn Abd al-Aziz under the orders of Caliph al-Walid in 709. Semicircular niches were used extensively in pre-Islamic times, most notably in classical architecture, where they usually contained statues, and similar niches like the one at Dura Europus, in Syria, occurred in Jewish synagogues where they formed a holy receptacle containing the scrolls of the Torah. Also a number of Christian monasteries, such as Mar Saba in Palestine, contained cells with prayer niches. In Islam the idea of the niche as a holy station, or receptacle, may have been inspired by the 'Light' verse of the Qur'an frequently found inscribed around the *mihrab*.

The image of the lamp in the niche provides one of the few recurrent symbolic images in Islamic art, but as far as the *mihrab* is concerned the general consensus is that it serves an honorific function commemorating the place where the Prophet stood leading the prayers.

Robert Hillenbrand suggests that the wider centralised aisle, or nave, leading towards the *mihrab* may have been introduced to function as a processional way and reflects something of the pomp and ceremony of the Friday prayers established in Damascus. He states that the dome placed over the *mihrab* also takes on an honorific function, and the introduction of a further dome at the other end of the nave gradually added more weight and importance to the processional axis of the central aisle. The dome in front of the *mihrab* at Qairawan is of great architectural significance, as well as possibly being the oldest masonry dome of its type. The zone of transition from square bay to circular dome is an intermediary octagon formed by the corner squinches and four sides of the bay. Radiating from the corners of the bay are four deeply cut shell squinches between which are set multi-foiled window spaces pierced by six lobed rosettes. Above this the drum, supported on further squinches, is pierced by a number of elaborately carved windows and blind panels surmounted by a beautifully proportioned ribbed dome. The whole ensemble is like a flowering plant with its repeat motifs of ribbed, lobed and scalloped forms, naturally opening out from one plane of transition to another.

Next to the *mihrab* stands an equally important wooden *minbar*, which is the oldest surviving example of its type. Abu Ibrahim Ahmad who installed the *mihrab* also had the *minbar* constructed out of the original consignment of imported teak. The delicate openwork carving in the vertical wooden panels of the *minbar* mirrors the arabesques and geometric configurations in the *mihrab* panels. The *minbar* consists of eleven steps leading up to a throne. Titus Burckhardt explains that according to tradition the first *minbar* consisted of a three-stepped platform on which the Prophet would sit addressing the congregation, resting his feet on the second step. When Abu Bakr succeeded to the caliphate, in deference to the Prophet he sat on the second step resting his feet on the third, and Omar in deference to both the Prophet and Abu Bakr sat on the third step with his feet

Tunisia, Qairawan: *riwaqs* around the *sahn* of the Great Mosque

on the floor.[10] According to Robert Hillenbrand the *minbar* functioned as a throne, from which a ruler would address his subjects, and therefore it fulfilled a political as well as a religious purpose. The Friday sermon, or *khutba*, frequently served political ends, as it does today, and the legitimacy of a newly installed ruler depended on formal confirmation in the Friday *khutba*.[11]

Beside the *minbar* is a latticed wooden structure of the same date known as a *maqsura*. This was a protected enclosure for the ruler and became a common feature in early mosques following the assassinations of the first caliphs. *Maqsuras* were invariably made of open lattice work so that the ruler could be seen participating in the daily prayers while maintaining a degree of princely aloofness and privacy. Such features are generally only found in the great Friday and imperial mosques. Later, as in Ottoman times, members of the ruling family were generally more discreetly out of sight in their own loggia, or gallery, with separate access.

The full architectural impact of this mosque is gained from the *sahn*, a vast open public space. Standing at one end, the prayer hall and flanking *riwaqs* face and

reach out in a huge embrace similar to that of Bernini's great colonnade curving around the Piazza of St Peter's in Rome. The *riwaqs* produce what amounts to a double aisled portico, like a cloister, around the *sahn*, but what is so delightful about this building is its many irregularities in plan, structure and detail. Most of the outer arches facing the *sahn* spring from piers faced with double columns, whereas the arches of the northern *riwaq* rest on single columns. The east and west *riwaqs* differ internally: the central arcade in one runs on double columns, and the other is on single columns crossed by transverse arches. These irregularities endow the building with character, as does the diversity of detail provided by a rich variety of recycled classical and Byzantine columns in all shapes and sizes; many columns have different sized impost blocks to bring them to a uniform height.

In the centre of the northern *riwaq* facing the prayer hall is the towering stone minaret, which is the oldest feature of the mosque. It is built in three storeys; the first two probably date from 724–27, when Caliph Hisham approved the purchase of land for its construction. The first storey is slightly tapered, the two smaller upper

Tunisia, Qairawan: the Great Mosque

storeys are crenellated, and the whole is capped with a fluted dome of later date.

A small entrance to the minaret is made up of fragments of Roman masonry, above which are a number of horseshoe-shaped relieving arches and three window openings that get progressively larger as they ascend. This is the oldest minaret of this scale, and its solid tower, 35 metres high, establishes the characteristic tower form of the North African and Spanish minaret. It is generally assumed that the origin of this form of minaret can be found in the stone towers of Syrian churches. During the Prophet's time, the call to prayer was inaugurated by Bilal, whose stentorian voice made the call from the roof of Muhammad's house. Thereafter the rooftops of mosques served that purpose until the corner towers of the *temenos* at Damascus were used. According to both Oleg Grabar and Robert Hillenbrand the evolution of the minaret may have been governed more by a desire for an outward display of Islam's presence, rather than by

purely functional considerations.[12] This makes sense because the cry of the *muezzin* cannot be heard effectively from very tall minarets, and all kinds of minarets provide very striking audio-visual landmarks on the skylines of so many Muslim cities. A number of writers make the point that the word *manara* is Arabic for lighthouse, and the minaret might have its formal roots in the lighthouses of late antiquity. With its three-tiered form, it has been suggested that the Qairawan Mosque minaret was inspired by the Pharos Lighthouse in Alexandria, and there is no doubt that minarets like this doubled up for defensive purposes as watch-towers and lighthouses.

The Great Mosque at Qairawan provided a model for most of the large congregational mosques in Tunisia. Next in importance is the Zaituna Mosque in Tunis, which was built by Abu Ibrahim Ahmad (856–63). Like the Great Mosque at Damascus, it is at the heart of the bazaar with the souks crowding in on all sides except one. The *riwaqs* form an irregular trapezoid plan, but the

Tunisia, Susa: the Great Mosque

prayer hall follows that of Qairawan in the T-formation of the central nave and transverse aisle along the *qibla* wall. The processional way through the nave is marked externally at each end by two melon-shaped domes. The *mihrab* dome is similar to that at Qairawan but is more elaborate and, according to George Michell, was erected during the Zirid period in 991.[13] The prayer hall columns are antique, with tall impost blocks and abacuses supporting transverse and perpendicular arches made of brick. The Zaituna was also a great seat of learning, competing with the al-Azhar in Cairo and the Qarawiyin in Fez. The Qairawan Mosque was to have a continuing influence into Fatimid times and the Great Mosque at Mahdiya, also in Tunisia (916) follows its example. The north façade is broad, solid and low slung, with a strong projecting central portal and two cubic corner towers (one is slightly trapezoidal) which contained cisterns. The central portal, a Fatimid innovation, is pierced by a horseshoe arch flanked on two storeys by four narrow blind niches. Similar niches punctuate the prayer hall façade above the arcade, foreshadowing such decorative devices in Fatimid Cairo. The *sahn* has four *riwaqs*, and the compact cubic organisation of space and mass gives this building a fortified character appropriate to its coastal location and in keeping with the city walls and ramparts.

A similar fortified aspect can be seen in the Great Mosque at Susa (Sousse) on the coast of Tunisia, with its ramparts, crenellations, corner bastions and towers. For the Aghlabid rulers the harbour at Susa was strategically crucial, as it was the main outlet to the Mediterranean

and became the springboard for the conquest of Sicily in 827. For this reason the city walls, the *ribat* and mosque, overlooking the harbour, all contributed in some defensive capacity. The mosque, dating from 850–51, has much in common with the Qairawan; it has a prayer hall of thirteen aisles leading towards the *mihrab* with a wider central aisle supporting two domes. The east, west and north *riwaqs* around the *sahn* have pronounced horseshoe arches set on squat piers. The arcade forming the façade of the prayer hall was built much later and has slightly pointed arches set on columns. Around the whole *sahn* is a splendid Kufic inscription, one of the earliest manifestations of calligraphy in an architectural setting on this scale. A staircase leads up to the roofs of the *sahn* arcades, these function as crenellated ramparts giving access to the domed octagonal corner towers which could be watch-towers and beacons.

The *ribat* near the mosque was a significant contribution to the harbour defences. *Ribats* are a distinctive feature of early Tunisian architecture and bear witness to the military activity during this early period of conquest, occupation and consolidation. They have been described as fortified monasteries functioning as military bases for soldiers prosecuting holy war (*jihad*). But Islam has never formally endorsed the notion of religious and military orders, and closed monasticism has never been encouraged in the Muslim world. The nearest equivalent to a monastery in architectural terms is the *tekke*, or *khanqah*, which provides accommodation for Sufi dervishes. The Sufi orders are confraternities, rather than monastic orders in the western sense, and access to them is open to the laity. It was commonplace for craft guilds and professions to seek affiliation with Sufi orders, including military units, such as the Turkish Janissaries, who were linked with the Bektasi order. However, the architectural form of the Susa *ribat* more appropriately resembles a caravansarai, or *han*, rather than a monastery.

As with the early palaces, the Susa *ribat* demonstrates the open-ended, multi-purpose character of certain categories of early Islamic architecture. A caravansarai protects a caravan, but the same building format can also function as a barracks, and the Susa *ribat* amounts to a fortified caravansarai for soldiers. It is square with eight semicircular towers, four at each corner and four in the centre of each wall. From the entrance, flanked by antique

ABOVE
Tunisia, Susa: the *ribat*

RIGHT
Tunisia, Qairawan: the Aghlabid Cisterns

Corinthian columns, the guard-rooms give on to a courtyard around which is an arcaded portico leading into twenty-six windowless rooms. A staircase from the courtyard gives access to the second storey, where barrel-vaulted rooms, or cells, are arranged around the east, west and north sides, while the whole of the south side is taken up by the prayer hall of the mosque. The windowless rooms on the ground floor served for storage and stabling, while the mosque and cells, in place of communal barracks, indicate the religious nature of the community that served here. In the south-east corner is a circular tower over 15 metres high which bears an inscription stating that it was built by Ziyadat Allah (who built the Great Mosque at Qairawan) in 822. It is essentially the mosque and cell accommodation that endows this building with its monastic character and distinguishes it from more secular *hans* and caravansarais. Nevertheless, as the need for military accommodation declined, such buildings in many other parts of the Muslim world were easily adapted to civilian purposes.

Among other outstanding monuments of the Aghlabid period are the two great water cisterns of Qairawan (860–63). The largest is a forty-eight sided polygon, over 1 kilometre in diameter and 8 metres deep, with rounded buttresses anchored internally and externally at each angle. An opening channel in the side connects this to the smaller cistern, which is a seventeen-sided polygon buttressed in similar fashion. The smaller cistern was fed by an aqueduct bringing water from Wadi Merj al-Lil; it functioned as a decanter, filtering the water through mud before it was passed into the larger cistern. In the centre of the main reservoir is a column which may have supported a pavilion providing a cool summer retreat or vantage point to view water sports. The building material is rubble coated with cement, and the cylindrical buttresses which rhythmically encircle these huge reservoirs create a monumental simplicity that echoes the spirit of the Great Mosque. Fifteen cisterns supplied the city; their scale recalls their Roman antecedents (the largest is comparable in dimension to the cistern at Bosra in Syria). Tunisia, the Roman province of Ifriqiyya, had been the bread basket of Rome. It contained a wealth of spectacular architectural monuments from Carthage to El Djem, which the Muslim builders used freely. The Aghlabid cisterns demonstrate that in Tunisia, as elsewhere, the Arabs sustained and developed methods of irrigation and hydraulic engineering that were essentially a part of their Roman heritage.

It could be said that military confrontation and expansion were the determining factor in Aghlabid architecture. They account for its essential austerity and

Tunisia, Susa: the *ribat*

simplicity. The *ribat* at Susa reveals the asceticism and rigours of frontier life. The same simplicity is expressed in the mosques of Susa, Qairawan, Tunis and Mahdiya. If worldly ostentation existed in Aghlabid architecture it would have been found in the royal cities of Raqqada and al-Abbasiyya, but like most later royal complexes these were constructed of insubstantial materials and little has survived. Tunisian architecture is stated principally through its mosques and fortifications which embody the dignity, energy and integrity of the Muslim faith at a time of expansion before the Aghlabids were ousted by the Fatimids.

CHAPTER 4

TULUNID AND FATIMID EGYPT

Unlike Baghdad and many other parts of the Muslim world Egypt was spared the ravages of the Mongol invasions in the thirteenth century when Egyptian forces led by Baibars and Sultan Qutuz defeated Kitbugha's Mongol army at 'Ayn Jalut in Syria in 1260. For this reason Cairo was never sacked and its buildings are preserved, providing us with an extensive and unique legacy of Muslim architecture ranging from the ninth to the nineteenth centuries. Cairo contains some of the world's greatest buildings, yet many have been much neglected while so much archaeological interest and architectural preservation has been devoted to Egypt's Pharaonic past. Western scholarship has been largely concerned with ancient Egypt, and as Edward Said has observed, the West has appropriated the world of the Pharaohs as a part of its own cultural legacy, leaving Egypt's Islamic identity somewhat marginalised.

The Muslim conquest of Egypt was led by Amr ibn al-As, who defeated the Byzantine forces at Heliopolis (now a suburb of modern Cairo) and secured a military base to the south at the Roman fortress of Babylon in 641. A year later Alexandria capitulated, and the Arabs were generally welcomed by the Monophysite Copts, who like the heterodox Christians of Palestine and Syria regarded them as liberators from the oppressive orthodoxy of Byzantium. After 646 it was decided to establish the new capital at Babylon, as being less vulnerable and more accessible to Arabia. The new garrison city which grew up around the fortress of Babylon was named al-Fustat (now the Coptic area of Cairo), and it was here that Amr established his headquarters and built his mosque.

Nothing of Amr's original mosque survives today because it was pulled down thirty-two years after his death and rebuilt to accommodate a larger congregation. The Caliph Mu'awiya ordered four corner minarets to be built; architecturally they are likely to have been similar to those at Damascus, amounting to little more than corner buttresses slightly raised above the roof-line. The mosque has undergone numerous demolitions and reconstructions since, and the present building broadly occupies the plan of the reconstructed mosque of 'Abd Allah ibn Tahir dating from 827. Creswell attributed some of the southern wall with its bricked-up windows to this period. The prayer hall today is a nineteenth-century reconstruction with twenty aisles running perpendicular to the *qibla* wall, unlike the original mosque where the aisles were parallel, as at Damascus. The arches spring from columns, and in the Cairene manner are reinforced with wooden tie-beams. To the right of the prayer hall are the remains of wooden beams carved in the Hellenistic style, with scroll-work similar to the pier cornices of the Dome of the Rock. These beams, with broken fragments of tie-beam, provide evidence of the original parallel arrangement of the arcading and most likely date from 827.

In the tenth century Muqaddasi reported that the mosque walls were covered in glass mosaic, evidence that the use of mosaic was more extensive in early Islamic architecture than many surviving buildings suggest. Doris Behrens-Abouseif says that gold and silver were used at various times to decorate the mosque.[1] Like the Dome of the Rock and the Qala'un Mausoleum, also in Cairo, the capitals of the columns were gilded, and during Fatimid times the *mihrab* and columns were embellished with silver. This lavish treatment indicates the veneration and respect for this mosque by successive generations, both Sunni and Shi'ite. Over the centuries prominent restorers have included Salah al-Din, Baibars, Qala'un, Qa'it Bay and Murat Bey, who virtually rebuilt the whole mosque in 1800. The mosque has been an important centre for teaching theology and law, and Imam Shafi'i, a founder of one of the four orthodox Sunni schools of law, taught here for many years in the eighth century.

Most of what we see in the mosque of Amr dates from the early nineteenth century, but one of Cairo's finest and oldest surviving Islamic monuments is the Nilometer on the Rawda Island. This was the instrument that measured the height of the Nile waters during the annual inundation and so determined irrigation policy. It was built by the Caliph al-Mutawakkil in 861. The Nilometer is a stone-lined pit, circular at the bottom and rectangular at the top, from which three lateral tunnels at different levels connect with the Nile from the east. Twenty-four steps lead down to a landing which faces four recessed arches. These pointed arches, framed with colonettes, are described by Creswell as 'tier point' arches, identical in form to those used by Gothic architects three centuries later.[2] The whole unit was capped by a wooden dome, and in the centre of the pit is an octagonal measuring column with a composite capital held at the top by a timber beam and secured at the bottom in a granite millstone. The measuring column is divided into 19 cubits, with the 16th-cubit mark representing the ideal flood level. The Nilometer is primarily an instrument of measurement, in which function determines form with a demanding precision.

In 868 the course of Egyptian history and its architecture fundamentally changed with the appointment of Ahmad ibn Tulun as governor. Ibn Tulun was a product of that slave meritocracy which brought about the downfall of the Abbasid caliphate. His father had been a slave from Central Asia who rose in the Abbasid court, becoming commander of the household of guards. Ibn Tulun received his military and theological education in Samarra before coming to Egypt, and this Samarran background is the key to understanding the architecture of his great mosque. When he arrived from Samarra Ibn Tulun had very limited powers, but after becoming financially independent of Baghdad, and building up a considerable army of Turkish, Sudanese and Greek troops, he clashed with the Abbasid co-regent, al-Muwaffak, and occupied Syria. The struggle for Egypt's autonomy remained unresolved when he died in 884, but his power base allowed his son, Khumarawaih, to take control. Khumarawaih signed a treaty with al-Muwaffak guaranteeing him and his descendants the right to rule Egypt, Syria and other territories for thirty years. He married his daughter to the new caliph and ruled a semi-independent empire which extended into Mesopotamia and Cilicia. The Tulunid dynasty lasted until 905 when, weakened by internal intrigues and insurrection in Syria, the imperial army stepped in and direct rule from Baghdad was re-established.

Cairo, the mosque of Ibn Tulun: central fountain and *ziyada*

After Ibn Tulun arrived in Egypt he moved the centre of government from al-Fustat to a new site north-east of Fustat called al-Qata'i and built a new city which included a palace, garrison, hippodrome, hospital, mosque and aqueduct. Only the mosque and aqueduct survive today, but there are descriptions of the palace and gardens laid out by Khumarawaih that suggest great indulgence and luxury on the Samarran scale. The mosque, built between 876 and 896, is the largest, oldest and in terms of grandeur, dignity and monumental simplicity the finest in Egypt. It is distinctly Samarran in style, and unlike any other Cairo mosque, and with the exception of the stone minaret, is made of brick faced

with stucco. The use of brick piers, rather than columns, to support the arcades is also a characteristic feature of Samarran architecture. Creswell quotes an unlikely story of a Christian who suggested the idea of brick piers in order to prevent the Muslims from plundering local churches for their columns. However, the mosque is obviously a Mesopotamian import, and Ibn Tulun brought with him his Samarran tastes and preferences as well as many Iraqi builders and craftsmen. It is a hypostyle mosque with four *riwaqs*, five aisles deep on the *qibla* side and two aisles deep around the rest of the *sahn*. The arcades of the prayer hall are made up of seventeen arches that run parallel to the *qibla* wall, and

the *sahn* is a square with an arcade of thirteen pointed arches on each of the four sides. The arcade on the side of the prayer hall is identical to the others, and there are no distinguishing features, such as a larger central aisle or dome, to emphasise this façade.

The whole mosque is enclosed in an outer perimeter wall known as a *ziyada* which isolated it from the noise of everyday life. This is also a feature of the Samarran mosques, but Creswell suggests that the *ziyada* may have more ancient origins in the sacred enclosure of the Roman *temenos*. In Hellenistic times the streets of a city would frequently terminate at the gates of the *temenos*, and Creswell suggests that in ninth-century Egypt the main streets of the bazaar probably converged on the doors to the *ziyada*. Originally the mosque was in a dense and crowded urban centre, but today the deep expanse around the imposing walls of the *ziyada* is clear and makes a worthy prelude to the immense space of the *sahn*. On a more mundane level, a part of the *ziyada* precinct was used for washing, and the original central fountain of the *sahn*, with its gilded dome, marble columns and basin, was purely ornamental. The present fountain in the centre of the *sahn* is the thirteenth-century work of Sultan Lajin.

The stone minaret stands off centre between the north-west wall of the mosque and the *ziyada* wall. It is a four-tiered structure with a square base and external staircase winding in an anti-clockwise direction up to a cylindrical tier which is topped by a two-storeyed octagonal section with a Mamluk pepperpot cap. It begins with a square plan and spirals into the cylinder, with stylistic roots in Samarra. In the eleventh and twelfth centuries contemporary writers commented on the similarity between this and the minaret at Samarra. There are some doubts about whether the existing minaret is original or a thirteenth-century reconstruction by Sultan Lajin or a mixture of both. Al-Mansur Lajin took refuge in the abandoned mosque of Ibn Tulun in 1296, following his assassination of Sultan al-Ashraf Khalil, and vowed that if he survived to take the throne he would restore the mosque. He did survive, became sultan the following year and began the restoration of the mosque.

There are many sections of the mosque which can obviously be attributed to the thirteenth century, most notably the *sahn* fountain and the top of the minaret. Creswell originally thought that the minaret was a

Cairo, the mosque of Ibn Tulun: the fountain with the Muhammad Ali mosque in the distance

Cairo, the mosque of Ibn Tulun: arabesque in the soffit of the arch

mixture of work by Ibn Tulun and restoration by Lajin. However, the underlying construction is a unified whole; if it had been totally reconstructed by Lajin it would have been built, like the fountain, in the thirteenth-century style, and as Behrens-Abouseif points out there would have been some commemorative inscription. From the side, it looks as if it would have been free standing, like the Samarran minarets, but it is connected to the north-west wall of the mosque by an arched bridge, which seems an intrusive addition clumsily blocking up one of the mosque windows. Also there are Andalusian-style windows, corbels and arches, which did not appear in Egyptian architecture until the thirteenth century. On this evidence, perhaps Creswell was right in his first assumption that the minaret is a mixture of original work by Ibn Tulun and restoration by Lajin.

The remarkable stucco decoration is an import from Samarra, which demonstrates that here and in Samarra Islamic art matured and developed its own unique decorative language. There may still be lingering traces of Byzantium and Persia, but the fusion of all these traditions generated an entirely new organisation of patterns, a new category of art. This is the earliest major manifestation of Islamic arabesque *in situ* on this scale. Plenty of fragments of stucco survive from the Jausaq al-Khaqani and Balkuwara palaces in Samarra, but here it functions within its original architectural framework in a remarkable state of preservation. The soffits of the arches demonstrate a densely patterned equation between geometry and arabesque. Vegetal motifs, consisting of vines, grapes, palmettes and stalks, are locked into geometric patterns in such a way that the competing elements co-exist in concord on the surface.

The new element – and this is characteristic of all Islamic design – is the resolution of opposites – static and dynamic, organic and geometric. Geometry acts as a trellis supporting the design, but it is never closed, crystallised or static. It is invariably dynamic and open ended and rarely seeks to find a point of rest or termination. The floral and vegetal arabesques are stylised and two dimensional, respecting the flat plane of the surface to be decorated, unlike Hellenistic ornament, which tends towards naturalism. As Owen Jones points out in *The*

Grammar of Ornament, the flowers and leaves of Greek scroll-work grow out of the surface while Islamic design is locked into it.[3] Owen Jones wrote his book in order to improve British design in 1856 and devoted a whole page on Arabian ornament to the mosque of Ibn Tulun. He believed the West could learn from Islamic art, and maintained that the Ibn Tulun marked a significant stage in the evolution of decorative art, which reached its peak in the Alhambra Palace in Granada.

Each pier in the Ibn Tulun, like those at Samarra, has a colonette in each corner, the capitals of which consist of vine-leaf motifs, which also form the central scroll-work in the delicate band of ornament that frames the face of each arch and forms an articulating band around the top of each pier above the capitals. The spandrel of each arch is pierced by a window framed with colonettes, flanked by rosettes and occasional square-patterned panels. Between two mouldings the rosette motif also provides a continuous frieze around the top of the *sahn* arcading and on the outer walls of the mosque. Also, beneath the crenellation runs a frieze of circles within a recessed square similar to those on the external walls of the Great Mosque at Samarra. All four walls of the mosque are pierced by over a hundred and twenty pointed arched windows which contain grills from many periods, and Creswell identifies four as original by their compass-work design similar to the marble window-grills of Damascus.

There are certain buildings like the Great Mosque at Cordoba and the Masjid i Jami in Isfahan which overwhelm us by a sense of their accumulated history. For this reason they do not always cohere in terms of style, but carry with them the residue of centuries which adds richness of form and association. Ibn Tulun's antiquity impresses in a different way, because it has retained its original form and much of its detail. It has a magnificently proportioned architectural unity, and its fundamental simplicity paradoxically makes it a visually complex building. The deep perspectives and the ranks of arcades frame an endless variety of vistas, making this one of the most photogenic buildings in Cairo. The one feature that does not conform to the Tulunid period is Lajin's fountain, which dominates the centre of the *sahn*, but this is successfully assimilated and forms an interesting counterpoint, making its own contribution to the many satisfying architectural alignments and groupings in the *sahn*. The

Ibn Tulun Mosque combines subtlety and refinement with grandeur of scale and is one of those buildings that reveals more on greater acquaintance.

The Tulunid dynasty, and the Ikhshidids who followed, re-established Egypt as a major independent power, something she had not enjoyed since the age of the Ptolemies. With the Fatimid conquest, Egypt became the centre of a considerable empire, and all formal links with Baghdad were severed. What emerged then too was an architectural independence that is uniquely Egyptian. The Fatimids were the most successful of the Ishma'ili sects which had wrought havoc in many parts of the Muslim world challenging the authority of the Sunni caliphate. They had been the most extreme sect of the Shia, believing in the infallibility of their Imams, evolving an esoteric interpretation of the Qur'an and managing their affairs with a masonic secrecy which made them very effective subversives. Because they refused to acknowledge the Sunni caliphate, the first Fatimid ruler of Tunisia, Imam Ubaidallah, claimed the title of caliph in 908. Like any radical opposition they had to moderate their more extreme doctrines when they achieved power and had to face the political and economic realities of office. This did not always satisfy their more zealous followers, and they encountered some pockets of resistance from fellow Ishma'ili groups such as the Carmathians in Syria. The Fatimids carved out a huge empire in North Africa, Syria, Palestine and the Hijaz, which became more powerful than that ruled by the Sunni caliphate. Mu'izz, the fourth Caliph, captured Cairo in 969 with the help of Jawhar al-Siqilli, his general, and a Jewish convert, Ya'qub ibn Killis, a brilliant economist who set up the financial and administrative base of the empire.

Jahwar was given the task of building a new city north of al-Qata'i called al-Qahira, from which modern Cairo gets its name. The walled city of al-Qahira became the political centre for the new dynasty with a major palace complex and several mansions for the ruling elite, while al-Fustat remained the economic hub of the expanding metropolis. Only some notable gates and fragments of the Fatimid city walls remain today, but much of old Cairo falls within those old boundaries, and the alignment of Fatimid streets remains the same, containing many of Cairo's most important medieval buildings as well as the craft and commercial area known

as the Khan al-Khalili, which is built on the site of the royal Fatimid cemetery. Jahwar was also entrusted with building a congregational mosque to serve the new city, with the added remit of making it a centre for higher learning. This was the al-Azhar Mosque which still remains the principle centre for Islamic theological scholarship in the Muslim world.

The mosque of al-Azhar was founded in 970 and named al-Azhar ('the radiant'), in honour of the Prophet's daughter Fatima al-Zahra, from whom the Fatimid dynasty claimed descent. It was established as a seat of higher learning, and along with the Qarawiyin Mosque and Madrasa in Fez al-Azhar is one of the oldest universities in the Muslim world (considerably pre-dating the foundation of European universities).[4] It was the Fatimid vision and mission to convert the whole Muslim world to the Ishma'ili faith and overthrow the Sunni caliphate in Baghdad. For this reason Ishma'ilism was strongly evangelical, and missionary activity was a major force. The caliph ruled by divine right and his government was

ABOVE
Cairo, the minarets of the mosque of al-Azhar

OPPOSITE
Cairo, the mosque of al-Azhar

divided between the military, administrative and religious hierarchies. Heading the religious sector was a missionary-in-chief who was responsible for organising a pan-Islamic network of missionary activity, as well as having responsibility for propaganda and education. Religion was highly politicised, and the establishment of al-Azhar as a major focus for Shi'ite learning represented a very significant religious and political threat to Sunni Islam. Its foundation triggered off the establishment of numerous *madrasas* throughout the Sunni Muslim world as they picked up the challenge of Ishma'ili Shi'ism, and set about securing and reinforcing the foundations of their own faith.

After Salah al-Din overthrew the Fatimid regime and restored the Sunni orthodoxy, al-Azhar fell into a ruinous state until Baibars carried out restoration work in 1266. Salah al-Din's neglect was indicative of his antipathy towards Shi'ism, but the mosque's former distinction as a university lingered, and it was subsequently rededicated to Sunni Islam and continued as a major seat of theological learning. Since then various rulers have considered it their religious duty to make their contribution to the mosque and as a consequence very little of the original Fatimid mosque remains today. The first mosque was in the North African style with a prayer hall five aisles deep running parallel to the *qibla* wall and *riwaqs* of three aisles' width around the south-east and west of the *sahn*. Like at the Qairawan, a wide transept perpendicular to the *qibla* wall leads towards the *mihrab*. Originally it had three domes, one over the *mihrab* and two in the corners of the prayer hall. In the later Fatimid period Caliph al-Hafiz li Din Allah added another arcade around the *sahn* which widened the *riwaqs* to four aisles and created a new arcaded aisle to the north. Unlike the earlier rounded arches, these arcades employed the keel arch, shaped like an upturned boat, which became the most distinctive feature of Fatimid architecture and for decorative purposes was retained late into the Mamluk period.

Of the original Fatimid mosque, only the stucco work remains and this cannot be precisely dated. It is generally agreed that the hood of the *mihrab* dates from the foundation of the mosque, and the decoration beneath the transept dome forms a part of the new *sahn* arcading put in by al-Hafiz in the mid-twelfth century. This dome, raised on four squinches without an intermediary drum,

Cairo, stucco work in the mosque of al-Azhar

Cairo, the *mihrab* of Katkhuda in the mosque of al-Azhar

contains some beautiful foliate stucco work and also some of the earliest surviving stained glass of the period. Inside the prayer hall on the west wall opposite the *mihrab* are several round-headed panels of Fatimid stucco work with palm trees and scroll-work framed by bands of Kufic inscriptions. The mosque was damaged by earthquake in 1303, and further restoration took place, including the Mamluk stucco work around the first *mihrab*. Major work took place in the eighteenth century when Amir 'Abd al-Rahman Katkhuda extended the prayer hall four arcades deep at a higher level behind the *mihrab*.

This irregular extension, with its off-centre *mihrab*, breaks the symmetry of the original design and neutralises the formal and processional aspect of the transept. Orientation is no longer focused on the original *mihrab*, and the space across the prayer hall is decentralised and more diffuse. The pointed arcades, arranged parallel to the *qibla* wall, are held together by wooden tie-beams which emphasise the lateral distribution of space around the first *mihrab*. Each bay, containing a red

carpet with a central medallion, forms a space frame marked out by four Corinthian columns and overhead tie-beams. These discrete units within the informal spatial disposition of the prayer hall make ideal teaching spaces where, by tradition, the teacher sits against a column with his students seated on the floor around him. Muqaddasi in the tenth century noted one hundred and twenty such groups in the al-Azhar. Outside the prayer hall, but within the main body of the mosque, are a number of *riwaqs* and small *madrasas*. The *riwaqs* of Sharkiyyah, Hanafiyyah and Abbas are nineteenth-century additions to the al-Azhar Mosque providing extra teaching space for students as well as rooms for the Mufti and officials of the mosque. The *madrasas* of Taybars (1309), Aqbugha (1339) and Jawhar (1440) provide further accommodation for teaching the religious sciences, which include *tafsir* (exegesis), *hadith* and *fiqh* (law) as well as Arabic. The Taybars Madrasa is the centre for teaching the Maliki and Shafi'i rites of orthodox Sunni law.

Cairo, the interior of the mosque of al-Azhar

The much restored *sahn* arcades consist of keel arches, joined by tie-beams springing from slender columns, typical of this lighter Fatimid style. In the spandrels of the arches are blind keel-arched recesses with scalloped hoods and colonettes framed with Kufic script. Between these are roundels containing a scalloped sunburst with a delicate border pattern similar to the arabesques that appear on contemporary pottery. On the prayer hall side of the *sahn* al-Hafiz introduced a *pishtaq* – that portion of the façade built higher than the rest, which gives emphasis to the central transept. This feature, also at Ukhaidir, is normally associated with eastern Islamic architecture. Above the main entrance to the *sahn* is the Mamluk minaret of Qa'it Bay (1483) constructed in three tiers, separated by two fretted balconies supported on stalactite corbels known as *muqarnas*. The lower two tiers are octagonal and the upper tier cylindrical. This minaret displays some of the finest stone carving of the period, with keel arches cut into the first tier and delicate lace-like carving between the colonettes. The second tier has plaiting, and the last tier is

Cairo, the mosque of al-Azhar

plain, pierced with four arches and crowned with a bulb. Next to this is the taller minaret of al-Ghuri (1510), which is built on two octagonal tiers and the third, a divided rectangular shaft with two bulbs, is typical of the late Mamluk period. The lower tier has keel arches, and the second tier is decorated with blue faience. This is a sturdier, simpler, stronger construction, and the two minarets, representing the best of later Mamluk architecture, complement each other magnificently.

Over the centuries supplementary buildings, including kitchens and residential accommodation, have been added to al-Azhar. The university has considerably expanded to include, since the 1960s, faculties of medicine, agriculture, engineering and commerce. Despite this degree of secularisation, al-Azhar remains pre-eminent as a centre for Islamic studies, attracting an international community of scholars, and the director remains one of the most senior religious authorities in the Muslim world. Al-Azhar is also responsible for primary and secondary education, and the presence of younger children attending Qur'an school is a feature of the working atmosphere of the mosque.

Time has eradicated the North African origins of the al-Azhar Mosque, but not that of al-Hakim. There is a

TOP
Mosque of al-Hakim by Prosper Georges Marilhat (Louvre Collection)

ABOVE
Cairo, the minaret of the mosque of al-Hakim

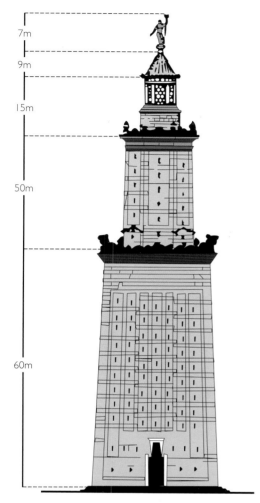

7m
9m
15m
50m
60m

Alexandria, the Pharos lighthouse

very evocative painting in the Louvre of the ruins of the mosque of al-Hakim by Prosper Georges Marilhat in 1840. For those who visited the mosque before the 1980s, and those familiar with Marilhat's picture, it comes as a surprise today to find this mosque completely rebuilt and in mint condition. It raises a number of fundamental questions about the purpose, function and desirability of restoration in situations where it might be argued that a monument's aesthetic value lies principally in its ruinous condition. The mosque was founded by al-Hakim's father in 990 and completed by al-Hakim twelve years later. In many respects this mosque suggests a stylistic return to Ibn Tulun because, with the exception of the stone-built north wall and minarets that form a part of the city walls, it is built throughout in brick. Like at Ibn Tulun, the pointed arches spring from brick piers, but the proportion is generally taller and there are planning features that are much closer to North Africa than

Mesopotamia. As at al-Azhar, there is a central transept perpendicular to the *qibla* wall and three domes placed over the *mihrab* and corners of the prayer hall in the Tunisian manner.

The original corner minarets have been encased in rectangular stone bastions with battered sides like ancient pylons. These massive bases support the shafts of the fourteenth-century minarets of Baibars al-Jashankir which vary in their divisions of octagonal tiers and decorative banding. The north minaret has three octagonal tiers pierced by windows and banded with *muqarnas* crowned with a ribbed keel-shaped dome. Each tier of the shaft of the northern minaret is appropriately proportioned allowing for greater elaboration towards the top and culminating in the deep relief of the band of *muqarnas* and the rich texture of the ribbed dome. Hillenbrand argues that the multi-partite division may have its roots in the Pharos Lighthouse, which was a well-known landmark.[5] The Pharos, built by Ptolemy II (c. 279 BC), in its time was damaged by earthquakes, but it was restored by a number of sultans, including Ibn Tulun, before it finally disappeared following the earthquake of 1307. It was made up of three main shafts – square, octagonal and cylindrical – and something of its appearance may be gleaned from the ruin of a surviving Ptolemeic lighthouse with a similar three-tiered structure at Abu Sir. The Pharos was well known to the seafarers of Tunisia and its possible impact on the Qairawan minaret has been noted. Tunisian architecture has influenced al-Hakim's mosque in both its plan and in the decoration on the original north minaret which is similar to that on the minaret of the Great Mosque in Sfax.

The processional aspect of the transept was exploited to the full by Hakim who frequently preached the Friday *khutbar* against an extravagant background of pageantry and ceremony. According to Suni historians he was a despotic and volatile ruler who routinely persecuted Jews, Christians and Suni Muslims during his twenty-five year reign of terror. He confiscated church property, ordered the demolition of the Church of the Holy Sepulchre in Jerusalem, and passed a series of arbitrary laws, including one forbidding women to leave their houses. He declared that he was an incarnation of God and the mayhem and insurrection which followed this proclamation led to the destruction of much of the city.

TOP
Cairo, the mosque of al-Aqmar: façade

ABOVE
Cairo, the mosque of al-Aqmar: detail of the façade

He eventually disappeared in the Muqattam Hills where he was probably assassinated. However a group of his followers believed that he went into occultation and, like the *Mahdi*, would return to rule. When he proclaimed his divinity, he sent his religious adviser al-Darazi to Syria where he founded the sect of the Druzes. This now forms a significant religious and political minority in modern Lebanon and Syria.

With some notable exceptions, like Ottoman Turkey, the architecture of the mosque across the Muslim world rarely exhibits ostentatious exterior form. They are mainly introverted structures, experienced from within the *sahn*, and often, like Damascus and Tunis, hidden from public view in the centre of crowded bazaars. As Hillenbrand explains, the rights of private property, and the absence of a public domain in terms of town planning, did not allow for the design of much public space where large buildings could be sited.[6] Streets in the traditional Muslim city are shaded and narrow, consequently the visual impact of many mosques is greatest through a gate or portal and not across a square or piazza. The façade of the mosque of al-Aqmar (1125) is an exception and an architectural composition of great distinction and beauty. The plan is bent in order to align the façade with the street and ensure that its body points towards Mecca.

The tripartite façade has a projecting portal consisting of a keel-arched niche with deeply cut fluting, horizontal at the bottom and radiating to a sunrise from a central medallion. The medallion consists of open-work filigree focused on the name of Ali in the centre, encircled by the repeated names of Muhammad carved in Kufic script, with an outer circle of scroll-work carved into solid masonry. This medallion is one of the most refined and perfectly balanced motifs in Islamic art, forming a finely meshed centre from which the rest of the design radiates until it terminates at the scalloped edges of the keel arch, framed with a band of delicate interlaced circles. The design of this niche is a sculptural triumph, with a perfect ordering of solid, void, surface decoration and depth of relief. Flanking this niche are smaller ones crowned by square panels of *muqarnas*, showing the earliest use of these elements for decoration. The left wing of the central portal also contains a slightly smaller and shallower niche containing a fluted hood with a central medallion. The top of the façade is banded with a foliated Kufic inscription and a similar, narrower horizontal band cuts across on a level with the springing of the keel arches. This is a beautifully proportioned façade, and the architects understood how to mould the various surfaces and exploit the play of sunlight and shadow, scooping out the deeply hollowed niche in the centre, balancing it with the shallower flanking niches, and articulating the composition with selected areas of refined surface decoration.

The Fatimid dynasty claimed descent from Fatima and paid particular attention to any tomb associated with the Prophet's family, so the shrines and mausolea dedicated to the descendants of the Prophet had powerful religious and political significance. The Mashhad of Sayyida Ruqayya (1133), built in the southern cemetery, is supposed to be the grave of Sayidda Ruqayya, daughter of Ali and step-sister of Zeinab. Its plan consists of a domed central chamber, flanked by *iwans* leading to two rectangular side chambers. The façade of the tomb, which originally faced a courtyard, has a three-arched opening with prayer niches on either side of the entrance. Above the façade is an octagonal drum pierced on four sides by paired lobed windows, and above this springs a keel-shaped dome, fluted inside and out. The stucco *mihrab* of the dome chamber recalls the façade niches of the al-Aqmar Mosque and is one of the finest of the period, consisting of a deeply cut fluted hood, radiating from a central medallion containing the names of Ali and Muhammad. It is framed with three bands of *muqarnas* set in a panel of arabesque with spandrel bosses and Kufic script. Further south is another tomb associated with the holy family, that of Yahya al-Shabih (1150), a descendant of the Prophet through Husain. This tomb has a fluted dome similar to that of Sayyida Ruqayya, but here it is placed over a stepped zone of transition rather than an octagon. Its plan consists of a central chamber, with five tombs, surrounded on three sides by an ambulatory which contains on the *qibla* side three *mihrabs* of similar design to that at the Sayyida Ruqayya.

Fatimid links with the descendants of the Prophet were further strengthened when the relic of Husain's head was brought to Cairo from Askalon for safe keeping. The intention was to enshrine the relic in a mosque founded for this purpose in 1150 by Vizir al-Salih Tala'i.

However, Caliph al-Faiz intervened and insisted that it should be buried in a *mashhad*, or shrine, in the grounds of his palace. Today the nineteenth-century mosque of Sayyidna al-Husain occupies this palace site, where it serves as one of the principal mosques of Cairo, used on state occasions, as well as being a major centre of pilgrimage for Shi'ite Muslims. Legend also has it that the relic of Husain's head is interred in the Great Mosque at Damascus near the niche where Yazid placed it for public view after the battle of Karbala. Other accounts say that after the head was exhibited, and Husain's sister, Zeinab, humiliated, the Umayyads sent it to Medina for burial. Whatever the truth, there were strong religious and political reasons for the Shi'ite Fatimids to take responsibility for its protection and enhance the prestige of Cairo with the possession of this sacred relic.

The mosque of al-Salih Tal'i is a free-standing rectangular solid enclosing the rectangular void of the *sahn*. Unusually it is constructed over vaulted shops, anticipating a practice in Ottoman architecture. Another unusual feature is the façade, composed of an open five-arched gallery forming the portico of the mosque. The five-keel arches, springing from antique columns, are flanked by two shallow blind recesses with scalloped-keel arched hoods and square iron-grilled windows just above floor level over the basement shops. The portico is screened inside with a modern copy of *mashrabiya*, or screens, which originally formed a part of the *maqsura* in the prayer hall. The other exterior walls present a solid mass made of brick with stone facing. They are relieved in the north-east and south-west by central portals flanked by keel-arched recesses with square (bricked-up) windows and basement shops like those flanking the entrance façade. The minaret above the entrance was destroyed in the earthquake of 1303 and hardly anything remains of the stepped crenellation that crowned the building. Inside, the arcades of the *riwaqs* are built of brick, framed with Kufic script with fluted medallions above the apex, and with keel-arched panels in the spandrels. The prayer hall is three aisles deep, and the *mihrab* penetrates deeply into the *qibla* wall, creating a slight salient on the external wall – a feature established in the Mahdiya Mosque in Tunisia and developed in a number of subsequent Fatimid mosques. Near the *minbar* is a *malcaf*, or wind vent, a shaft connected to the roof which catches the cooler air and circulates it through the prayer hall.

The walls and gates of the city of al-Qahira form the most imposing legacy of the Fatimid era. The original walls were built of brick, but from 1087 to 1092, according to the fifteenth-century historian al-Maqrizi, al-Jamali replaced them with stone with the help of two Armenian architects.[7] Little survives today except the Bab Zuwaila in the south and the northern gates of Bab al-Nasr ('Gate of Victory') and Bab al-Futuh ('Gate of Conquest'). The northern section between Bab al-Nasr and Bab al-Futuh provides an impressive and varied massing of the solid geometries of architectural form, with the rectangular bastions and towers of Bab al-Nasr complementing the semicircular rhythms of Bab al-Futuh and the octagonal shaft of Baibars al-Jashankir's minaret. Bab al-Nasr consists of two rectangular towers, the lower sections of which are of solid masonry of dressed stone over a rubble core. A semicircular entrance leads into a cross-vaulted hall, and the upper towers are roofed with domes set on pendentives. The use of domes and vaults suggests Byzantine influence, and the relief decoration of shields in the Byzantine and Norman style is further evidence of contact between the cultures of the East and the West. These shield motifs are symbols of protection and also function as talismans, like the heraldic serpents and beasts that adorn so many other Muslim gates and fortifications.

The Bab al-Futuh has two massive semicircular towers, and the semicircular arch provides a decorative compositional motif on the lower storey, which consists of a series of shallow arched recesses looping around the whole outer surface, pierced in the centre by the arched doorway which leads to a domed vestibule. The flanking inner walls of the main gate contain recessed arches made up of cushion voussoirs (or gadrooned arches), which became a feature in both later Islamic and Crusader architecture. They appear on the façade of the Church of the Holy Sepulchre in Jerusalem, on the entrance portal of the mosque of al-Zahir Baibars, and in a more decorative form on the blind arches adorning the minarets of the *madrasas* of Qala'un, and Amir Sanjar al-Jawli in Cairo. The sense of architectural weight and mass is enhanced by the nearby presence of the supporting bastion and minaret of the al-Hakim, and the massing of these elements provides one of the most striking architectural ensembles in Cairo.

Cairo, the Bab al-Nasr

The southern walls of al-Qahira are pierced by the Bab Zuwaila (1091–92), which has semicircular towers joined by an arch supporting a crenellated platform, which may have accommodated musicians. Another open rounded arch above this joins the two towers at the top, and both towers now support two imposing Mamluk minarets (1420) which serve the adjacent mosque of Mu'ayyad Shaykh. The inner porch of this gate is also roofed by a shallow dome placed on pendentives. The extensive use of vaulting, domes and pendentives in these fortifications has led to a general view that Byzantium provided the architectural model. Byzantine military architecture, so spectacularly manifest in the fourth-century walls of Theodosius at Constantinople, has long been assumed to be the source for both Islamic and Crusader fortifications. T. E. Lawrence set out to disprove this theory with regard to Crusader castles, but it seems likely that Byzantine influence is manifest here in Cairo, just four years before the beginning of the First Crusade.[8]

Although Egypt was attacked by the Crusaders, the Fatimid walls never had to bear a sustained siege, and Cairo was spared the fate of many other parts of the Muslim world which had to face two invasions from the Crusaders in the west and the Mongols in the east. The ultimate downfall of the Fatimid rulers was due to their general impotence and dissembling politics. Their hold on Syria and Palestine had always been fragile, and the advance of the Franks through these territories was met with no effective resistance. Enmity between the Fatimids

Cairo, the Bab al-Futuh

and the Sunni Seljuk Turks was so intense that the Fatimids preferred to form alliances with the Christian Franks, finding that the Crusader kingdoms provided convenient buffer states between them and the detested Seljuk sultanates. Egypt had ceased to be an effective military power, and the Muslim world, now dominated by Seljuk Turks, was so disunited and disorganised that it was incapable of withstanding the ferocity and fanaticism of the Frankish invasion. It took some considerable time for them to find the will to recover, unite and counter-attack. The beginnings of that revival began with the rise of a Turkish officer called Imad al-Din Zangi who was governor of Mosul. With his power base in Mesopotamia, he eventually extended his rule over northern Syria, taking Aleppo, Homs and the Crusader stronghold of Edessa. Edessa was the first territory to be reclaimed from the Christians, and this process of reconquest was to continue with Zangi's son, the virtuous and pious Nur al-Din, his brilliant Kurdish general, Shirkuh, and Shirkuh's nephew, Salah al-Din (better known as Saladin). They effectively led a powerful *jihad* (holy war) against the Frankish Crusaders and in so doing brought down the Fatimids in Egypt.

CHAPTER 5

UMAYYAD, ALMORAVID AND ALMOHAD ARCHITECTURE IN SPAIN AND MOROCCO

The Christian onslaught on Syria and Palestine was an ultimate failure, but the same impulse did bring success in Muslim Spain (called al-Andalus by the Arabs). The first attempts at the reconquest of Spain precede the Crusades, and a number of knights, like Raymond of Saint-Gilles, Count of Toulouse, began their holy wars there before responding to Pope Urban's summons to march east to Jerusalem. As Montgomery Watt observes, the very notion of crusade, or holy war, may well be derived from *jihad* through western contact with Muslim Spain.[1] Of the two higher cultures that western Christianity encountered, Spanish Islam and Byzantine Christendom, it was Muslim Spain which was closer and more familiar to the Christians. The attitude of western Christianity towards Spanish Islam was a mixture of contempt and admiration, not dissimilar to that felt by the Arabs when they first came to terms with the superiority of Byzantine culture. Ultimately western Christendom triumphed, and in forcing the Muslims out of Spain the West caused the most serious territorial retreat for Islam after centuries of invincible expansion. The reconquest, however, involved the wholesale diaspora of Muslims and Jews and eventually those Arabs, Berbers and Jews who had converted to Christianity. It was a racial as well as a religious purge, and Christian militancy in the West destroyed a culture that in some large measure had contributed towards its own intellectual enlightenment and ultimate Renaissance.

The Muslim monuments of Spain bear witness to a remarkable culture which lasted in some parts of Andalusia for nearly eight centuries. It was a culture largely built on the creative interaction of racial and religious diversity, made possible within that climate of religious tolerance exercised under Muslim rule. The Arabs represented a small ruling elite, and the vast majority of those who made up the Muslim invasion forces consisted of Berbers. The Arabs themselves have never been homogeneous, and tribal diversity in Spain was represented principally through the Qaysite and Kalbite factions which originated from the Yemen and Syria. Of the indigenous people there were the Romance and Latin-speaking Christian Hispano-Romans, who became culturally Arabised as they gradually adopted the Arabic language and customs and became known as the Mozarabs. There were Muslims who learned Latin and

Romance, and collaboration between Muslim, Christian and Jewish scholars produced vibrant centres of multi-lingual scholarship, principally in Seville and Toledo. The Mudejars were Arab minorities who retained their religion and law within Christian society and later under Christian rule. The Moriscos were those Berbers and Arabs who had converted to Christianity. The Jews were a long-settled minority who contributed to trade and commerce despite frequent Visigothic persecution. Such was the racial, religious and cultural mix in Spain under Muslim and Christian rule.[2]

It was this cultural diversity, and coalition between Muslim, Christian and Jewish scholars and artists, that explains the flowering of the visual arts, poetry, philosophy and theology and a revival of the Greek sciences. Without the cultural transmission of this artistry and learning to the West, the intellectual life of medieval Europe and the subsequent Renaissance would probably not have been possible. The visual arts of Muslim Spain enriched the West through the export of its crafts, tapestries and ceramics, and Muslim architecture had a major effect on the development of multi-foiled arches, ribbed domes and vaulting in Romanesque and Gothic churches. The pilgrimages to the shrine of St James at Santiago de Compostella, northern Spain, popular with English pilgrims, may have played a key part in conveying other architectural forms, such as interlacing blind arches, to the cathedrals of England. Spanish mystic poetry, and accounts of the *miraj* (the Prophet's 'night journey' or visions), are said to have inspired Dante, and Islamic poetry and music influenced the troubadours of the West. In his *Divine Comedy*, Dante refers to Averroes (1126–98) as the Commentator, acknowledging him as the greatest authority on Aristotle. The philosophical works of Averroes had a profound influence on western scholastic philosophy, and his works on medicine were widely read in the West. The Arabs conserved and developed medical knowledge based on Graeco-Alexandrian, Persian and Syriac medicine, and the works of Averroes, Maimonides and Ibn Sina were transmitted to the West and taught in the western schools of medicine.

The Muslims believed in an undivided, holistic and symbiotic relationship between mind and body, and the notion of the physician/philosopher is combined in the person of the *hakim*. For this reason, great polymaths, whom we normally associate with the Italian Renaissance, emerged centuries earlier in western Islam in such personalities as Averroes, Ibn Tufayl, Ibn Hazm and Maimonides. Averroes (Ibn Rushd) was a twelfth-century philosopher, physician and astronomer, and the translations of his work and thought, from Arabic to Latin and Hebrew, made the dissemination of Aristotle's ideas possible in Europe. He was also creatively engaged in philosophical debate within the wider Muslim world, writing a book defending his philosophical position against that of al-Ghazali (1058–1111) in the great work *The Inconsistency of the Philosophers*. Averroes's medical works included commentaries on Galen, as well as the *Kitab al-külliyyat*, a book on general medical principles that became a standard text in the West. Another physician and friend of Averroes, Ibn Tufayl, was also a major philosopher as well as vizir to the Almohad ruler Abu Ya'qub Yusuf. The theologian Ibn Hazm, a vizir in both Valencia and Cordoba, wrote extensively on comparative religion and is best known for his treatise on love, called the *The Dove's Necklace*. The Jewish physician and philosopher Maimonides (1135–1204) wrote many classic works on medicine and became the personal physician to Salah al-Din and his family.

Before the Arab and Berber invasions, Spain had been ruled by the Visigoths, who had entered the country from Germany in 414. With the indigenous Hispano-Roman aristocracy they ruled the whole of the peninsula and part of southern France. The Visigothic monarchy was weak with no secure means of succession, due to constant disputes as to whether the monarchy should be inherited or elected. They ruled over a large underprivileged peasantry and a considerable population of Jews who had been subjected to frequent arbitrary persecution. It was this large oppressed and disaffected population that colluded with the Arabs, whose coming was regarded here as liberation. The first Arab invasion occurred in 711 led by a Berber called Tariq ibn Ziyad whose name has given rise to Gibraltar (Jabal Tariq, or mountain of Tariq). The first Muslim victory over the Visigoths near Algeciras was decisive, and thereafter they met little serious resistance and eventually captured the Visigothic capital of Toledo. By 715 the bulk of the Iberian Peninsula, with the exception of the north, was in Arab hands, and by 732 they had penetrated into France

and were eventually repulsed by Charles Martel between Tours and Poitiers.

Spain achieved independence from Baghdad under a new Umayyad dynasty founded by Abd al-Rahman, a surviving member of the Umayyad family, who escaped from Iraq and Syria and made his way along the North African coast. For a time he sought refuge near the Moroccan coast with relatives of his Berber mother and sent emissaries to Spain seeking support from various Arab factions. Eventually he crossed the Straits of Gibraltar and contacted fellow Syrians already settled in the valley of the Guadalquivir, and with their help captured Cordoba and proclaimed an independent Umayyad emirate which lasted for over two hundred years. Most of his reign was spent waging incessant wars in order to stamp his autocratic rule over the anarchic tribal factions under his domain. This gave him little scope for building, but he did recognise the symbolic importance of establishing a large congregational mosque in Cordoba which could unite all the disparate Muslims in one communal act of prayer.

Cordoba, the Great Mosque

The Great Mosque of Cordoba was begun by Abd al-Rahman I in 785 and was extended and embellished by subsequent rulers during a period of just over two hundred years. It follows the hypostyle hall model of the congregational mosque and shows the adaptability and flexibility of this form of building in that it allowed extensions southwards and eastwards to accommodate an expanding Muslim population. Tradition has it that the Muslims and Christians shared the Visigothic church of St Vincent until Abd al-Rahman I, like Caliph al-Walid in

Cordoba, the Great Mosque at Cordoba: interior

Damascus, bought out the Christians and built the mosque over the site. This story is probably apocryphal, being a fanciful attempt to link the foundation of this mosque with that of Damascus.

The original mosque of Abd al-Rahman I consisted of a *sahn* and a prayer hall divided into eleven aisles by ten arcades each with twelve arches running perpendicular to the *qibla* wall. There was no minaret and no *riwaqs*, and it is assumed the present *riwaqs* were added at the time of Abd al-Rahman III before the minaret was

constructed after 952. The arcading of the *riwaqs* consisted of arches springing from paired columns alternating with piers, and they served various purposes, from the reception of petitions by the *qadis* (judges) in the east *riwaq*, to teaching in the west. Averroes taught in the western *riwaq*, and there are accounts that his controversial teaching, in which he attempted to reconcile Aristotelian philosophy with Islamic dogma, generated so much public hostility, incited by the Almohad clergy, that he was eventually driven from the mosque. The minaret was built by Abd al-Rahman III and was made of stone with two separate staircases, one each for ascending and descending. Nothing of the original minaret can be seen today, because it was converted into a bell tower and is encased in the masonry of the present Baroque tower built in the seventeenth century. The *sahn* is now known as the Patio de los Naranjos, but according to Rafael Castejon orange trees were not introduced into Spain until after the reconquest, and the original *sahn* was planted at the time of Abd al-Rahman III with olive, cypress and laurel trees.[3]

The horseshoe arches of the prayer hall façade spring from piers flanked by columns, which are now walled in, with the exception of the two entrances. This means that less light is now admitted into the building. As you enter the prayer hall you are confronted by a seemingly infinite forest of regular columns which fan out rhythmically in a lateral spread with no apparent defining directional axis. This sense of a dynamic diffusion of space is heightened by the contrasting neutrality of the perimeter walls, which do not significantly limit or terminate the space but appear at certain points to fade in the shadows, thus sustaining a sense of boundlessness. It is a space reminiscent of Justinian's Yerabatin Cistern in Constantinople (532) where there is a similar vastness and regularity of spatial division with boundary walls dimly perceived at the periphery of vision. There the comparison ends, because what makes Cordoba extraordinary is the sequential rhythmic springing of the arcades, which radiate and branch in all directions like fronds in a lush palm grove.

The setting of the columns and the springing of the arches has no architectural precedent. Richly diverse, the recycled antique columns, Corinthian and Composite in style, are varied in colour and smooth or occasionally cut into fluted spirals. They are more or less of equal size, but they were not high enough to roof such a vast enclosure, so the architect doubled the height by placing an impost block on each column and then setting a square pier on top. From the impost blocks spring round horseshoe arches with radiating wedge-shaped voussoirs of alternating white stone and terracotta brick. The second tier of arches springs from the piers; they are almost pure semicircles but lack that extension of the inscribed semicircle at the base that defines the horseshoe form. It has been sug-

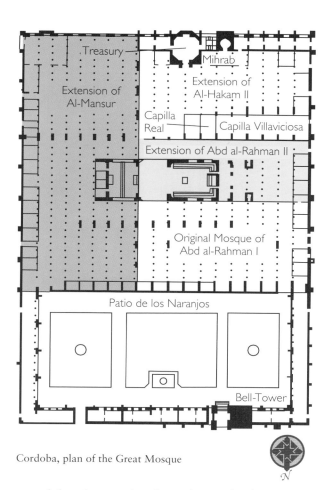

Cordoba, plan of the Great Mosque

gested that the two-tiered arcade may be derived from the Roman aqueduct, or the double-tiered arcade in the Damascus Great Mosque, but what is so distinctive about this building is the openness of the lower arches.[4] They spring lightly and freely, like semicircular tie-beams, with no masonry infill in the spandrels, so that there is none of the usual solid horizontal coursing of stone above the crown of the arch.

The light, agile, double springing of the arches, and the radiating pattern of the voussoirs, set up a series of dynamic rhythms as the eye pans across the space and experiences a sensation of multi-point perspective. The eye is never drawn to one centre of focus but is presented with multifarious projections and vistas as it is driven laterally across the space by a sequential alternation between the stabilising verticals of the columns and the expansive outreach of the arches. This is a complex visual structure which evolves more intricate elaboration through the extensions built by Abd al-Rahman II (848) and al-Hakam (965). In the Capilla Villaviciosa, which contained the second *mihrab*, the arches are lobed with

delicate surface decoration, and inverted arches spring from the crowns of the lower arches and fan out into a rippling crescendo under the ribbed vault. The lobed arches progress with further elaboration and virtuosity towards the *mihrab* of al-Hakam, which is one of the most significant and beautiful in the Muslim world and the visual climax of the mosque.

Titus Burckhardt has expressed no surprise that the most magnificent part of the mosque was built by al-Hakam, who was one of the most cultivated and learned of the Spanish caliphs (the title caliph was assumed by his predecessor, Abd al-Rahman III).[5] He established the caliphal library, said to contain 400,000 volumes, which attracted scholars from all over the Muslim world. This

ABOVE
Cordoba, the Great Mosque: towards the *mihrab* of al-Hakam

LEFT
Cordoba, the Capilla Villaviciosa within the Great Mosque

OPPOSITE PAGE, LEFT
Cordoba, the *mihrab* of the Great Mosque

OPPOSITE PAGE, RIGHT
Cordoba, the dome over the bay in front of the *mihrab* in the Great Mosque

was just one of seventy libraries in Cordoba, and it is worth reflecting on this number of books by comparison with the Vatican Library, endowed by Pope Sixtus IV in 1475, which contained 1,527 volumes, and Oxford's principal library, founded by Sir Thomas Bodley in 1602, which opened with the grand total of 2,000 books. As well as seventy libraries, Cordoba boasted many public baths and was the most civilised city in western Europe, ranked in cultural splendour only with the cities of Baghdad and Constantinople. Trading contacts with Byzantium were important, leading also to cultural exchanges. When the Byzantine Emperor Nicephoras Phocas II ceased his hostilities against the Arabs in Crete, he turned his attention to cultural dialogue with Cordoba, and sent as a gift to al-Hakam master mosaicists and tesserae to give material and technical support for the magnificent *mihrab* in the Cordoban Great Mosque.

The *mihrab* is formed by a circular horseshoe arch enclosed in a rectangular frame forming a compositional device which is also characteristic of many Moorish doorways. Around the arch of the *mihrab* are radiating wedge-shaped decorative voussoirs containing mosaic arabesques in gold, red, blue and green. The scroll-work in these voussoirs suggests Byzantine influence, unlike the marble arabesque panels flanking and behind the *mihrab* arch. The lower voussoir mosaics are essentially naturalistic, within the Hellenistic tradition, showing a clear separation between figure and ground, whereas the marble panels display foliate forms with fine, lace-like stems and leaves distributed in equal measure over the whole surface and with a much tighter sense of abstract organisation. The marble relief panels exploit light and shadow and are cut with the same intricacy as contemporary ivory caskets, while the mosaic arabesques in the lower voussoirs, representing acanthus scrolls, are essentially pictorial. Those mosaics in the voussoirs nearer the crown of the arch are lighter, more emblematic and stylised, like those above in the *mihrab* dome. The *mihrab* arch springs from paired Corinthian red and bluish marble colonettes taken from the earlier ninth-century *mihrab*, and around the frame of the arch are two splendid mosaic bands of Kufic inscriptions in gold, set against cobalt blue, and enlivened with a border picked out in gold, copper and russet tones. Above this are panels of mosaic arabesques set in blind trilobed arches.

Behind the *mihrab* arch, instead of the normal semi-circular niche, there is a small seven-sided room lined with panels decorated with arabesques and trilobed arch recesses crowned with a shell half-dome. In front of and above the *mihrab* is one of a number of remarkable ribbed domes which are structurally innovative and foreshadow ribbed vaulting in Romanesque and Gothic architecture. The domes over the vestibule and *mihrab* consist of rib vaults in which semicircular ribs spring from the corners of an octagon inscribed within the square of the bay. The intersecting ribs spring from the squinches and side panels of the octagon and form eight-pointed arches alternating with eight narrow triangular pendentives, which enclose a central octagon supporting the ribbed dome of the *mihrab*. In the *mihrab* dome the whole surface, including the ribs, is covered in rich mosaic arabesques with a Kufic inscription running along the base of the central octagon. This dome crowns a glorious ensemble of iridescent forms in the *mihrab* area, providing a sumptuous visual crescendo towards which all the later architectural elaborations were directed. In marked contrast to the austerity and piety of the Qairawan, there is a courtly magnificence expressed here which reflects the wealth, splendour and confidence of the Cordoban caliphate.

The use of the ribbed vault and dome in this and a number of North African mosques is ceremonial and selective, in order to accentuate the *mihrab* area, or mark the processional axis of the central and *qibla* aisles. However, great ingenuity in ribbed vaults and domes can be seen in such smaller structures as the mosque of Bab al-Mardum in Toledo (999), where the whole nine-bay interior is rib vaulted. This is a compact and tightly

organised building, like an open sided pavilion, 6.5 metres square and 9.25 metres in height. Its nine bays are each vaulted with different patterns of rib vaults made up of varied combinations of lozenge, diaper and stellar formations. The central dome is set higher on four recycled Visigothic columns, and its ribs form an octagon enclosing an eight-pointed star with a shell at the centre. The cubic unity of the original structure was destroyed by the extension of the building and the addition of an apse in the *mudejar* style after the reconquest in 1085. The door openings on the front façade are varied, with trilobed, semicircular and horseshoe arches carrying a blind arcade of interlacing horseshoe arches surmounted by horizontal decorative bands of brick and rows of corbels under the eaves. At the sides, three open horseshoe arches, set in tall semicircular recesses, support an arcade of trilobed blind arches within which are set smaller horseshoe arches with terracotta and white voussoirs. In terms of scale this is a modest structure, but the inventiveness of its vaulted forms at this early date is significant and noteworthy.

ABOVE
Toledo, the Bab al-Mardum Mosque

LEFT
Toledo, cross-section of Bab al-Mardum

The full imperial splendour of the Cordoban caliphate found its ultimate expression in secular architecture when Abd al-Rahman III built the palace-city of Madinet al-Zahra six kilometres west of Cordoba in 936. It was destroyed by the Berber riots of 1010, and all that remains today is an archaeological site with just a few reconstructed sections. Our fragmented knowledge and image of the palace comes mainly from literary sources, which are full of the usual hyperbole. For instance, it was said that a court of 25,000 lived here, but as Robert Hillenbrand notes, archaeological evidence does not support this.[6] Nevertheless, it was the seat of a new and powerful caliphate, and it flourished while Umayyad Spain was at the peak of her power and influence. When Abd al-Rahman III took the throne at the age of twenty-seven, his position was insecure, because he was threatened by internal dissension as well as aggression from two important emerging external powers, Leon to the north and the Fatimid Empire in North Africa. Most of his reign was concerned with strengthening and consolidating his power within the peninsula, and this he certainly achieved. His reign marked the zenith of Umayyad power, with the northern Christian territory of Leon acknowledging his suzerainty. The rise of Fatimid power in North Africa, and its proclamation of a Shi'ite caliphate, persuaded Abd al-Rahman also to adopt the title of caliph in order to strengthen his authority in Spain and demand allegiance from the petty rulers of the Maghrib outside Fatimid control. The special power which the caliphate bestowed demanded a corresponding symbol of imperial authority in architectural terms, and so Abd al-Rahman built the palace-city of Madinet al-Zahra on a scale appropriate to his new office.

Titus Burckhardt quotes Muhyi d din ibn 'Arabi's account of a mission of Spanish Christians who were sent to negotiate with Abd al-Rahman. They were made to process between double ranks of soldiers lining a twenty-kilometre route until they reached the palace of Madinet al-Zahra, where they were conducted through rooms of increasing splendour. The Spanish retinue encountered seated courtiers dressed in silks and brocades of such regal magnificence that they were bemused as to which personage might be the caliph. Finally they were summoned to the fearful presence of the caliph, who was seated on the floor wearing a simple coarse robe reading his copy of the Qur'an.[7] We are told that in the Golden Reception Hall there was a pool of quicksilver, which the caliph would agitate in order to generate kaleidoscopic reflections in the sunlight. The shimmering impact of the hall was enhanced by the gold and silver drapery on the walls, the multi-coloured translucent marble and the doors set with gold and ebony. Suspended from the ceiling was a pearl the size of a pigeon's egg given by the Byzantine Emperor Leo. Perhaps such descriptions may not be so fanciful, because similar accounts of other palaces abound: we are told, for instance, that the Tulunid palace of Khumarawaih in Cairo contained a quicksilver pond 50 cubits square, and Hillenbrand notes that in 917 the Abbasid caliph in Baghdad had a lake of tin 20 by 30 metres square.[8]

As Leo's gift suggests, contact with Constantinople was not confined to the provision of the mosaic tesserae in the Great Mosque, because there are accounts of several gifts from Constantinople, including 114 columns and two fountains of gilt-bronze and green marble with

Cordoba, an overall view of Madinat al-Zahra

sculpted reliefs of human figures. When the marble fountain was installed, it was flanked by animal figures in the form of lions, stags, crocodiles, dragons and various birds spouting water from their mouths, foreshadowing the famous Court of the Lions in Granada. One third of tax revenues, estimated at 3,000,000 dinars, financed the building of the palace, and no expense was spared on materials. Marble was brought in from Carthage and Tunis, and over 4,000 columns were imported from France, Rome, Carthage, Tunis and Sfax, as well as locally quarried columns from Tarragona and Almeria.

Cordoba, the audience hall at Madinat al-Zahra

Madinet al-Zahra today is reminiscent of a Roman archaeological site, a reminder of the way in which the Arabs adopted the imperial legacy of Rome. Madinet al-Zahra was divided into three layered terraces, each with its own ramparts and fortifications. The palace enclosure was on top, the middle terrace was taken up with gardens and the lowest contained the mosque and quarters for palace servants. One of the major audience halls, the *dar al-mulk*, has been restored, and here there is a basilican hall divided into nave and side aisles by arcades of horseshoe arches springing from Corinthian columns. There is a sturdy nobility about this beautifully proportioned hall, which could, in lesser hands, appear top heavy with so much masonry piled on relatively slender marbled columns. The circular rhythms of arcade voussoirs attract the eye towards the radiant form of the horseshoe arch framed in the far wall. Other surviving sections include the *majlis al-gharbi*, another reception hall with a basilican plan of which only the piers and columns are left. Like many Muslim palaces the buildings are arranged

informally and linked by patios, water channels and pools. The complex included, after the Roman fashion, a number of baths and latrines with running water.

The distribution and control of water was a fundamental theme in Islamic architecture, fulfilling aesthetic as well as functional ends, and in the fountains, channels, basins and streams of the Alhambra Palace hydraulic engineering was elevated to a fine art. Evidence of Roman irrigation existed in the aqueducts at Segovia and Tarragona, and their irrigation systems in southern Spain were conserved and developed by the Arabs and other settlers who came from the desert of North Africa and beyond. In Cordoba remains of Arab *norias*, or water wheels, can still be seen on the banks of the Guadalquivir. They were designed to scoop up and deposit water into aqueducts and channels, and such devices can still be seen in the fifteenth-century *norias* of Hamma in Syria.

Well-irrigated gardens, water channels and patios provide the spatial context for palace architecture in Spain, where there is a distinct contrast to the formal, symmetrical plans of palaces in Syria and Iraq. The Roman villa, rather than the frontier fortress which the Arabs adopted, serves as an antecedent in Spain. In later palace architecture there is less emphasis on ceremonial, and the layout is often more relaxed and open ended, with pavilions replacing the formally structured basilican throne rooms. The external fortified aspect was not discarded, as the gates, towers, keeps and curtain walls of *alcazars* and *alcazabas* often formidably ring a citadel. Nevertheless, once inside these elaborate defences, even such long-standing fortifications as the *alcazaba* at Malaga yield to a more tranquil informality internally in residential quarters and pavilions grouped at various levels around courts, basins and gardens.

One exception to this general rule is the Aljaferia at Zaragoza, which is tightly sealed within its trapezoidal curtain walls and semicircular towers. This palace was built by one of the Berber Banu Hud *amirs*, Abu Ja'far Ahmed (1049–83). Its façade recalls the Syrian *qasr* (palace or fort) with its curtain wall of intermittent towers. The main entrance is composed of a horseshoe arch surmounted by a band of blind interlaced arches, over

which a simple cornice supports an open arcaded walk-way extending some length across the top of the façade and round the north wall as far as the keep. Entrance is by a forecourt beyond which is a large transverse open court with two pools at each end in front of the flanking royal apartments. On the east side of the northern quarters is a beautiful domed octagonal oratory with an inventive variety of arcades. Under the dome they are in the Cordoban style, with lobed arches springing from the apexes of paired arches below. At ground level horseshoe arches alternate with halberd-shaped arches composed of paired semicircular lobes at the base, carrying right-angled shoulders, and a blade-shaped head forming its apex. The oratory opens into arcades which surround the pool in front of the vestibule to the throne room. Here again there

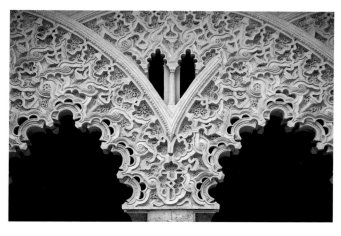

RIGHT
Zaragoza, the Aljaferia Palace: detail of interlaced arcades

BELOW
Zaragoza, the Aljaferia Palace

is a variety of arcades, interlaced in the Cordoban style in front of the throne room or lobed where they surround the pool. They stand on double columns and are beautifully proportioned and decorated with lace-like delicacy. The ornamentation in the rest of the palace, with its complex interlacing of lobed, cusped and vegetal forms, has been described as 'baroque', but it strikes me that its lightness of touch might more appropriately be called 'rococo'. It anticipates the fragile and incorporeal surface decoration in the fourteenth-century art of Nasrid Granada and Merinid Morocco.

After Abd al-Rahman III, the cultured al-Hakam was the last effective caliph of the Umayyad line. When he died his successor, Hisham II, was only twelve years old, and power fell into the hands of the unscrupulous Ibn Abi Amir, who assumed caliphal powers and later, as a consequence of many victories, became known as al-Mansur. His contribution to architecture was the major extension to the east of the Great Mosque at Cordoba, giving it as many bays as days in the year and moving the centre of government away from Madinet al-Zahra by building a new palace at al-Madina az Zahira. This administrative move effectively isolated and marginalised the young caliph, who eventually ceded power to al-Mansur's successor, Abd al-Malik, later known as al-Muzaffar. Al-Mansur and al-Muzaffar were both powerful, effective and dictatorial rulers who were largely successful on the battlefield and who kept the western empire together. When al-Muzaffar died after a brief reign, his ineffective brother succeeded and the country collapsed into a state of civil war. After Hisham II abdicated in 1009, six members of the Umayyad family held the title of caliph until the office was abolished in 1031. Thereafter Muslim rule in Spain disintegrated into the hands of regional dynasties such as the Zirids of Granada, the Hammudids in Malaga and Algeciras and the Abbadids of Seville.

The weakness of these new petty kingdoms is illustrated by their change of fortunes in relation to the Christian princes of the north. Under the Umayyad caliphate Christian princes paid tribute to the caliph, but now the situation was reversed, and the Christians saw their opportunity of seizing territorial advantage. The first significant reconquest was Toledo, which fell to Alfonso VI in 1085 and remained in Christian hands, although his

army was defeated at Zallaqa the following year by a combination of Muslim forces led by al-Mu'tamid of Seville and the Almoravid leader, Yusuf ibn Tushuf, from Morocco. Yusuf ibn Tushuf was the dynamic leader of an expanding Berber empire in the Maghrib. He expanded into Spain, and by 1091 he had eliminated his Muslim rivals by capturing Cordoba, Seville, Granada, Zaragoza and Valencia, thus inaugurating Almoravid rule in Spain.

The Almoravids, known as the 'veiled ones' (because of the head-cloths worn for protection against the desert winds), were originally nomadic Berbers of the Sanhaja tribe from south Morocco. Their conquests in the south had been driven by a form of Muslim evangelism, a mixture of Malikite jurisprudence and mysticism, as well as the lucrative trade of exchanging salt for gold in the sub-Saharan regions of Niger and Senegal. As their territorial expansion progressed, they were obliged to establish permanent settlements, and in 1062 Yusuf ibn Tushuf founded Marrakesh and the Kutubiya Mosque. Ibn Tushuf was a charismatic leader who was reputed to have lived for over a hundred years, but his successors, seduced by the luxuries of Andalucia, became weak and effete, and the Almoravids lasted for only eighty-five years. They were ousted by the Almohad dynasty, which was equally religiously zealous. Nothing remains of Ibn Tushuf's mosque in Marrakesh, and little has survived of Almoravid architecture, although the large congregational mosques at Nedroma, Algiers and Tlemcen, despite subsequent alterations, retain something of their original Almoravid character in general structure and layout.

All these buildings broadly follow the example of the Great Mosque of Cordoba, having the defining Maghribi characteristics of tower minaret, long gable-roofed prayer halls and relatively small rectangular transverse *sahns*. Despite the evolution of the deep prayer hall, the ultimate antecedent of these types is the Great Mosque at Damascus, and Umayyad influence still lingers in many of these buildings, possibly explaining the development of the distinctive tower minaret. This tower form probably has its origins in Syria, but no early Syrian examples survive, and the oldest standing Syrian minarets within this tradition are those dating from the eleventh century in Aleppo and Ma'arrat, which are distant relatives lacking the proportion, mass and grandeur of

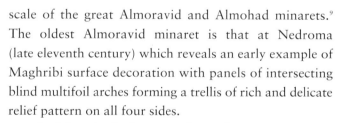

Marrakesh, the interior of the Kutubiya Mosque

Marrakesh, the minaret of the Kutubiya Mosque

scale of the great Almoravid and Almohad minarets.[9] The oldest Almoravid minaret is that at Nedroma (late eleventh century) which reveals an early example of Maghribi surface decoration with panels of intersecting blind multifoil arches forming a trellis of rich and delicate relief pattern on all four sides.

In Marrakesh the second Kutubiya Mosque was begun by Abd al-Mumene and completed in 1190 by his grandson, Yacoub al-Mansur. It is built of sandstone and is one of the largest mosques in North Africa, accommodating up to 20,000 people. Rectangular in plan, the vast prayer hall has seventeen aisles arranged perpendicular to the *qibla* wall. The central aisle and transverse *qibla* aisle form a characteristic North African T-plan, which is emphasised by a string of domes roofing the central aisle and five further domes situated three bays apart in the *qibla* aisle. Although the orientation of the aisles is perpendicular to the *qibla* wall, the arcades of pointed horseshoe arches spring transversely from their piers, and each aisle is framed with a lobed arch where it terminates

at the perimeter wall. Each arch and pier, with its pairs of engaged Corinthian columns, is identical, and the interior of the mosque is painted pristine white with a floor of simple rush matting. This is the most serene and spartan of interiors, with a breadth and scale reminiscent of Cordoba. Here, however, the comparison ends, because Cordoba is distinguished by its diversity, elaboration and courtly magnificence, whereas the cold regularity of this interior, with its boundless and unrelenting rhythmic repetition of pier and arch, solid and void, expresses the uncompromising spirit of unity and purity that is the heart of Almohad theology.

Like the other Almohad monuments, its most distinctive external feature is the minaret, 77 metres high, consisting of a crenellated rectangular tower crowned with a domed lantern and finial. This is a beautifully proportioned structure in which the combination of fenestration and surface decoration is organised with great refinement and elegance. On one face the main shaft of the tower is pierced and broken by four panels of blind arcading and windows. There are four storeys, and at the lowest level a rectangular recessed panel encloses three tall blind horseshoe arches divided by slender columns. Above this, three blind arches are set in a horizontal recess framed by a lobed pointed arch with a small rectangular window aperture placed below its apex. The third storey is pierced by paired windows set in a semi-circular arched recess, in turn framed by a moulded rectangular panel. The fourth storey is crowned by a strong horizontal band of four windows situated behind a screen of interlaced lobed arches. The warm sandstone of the tower is complemented at the top by a narrow strip of blue tiling underneath the crowning band of crenellation. The lantern, with its ribbed dome, has paired windows with lobed arches set in a latticed panel of interlaced arches. This sophisticated play and diversity of pattern, with its contrasts of surface pattern, shallow relief and deeply pierced windows, is sustained with different compositional formats on all four sides of the minaret.

The Hassan Tower, which forms the minaret of the Great Mosque at Rabat, was intended to be even taller, probably measuring over 80 metres. The mosque was founded by Yacoub al-Mansur in 1195 but was never completed. It would have been the second largest mosque in the Muslim world, measuring 180 by 140 metres (Samarra is 240 by 156 metres). All that survives today is the incomplete tower rising to 44 metres, three hundred and fifty column bases and masonry remnants indicating the position of the perimeter walls. Most of the enclosure would have been gable roofed with twenty-one aisles running perpendicular to the qibla wall. A slightly wider central aisle led to the mihrab, and three transverse aisles in front of the qibla wall accentuated the characteristic Maghribi T-formation. Stepped entrances flanked the minaret and a transverse oblong sahn led to the main prayer hall. One unusual feature was the addition of two smaller sahns, perpendicular to the qibla, which would have provided illumination to the sides of this vast roofed enclosure. The Hassan Tower is built of sandstone, and each face is relieved by surface decoration rather than by fenestration. The narrow horseshoe arched windows are little more than arrowslits arranged up the central axis of the tower and are subordinate to the main decorative scheme, which consists of varied arrangements of arched recesses and delicate interlacing.

The third great Almohad tower minaret in this series was also built by Yacoub al-Mansur in Seville. Known as the Giralda, this and parts of the sahn are all that remain of the mosque he established in 1172. After the Christian reconquest, the mosque was destroyed to make way for the present fifteenth-century cathedral of Sta Maria de le Sede, which is the largest Gothic building in Europe. Leading into the Patio de los Naranjos is the Almohad gate, the Puerta del Perdon, with splendid twelfth-century bronze doors containing beautiful door-knockers in pierced arabesque, but all that is left of the sahn are just two arcades of horseshoe arches springing from piers. The minaret now forms the bell tower, and the original Almohad structure is crowned by a Baroque belfry designed by Hernan Ruiz. Despite this incongruous addition the tower remains one of the finest minarets in the Muslim world. It is 50 metres high with an inner ramp that rises by right-angled turns.

The brick-built Giralda is magnificently composed and proportioned, and the fenestration up the central vertical axis is quite masterly. There are seven rooms arranged above each other, and every window aperture presents a different format, some single, most double, some recessed and each framed with different arches. The top four double windows are divided by slender columns and shaped in alternating lobed and horseshoe form. They are set in recesses with lobed framing arches of varied shape and flanked with decorative panels of intersecting lobed arches. The detail is very fine, particularly the varied arabesques in the spandrels around the framing arches of the windows. The balconies, like the belfry, are an insensitive sixteenth-century addition which disturb the architectural purity of the façade, although their presence prompts an interesting comparison between this and Venetian Gothic.

Relations with the Christian powers in Spain deteriorated, and conflict with the increasing power of Christian Leon, Castile and Aragon ensured that the Almohad grip on Andalucia was always fragile. The last assertion of Almohad power in the region was the battle of Alarcos at which the army of Alfonso VIII of Castile was decisively defeated in 1195. It was a defeat, however, that strengthened the resolve of the Christians, and in the ensuing peace they put aside differences, strengthened alliances and brought in reinforcements.

In 1212 the Christians assembled a combined force from Leon, Castile, Aragon and Navarre and defeated Muhammad al-Nasir at Las Navas de Tolosa. This battle effectively destroyed Almohad power in Spain, and after Muhammad's death the following year his successors were unable to hold the regime together. By 1269 the disintegration of Almohad rule in both Spain and the Maghrib was complete. The union of Leon and Castile in 1230 made possible a new Christian offensive which resulted in the fall of Cordoba in 1236 and Seville in 1248. It took a further twenty years for the Christians finally to extinguish Muslim rule in Spain – with the one notable exception of the kingdom of Granada, which miraculously managed not only to survive but to flourish until 1492.

ABOVE
Seville, the Giralda

LEFT
Rabat, the minaret of the mosque of Hassan

Nasrid, Mudejar, Marinid and Sa'dian Architecture in Spain and Morocco

The Nasrid dynasty was established by Muhammad ibn Yusuf ibn Nasr in the city of Jaen in 1231, and it was from here that he ruled over the province of Granada. In 1245 Ferdinand III of Castile laid siege to Jaen, and Muhammad, recognising Ferdinand's military superiority, retreated south to Granada and negotiated peace. The outcome was a remarkable alliance on which the survival of the kingdom of Granada was to depend for over two centuries. Muhammad became not only a vassal but also a companion of arms to Ferdinand, so that when Seville fell in 1248 it was to a besieging army of Castilian and Muslim forces led jointly by Ferdinand and Muhammad. Muhammad was not the only Muslim vassal of Ferdinand, but Granada survived because Muhammad became a useful and loyal friend, and it was in Castile's interest to preserve the *status quo* in Granada. Ferdinand recognised that a military conquest of Granada would be expensive, and for the time being it provided a useful refuge for Muslims fleeing Christian occupation elsewhere. Muhammad having bought peace nevertheless armed and fortified his kingdom and proved to be an effective ruler, investing in education, manufacturing, agriculture and trade and laying the foundations for Granada's subsequent enormous wealth.

In Visigothic times the population of the city was divided between Christians and Jews, with the latter occupying an area called *Garnatha Alyhud*, from which Granada probably derives its name. It was the Jewish population that facilitated Tariq ibn Ziyad's conquest of the city in 711. During the early years of Muslim rule, Elvira dominated the region, and Granada did not emerge as a provincial capital until the reign of the Berber Zirid dynasty in the eleventh century. The Zirid rulers, Habbus, Badis and Abd Allah, developed the city in the area of a former Roman fortress, known as Alcazaba Cadima, which is situated opposite the Sabika hill where the Alhambra Palace stands. According to Oleg Grabar a palace was built on the Albaicin hill above the Alcazaba, which had a weather-vane imitating that of al-Mansur's palace in Baghdad.[1] The Albaicin and the Sabika hills are separated by the valley of the river Darro and form spurs from the Sierra Nevada mountains. Muslims settled on the Albaicin hill in Zirid times. The Sabika forms a natural citadel, but little is known about any development there until the Jewish vizir, Yusuf ibn Nagrallah, built a

palace in the eleventh century. Although only fragments remain of Nagrallah's palace, it was culturally significant, because, according to Frederick Bargeburh, it expressed an architectural vision of Solomon's palace which had a lasting impact on the subsequent building of the Alhambra Palace in the fourteenth century.[2]

Granada, distant view of the Alhambra

The best general view of the Alhambra Palace is from the top of the Albaicin hill against the backdrop of the snow-capped Sierra Nevada mountains. It is a setting described by Ibn Zamrak:

> Sabika is the crown of Granada's brow, and the
> stars of heaven yearn to be its jewels;
> And the Alhambra, may God protect it, is the
> central ruby of its crown.[3]

The Alhambra is self-consciously steeped in poetry, and the genesis of that poetic mood can be found in the eleventh-century verses of the Jewish poet Solomon ibn Gabirol, whose evocations of Solomon's splendour in his descriptions of Nagrallah's palace explain something of the Alhambra's imaginative context. The poetic narrative is taken up in the fourteenth century by Ibn Zamrak, whose verses festoon the Alhambra providing oblique clues to its meaning. There is also a remarkable concordance in the Granadan court between poetic expression and visual form, and both represent in their separate ways the flowering and swan-song of Muslim culture in Spain. The refined and luxurious court of Nasrid

Granada cultivated the arts of poetry and music, and reminisced over Islam's glorious past.

The panegyric literature of the Muslim court so often distorts the reality of the past. In the case of the Alhambra, however, poetry and hyperbole are now defining and fundamental aspects of its reality. To borrow Heinrich Klotz's phrase, it is a case of architectural form following fiction rather than function.[4] And it is a fiction that has spawned fiction, making possible the Romantic literature of Washington Irving, Chateaubriand and Victor Hugo, as well as the architectural mythologies of the Granada and Alhambra dance halls and cinemas of the twentieth century.

The first palace on the Sabika hill, built by Yusuf ibn Nagrallah in the eleventh century, is indicative of Jewish power and influence. Yusuf's father, Samuel, was an outstanding scholar, poet, military leader and statesman, holding the rank of vizir under the sultan and the title of *han-Naghidh* (leader of the Jews) among his own community. Samuel brought a number of Jews into high government office, and their political power was complemented by a cultural flowering of Hebrew literature and scholarship. Samuel established an academy of Jewish scholars, and became patron to the poet and Neo-Platonic philosopher, Solomon ibn Gabirol. Yusuf inherited most of his father's gifts and rose to become the power behind Badis's throne, but he indulged in various intrigues that failed. His actions precipitated a wave of anti-Semitic violence which resulted not only in his own murder in 1066 but also in the slaughter of many of the Jewish community.

Yusuf ibn Nagrallah's palace on the Sabika was a powerful symbol of his political ambitions, and its magnificence, which exceeded Badis's own palace on the Albaicin, no doubt nurtured the resentment which led to his downfall. Frederick Bargeburh suggests that Samuel and Yusuf may have harboured Messianic ambitions for a revival of a Solomonic kingdom in Spain, and the symbolism of the palace, expressed through Ibn Gabirol's poetry, provides evidence for this.[5] One of his nature poems is loaded with Solomonic symbolism, evoking the image of a palace that vividly foreshadows the Alhambra.

The buildings are built and decorated
with openwork, intaglios and filigrees,

Paved with marble slabs and alabaster –
I cannot count its many gates.

The doors are like those of ivory mansions
reddened by palatial algum woods.[6]

We do not know whether the poem describes a real or imaginary palace, but the descriptive detail suggests that some of it may be grounded in fact. The following passage is such a precise description of the famous Lion Fountain in the Alhambra's Court of Lions that scholars now attribute it to the original fabric of Yusuf's eleventh-century palace:[7]

And there is a full sea, like unto Solomon's Sea,
though not on oxen it stands,

But there are lions, in phalanx by its rim,
as though roaring for prey – these whelps

Whose bellies are wellsprings that spout forth
through their mouths floods like streams.

And there are hinds embedded in the channels,
hollowed out as water spouts.[8]

The Old Testament reference to the Sea of Solomon describes a bronze tank situated in the precincts of the temple, 30 cubits round and resting on twelve oxen (I Kings 7: 23–25). In Ibn Gabirol's poem, lions have replaced oxen, and Bargebuhr suggests that the Lion Fountain is essentially a composite regal image that synthesises Solomon's Sea with Solomon's throne. In the Bible Solomon's throne is described with some precision, having two flanking lions and twelve standing on each side of six steps (I Kings 10: 18–20).

Solomonic association is not unique to the Alhambra, and the splendours of Solomon's temple and palace, so vividly described in the Old Testament and the Qur'an, for long captured the imagination of Muslim builders.[9] According to the Qur'an, Solomon's palace had a glass floor which the Queen of Sheba mistook for a pool of water. Shimmering surfaces, pools and glass floors form a part of the visual and spatial repertoire of many Muslim palaces. Solomon's lavish court provided a sublime image of authority and wealth, and Muslim rulers were mindful of this symbolism of power. At Madinet al-Zahra ambassadors responded to its awesome splendour in much the same way that the Queen of Sheba reacted to the court of Solomon. However, in the Alhambra reference made to Solomon's splendour is more an expression of nostalgia, subsumed under a palatial magnificence that is complex, lyrical and light in feeling. It is not the expression of power as demonstrated in earlier palace architecture but a cultivated refinement more in keeping with a dynasty that lacked political clout.

On first acquaintance the Alhambra Palace appears to be a heavily fortified citadel, but like Mshatta and Qasr al-Hair West, in places the fortifications are more apparent than real. Many of the towers in the curtain walls are robust, but as Grabar observed, the interior rooms are frequently designed more for pleasure than defence, and sections of wall looking out from the palace are quite insubstantial.[10] Undoubtedly the Alcazaba, projecting like the prow of a ship on the western side of the hill, is strongly fortified. It is mainly pre-Nasrid, the earliest part of the palace complex, built principally in the twelfth century, with Zirid foundations of striped masonry forming possibly a part of Yusuf's original palace.[11] With its thick curtain walls and towers, the Alcazaba is self-contained, separate from the main palace buildings. There are ramparts and five towers: the Adarguero, the Quebrado, the Homenaje, the Polvoro and the Vela, the last of which is a dominating watch-tower containing the barracks and prison. This section of the Alhambra has always functioned as a fortress with stables, storage areas and barracks.

The Alcazaba forms one of the three main sections of the Alhambra. The second is the royal palace proper and the third, now largely disappeared, consisted of residential buildings for the court and its servants. A further palace on land adjacent to the Alhambra citadel is the summer residence of the Generalife, consisting of pavilions set in lush and luxuriant gardens. The whole Alhambra complex, including the Generalife, is connected, and its irregular plan provides a constant element of surprise and wonder through the right-angled set of the

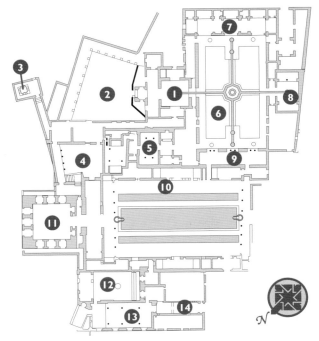

KEY

1	Hall of the Two Sisters	8	Hall of the Abencerrajes
2	Mirador de la Daraxa	9	Hall of the Stalactites
3	Tocador de la Reina	10	Court of the Myrtles
4	Patio de la Reja	11	Hall of the Ambassadors
5	Baths	12	Patio del Cuarto Dorado
6	Court of the Lions	13	Mexaur
7	Hall of the Kings	14	Entrance

Granada, plan of the Alhambra

Granada, Alhambra: the Alcazaba

principal courts, the bent entrances and the labyrinthine disposition of halls, patios and gardens. It is the opposite of Versailles, where symmetry and monumental mass proclaim absolute power. Here the diminutive proportions, the weightless fragility of the fabric and the introverted organisation of space induce feelings of transience and intimacy. There is a fluid and relaxed communication between open and enclosed space, and the use of light gabled porticos and arcades provides an indeterminate demarcation between exterior and interior. This ambiguity of inside and outside space is reinforced by the landscaping of the court, and the network of interconnecting water channels, fountains, pools and basins of water. The gardens are brought into the heart of the building and architectural regularity is softened and complemented by natural informality. The sense of intimacy is also sustained in the Partel Gardens and Generalife where paths, hedges and shrubberies allow just a few people at a time.

The open-ended nature of its form and plan is matched by uncertainties and ambiguities regarding its function. Despite its miraculous state of preservation, the meaning and purpose of the individual components of the building remain largely a mystery. Tradition has produced a variety of named halls and courts: the Hall of the Two Sisters, the Hall of the Abencerrajes, and the Court of the Myrtles, but these names are the stuff of romance. With the exception of the baths, the oratories, the Mexuar and the Hall of the Ambassadors, the identity of individual rooms and quarters is mainly conjecture. There is reasonable consensus that the palace proper can be broadly divided into three sections, moving from public to private domains. The entrance buildings of the Mexuar were used for the administration of justice, the Court of the Myrtles provided the focus for the sultan's official duties and the private harem quarters were clustered around the Court of the Lions. This follows the tradition of earlier Muslim palaces, but beyond this there is no documentary evidence to explain the detail. The only written clues are Ibn Zamrak's poetry, and Qur'anic inscriptions in many parts of the palace. Much of the poetry is oblique in its meaning, eulogising the principal builders of the palace (Yusuf I and Muhammad V) and celebrating the regime's rare military achievements. Rather than explaining the building, these inscriptions contribute

to its mystique and, as Mallarmé would approve, they suggest rather than define.

The visitor enters the royal palace through the partly restored courts of the Mexuar into a public domain which served as an audience hall and place for tribunals. The first room was rebuilt by Muhammad V in 1365, but it has been altered several times and lacks decorative coherence. The wooden gallery was installed in the sixteenth century, and the tile decoration is made up of work moved from other parts of the palace. On the north side of the room is a small oratory with an exquisite stucco decorated *mihrab*. The next section of the palace is the Cuarto Dorado ('Golden Court'), which contains a central fountain, a three-arched portico on the north side and a south façade with two entrances leading to the Palacio de Comares. Many elements date from different periods, but this small court encapsulates most of the visual themes in the palace. The building materials are fragile: glazed tiles, slender columns, brick, stucco, plaster and wood, assembled in such a way as to deny any sense of architectural weight and mass. This immateriality and weightlessness are made possible by the yielding nature of the materials which allows for elaboration, complexity and fine textural modulation. Colour, present in the form of glazed tiles, introduces an heraldic and courtly note to match the palatial function.

The north portico, set on two free-standing and two engaged columns, has fine fretted lace-like stucco panels above the flanking arches. The lower registers of the north and south walls contain wainscoting of geometric tile mosaic forming complex optical patterns which offset the fluid arabesques and calligraphy in the stucco work above. Spanish and north-west African tile mosaic is exclusively geometric and never employs the floral motifs and arabesques commonly used in the tilework of the eastern Muslim world. The south wall represents a masterly synthesis of those three elements of Islamic design: arabesque, geometry and calligraphy. Among the arabesques appears a motif of intertwined ribbon, known as *lacaria*, and the calligraphy is in both Kufic and Naskhi form. The interlaced geometry of the ceramic tile mosaic extends up from the wainscot to frame two rectangular doors, and above these on the upper storey are two paired latticed windows flanking one in the centre. This is a beautifully proportioned wall broken by panels of vertical

ABOVE
Granada, Alhambra, the Cuarto Dorado: north wall (detail)

LEFT
Granada, Alhambra, the Cuarto Dorado: south wall

BOTTTOM LEFT
Granada, Alhambra, the Cuarto Dorado: south wall (detail)

and horizontal arabesques of stucco crowned by a horizontal *muqarnas* frieze and deep projecting wooden eaves. The stuccoed arabesques form a fine honey-coloured tapestry today, but originally the whole surface would have been animated by bright colours, providing chromatic coherence with the tile mosaic below. The first colour analysis of the Alhambra's decoration was made in the nineteenth century by Owen Jones in *The Grammar of Ornament* (1856).

> The colours employed by the Moors on their stucco work were, in all cases, *the primaries, red, blue and yellow (gold). The secondary colours, purple, green, and orange, occur only in the mosaic dados*, which, being near the eye, formed a point of repose from the more brilliant colouring above.[12]

Grabar describes this wall as a monumental gate with a ceremonial function leading to the more official parts of Muhammad V's palace. The regal tone is set by the 'Throne' verse (*Sura* 2:255) of the Qur'an, and poetic inscriptions describe it as a 'gate where [roads] bifurcate and through [which] the East envies the West'.[13]

The entrances lead to two separate destinations. The right hand door leads back to the Mexuar complex, and the left through two right-angled turns to the Patio de Comares, or Court of the Myrtles. The Court of the

Myrtles is the largest internal space in the palace and was the ceremonial focus for the sultan's official duties. Framed by the low horizontal lines of two myrtle hedges, low fountains spurt into a large rectangular pool creating ripples which blur and soften the reflected image of the architecture above. Water cools and tranquillises the senses, as well as adding a crucial spatial and poetic dimension to the palace. The long eastern and western walls have irregularly placed doors giving access to rooms used by the wives of the sultan. The south façade is an elegant structure pierced at ground level by an arcaded portico, surmounted by a band of seven windows on the second storey and a lofty, open, arcaded gallery on the third. The north façade of the court, leading to the Hall of the Ambassadors, is the most imposing. Here there is a satisfying balance between solid mass and open form, where the lightness of the arcaded portico is complemented by the weight of the crenellated Comares Tower at some distance behind. Inside the portico is a fine ceiling of wooden marquetry, and flanking left and right are two beautifully composed recesses with *muqarnas* hoods, friezes and tiled mosaic wainscots.

Another splendid ceiling of wooden marquetry is in the Sala de la Barca, a long transverse ante-room which provides an intermediary space between the portico and Hall of the Ambassadors. Inscriptions in the portico and the Sala de la Barca are full of hyperbole praising Muhammad V and his great victory at Algeciras in 1369. The Hall of the Ambassadors, built by Yusuf I before 1354, is a large square room with nine deeply recessed windows, like niches, overlooking the Darro valley on the north, east and west sides. This great ceremonial space is crowned by a ceiling of wooden marquetry depicting a galaxy of stars representing the seven heavens. The clue to this symbolism is found in an accompanying *sura* from the Qur'an: 'He created seven heavens, one above the other. His work is fautless' (*Sura* 67:3).

In addition to Qur'anic verses, the poetic inscriptions allow the various parts of the building to speak for themselves. The central window recess on the north side has greater decorative elaboration, and the poetry identifies this space as the throne niche.

Leaving the Court of the Myrtles and the grandeur of the throne room, we move to the more private domain of those buildings built by Muhammad V which surround

TOP
Granada, Alhambra: south façade of the Court of the Myrtles

MIDDLE
Granada, Alhambra: north façade of the Court of the Myrtles

ABOVE
Granada, Alhambra: detail of the ceiling of Sala de la Barca

TOP
Granada, Alhambra: the Hall of the Ambassadors

ABOVE
Granada, Alhambra: the Lion Fountain

the Court of the Lions. Here the scale is more intimate, and the design more complex, rich and finely wrought. The Court of the Lions is rectangular, surrounded by a continuous portico broken on the east and west sides by two projecting pavilions. The court is cut in four by a cruciform arrangement of water channels at the centre of which is the Lion Fountain. Ibn Gabirol's poem suggests that the lions are eleventh century and came from Naghrallah's palace, although the basin which the lions now support was placed there by Muhammad V. The original basin is possibly the one that now occupies a space in the Hall of the Abencerrajes, and if this is so it

would have been placed lower, on the backs of the lions.[14] The present basin is inscribed with a long poem by Ibn Zamrak, which adds other poetic layers of meaning and association to those already identified with Solomon's sea and throne.

> . . . A running stream evokes the illusion of being a solid substance and one wonders which one is in truth fluid.
> Don't you see that it is the water which is running over the rim of the fountain, whereas it is the monument which offers long channels for the water; like one in love whose lids overflow with tears and who curbs the tears in fear of a slanderer.
> What else is it in truth but a mist which sheds forth from the fountain drenching towards the lions?
> It resembles in this the hand of the caliph when it happens that it sheds forth supports towards the lions of Holy War.
> O thou who beholdest the lions while they are crouching, timidity preventing them from becoming hostile;
> O thou heir of the Helpers and thus not through distant kin, a heritage of glory you raise to the well-rooted [mountains],
> God's blessing upon thee and mayest thou be blessed eternally to reiterate celebrations and to wear down thine enemies.[15]

The concept of water as a sculptural medium is a strikingly modern one – more to be associated with

ABOVE
Granada, Alhambra, the Court of the Lions

TOP RIGHT
Granada, Alhambra, the Court of the Lions: stucco decoration

RIGHT
Granada, Alhambra: the dome of the Hall of the Abencerrajes

Naum Gabo and Marcel Duchamp than fourteenth-century Muslim Spain.[16] And it is not just in the isolated detail that the Alhambra begs comparison with modernist thinking. Its fluid spatial organisation conceptually relates to Cubism and Le Corbusier, and the integration of natural and built elements calls to mind Frank Lloyd Wright's Kaufman House and Taliesen West.

The arcaded porticos and pavilions in the Court of the Lions are supported on slender paired and single columns with tall attenuated impost blocks. Lambrequin arches are surmounted by panels of fretted interlaced trellis. The pavilions on the east and west project deeply into the interior space of the court, so that from certain vantage points there are wide vistas and deep clusters of slender elegant columns supporting ascending rhythms of arabesques. The perforated stucco becomes a weightless filigree admitting pin-pricks of light which scatter over the lace-like surfaces of the inner arcade. Inside the porticos these illuminated surfaces of stone and stucco resonate

with subtle colour variations of gold, honey and ivory, and the whole space has a feeling of extraordinary incorporeality. As Titus Burckhardt aptly describes it, the Court of the Lions 'sets the example of stone transformed into a vibration of light'.[17]

The theme of light is expressed in the most sensational way in the domes of two rooms flanking the Court of the Lions: the Hall of the Abencerrajes and the Hall of the Two Sisters. The *muqarnas* dome in the Hall of the Abencerrajes is a nebulous structure of infinite crystalline complexity constructed on an eight-pointed star. It is a celestial dome suspended over sixteen windows which admit the transforming light, as the sun and moon move their positions throughout the day and night. In its constantly changing aspect, it is an exquisite abstract expression of the cosmos, acting as a visual metaphor for those apocalyptic passages in the Qur'an referring to the scattering of the heavens.

> I swear by the turning planets and by the stars that rise and set; by the fall of the night and the first breath of morning . . . (*Sura* 81:15–18).

As well as Qur'anic verses the iconographic context of the dome may also be explained by the following passage from Ibn Gabirol's poem:

> And there are windows, transparent above them, skylights where dwell the luminous planets.

> The dome is like the palanquin of Solomon hung above the glories of the chamber.[18]

Under this palanquin – this celestial dome – is an octagonal fountain which reflects and distorts through its rippling surface the kaleidoscopic pattern above.

The *muqarnas* dome in the Hall of the Two Sisters equals in splendour that of the Hall of the Abencerrajes. This one is placed on an octagon instead of an eight-pointed star, and in both cases the structural build-up to the visual crescendo in the dome is achieved in the first instance by the upward surge of *muqarnas* which fill the squinches in the zone of transition. Stucco *muqarnas* also feature in the three square lanterns lighting the Hall of the Kings, which extends along the east side of the Court of the Lions. The space of this long room is broken on the east side by three broad alcoves separated by small rooms. On the west side triple arcaded openings look out to the Court of the Lions, and here there is the fluid mingling of exterior and interior space and light. The Court of the Lions provides a well of light to one side, and within the hall there is further overhead illumination

ABOVE LEFT
Granada, Alhambra: ceiling painting in the Hall of the Kings

LEFT & ABOVE
Granada, Alhambra: Generalife gardens

from the three lanterns. The whole space of the Hall of
the Kings is partitioned into arched patterns of alternating
light and dark, shaped by the shadowed recesses between
the lambrequin arches and the illumination above. The
alcove ceilings above the east wall contain brilliant
decorative paintings of castles and jousting knights,
which are European in style and reminiscent of French
tapestries and illuminated manuscripts. The chivalric
iconography of these paintings is largely unknown, but
Godfrey Goodwin identifies one in which a Muslim
knight wins the hand of his lady from her Christian
lover.[19] The western style of these paintings, with their
romantic sentiments and courtly splendour, corresponds
perfectly with the mood of the palace.

One of the finest decorated rooms in the Alhambra
is the Mirador de la Daraxa which is to the north of the
Hall of the Two Sisters. It forms a look-out to the garden
below, which is post-conquest in its design and layout.
From the Court of the Lions to the east is the Partel,
which is one of the oldest parts of the palace and now
functions as a pavilion. It is situated by a pool with spouting lions, and the gardens and pools which extend from it
need to be considered in general terms with the
Generalife. Today these gardens owe much to post-
conquest, nineteenth-century and modern layouts and
bear little relationship to the original Nasrid designs.
Goodwin describes the present lush setting of the
Generalife as a nonsense, pointing out that it originally
functioned as a farm with orchards and vegetable
gardens.[20] The garden settings of the Alhambra and
Generalife are crucial to our appreciation and understanding of the whole, and have to be considered in equal
measure with the architecture. But how can this be
judged when the present gardens lack authenticity? My
own view is to ask whether the architecture works with
the landscape – any garden landscape – and to say that
authenticity is not crucial. In the Alhambra landscape,
water and architecture form a visual continuum, and
within the regularities of its open architectural frame
nature offers that transient and ephemeral dimension
which gives the building its poetry. It is the changing
nature of the garden setting, Nasrid, nineteenth-century
or modern, which defines the palace. The Alhambra is a
living monument designed to accommodate change, and
what we see today may not be as it was in Nasrid times,

but it is splendid in its own terms, and the Alhambra
and Generalife buildings accommodate the landscape
magnificently. They show that you can put new wine into
old bottles.

We are not, however, entirely ignorant of what
Nasrid gardens were like because of the detailed and vivid
descriptions in the contemporary poetry of Ibn Layun,
which is full of practical gardening advice. For a more
visionary understanding of the gardens, we must turn
to the Qur'an. The Alhambra and Generalife represent an
earthly vision of the Qur'anic paradise, and in this respect
they constitute a major genre within Islamic art and
architecture. Paradisial imagery permeates Islamic art
in arabesque, tilework, garden carpets, illumination,
illustration and the layout of gardens. The pavilions,
fountains, streams and gardens of the Alhambra and
Generalife are a perfect mirror of Qur'anic descriptions
of paradise, such as that found in *Sura* 55: 46–78 ('The
Merciful'), and in this respect they could be described as
vivid examples of representational art.

The Alhambra is undoubtedly the great cultural
achievement of Muhammad V's reign, which lasted with
a brief interruption from 1354 to 1391. It marks the high
point of Granada's culture, and it is tempting to interpret
this splendid citadel as a symbol of Granada's political
and cultural isolation. However, isolation was far from
the case, because during that period Granada absorbed
Christian culture (as witnessed in the roof paintings in
the Hall of the Kings) and exported much of its own.
Moorish art was much admired in the Christian domain
and Muslim craftsmen were sought after by Christian
patrons. In many of those territories reconquered by the
Christians the vast majority of the population remained
Muslim, and the Christian rulers were obliged to exercise
tolerance and protection because they were economically
dependent on the commercial expertise and artistic skills
of these people. The Muslims under Christian rule,
before their gradual expulsion, occupied a position
similar to the *dhimmis* in Muslim society. They were a
protected community which paid a poll tax for the
privilege of exercising their religious freedom, laws and
customs. A number of Muslim artists thrived under such
circumstances, and the term used to describe the art of
Muslim architects and craftsmen working for Christian
patrons is *mudejar*.

Seville, Alcazar: the Court of Stucco

One of the best preserved examples of *mudejar* architecture is the Alcazar in Seville, built for Pedro I (the Cruel) in the fourteenth century. It is contemporary with the Alhambra (1364), and Muhammad V helped supply craftsmen. The original Alcazar was established earlier, in the eighth century, and some of the present walls date from the time of Abd al-Rahman II in the ninth. The oldest part of the palace complex is the Court of Stucco, which is Almohad and dates from the twelfth century. This is a quiet, inconspicuous courtyard with a sunken pool surrounded by a low hedge. Facing two sides of the court are large multifoil arches, like *iwans*, springing from low piers framed with patterns of interlaced lozenge trellis. On either side of the arches are three smaller arches supported in the centre by two slender columns and panelled above by a pattern of open-work trellis. The rest of the Alcazar is the fourteenth-century palace commissioned by Pedro with Muhammad's help. Over the centuries it has been much altered and suffered from fire and earthquake damage, which accounts for the somewhat artificial and over-restored look of the present building.

The Alcazar differs from the Alhambra not so much in its detail but in its composition and layout. The Alhambra has a relaxed charm and informality, being full of unexpected vistas as it meanders in its leisurely and ex-pansive way from court to court. It incorporates its own landscape, while the Alcazar in Seville is experienced as a group of interiors which are more compact and formal, with a greater sense of symmetry in its distribution of space. Because of restoration and refurbishment, there is a

newness and richness of materials as well as a greater density of colour. Its palatial status is announced by the Puerto del Leon set in an imposing façade, which like the Great Mosque in Damascus is similar in composition to the Byzantine palace illustrated in the famous San Vitale mosaic. The rectangular entrance is flanked by two blind multifoil arches springing from low colonettes set in trel-lis panels, above which are horizontal bands of blind arches and trellis work. Beneath the deep projecting eaves and horizontal courses of *muqarnas* decoration is a group of windows which are analogous to the *piano nobile* of a Venetian palace. This solid central façade is flanked by two wings of open arcades. On entering the building you are unexpectedly obliged to turn at right angles into a laterally arranged corridor. These blind entrances may derive from the plan of military gates, designed so that an invader would be impeded or trapped in the confines of the right-angled access.

The corridor leads to the Court of the Maidens, which is the main court of the palace. Four scalloped arches, flanked by smaller paired arches on the short side and triple arches on the long side, face the court like *iwans*. All the arches spring from slender paired columns and carry a façade made up of rich moulding with shells, cones and bosses enmeshed in an arabesque arranged in lozenges similar to that in the Court of the Lions. Much of the detail is not Islamic; it consists of faces and heraldic devices displaying the shields of Castile, Leon and Trastamara. Above the stucco façade is a cumbersome, overweight upper storey, built in the sixteenth century, which completely negates the impact of the fragile

Seville, Alcazar: the Court of the Maidens

Seville, Alcazar: the Hall of the Ambassadors

elegance displayed in the *mudejar* work below. The wainscoting in the inner walls of the court is covered in complex geometric patterns of tile mosaic. The main axis of the Court of the Maidens, like the Court of the Myrtles in the Alhambra, points to the ceremonial centre of the building, the Hall of the Ambassadors.

In the Hall of the Ambassadors the geometry of the tiled wainscoting complements the rich stucco panels of arabesque placed above, and paired columns support heavier triple horseshoe arches of the Cordoban type (a feature that is not seen in the Alhambra). The Cordoban arches are a revival of those at Madinat al-Zahra, and it is thought that a number of columns and capitals were imported from the site. This ornate room is crowned by a fifteenth-century wooden dome, the complex geometry of which is constructed in such a way as to represent the star-like clusters of the cosmos. Triple arcades of Cordoban arches can be seen in the Hall of Moorish Kings, where deep alcoves provided space for beds. The tall, elegant Court of the Dolls, which forms part of the harem, is open to the sky and provides a deep well of light. Like the Alhambra, the Alcazar is more than the sum of its parts and its visual impact is through the endless vistas that open up as one space penetrates another. Space is never closed or terminated. Arched doorways provide keyhole views through several rooms at once and the perception of receding space is often like the illusion of infinite depth viewed between two mirrors.

If the Alhambra was the swan-song of Moorish architecture, the Alcazar symbolises its inevitable demise; it appears like an imitation of Moorish architecture at its flowering, rather than the genuine article. To some extent

this is explained by the over-restoration, but there are elements, like the Cordoban arches, that are revivalist rather than original. We see a well-rehearsed repertoire of architectural forms adapted and modified for the convenience of a new court and political regime. It satisfied the bidding of a Christian ruler for courtly indulgence and became a fancy dress parade for a foreign power. Severed from its cultural roots, Moorish art had no natural or organic way to change and develop meaningfully, and without a functional base it only survived as a second-hand style of decoration.

The oldest *mudejar* population was in Toledo, which fell to Alfonso VI in 1085, and under Christian rule it became a model of cultural cohesion. The Jews formed a very important part of the population, and the city became a brilliant intellectual centre due to the close linguistic collaboration of Christians, Muslims and Jews. The cultural impact of Toledo cannot be underestimated because it was from here that much Arab learning, based on Greek philosophy and science, was transmitted to the West. Multilingual scholarship made possible the translation of Arabic texts into Romance, Hebrew and Latin. The works of al-Farabi (d. 950 in Damascus), Ibn Sina (or Avicenna (980–1037), Averroes, Ibn Gabirol (1020–c. 1070), and al-Ghazali (1058–1111), were translated into Latin. Translations of Averroes' commentaries on Aristotle by Michael Scotus and Hermannus Alemannus had a significant impact on the Italian universities, where his work was widely read until the seventeenth century. Thomas Aquinas was particularly responsive to Averroes, although he ultimately refuted Averroes' work, arguing that Aristotelian thought had to be compatible with Christian dogma. The Neo-Platonic philosophy of Ibn Gabirol also provoked a critical reaction from Aquinas, who wrote *De Ente et Essentia* as a rebuttal of Gabirol's *Fons Vitae*, translated from Arabic. Ibn Sina (placed in Dante's *Inferno* alongside Averroes in the Limbo of the Philosopher) inspired Duns Scotus later, and his commentaries on Aristotle, Galen and other works influenced thirteenth-century scholasticism, medicine and ideas of courtly love. The Toledan translation of Muhammad ibn Musa al-Khwarazmi's *Algorismi de numero indorum* introduced the West to Indian numerals and such terms as the cipher and algorithm. Gerard of Cremona translated several astronomical works, including Jabir ibn

LEFT & TOP
Toledo, Sta Maria la Blanca

ABOVE
Toledo, the El Transisto Synagogue: detail of frieze

Aflah's *Kitab al-Haia* and Ptolemy's *Almagest*, which laid the foundations of Islamic astronomy. It was Averroes who made the West aware of the theories of dynamics of Ibn Bajjah (known as Avempace), which considerably influenced Galileo's *Pisan Dialogue*.

Toledo's golden age of cultural consolidation took place in the thirteenth century during the reign of Alfonso X (the Wise), who encouraged many scientific works as well as the Bible, Qur'an and Talmud to be published in Castilian rather than Latin. The architectural evidence of this cultural cohesion in Toledo can best be seen in two synagogues. The church of Sta Maria la Blanca was once a thirteenth-century synagogue, and its striking interior is divided by four powerful arcades of round horseshoe arches springing from octagonal piers. The unusual capitals are basket shaped, with curling volutes like pine cones, pulled into a tight weave of drilled strapwork. The spandrels of the arches contain fluid interlace designs with fine meshed medallions, and above the arcade alternate aisles carry friezes with reticulated patterns and blind trilobed arches. In all its pristine whiteness, it has, as Godfrey Goodwin has observed, the striking appearance of a North African mosque.[21] In contrast, the finely wrought stucco of the other synagogue, El Transisto (1357), is more obviously contemporary with the Alhambra and the Alcazar at Seville. It was built by Don Meir Abdeil for Samuel Levi, the treasurer of Pedro the Cruel. It consists of an open hall 23 metres long and 17 metres wide, with a north wall decorated with three vertically hanging stucco panels. The central panel is a lozenge trellis with three multifoil blind arches beneath. An exquisite frieze runs around the hall with a tree of life motif bordered by Hebrew inscriptions. Gothic, Moorish and Hebrew elements synthesise in the detail. In one panel, bordered with elegant Hebrew characters, an heraldic Castilian shield, wreathed in Gothic oak leaves, is contained in a multifoiled ribbon of Arabic calligraphy. Above the frieze is a continuous arcade of seven lobed arches with lattice windows set in dense, finely wrought arabesques.

Elsewhere in Toledo *mudejar* craftsmanship is evident in a number of Christian buildings. Distinctive horseshoe arches form the aisles and nave of San Roman, and Santiago del Arabel has a *mudejar* porch set in a frame surmounted by interlaced multifoil blind arches. The cathedral's *mozarabic* chapel bears witness to the continuous tradition of Christian worship before and after the reconquest (there were six churches operating under Muslim rule), and the chapter house displays a fine *mudejar* ceiling. The monastery of Sta Isabel la Real has *mudejar* stucco decoration and woodwork, and its structure and room plan resemble Moorish domestic architecture and caravansarais like the Corral del Carbon in Granada. Outside the religious sphere are the impressive gates of Toledo, where distinctive horseshoe arches can be seen in the Puerta de Alfonso VI and the Puerta del Sol. *Mudejar* work elsewhere in Spain has made a lasting impact on the decorative and structural development of Spanish architecture. In Burgos the monastery of Las Huelgas has *muqarnas* domes, a domical vault with stellar patterned ribs and elaborate multifoil arches in the chapels. Interlaced *mudejar* blind arches adorn the façade of the cathedral (La Seo) in Zaragoza, and the octagonal lantern has a stellar rib structure similar to the *maqsura*

dome in the Great Mosque in Cordoba. Structures like this, and the ribbed vaulting in the Church of the Holy Sepulchre at Torres del Rio, Navarre, provide clear evidence of Moorish influence on the subsequent development of ribbed vaulting in Romanesque and Gothic architecture.

Cultural cohesion like that in Toledo did not last. After the union of Aragon and Castile, and the fall of Granada in 1492, Ferdinand and Isabella pursued an uncompromising policy for a unified Catholic identity in Spain. The year 1492 is auspicious, because it also marks the voyage west of Christopher Columbus and the expulsion of the Jews. These events, are not totally unconnected, as Christopher Columbus related in his memoirs.

> On 2 January in the year 1492, when your Highnesses had concluded your war with the Moors who reigned in Europe, I saw your Highnesses' banners victoriously raised on the towers of the Alhambra, the citadel of that city, and the Moorish king come out of the city gates and kiss the hands of your Highnesses, and the prince, my Lord . . . And later in that same month . . . your Highnesses . . . decided to send me, Christopher Columbus, to see those parts of India and the princes and peoples of these lands, and consider the best means of their conversion, and your Highnesses ordered that I should not travel overland to the east, as is customary, but rather by way of the west, whither to this day, so far as I know, no man has ever gone before. Therefore, having expelled all the Jews from your domains in the same month of January, your Highnesses commanded me to go with an adequate fleet to these parts of India.[22]

Ferdinand and Isabella's quest for trade routes in the west marked a decisive move to bypass the Muslim world, and the subsequent success of the western routes meant that the Spanish Christians became less dependent on the indigenous Muslim population. After centuries of growing suspicion, forced conversion to Christianity and oppression, finally the ethnic cleansing of Spain was completed between 1609 and 1614, when the Moriscos (converted Muslims, who still secretly retained their faith) were forced to leave.

The exodus of Spanish Muslims had been taking place since the beginning of the reconquest. Most settled in North Africa, but despite being among co-religionists, many felt more Spanish than North African and retained much of their Andalusian identity. Some felt a sense of cultural superiority, but their distinctive presence had an enriching and continuing influence on the character of North Africa. Since the end of the caliphate, Spain's fortunes had been closely tied up with North Africa, and this symbiotic relationship continued well into the fifteenth century. The Marinid dynasty of Morocco periodically offered political, diplomatic and military support to Granada, and cross-cultural exchange was frequent. The circularity of this contact is exemplified by the great historian Ibn Khaldun. He was born in Tunis in 1332. His forebears had played a leading role in Spanish politics before the fall of Seville in 1248. He was heir to the intellectual legacy of this family of scholars and courtiers and went on to hold high office in the courts of Tunisia, Algeria, Morocco and Granada. The visual evidence of this cultural symbiosis can clearly be seen in the later architecture of the Marinids and Sa'dians, in which Nasrid influence survived into the seventeenth century.

The Berber tribe of Beni Marin, or Marinids, entered Morocco from the east and overthrew the Almohads in 1269. Fez became their capital, and a new walled city, Fez Djid, was built alongside the old in 1276. Fez Djid was essentially a centre of government and administration containing the royal palace and military headquarters. For strategic reasons the first significant buildings of the Marinid dynasty were constructed in Taza and Tlemcen in order to strengthen and consolidate their presence on the eastern borders. At Taza the Great Mosque (1294) was doubled in size to accommodate the expanding population by extending the *qibla* wall by four bays and adding aisles to the east and west. It follows the Tunisian model, with domes adding ceremonial importance to the central aisle. The inside of the *mihrab* dome in particular is a *tour de force* of virtuoso stucco carving. Light is diffused through a delicate filigree of lace-like tracery held in place by sixteen slender ribs which divide half way up into intersecting branches forming a crown of *muqarnas* at the apex. The fragile elegance of this structure is in marked contrast to the ruined minaret at al-Mansura near Tlemcen. This mosque was built by the

Fez, the Bou Inania Madrasa

Marinids to serve the small garrison town which grew up during the eight-year siege of Tlemcen. Its function as fortification is expressed in its sturdy form, but all that stands today are a few walls and the impressive ruined minaret 38 metres high. Divided into four unequal storeys, this minaret represents one of those masterly compositions of varied and restrained surface decoration in the Almohad tradition.

The most significant architectural contribution of the Marinids was the introduction of the *madrasa* into Morocco in order to check Sufi influence and ensure a more temperate orthodoxy following the excesses of their zealous Almoravid and Almohad predecessors. The finest example is the Bou Inania Madrasa in Fez (1355), built by Sultan Abou Inan to accommodate students of the Qarawiyin university. This is contemporary with Muhammad IV's work at the Alhambra, and the stylistic similarities are manifest. It is situated on one of the main streets in Fez el Bali (Old Fez), and its entrance is flanked by shops. The entrance hall, covered with a wooden *muqarnas* dome, leads into a two-storeyed courtyard which is elaborately decorated in plaster, cedarwood and mosaic tiles in the Nasrid fashion. The effect is warmer and more subdued than in the courts of the Alhambra, due to the greater proportion of wood and more sparing use of tile mosaic. Wooden marquetry screens fill the ground floor arcades, which enclose a corridor on three sides leading to the students' rooms. At the centre of two sides of the court, wooden doors open to reveal lambrequin arches leading into two-storeyed lecture rooms. The façade opposite the entrance is pierced by a single arcade of five tall pointed horseshoe arches which lead over a water channel to the mosque. The mosque has two transverse aisles divided by four columns and is roofed by a wooden vault. The combination of a *madrasa* with a substantial mosque is quite unusual, and for this reason the Bou Inania is the only *madrasa* in Fez to have a minaret.

The Attarine Madrasa (1325) in Fez is much smaller than the Bou Inania, and instead of a mosque we have a small oratory. Nevertheless it is a gem of a building, in which all of the decorative elements of the courtyard are beautifully orchestrated in a balance of intricately carved

ivory-coloured stucco and deep, rich woodwork, complemented by the optical vibrance of the floor and tile mosaic. Although the structure, materials and composition recall Nasrid architecture, the use of wood in the upper windows, and its decorative role in the panels framing the arches, give it a distinctive Moroccan flavour. As well as *madrasas*, the Marinids made their contribution to the huge Qarawiyin congregational mosque in Fez. Its final plan is thirteenth-century Marinid, but it was founded in 859 and is the product of numerous extensions. It is the largest mosque in Morocco, accommodating up to 20,000 people and forms the nucleus of the oldest university in North Africa. The vast Almohad prayer hall, with its horseshoe arches on plain columns, is austere in its simplicity, relieved only by the complexity of the *muqarnas* vaults. The lateral plan of the rectangular *sahn*, like that in a number of North African mosques, is modest in size and follows Damascus in its orientation. It was built by the Sa'dian dynasty in 1624 and is distinguished by two pavilions which project into

Fez, the Attarine Madrasa

Fez, the Qarawiyin Mosque

its richly tiled space, containing a central ablutions fountain. They cover two rectangular pools and bear a striking resemblance to the pavilions in the Alhambra's Court of the Lions. These, however are much sturdier, with heavier timber cornices supported on single, rather than paired columns. Nevertheless, they demonstrate a lingering cultural consciousness of the Nasrid style over two hundred and fifty years later.

Ottoman influence in west North Africa was minimal. Moroccan architecture stayed relatively homogeneous, even if it lost its capacity for change and innovation. The Sa'dian dynasty continued to build well into the seventeenth century beautiful *madrasas* and tombs in a conservative Nasrid tradition. It can be seen in the largest *madrasa* in Morocco, the Ben Yusuf Madrasa (1565) in Marrakesh, which claimed to house up to eight hundred students. The *madrasa* is entered by a long corridor which leads to a vestibule from which stairs give access to student accommodation on the second floor, and corridors extend round the court leading to the cells and service rooms. Instead of an ablutions fountain, a

rectangular pool occupies the centre of the court, and the façades on the east and west sides are broken on the ground floor by arcades springing from heavy piers. Like the Bou Inania, the decorative scheme has a warmth and richness from the juxtaposition of ivory-coloured stucco sandwiched between mosaic tilework and deep brown cedarwood. Cedarwood plays a major role, crowning the court with its heavy projecting cornice, framing the principal arches and forming the lintels above the side arcades. The south façade leads to the wooden vaulted rectangular prayer hall, which is divided into three aisles by four columns. The horseshoe shaped *mihrab* is pentagonal in plan and projects out of the *qibla* wall in the manner of the early Fatimid mosques.

Besides *madrasas*, tombs played a significant part in the architectural repertoire of the Marinids and Sa'dians. There are dynastic tombs and those that honour the memory of Sufi mystics. Many of the latter formed centres of pilgrimage, and whole collections of buildings grew around them. One of the most important early Marinid tomb complexes was built for the mystic Abu Maydan outside Tlemcen in 1339. It is one of the best preserved, comprising a tomb, mosque, *madrasa*, hospice

Marrakesh, the Ben Yusuf Madrasa

Marrakesh, gateway to the Ben Yusuf Madrasa

and ablutions facility. Similar complexes were built by the Sa'dian dynasty, which maintained close links with the Sufi orders. One such order was founded by al-Juzuli, whose tomb has been an important centre of pilgrimage in Marrakesh since its foundation. The Sultan Ahmad al-A'raj instigated the building of the *zawiya* or retreat, of Sidi'l Jazuli in 1529, where he arranged for his father to be buried. The buildings include the saint's tomb, a cemetery for his followers, a mosque, school, hospice, ablutions facility and baths. Sixty-six members of the Sa'dian ruling families are buried in tombs contained within two buildings as well as the garden enclosure. The east tomb was built for the founder of the dynasty Muhammad al-Shaykh I and enlarged in 1570 by Ahmad al-Mansur for the interment of his mother, Lalla Masouda. The west tomb is made up of three sections: tomb, lecture hall and oratory, with the body of al-Mansur and his sons at the centre and those of his wives and other children nearby. The central chamber is built around twelve marble columns which enclose three marble cenotaphs marking the burial place of the sultan and his sons. They stand on a tiled floor of fine geometric patterns which harmonise perfectly with the radiating stellar motifs in the mosaic tiled wainscot. The interior is well preserved, and the stuccoed walls, lozenge trellis, lambrequin arches, gilding and cedarwood vault provide further evidence of the longevity of the Nasrid tradition.

Over two hundred and fifty years after the Alhambra, the examples of Nasrid survival in the Sa'dian Tombs and Qarawiyin Mosque represent the reproduction rather than development of Nasrid tradition. Within that tradition excellent standards of design and craftsmanship were sustained, but there is a crystallised finality in the design which suggests that all options were closed, and like the Alcazar at Seville they affirm the end of a chapter. Crystallisation is a defining characteristic of inanimate, rather than organic form. Good architecture should be organic, and while it may be regulated by tradition, it has to operate within a canon that admits the need for the human spirit to breathe. Unfortunately, in later Moroccan architecture the Nasrid tradition became a repetition of either sterile forms of revivalism or surface decoration which showed little regard for structural integrity. Where changes did occur they tended to be manifest in coarse recombinations of old themes – Almohad, Marinid or Nasrid. To some extent this can be seen in the remains of the palace complex of Mawlay Ishma'il (1672–1727) at Meknes. Here this despotic ruler expressed his authority by building a huge royal city consisting of three major palaces, military headquarters, mosques and numerous ancillary buildings set in extensive gardens. Constructed quickly and cheaply out of a body of clay mixed with gravel, its surfaces were covered with stucco, tiles and terracotta. Much of it was destroyed immediately after his death, and all that remains today are the ruins. Something of the ostentation of this complex can be judged by the surviving ceremonial gate of Bab al Mansur (1732), which was completed by Mawlay Ishma'il's successor. Built to impress, this gate is decorated with blind arches and lozenge trellis work embellished with green, black and white tiles. It expresses the inexorable decline of Moroccan architecture in its heavy-handed restatement and recombination of Almohad themes, and its cumbersome form anticipates the architectural pomposities normally associated with the nineteenth century.

Marrakesh, the Sa'dian Tombs

Meknes, the ceremonial gate of Bab al Mansur

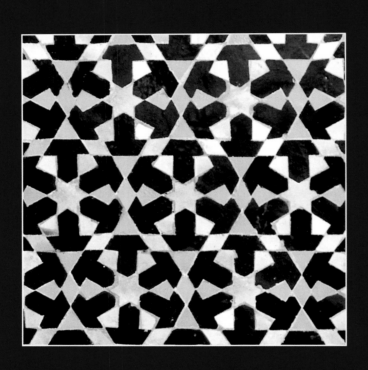

CHAPTER 7

AYYUBID AND MAMLUK ARCHITECTURE

Salah al-Din, founder of the Ayyubid dynasty, is best known for his defeat of the Crusaders and the re-clamation of Syria and Palestine for Islam. However, throughout most of his military career his energies were directed against Muslim enemies rather than Christians, because his objective was to secure and dominate a Muslim power base uniting Egypt, Syria and Palestine. Throughout his struggle with Muslim adversaries, Salah al-Din had been circumspect in dealing with the Franks, but it was Raynold of Chatillon's violations of peace treaties and attacks on Meccan caravans that finally pro-voked him into action against the Crusader states. Salah al-Din united an effective Muslim force which decisively defeated the Franks at the battle of Hittin in 1187, and it was this victory that made possible the subsequent Muslim conquest of Acre, Ascalon and Jerusalem. What remained of the Crusader kingdoms was a coastal strip of the Levant, ruled from Antioch, Tyre and Tripoli, where the Franks sustained a dwindling presence for another hundred years until the final campaigns of Baibars, Qala'un and Khalil.

Cairo, the tomb of Shafi'i: interior of the dome

In Egypt, following the overthrow of the Fatimids, Salah al-Din's first objective was to restore Sunni ortho-doxy and re-establish the caliphate of Baghdad as the ultimate religious authority. The al-Azhar mosque and *madrasa*, a pre-eminent centre of learning, was converted to Sunni Islam. It was a time of cultural revival and many new Sunni *madrasas* were established to ensure the hegemony of orthodox doctrine. The first to be built by Salah al-Din was dedicated to Imam Shafi'i and situated near his mausoleum, which the sultan began to restore. The Fatimids had erected numerous mausoleums for those members of the Prophet's family from whom they claimed descent, and for this reason monuments of this type bore significant political as well as religious authority. It was therefore politically necessary for the Ayyubids to honour the Sunni saints with notable shrines, and Salah al-Din regarded Shafi'i's tomb as particularly sacred. He buried his wife, Princess Shamsah, and son, Sultan al-Aziz, inside the mausoleum, no doubt in the belief that they might absorb something of the saint's *baraka*. The mausoleum was substantially rebuilt by Salah al-Din's nephew, al-Malik al-Kamil, son of al-Malik al-Adil, Salah al-Din's brother and successor. He carried out the work in 1211, the year of his mother's death, and buried her there, reserving a tomb for himself which he never occupied, because like his uncle he died in Damascus, where he is buried. What began as a restoration of a religious shrine became a significant royal mausoleum.

Imam Shafi'i was born in Gaza in 767 and was founder of the Shafi'i school of law. His earliest education consisted of learning grammar and poetry from the bedouin before going to Medina to study religious law under Malik ibn Anas, founder of the Maliki *madhhab*. During the reign of Haroun al-Rashid, Shafi'i taught in Baghdad, and became mentor to Ahmad ibn Hanbal, who established the third great *madhhab* of Sunni Islam, the Hanbali school. In 815 Shafi'i settled in Egypt where he taught at the Mosque of Amr ibn al-As until his death in 820. His mausoleum, in the south cemetery near Fustat, is in constant use, venerated by a steady stream of individuals (mainly women) saying prayers of intercession and supplication in addition to the daily liturgy. As in so many Muslim shrines, the holy presence of the Imam provides a focus for devotional prayer, also serving as an accessible intermediary between the devotee and God.

It is a unique monument, steeped in historical association, in which an atmosphere of profound sanctity is conferred by constant and casual daily usage.

The tomb has been restored by so many rulers that it is not easy to isolate the original Ayyubid work. The tomb is square, with heavy masonry walls supporting a transitional inset second tier with chamfered corners, from which springs the wooden dome covered with lead sheeting. The profile of the dome is distinctly Ayyubid in that it curves continuously from its base, unlike the Fatimid domes, which curve gently from a circular drum. The façade of the first storey is pieced by a central pointed arched window flanked by blind rectilinear and pointed arched niches. Above this runs a geometric horizontal course supporting a balcony of similar interlaced geometric design. The second tier is decorated with keel-arched niches with scalloped hoods between which alternate decorative rosette roundels and lozenges. Above these is another horizontal course of geometric interlace supporting finely pierced merlons. At each chamfered corner keel-arched doorways, flanked with delicate stucco decoration, give access to the balcony.

The dome, built of two wooden shells, similar to the Dome of the Rock, is covered with lead sheeting dating from 1772. It is surmounted by a finial in the shape of a boat, which is said to have contained water and seed for birds. There is some debate about the interior support of the dome, which Creswell attributed to Qa'it Bay of the late fifteenth century, but Behrens-Abouseif argues that it may be original Ayyubid work. Green tiles were found under the lead sheeting, and these have been attributed to Sultan al-Ghuri who restored the dome in the early sixteenth century, covering it with tiles similar to those in his own mausoleum. Inside the mausoleum is an original Kufic frieze from which project eight finely carved beams. These support an octagonal frame carrying the mosque lamps. There are three *mihrabs* on the south-east wall with Mamluk decoration, and a further *mihrab* was added to compensate for the faulty alignment of the tomb to Mecca. The wooden teak cenotaph on Shafi'i's tomb, commissioned by Salah al-Din and carved by Ubayd al-Najjar Ibn Ma'ali in 1178, is one of the finest pieces of medieval wood carving in Egypt. Its geometric panels are banded with Kufic inscriptions, as well as some of the earliest flourishes of cursive Naskhi script, introduced into Egypt at this time.

It was inevitable that throughout the period of the Crusades, military architecture played a significant role not just in Egypt but throughout the Ayyubid territories, which included Syria and Palestine. The Crusader fortresses, which are outside the scope of this book, made their own extraordinary contribution to the architectural landscape of the region and influenced in some measure Muslim military architecture. Salah al-Din's major architectural contribution to the city of Cairo was the building of the Citadel on the Muqattam Hill, but before he embarked on this undertaking, he unified the cities of Fustat and al-Qahira by extending existing walls, intending to encompass both cities and connect them with the Citadel. His premature death prevented the completion of the plan. Neither did he live on the Citadel, which served as a barracks and royal palace up until the reign of Muhammad Ali in the nineteenth century. This commanding structure is the most enduring symbol of Salah al-Din's reign, and remained under military command well into the twentieth century.

The Citadel roughly divides into two, the military northern enclosure and the residential southern enclosure. The northern enclosure, which juts out to the east, is surrounded by a curtain wall to the south and east, built by Salah al-Din and al-Malik al-Adil, consisting of square and round towers (Creswell attributes the round towers to Salah al-Din and the square towers to al-Malik al-Adil). The Arabic word for tower is *burg*, from which derives the name Burgi, used to refer to the Mamluk corps of soldiers barracked in this enclosure who later established the second ruling Mamluk dynasty of Egypt. The towers were built of locally quarried stone as well as material taken from the smaller pyramids at Giza, and surface differences can be seen by the use of rusticated blocks

Cairo, the tomb of Shafi'i: exterior view

TOP
Aleppo, the Citadel

ABOVE
Cairo, the Citadel walls

in the square towers and smoother dressed stone in the circular towers. One of the original gates to the northern enclosure, the Bab al-Mudarraj, contains an early Naskhi inscription dated 1183, stating that Vizir Qaraqush built the gate under the orders of Salah al-Din and al-Adil. The southern enclosure was mainly residential, but nothing survives from the Ayyubid period except the Bir Yusuf, Salah al-Din's impressive 90-metre deep well. This is the only remnant of a complex programme of hydraulic engineering initiated by Salah al-Din, bringing water to cisterns on the Citadel via aqueducts from the Nile.

Undoubtedly the most dramatic and impressive fortified citadel of the Ayyubid period is that which dominates the city of Aleppo in northern Syria. It consists of a mound, part natural, and part artificial, rising 55 metres above the city. The upper part has been moulded by the action of numerous periods of settlement, and among the earliest remains archaeologists have found fragments of a Hittite temple. The Romans and Byzantines garrisoned and fortified the site, but all that remains of this period are the bases of a number of Byzantine cisterns. After the Arab conquest the walls were periodically refortified and what we see today dates principally from the Ayyubid and Mamluk periods. This imposing Citadel is to some extent a monumental symbol of the Muslim revival and *jihad* against the Franks. The success of the early Crusades was due mainly to the disarray, incompetence and internal strife among the Seljuk principalities and their total inability to unite against a common Christian foe. The first effective challenge to the Franks came from Imad al-Din Zangi, who established Aleppo as his base for territorial expansion, making possible the change of Muslim fortunes which gave rise to the victories of his son, Nur al-Din, and the consequent success of Salah al-Din. The rebuilding of the Citadel at Aleppo owes much to Salah al-Din's son, al-Zahir Ghazi, who with his father successfully captured the Crusader stronghold of Saone.

Al-Zahir Ghazi's gate to the Citadel was constructed in 1211 and is one of the finest examples of military architecture in the Muslim world. This well composed and proportioned structure is a supreme example of how architectural nobility can be determined by functional necessity. Its solid, crenellated cubic mass is pierced by the deep shadowed recess of the tall central gate, surmounted by a shallow four-centred arch, giving access to a passage which deviates via five 90 degree turns, to the Citadel beyond. Each of these right-angled passages can be blocked and a potential invader halted, boxed in and attacked with arrows and other missiles from above. Also the sequence of short passages created by this configuration limits space, making it impossible for an assailant effectively to swing a battering ram against the inner gates. The bent entrance, previously noted in Moorish gates, was a pattern used in both Arab and Crusader architecture during this period, and the most impressive Frankish use of this device can be found in the long vaulted entrance passages of Krak des Chevaliers near the coast in Syria.

Arab fortresses during this period also used machicolation. Early forms of machicolation appeared in Umayyad monuments, such as Qasr al-Hair East, but it now became commonplace in both Muslim and Crusader fortifications. The Ayyubid gate at Aleppo is flanked by six box machicolations, three on each side, supported by

four stepped corbels, almost identical in design to those on the outer face of the western curtain wall at Krak des Chevaliers. Arrow slits pierce each machicolation, as well as the spaces between, above and below at bridge level, where they form a slightly different alignment. The storey above the central gate is broken by a large vertically placed rectangular central window framed with alternating courses of *ablaq* (two-toned) masonry above which is a cartouche made up of decorative strapwork surmounted by a small pointed window framing a thin arrow slit. This vertical alignment of features is set in a recessed moulded panel crowned by a horizontal course of *muqarnas* surmounted by the projecting corbels of a machicolation. This central panel is flanked at the bottom by six smaller rectangular windows, and at the top by two small arched windows and two pointed cylindrical machicolations which project from the surface like the helms of two knights. This is a remarkably varied and

TOP
Aleppo, the entrance gate to the Citadel

ABOVE
Aleppo, the serpents on the Citadel gate

tense composition of architectural elements in which the flat surface is broken by a sophisticated juxtaposition of pierced, projected and recessed forms, punctuated and articulated by the shadows cast in the strong Syrian sunlight.

The defensive power of the gate is reinforced on a symbolic level inside by the presence of two beautifully carved interlaced, serpentine dragons above the entrance of the first gate of the passage. The passage proceeds through its various right-angled turns to the final gate, which is flanked with the projecting heads of two lions. Michael Rogers suggests that these beasts may have their origin in Mesopotamian symbols of royalty, and he draws a comparison between the dragons on this and the thirteenth-century Talisman gate at Baghdad (now destroyed).[1] Such beasts represent scarce examples of stone sculpture, which for the religious reasons outlined in Chapter 1 is the least developed and exploited art form in the Muslim world. Lions, eagles and dragons appear in the secular precincts of palaces and more frequently on fortifications. Contemporaneous with the Aleppo serpents and lions are some remarkable examples of double-headed eagles and human-headed lions placed on the towers of Diyerbakr in south-east Turkey by the Ortokid ruler Malik as Salih Mahmud. Other notable lions appear on the Lion Gate in Jerusalem, at the base of the tower of Sultan al-Zahir Baibars on the Cairo Citadel and in the Court of the Lions at the Alhambra. On fortifications these mythic creatures have a talismanic function, acting as palladiums and performing the ancient role of protective guardians.

The Ayyubid gate is the climax to a magnificent architectural ensemble leading up to the Citadel, which includes the Mamluk entrance tower, built by Sultan Qansuh al-Ghuri in 1507, guarding a sloping bridge set on tall, slender, pointed arches. The bridge, built at the same time as the Ayyubid gate, looks down on the moat and smooth stone-faced glacis which inclines steeply up from the base of the mound. Two further imposing Mamluk towers, built by Sultan Faraj ibn Barquq at the beginning of the fifteenth century, are situated near the base of the mound on the north and south sides. These free-standing towers form island bastions which were originally connected to the Citadel by drawbridges. These

gates and bastions represent military architecture at its best, but the real impact of the Aleppo Citadel lies not so much in the finer points of architectural detail but in the dramatic scale of the mound which forms a truncated cone, ringed at the top by the extensive walls and fortifications. The mound itself has a strong, varied and undulating relief, formed by the smooth face of the glacis, which gradually breaks up and gives way higher up to natural ground, where the steep incline of the mass is deeply scored and shadowed by furrowed rivulets snaking down the surface.

The Citadel housed the Hamdanid court in the tenth century, but most of the principal buildings we observe within the walls today, consisting of a mosque, shrine and palace, date from the Ayyubid period and are in a ruinous state. The Ayyubid palace was originally built by al-Zahir Ghazi, but it was burnt down in 1212 and rebuilt in 1230 by al-Malik al-Aziz. The palace was destroyed by the Mongols, but recent restoration and rebuilding reveals an impressive bath complex, and the main entrance portal is well preserved, displaying handsome *ablaq* masonry of basalt and limestone, strapwork panels and a *muqarnas* hood. The top room of the Ayyubid gate was reserved for receptions and ceremonial purposes and has recently been somewhat over-restored in the late Mamluk style of Qa'it Bay. The ruins of the small mosque of Abraham date from the time of Nur al-Din (1168) and honours the place where Abraham milked his flocks. The larger mosque, built by al-Ghazi, also has Abrahamic associations, as it once supposedly contained the altar where Abraham sacrificed Isaac (or Ishmael). It is simple and beautifully proportioned, consisting of a cloister plan made up of a courtyard giving access to a vaulted prayer hall one bay deep, which runs laterally along the *qibla* wall with a central dome placed over the *mihrab*. The minaret is a simple square tower of the Syrian type.

The Ayyubid dynasty was overthrown by the Mamluks, a military caste which had formed a *corps d'élite* under previous sultans. Like similar troops employed by the Abbasid caliphs, they were originally Turkish slaves from Central Asia who were specially recruited, trained and subsequently freed to serve the

OPPOSITE PAGE
Aleppo, the Citadel gate

TOP
Cairo, the mosque of Qala'un

ABOVE
Damascus, the *maristan* of Nur al-Din

Egyptian sultans. They proved to be more loyal and dependable than the mixed contingents of Kurdish, Berber and Sudanese troops that had made up the bulk of Egyptian armies. However, as witnessed in Baghdad, Mamluk forces could occasionally turn into a double-edged sword. The Ayyubid sultan al-Malik al-Salih established on the island of Rawda a powerful Mamluk army (known as the Bahri Mamluks) which became fiercely loyal to him and his family. The next sultan, Turan Shah, imported his own Mamluk troops from Mesopotamia, so a group of Bahri Mamluks, led by al-Zahir Baibars, murdered Turan Shah and declared al-Salih's widow, Shajar al-Durr, the new ruler. This extraordinary elevation of a woman to the sultanate of Egypt proved unacceptable to both the caliph of Baghdad and the Syrian Ayyubid princes, so a marriage was arranged enabling joint rule between Shajar al-Durr and her commander-in-chief, Aybeg. It did not work, and both were murdered leaving an opportunity for Qutuz, the leader of Aybeg's Bahri Mamluks, to seize power.

As soon as Qutuz came to power, he and his brilliant commander, al-Zahir Baibars, faced the onslaught of the Mongol invasions, which were far more devastating to the Muslim world than the Frankish occupation of the Levant. The first waves of Turcoman incursions had begun in the eleventh century. In the thirteenth century, Mongol invaders swept down from the Muslim east, overthrew Seljuk Persia and sacked Baghdad in 1258. The Franks formed alliances with the Mongols, and with Armenian help they occupied northern Syria, taking Aleppo and Damascus. The Mongols then demanded the submission of Egypt, but Sultan Qutuz refused, and in 1260 he and Baibars routed Kitbuga's Mongol army at Ayn Jalut. This battle, the first major defeat of the Mongols, stemmed the tide of their relentless western advance. The victorious Mamluk army went on to liberate Aleppo and Damascus before returning to Egypt where Baibars, with characteristic opportunism, assassinated Qutuz. He was proclaimed sultan, and it was Baibars' brilliant leadership that consolidated Mamluk power in Egypt, Syria and Palestine. He repulsed further Mongol attacks, weakened the resistance of the remaining Ayyubid princes and continued his campaign against the Franks in the Levant. After Salah al-Din, Baibars was the most effective leader to emerge from Egypt. He restored the caliphate, secured the allegiance of the *sharif* of Mecca and gave Egypt enormous political influence over the Hijaz. Salah al-Din was the perfect knight, but it was Baibars' ruthless action in meeting Frankish and Mongol barbarity with barbarity in equal measure that most effectively rid Syria and Palestine of these invaders. He also laid the foundations for the dynasty of Bahri Mamluks which ruled Egypt for over a hundred years.

Sultan al-Zahir Baibars, like Salah al-Din, devoted his life to building an empire rather than monuments. Nevertheless, his huge mosque in Cairo, built in 1269, and now ruined, with its buttressed walls and heavy gates, expresses a solid, cubic, fortified bulk, which is in keeping with his austere character and that of his reign. It later proved a suitable stronghold and barracks for soldiers during the Napoleonic occupation. Its plan is similar to that of al-Hakim's Mosque in Cairo, with one major innovation in the large dome over the central aisle in front of the *mihrab* taking up a space equivalent to nine bays. This wooden dome, much larger than any used previously in this position in the western Islamic mosque, is similar in scale and concept to the domed sanctuaries of the Seljuk mosques of Persia and Anatolia. Another innovation is the use of *ablaq*, a very distinctive feature of later Cairene architecture. The projecting main entrance retains something of a Fatimid feature, but the cushion voussoirs in the arch, similar to those in contemporary Crusader architecture, provide evidence of some exchange in architectural language during this period of conflict.

So far the buildings we have considered have largely been self-standing, autonomous structures with specialised functions – congregational mosques, *madrasas* and mausolea. One important form to emerge in Mamluk architecture was the joint foundation combining mosque, *madrasa*, *maristan* (hospital) and mausoleum. It expresses the continuity of those religious, intellectual and social values established in Muhammad's mosque in Medina and also marks a change in patronage as well as in architectural form and plan. The establishment of numerous congregational mosques in a city like Cairo gradually obviated the need for large prayer halls in new buildings, so there was a relative reduction of prayer space within these new complexes; the mosque area became more intimate, serving as an oratory rather

than a space for mass prayers. One of the earliest and greatest architectural manifestations of this innovation is the mosque, *madrasa*, mausoleum and *maristan* complex of Baibars' successor, Qala'un, built in 1284.

The most beautiful feature is the mausoleum, but in its time the Qala'un complex was famous for the *maristan*, of which nothing remains. Muslim medicine, developed from the Greek tradition, was far in advance of that of the West, and close links were established at this time between medical centres in Syria and Egypt. Qala'un had received treatment at Nur al-Din's famous *maristan* in Damascus and when he returned to Cairo he established a similar institution. Nur al-Din's *maristan* (1154) was a hospital and teaching centre in Damascus well into the nineteenth century. The building today is a museum of medical science and is difficult to date because of its extensive thirteenth and eighteenth-century restoration. It retains much of its original character with its large teaching *iwan*, the recycled classical lintel set in the *muqarnas* entrance portal and its distinctive dome with clusters of *muqarnas* on the outside in the Mesopotamian fashion. This particular form of *muqarnas* construction, which also appears on the dome of his nearby mausoleum, was imported into Syria by the Seljuks from Mesopotamia and Persia. There, such forms can be seen in buildings like the Mausoleum of Sitt Zubaida in Baghdad and the so called 'sugar-loaf' towers on the island of Karg in the Gulf.

Qala'un's *maristan* in Cairo provided medical attention, food and accommodation, free of charge, to patients of either sex, regardless of age, social class, religion or nationality. The sexes were separated, different wards provided for specified illnesses, and staff were constantly on duty. It was a leading centre for medical research, being generously provided with lecture halls, laboratories and a library. Attention was given to all patients' physical and emotional needs, with story-tellers providing entertainment and music offering solace and therapy (following the Greek tradition). The modern Ophthalmic Hospital, which occupies the site of the original buildings, sustains medical provision here, which has lasted for seven hundred years. The mosque provided a public library and public lectures promoted by the law schools, as well as kindergarten classes and a Qur'an school for children.

Cairo, the façade of the mosque of Qala'un

This complex represents one of the most impressive examples of medieval architecture in Cairo, and its façade shows the influence of western Gothic. Qala'un continued Baibars' policy of strengthening contacts with the West while simultaneously continuing his *jihad* against the Franks. In the process of cultivating diplomatic links with Genoa, Castile, Sicily, Byzantium and the Holy Roman Empire, Qala'un took the Crusader fortress of Marqab in Syria. As they fell, Crusader castles were occupied by Muslim forces, who extended and adapted existing buildings as well as adding new complexes. In the case of Saone, substantial Muslim additions dating from the late twelfth and thirteenth centuries, partly attributed to Qala'un, include a mosque, baths and palace.[2] The close proximity of Muslim and Crusader buildings in circumstances like this, as well as growing diplomatic relations with western powers, may account for the Gothic influence in the long façade of Qala'un's building in Cairo. The façade is broken vertically by recessed panels crowned with pointed arches of similar shape to those in contemporary Crusader buildings, such as the Church of the Holy Sepulchre and the portico of the Aqsa Mosque in Jerusalem. Within these recesses are three tiers of windows, rectangular at the bottom, pointed in the centre and tall double lights surmounted by a small oculus at the top. The upper windows contain delicately pierced stucco, but their general composition is distinctly Gothic, and Creswell suggests that the influence may be Sicilian.[3] Further western influence has also been identified in the window grill above the main entrance, which has been attributed to Crusader craftsmanship.

Cairo, the façade of the mosque of al-Nasir Muhammad

From the front entrance a narrow passage divides the mausoleum from the mosque, *madrasa* and *maristan*. The mausoleum is reached through a small courtyard on the right and its entrance is surmounted by some of the finest and best preserved stucco work in Cairo. The mausoleum resembles the Dome of the Rock, although its pointed arches accentuate its narrower and taller proportions. The central section of the Dome of the Rock rests on a circular arrangement of drum, columns and piers, whereas here there is an octagonal drum supported by four columns and four piers. The pink granite columns are capped by gilded Corinthian capitals with impost blocks, and the whole octagonal arrangement is visually and structurally braced by timber tie-beams. The cenotaph of Qala'un and his son is surrounded by wooden screens of delicate *mashrabiya* work which was commissioned by his successor, al-Nasir Muhammad.

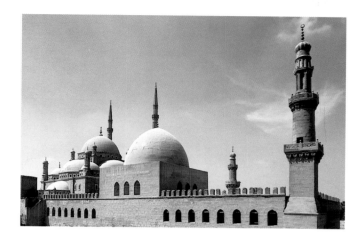

TOP
Cairo, the Citadel mosque of al-Nasir Muhammad

ABOVE
Cairo, the Citadel mosque of al-Nasir Muhammad: the *sahn*

The interior decoration of inlaid marble, mother-of-pearl, gilding and mosaic is both opulent and restrained. The decorative focus of the mausoleum is the large, deep recessed *mihrab* which is inlaid with mother-of-pearl and marble and flanked by three pairs of columns and polychrome marble panels.

The *madrasa*, now badly damaged, and mosque form parts of one continuous space. The arrangement shows the emerging cruciform *madrasa* plan that became so characteristic of Cairo's later buildings. The *sahn* is flanked north and south by two unequal *iwans* and east and west by recesses that anticipate the four-*iwan* cruciform plan. The eastern and western sections of the *sahn* provided three storeys of tunnel-vaulted rooms for students. The large sanctuary *iwan* has an unusual façade of two tiers of triple arches, behind which spring two arcades, running the length of the sanctuary perpendicular to the *qibla* wall, thus dividing the sanctuary space into nave and side aisles like a basilica. The *mihrab*, made up of marble panels, is flanked by two columns supporting a stilted round-arched hood containing glass mosaic. The deep recessed form of the *mihrab* holds a central position in an impressive composition of pointed recessed panels, colonettes and stucco arabesques.

The minaret of al-Nasir Muhammad's *madrasa* next door has recently been restored. It consists of three storeys; the first shaft is rectangular and the second octagonal, constructed of brick and covered with some of the most exquisite stucco work in Cairo. The lower rectangular storey is divided vertically by three keel-arched recesses containing lobed arches full of delicate geometric decoration. Above are lozenges, panels, Kufic inscriptions and a central sunburst medallion set in arabesque. The whole composition is contained at the top by two horizontal bands of blind lobed arches and Naskhi calligraphy capped by a crown of rich and dense *muqarnas*. The door to the *madrasa* is a significant trophy of Crusader origin, removed from the church of St George in Acre after the siege and capture of the city by Sultan Khalil in 1291. After the capitulation of Acre, the remaining Crusader cities surrendered, including Tortosa, the last stronghold in the Levant of Crusader power. The knights left the city and settled on the nearby island of Arward, where they maintained some resistance before finally withdrawing to Cyprus in 1303.

Al-Malik al-Nasir Muhammad was the son of Qala'un, and he reigned from 1293 to 1340 despite two interruptions by usurpers. He was a great builder and restorer and his most important surviving monument is his mosque built on the Cairo Citadel in 1318, which served as the royal mosque of the city. Its exterior presents an unadorned, austere cubic mass relieved only by the entrance portal with its *muqarnas* hood and a row of pointed upper windows. The two minarets with their bulbous crowns are unusual. The western minaret has three cylindrical shafts, the first of which is carved with a vertical arrangement of chevrons and the second with horizontal chevrons. The third shaft is a ribbed and tapered cylinder (similar to a section of the Qutb Minar in Delhi) with a band of Naskhi, crowned by a melon-shaped bulbous dome with blue, green and white mosaics. Behrens-Abouseif suggests that this melon-shaped form, which occurs nowhere else in Cairo, may have

TOP
Cairo, the mosque of Sultan Hasan

OPPOSITE PAGE
Cairo, the *qibla* wall of the Sultan Hasan mosque

come from Tabriz, because craftsmen were brought from that city, and a thirteenth-century Persian illustration of Tabriz confirms that such minarets existed.[4]

Along with the Maridani and Aqsunqur mosques, this is among the last of the hypostyle type with a *sahn* surrounded by arcades supporting a row of arched windows. The voussoirs of the lower arches and upper windows are articulated in alternating patterns of *ablaq* masonry, and the whole *sahn* is crowned by rows of stepped merlons. There is a simplicity and nobility to this building which is enriched by ancient Egyptian granite columns supporting the sanctuary dome and a number of marble columns bearing pre-Islamic capitals. The *sahn* is surrounded by *riwaqs* two arches deep on the north, east and western sides, and the sanctuary is four arches deep. The wooden dome over the *mihrab* is modern, but the original, which was covered in green tiles, collapsed in 1468 when it was restored by Qa'it Bay, and then fell again in the nineteenth century.

If al-Nasir Muhammad's Mosque represents one of the last of the hypostyle models, Sultan Hasan's mosque, *madrasa* and mausoleum (1356–61) announces the arrival of the cruciform plan which developed from Qala'un's complex. Next to Ibn Tulun's Mosque this is perhaps the greatest architectural masterpiece in Cairo. Situated at the foot of the Citadel, near the hippodrome, it is the largest mosque in Cairo, incorporating *madrasas* for all four law schools which originally housed four hundred students. Its strategic position and defensive bulk have made it susceptible to seizure by insurgents. Military action, bombardment and reconditioning have periodically mutilated, damaged and weakened the structure, indirectly causing the collapse of the dome and minarets. Nevetheless, it represents Mamluk architecture in its most mature and monumental form, as well as possessing features that reveal its position within an emerging international architectural language.

Sultan Hasan's cruciform plan, which became a common format for most Mamluk mosques, consists of four great *iwans* facing a central *sahn*. It is an arrangement seen in most Persian mosques, except that the Mamluk plan is more compact with proportionately larger *iwans* close together in one cubic space with short, connecting right-angled wall sections. In the Persian mosques the *sahn* is larger and the *iwans* are joined by longer lower ranges of double-tiered arcades. Also the *iwans* in Mamluk architecture form deep recesses, used for prayer or instruction, whereas the Persian *iwans* act as grand portals, marking transitional zones leading to interior spaces, such as the domed sanctuary. Sultan Hasan's mosque establishes the use of an enlarged *qibla iwan* as a prayer hall. The cruciform format does introduce a fluid use of internal space so that accommodation for prayers could spill out from the *qibla iwan* into the *sahn* and teaching areas if necessary. The *qibla iwan* of Sultan Hasan is immense, and as Behrens-Abouseif points out, it calls to mind its pre-Islamic origins; it is slightly larger than the great Sasanian *iwan* of Ctesiphon, which at 26 metres still stands as the largest brick span in the ancient world.[5] The remaining three *iwans* separate the four *madrasas* which occupy the corners of the *sahn*. These *madrasas*, of unequal size, are devoted to the four law schools, forming small independent units behind the central *sahn*, with their own student accommodation facing private inner courts.

The *qibla iwan* contains magnificent polychrome marble richly veined in grey white, antique green, yellow, maroon and pink. The *mihrab* is flanked with columns of Crusader origin, and the hood is framed by two pointed arches which radiate with zigzag chevrons of polychrome marble. Above the marble panels, running around three walls of the sanctuary is a beautiful stucco monumental Kufic inscription set in fine arabesque. Behrens-Abouseif says that its Chinese lotus motifs reflect contemporary minor arts, and Martin Lings identifies similar flowers in illuminated Qur'anic manuscripts.[6] Lotus flowers and chrysanthemums carved in shallow stone relief frame the great portal of the mosque, and both these features are indicative of the extent of Ilkhanid penetration in the west. Behind the *qibla iwan* is the unusual feature of a domed mausoleum, and Behrens-Abouseif makes the observation that this arrangement, with the direction of prayer pointing towards the founder, may constitute a breach of Islamic orthodoxy. In Persian mosques the *qibla iwan* always respectfully leads to a domed sanctuary, but the placing of a tomb behind the *qibla* wall is not uncommon in Anatolian *madrasas*. Such an arrangement can be seen in the Çifte Minare and Yakutiya *madrasas* in Erzurum, and there are other features in Sultan Hasan suggesting Anatolian influence. Sultan Hasan's is the largest domed mausoleum in Cairo, and its projection

Iraq, the *iwan* of the palace at Ctesiphon

from the south façade of the mosque presents an imposing cubic mass which is now crowned with a modern elliptical dome framed by two minarets. The original dome was made of wood and its bulbous shape was possibly similar to the dome of the fourteenth-century fountain which occupies the centre of the *sahn*.

The minaret to the left of the dome, consisting of three octagonal shafts, is the tallest in Cairo and was paired by an identical minaret to the right which fell down in 1659 and was replaced by the existing smaller minaret. Two more minarets were designed to go over the great portal, in the Seljuk manner, but one collapsed. The great portal has been compared to that of the Gök *madrasa* at Sivas in central Anatolia, but its height of 37 metres makes it proportionately much taller. The deep recess of the Gök *madrasa* portal is crowned with a typical Anatolian conical hood filled with *muqarnas*, whereas Sultan Hasan's portal hood, like the hoods of the window recesses of the mausoleum, has conical shoulders in which a rich concentration of *muqarnas* support a smooth semi-domed head. Framing the portal are tall narrow colonettes set against a lace-like moulding with a light, delicate, geometric pattern similar to those in such Anatolian Seljuk buildings as the Khwand Khatun complex at Kaysari. The side panels of the portal consist of large geometric patterns, and the façade is further enlivened with medallions and borders of Chinese lotus flowers and trefoil scrolls. Traces of tile mosaic by Tabrizi craftsmen have been found in the windows of the mosque, and the Syrian-style serpentine interlace around the mausoleum windows further adds to the synthesis of pre-Islamic, Chinese, Persian, Anatolian and possibly Syrian influences. However the parts of this mosque have been orchestrated into a monumental masterpiece which is distinctly Mamluk.

Of Sultan Hasan's turbulent reign we know very little, except that he was declared sultan at the age of thirteen in 1347 and was deposed four years later. He was restored to the throne in 1354, but after failing to curb the power of the amirs and other court factions, he was imprisoned and assassinated in 1362. Sultan Hasan was never buried in his mausoleum, and his weak hold on government was characteristic of many of Qala'un's successors. The last of the Bahri Mamluks was al-Salih Hajji who was deposed in 1382 by the Circassian

Cairo, the *sahn* of the Sultan Hasan mosque: illustrating the fountain

Mamluk al-Zahir Barquq. Most of the Bahri Mamluks had been Kipchak Turks from north of the Black Sea, but Mamluks were conscripted from other Turkish tribes as well as from Circassians, Kurds, Mongols, Greeks and other Europeans. The other group of Mamluks, known as the Burgi Mamluks, were Circassians who came from a regiment garrisoned on the Citadel which had originally been formed by Qala'un. These Circassians led by al-Zahir Barquq were to establish a new dynasty which ruled Egypt for the next hundred and forty years until the Ottoman Turks arrived in 1516.

Al-Zahir Barquq built a mosque, mausoleum and *madrasa* on Sharia al-Mu'izz, next to al-Nasir Muhammad's *madrasa* and Qala'un's complex but later expressed a wish to be interred in the northern cemetery, where a number of holy sheikhs are buried. This prompted his son, Faraj, to build a huge funerary complex to meet his father's wishes. The northern cemetery, or City of the Dead, is of remarkable architectural interest. The other great necropolis is the southern cemetery which contains the tomb of Shafi'i. The City of the Dead is anything but dead, because many of the mausolea are occupied by the living, and funerary monuments exist

cheek by jowl with ramshackle housing, shops and streets full of children. It is essentially a residential suburb, and to some extent always has been, with mosques serving the local community, houses built for visitors and many religious foundations providing accommodation for families, students and Sufis. The tombs of the sheikhs have always attracted large numbers of visitors, and families today pay their respects to deceased relatives with regular outings and picnics. It is doubtful whether it ever conformed to that evocative western vision of haunting desolation, so vividly expressed in the Romantic nineteenth-century paintings of David Roberts, Thomas Seddon and Jean-Leon Gérôme.

The funerary *khanqah* of Faraj ibn Barquq (1400–11) represents a category of Cairene architecture in which the mausolea have a high profile. It is uncertain whether this complex also served as a *madrasa*, and the distinction between *madrasa* and *khanqah* is not always clear. A *khanqah* provides Sufis with space for prayers, meetings and communal living, as well as supplying accommodation for occasional travellers on a limited and seasonal basis. The sheikh who governed the institution was a spiritual mentor, and teaching was central within the *khanqah*, so its function frequently overlapped with that of the *madrasa*. After the fall of the Fatimids the Sufi orders were given official encouragement and patronage in Egypt because they were regarded as upholders of Sunni orthodoxy. However, later Sufi practice was frequently at odds with both Sunni and Shi'ite orthodoxy, and Michael Rogers suggests that the Mamluk sultans brought the *khanqahs* and *madrasas* together under one roof to ensure a degree of Sufi conformity. He points out that we do not know which Sufi orders occupied which premises, and this suggests that state control, in its appointment of sheikhs, discouraged continuity within individual *tariqas* or Sufi traditions.[7]

Unlike most Mamluk buildings hemmed into medieval streets, Faraj ibn Barquq's complex is in a spacious location where the imposing symmetry of this free-standing structure can be appreciated at some distance. The main north-west façade supports a pair of tall minarets which are balanced on the opposite south-eastern *qibla* side by two striking stone domes flanking the prayer hall. These are the largest stone domes in Cairo, measuring 14 metres in diameter, and with their zigzag patterns they demonstrate

Cairo, the funerary *khanqah* of Faraj ibn Barquq

the growing confidence and ingenuity of the stonemasons at this time. The north-eastern dome contains the tomb of al-Zahir Barquq and his second son, and the south-western dome contains those of his wife and daughter. In contrast to the austerity and simplicity of the rest of the building these mausolea are richly endowed inside with polychrome marble and pendentives, decorated with *muqarnas* and support inner domes with richly painted arabesques and medallions. Unfortunately Faraj was assassinated in Syria and was never interred with his father and brother.

The main north-west façade is flanked by two *sabil kuttabs*, common features of later Mamluk and Ottoman architecture. *Sabil kuttabs* are attractive two-storey buildings, the upper storey consisting of a Qur'an school, with open windows and balconies over a ground floor containing a public fountain and iron window grills for free distribution of water. Next to the *sabil kuttab* the western portal leads to a vestibule and passage which turns left into the main *sahn*. The sanctuary, consisting of twenty-one domed bays, is situated between the two great mausolea and is of the hypostyle type with seven aisles three arches deep arranged perpendicular to the *qibla* wall. A small dome covers the *mihrab* bay, but the central

aisle is no wider than the rest. The absence of decoration gives the whole interior space of the mosque a simplicity reminiscent of al-Nasir Muhammad's mosque on the Citadel. Among the few relieving features in the sanctuary are the *dikka* (raised platform used by prayer leaders) and stone *minbar* installed by Qa'it Bay. The side *riwaqs* are one aisle deep, with tall pointed arcades supporting shallow domed bays behind which are situated the cells of the Sufis arranged in two storeys.

Stone domes of the complexity and scale of Faraj's mausolea are unique to Mamluk architecture and indicate remarkably sophisticated technology. Architects set themselves mathematical challenges by applying complex stellar patterns, more commonly seen in illuminated manuscripts, to the concave under-surface of the dome in order to wrap a two-dimensional design around a three-dimensional surface which decreases in size towards the apex. Their ingenuity can be seen in later fifteenth-century domes and particularly in the Barsbay funerary complex near Faraj's mosque. According to Behrens-Abouseif the problem is solved by different calculations relating to interlocking seven, eight, ten, and twelve-pointed stars.[8] Barsbay's complex is part of a magnificent ensemble that includes the mausoleum of Amir Ganibak al-Ashrafi and the recently restored tomb of Amir Qurqumas. Amir Ganibak's Mausoleum is in essence a domed cube, but the zone of transition from cube to circular drum, with its crystalline facets pierced by paired windows and oculi, shows a masterly handling of geometric volume. The clarity of this geometry is complemented by the glorious intricacy of the stellar-patterned dome which sits lightly on the stone mass below. The magic of Barsbay's complex, like the necropolis as a whole, lies not so much in the merits of individual buildings, but in their collective impact and how they relate to each other.

Perhaps the finest building on the necropolis is Qa'it Bay's funerary complex (1475). Al-Ashraf Qa'it Bay was a great builder and patron, who ruled Egypt for twenty-eight years, during which time Mamluk architecture reached the peak of ingenuity and refinement which this building so beautifully exemplifies. The dome and minaret both display remarkable qualities of stone carving on the outside. The dome is a harmonic balance of geometry and arabesque with an interlace of sixteen and ten-pointed stars enclosing a fluid grooved arabesque. The transitional zone is enlivened by the triangular ripples of the scrolled corners and deep piercing of the triple windows and oculi on all four sides. The decorative carving on the minaret punctuates those formal changes and transitions which rise elegantly from square base to octagonal shaft, to solid cylinder and eight-pillared pavilion. The structure is enriched and articulated by geometric patterns, keel-arched niches and fretted balconies supported by clusters of *muqarnas*.

The intricate surface carving on the dome and minaret tends to overshadow the refined and disciplined proportions of the rectilinear solids and voids which make up the rest of the exterior and complement the detail. The hood of the vaulted entrance portal, next to the *sabil kuttab*, presents a particularly satisfying kaleidoscope of *muqarnas* and *ablaq* inlay. The interior of the mosque is cruciform in plan, and the four-*iwan* vaults spring from brackets forming four impressive horseshoe arches with *ablaq* voussoirs. The side *iwans* are reduced to recesses, and the main orientation and emphasis is towards the *qibla iwan*. The whole interior space is typical of later smaller Mamluk complexes in which the *sahn* and *iwans* are completely roofed. Situated over the richly marbled

Cairo, the funerary complex of Qa'it Bay

Cairo, the *wakala* of Sultan al-Ghuri

sahn, the climax of this central space is an octagonal wooden lantern enclosing a fine gilded interlace of eight-pointed stars. This lantern casts a warm and diffuse light on a well-preserved unified interior, in which the colours and patterns of the painted and gilded ceiling find correspondence in the polychrome marble, red and black panels, stained glass, woodwork and inlaid ivory which make up the rest of this rich interior. The *minbar* is a particularly fine example of Egyptian woodwork with stellar patterns inlaid with delicately carved ivory (a sister *minbar*, of the same date, can be seen in the Victoria and Albert Museum in London).

Robert Hillenbrand describes how the evolution of late Mamluk buildings, like Qa'it Bay's funerary complex, was determined by a growing demand for greater flexibilities and economies of space.[9] In other parts of the necropolis where there is less pressure on space, interesting extensions of the Qa'it Bay plan present buildings of extraordinary length and monumental grandeur. The central plan of the funerary complex of Amir Qurqumas, with its compact

grouping of mausoleum, mosque and minaret, is almost identical in design to the Qa'it Bay, but there are two long, lower flanking wings that provide residential accommodation for Sufis, or for foundation staff and their dependants. Accommodation in the northern wing consists of apartments (known as a *rab'*), built over two storeys with their own staircases and lavatories. The long sweep of this complex joins the earlier funerary complex of Sultan Ashraf Inal with its ruined *khanqah*, and both buildings form an impressive monumental ensemble along the main road at the northern extremity of the necropolis.

The best preserved apartments, are found in the *wakala* of Sultan al-Ghuri (1504/5) near the al-Azhar mosque (a *wakala* is the Egyptian term for *han*, or urban caravansarai and warehouse). The *wakala* al-Ghuri is a magnificent example of secular architecture and an appropriate building to conclude this survey of Mamluk architecture. It consists of a large multi-storeyed stone cube enclosing a courtyard which forms a deep well of space and light illuminating the introverted apartments.

Cairo, the mosque of Muhammad Ali

Through the imposing portal is a beautifully propor-tioned courtyard with a central octagonal fountain bounded by a *riwaq* on three sides forming a tall pointed arcade supported on octagonal piers. This arcade rises through two storeys divided horizontally by a balcony made up of *mashrabiya* work. The *riwaqs* function as the caravansarai, providing storage space on the ground floor and accommodation above. The *rab'* occupies the upper three storeys and consists of three-roomed apartments connected by a staircase. The solidity of the building is lightened by the deep shadowed hollows of the arcade and the varied fenestration of the upper storeys, where oblong windows of light latticed *mashrabiya* work break up the façade. The windows on the top storey form projecting loggia, like machicolations, and round off the composition of the façade with an element of strong relief. Projecting *mashrabiya* windows are the *leit-motif* of Cairo's domestic architecture, guaranteeing light, ventilation and necessary privacy in the city's narrow crowded streets.

Al-Ghuri was the last effective ruler of a Mamluk dynasty. The Mamluks increasingly represented an older order of Islamic culture and failed to modernise or come to terms with the major political, economic and military changes taking place both in the Muslim world and Europe. The political and cultural leadership of Islam was now dominated by the Persians and Turks, and Europeans were gaining a naval hegemony which allowed them to trade directly with India and break Egypt's control over the spice trade. Thus Mamluk Egypt was in both economic and political decline, and the military were still clinging to medieval codes of chivalry and refusing to accept new technology. In 1453 the Ottoman Turks captured Constantinople, destroying the power of eastern Christendom and the last remnants of the Byzantine Empire. That success, however, marked just one significant stage in the rise of the Ottoman Empire, and soon Muslim powers, including Egypt, became vulnerable to the Turkish advances. On the pretext of invading Persia, the Ottoman Sultan Selim brought his troops, armed with cannon and muskets, to the northern borders of Syria. Here, in 1516, just north of Aleppo, al-Ghuri's Mamluk forces challenged the Turks, and failing to withstand the onslaught of Turkish firearms, his army was decimated. Al-Ghuri was killed in the conflict and a new Mamluk sultan, Tuman Bay, was proclaimed in Cairo. The following year the Ottomans inflicted a further defeat on the Mamluks at Raydaniya, and Selim entered Cairo and ordered the execution of Tuman Bay. Egypt lost her independence and became a province of the Ottoman Empire ruled by Turkish pashas.

This did not end the architectural story of Egypt, but it did effectively remove the state patronage that the Mamluk sultanate had provided, and although various Turkish pashas commissioned buildings, many of their pashas' mosques, like Süleyman Paşa (1543), are complete Ottoman imports. Mahmum Paşa's Mosque (1567), despite its Ottoman minaret, is Mamluk in style and makes a dignified contribution to that imposing group of buildings beneath the Citadel, which includes the Sultan Hasan mosque. Nevertheless, with the Ottoman conquest, Mamluk architecture lost its purpose, meaning and cultural foundation, and any attempt at sustaining this

tradition was bound to become mere reproduction or revivalism. With the exception of the *sabil kuttabs*, which have a charm of their own, Ottoman architecture in Cairo is mainly provincial and second-rate.

Napoleon's occupation of Egypt from 1798 marked the beginning of European domination over Egypt's affairs, and after the French withdrawal in 1801 her continued relationship with the Ottoman Empire became a mere formality. In 1805 Muhammad Ali founded a new dynasty and ruled with reasonable autonomy, paying lip service to Istanbul while modernising Egypt and cultivating European support and western technology. His mosque, an extravagant hybrid which dominates the Citadel and the city, symbolises this new position, trapped between East and West. The building bears no relationship to Mamluk tradition and like himself (he was born in Macedonia), it is a foreign import. To secure his own autocratic power Muhammad Ali ruthlessly massacred the remaining Mamluk leaders and in like manner cleared the Citadel of all architectural vestiges of Mamluk rule. What was left of their palaces was cleared for the building of the new mosque, and he commissioned a French architect, Pascal Coste, to design

Cairo, the mosque of Muhammad Ali: interior

it, but eventually he changed his mind and opted for an Armenian who produced an Ottoman design based on the Yeni Cami in Istanbul. Its shape is Ottoman but the detail, both inside and out, is an extravagant and clumsy form of French Baroque. The prayer hall is opulent to excess and the decoration is more in keeping with the ballroom of some Ruritanian prince than a place of worship. The clock tower in the *sahn* was a gift from Louis Philippe, and the fact that Muhammad Ali reciprocated by giving the French the obelisk that now stands in the Place de la Concorde speaks volumes regarding his sense of aesthetic values.

The Muhammad Ali mosque is a visual symbol of the architectural decline that the Turkish conquest precipitated, but as with the Mamluk dynasty itself, slow cultural decline had been evident in Egypt even before 1517. Since the early eleventh century, when the first Turcoman invasions took place, the Turks had been in the ascendancy, forming the military élite and ruling classes of much of the Muslim world. The Mamluk dynasties were themselves a proud example of this, but by 1517 they were a spent force. Dramatic decline had occurred in the Arab world. They were evicted from Spain, and the territories of the caliphate, including Baghdad, were taken over in the tenth century by Daylamites and Persians who divided much of the region, and established the Buwayhid and Samanid dynasties before the arrival of the Turks. Under Buwayhid rule the caliph became a religious figurehead with no political power, a puppet with diminishing significance until the office and title were finally subsumed under the Ottoman sultanate. These upheavals, as well as the subsequent Turkish and Mongol invasions, released energies into the Muslim world that generated new architectural creativity. With the decline of Egypt and the Arab world in general, the story of Islamic architecture continues further east in those regions that were shaped by Turkish and Persian culture.

Cairo, the mosque of Muhammad Ali: exterior detail

SAMANID AND SELJUK ARCHITECTURE IN PERSIA AND ANATOLIA

The Arab conquest of Persia successfully converted most of the region to Islam, but Muslim rule never extinguished the cultural identity of the Persians or subdued their political ambitions. They had taken a key role in the overthrow of the Umayyad dynasty and as a result played an important part in the politics of the Abbasid caliphate. After Harun al-Rashid's death in 809, the empire was thrown briefly into a state of civil war, and the subsequent weakness at the centre of government allowed more scope for autonomy in the regions, where Persian aristocratic families began to take control. Tahir, a Persian general who had supported Harun al-Rashid's son Mahmun in the war of succession, was sent as governor to Khurasan, where he established a semi-autonomous province which was ruled by his successors from Nishapur until 873. The Tahirids were overthrown by the Saffarids who extended the territory further east into Sistan and Afghanistan. This short-lived dynasty was in turn overthrown and the Samanid Empire annexed Transoxiana and ruled from Bukhara.

Bukhara, the 'Tomb of the Samanids'

Under Persian Samanid rule art and literature blossomed. The Samanids claimed descent from the Sasanians, and their court encouraged Persian values and a revival of literature which found its most eloquent expression in the work of the poet Firdawsi. His *Shah-nameh*, or *Book of Kings*, is a national epic which continues the work of the poet Daqiqi, and recalls Persia's heroes and kings from legendary to Sasanian times. It is an assertion of national identity and a celebration of Persia's pre-Islamic history written in the pure Persian language with all Arab vocabulary (which had permeated daily speech) excised. Among the other arts to reach an unparalleled level of excellence was pottery. Nishapur and Afrasiyab, near Samarqand, were the major centres of production, and among their most distinctive wares were dishes decorated with various forms of Kufic script, including plaited and floriated. These epigraphic wares are equal in achievement to the best of Chinese ceramics and demonstrate a highly wrought degree of discipline, elegance and refinement. The inscriptions exemplify a perfection and profundity of visual form which is not matched by their literary content, which consists mainly of trite aphorisms.

Due mainly to destruction by the Mongols, no standing monuments survive from the Samanid period, except one notable building, the 'Tomb of the Samanids' (also called the tomb of Ismail Samanid) in Bukhara (907).

Tenth-century plate from Nishapur, Samarqand

The domed square format of this building became standard for many Persian mausolea, but this plan, along with the *iwan*, has its origins in pre-Islamic architecture. Besides the mausoleum, the domed square provides the structural basis for the prayer sanctuaries of the Persian mosque, and its origins can be found in the pre-Islamic fire temple, or *chahar taq*. One of the earliest, dating from Parthian times, is at Naisar; it consists of a dome over a cube pierced on all four sides by semicircular arches. The Tomb of the Samanids has the same compositional format although it is pierced each side with smaller pointed-arched doorways. The Samanid tomb is exceptional in the richness and ingenuity of the brickwork. Since ancient times brick has been a major building material in Persia, but its structural and decorative potential was developed to an unprecedented level over the next few centuries, and no other civilisation has used it so creatively.

The façades of the Tomb of the Samanids present a densely textured surface of sun-baked bricks forming courses of alternating vertical and horizontal patterns of headers and stretchers, producing a strong wicker-work pattern of enormous vitality. The pointed-arched doorways are set in shallow recessed panels constructed with bricks arranged in herringbone pattern framed by a moulding, resembling stringed beads, individually made up of small bricks radiating from a central space like the spokes of a wheel. Zigzags, twists and radial patterns decorate the voussoirs and colonettes of the arcaded gallery which crowns the façade with a more deeply hollowed and articulated band of relief. Cylindrical columns are engaged into the corners of the tomb and the thrust of the hemispherical dome is contained within the thick walls which are slightly inclined (battered). The surface richness does not detract from the building's magnificent volumes and proportions, reached with some degree of mathematical sophistication.

The Tomb of the Samanids is a landmark in Persian Islamic architecture and for this reason it is a puzzle. Like the Dome of the Rock, there is nothing formative about this building, and at this early stage it has enormous authority and maturity. What traditions and circumstances explain this remarkable harmonic synthesis of form and decoration? Hillenbrand clearly locates its form in Sasanian architecture and describes it as a fire temple in Islamic dress, but acknowledges the decorative use of brick as totally innovative.¹ In looking for earlier uses of brick, he identifies its extensive and inventive use in Ukhaidir in Iraq, but it is doubtful if this knowledge was exported to north-eastern Persia. Hillenbrand is emphatic that the sophisticated use of brick in the Samanid monument must have taken years to evolve, but accepts that there is simply no surviving architectural or archaeological evidence in the region to explain it.

Another architectural masterpiece is the Gunbad i Qabus (1006), the mausoleum of Qabus ibn Washmigir, which emerges, perfect in form and conception, from the semi-autonomous Ziyarid province in the Gurgan area, south-east of the Caspian Sea in Iran. The Ziyarids were Daylamites from the mountainous regions south-west of the Caspian Sea, and the founder of the dynasty, Mardavij ibn Ziyar, ruled much of northern Persia until his assassination in 935. Among his companions were the three Daylamite brothers who went on to conquer Baghdad and establish the Buwayhid Empire which governed most of western Persia and Mesopotamia. Qabus ibn Washmigir is described by Arthur Upham Pope as a great patron, scholar, poet, astrologer, linguist, chess player and warrior.² He was assassinated in 1012, and tradition has it that his glass coffin was suspended in his tomb tower 45 metres above ground under the conical roof containing a window which permitted the light of the rising sun to shine on his face. If true, the absence of inhumation and the elevated position of the body recall the Zoroastrian funerary practice of exposing corpses in isolated locations on top of *dakhmas* ('towers of silence'). This tomb tower, on an elevated site against the backdrop of the Elburz Mountains, is an austere tapered brick cylinder, 56 metres high, capped by a cone. The upward thrust of this rocket-like structure is accentuated by the varied stripes of deep shadow cast by ten sharp angular flanges vertically engaged in the surface. The only horizontal articulation is provided by two immaculate bands of Kufic inscription, one near the base, and the other beneath the cornice of the conical roof. The material of this opaque towering mass is hard-baked brick, variously described as *café-au-lait*, bronze or tanned gold in colour; there is a small window in the cone and a tall elegant pointed-arched door at the bottom. Robert Byron, in *The Road to Oxiana*, ranks this as one of the great buildings of the world.³

The Gunbad i Qabus marks the beginning of a number of distinguished mausolea in northern Persia. They vary considerably in size and format, but none reaches the height or follows the tall proportions of the Gunbad i Qabus. In some the angular flanges multiply and engage the whole surface of the cylinder, as at Rayy (1139), or the exterior may be vertically ribbed with round shafts like the Ilkhanid tomb tower of Radkan East (1280–1300), north of Mashhad. The Pir i Alamdar (1021) at Damghan, south-east of the Caspian Sea, is a domed brick cylinder decorated under the cornice with a horizontal Kufic inscription sandwiched between two courses of key patterned bricks. The richly patterned brickwork and proportions of this and later mausolea, such as those at Kharraqan, (1067 and 1096), suggest forms that may have their origin in nomadic Turkish yurts, tents and reed huts. Hillenbrand points out that the excavations at Tagisken, south-west of Tehran in Central Asia (third century BC) reveal yurt-shaped tombs and burial practices that foreshadow the mausolea of Persia and Anatolia. He suggests that the nomadic ritual of exposing the deceased in a tent before burial may explain the evolution of the two-tiered mausoleum in which the coffin is placed in a crypt beneath an empty chamber.⁴ Records of nomadic reed huts are vividly revealed in the drawings of Friar Rubriquis in *Travels in Tartary and China*, which gives an account of his visit to the Mongol court in 1253. They show portable horse-drawn wicker-work huts with conical roofs draped with felt. The shapes of these dwellings, their wicker-work texture and patterned felt panels correspond to the Seljuk mausolea of both Persia and Anatolia. According to Hillenbrand the two tomb towers of Kharraqan, with their two-tiered construction, ribbed frame and lattice-patterned brick, exemplify this translation of nomadic tent and burial practices into permanent architectural form.

Firdawsi's *Shah-nameh* (completed 1020) deals patriotically with ancient battles between Turks and Persians. His epic poem told of the long-standing struggle; and his contemporaries were still then repulsing attacks from Turkish tribes. In 1030 this threat became more serious when the Seljuk Turks began advancing mercenary contingents into eastern Persia. By 1040 the Seljuk leader, Tughril Beg, had taken control of Khurasan and proclaimed himself sultan. Eventually he took all of

Persia and in 1055 entered Baghdad by invitation of the vizir, Ibn al Muslima. His successor, Alp Arslan, consolidated and extended the Seljuk Empire, inflicting a major defeat on the Byzantines at the battle of Manzikert in 1071, which made possible the Turkish conquest and settlement of Anatolia. He was assassinated the following year and during the minority of his successor, Malik Shah, the empire was ruled by Vizir Nizam al-Mulk, who played a central role in government for twenty years. It was during Malik Shah's reign that the Seljuk Empire reached its zenith, penetrating Fatimid territory as far as Syria, Palestine and the Hijaz, reducing much of Anatolia to a vassal state and securing suzerainty over the Ghaznavids in Afghanistan. The Byzantine defeat at Manzikert was a devastating blow to eastern Christendom and this event, as well as the Seljuk conquest of Jerusalem, prompted Pope Urban's call in 1095 for a crusade. The Seljuk conquests of Fatimid territory caused enmity and division between Sunni Turk and Shi'ite Fatimid, and the bitter squabbles among the Seljuk princes within Anatolia, Syria and Palestine allowed the Christians to exploit Muslim disunity and successfully launch the first crusades.

The stability and success of the new Seljuk regime rested on the political skills of Vizir Nizam al-Mulk. He was a cultured Persian, a brilliant administrator and reformer, as well as a significant political philosopher, whose work *The Book of Government* is a classic of Islamic literature. He is best remembered for the number of *madrasas* he founded in cities throughout Persia and Mesopotamia known as Nizamiyas. These foundations were almost certainly established for political reasons in order to promote Sunni Islam in a region where Shi'ism has its strongest following, as well as to counter the Shi'ite evangelism of Fatimid Egypt. Despite the politics of the situation, they reflected and contributed to the enormous intellectual and cultural regeneration taking place in the Muslim world since the previous century. It is significant that the intellectual lead was taken by Persians and Turks and eastern Persia played an important role in encouraging this intellectual climate. The formative years of Ibn Sina (980–1037) were spent in Bukhara, where he studied law and medicine, and access to the sultan's library of Greek philosophy enabled him to develop his own contribution to Muslim thought. His understanding

of Aristotle's *Metaphysics* was enriched by the works of al-Farabi (875–950), a Turkish philosopher who had studied Greek science, Plato and Aristotle in Baghdad. Al-Ghazzali (1058–1111), perhaps the greatest Muslim philosopher, studied in Nishapur before he became professor of religious sciences at Nizam al-Mulk's most famous Nizamiya in Baghdad. It was al-Ghazali who reconciled the divisions between theology and mysticism, and his long spiritual quest owed much to the philosophy of his predecessors, al-Farabi and Ibn Sina.

Following Firdawsi, Persian literature was enriched by the poet Omar Khayyam (1050–1122). Born in Nishapur, Omar Khayyam is best remembered for his *Rubaiyat*, which was freely translated into English by Edward Fitzgerald in the nineteenth century. The *Rubaiyat* is now acknowledged as a work of Sufi literature consisting of over a thousand quatrains reflecting on humanity and nature. One interpretation of these verses is that they were poetic summaries of his lectures on science and philosophy, and it is less appreciated that he was one of the leading mathematicians of his day. He was a court astronomer who worked on the reformation of the calendar, wrote books on algebra and geometry, and was engaged in practical science concerned with the weight of gold and silver. Omar Khayyam's distinction in several fields of learning is symptomatic of the holistic philosophy of medieval Muslim science. In this respect he follows Muhammad ibn Zakariyya al-Razi, or Rhazes (865–925), a Persian scholar and physician who was born and educated in Rayy. Schooled in Greek science, al-Razi was an original scholar who used his own observations and deductions to question received knowledge. His medical writing was comprehensive, and in the field of alchemy he was the first scholar 'responsible for transforming alchemy into chemistry'.[5] His works were catalogued by the most universal scholar of the age, al-Biruni (973–1050), who wrote on mathematics, astronomy, mineralogy, pharmacology, linguistics, poetry and history. His translations brought Indian culture and science to the Muslim world.

The Seljuk conquest marked the beginning of Isfahan as the capital city of Persia, and her periodic enjoyment of this status over subsequent centuries secured a sumptuous royal patronage which led to an architectural legacy that equals Cairo in its brilliance. With the exception of the portal of Jorjir, built under the

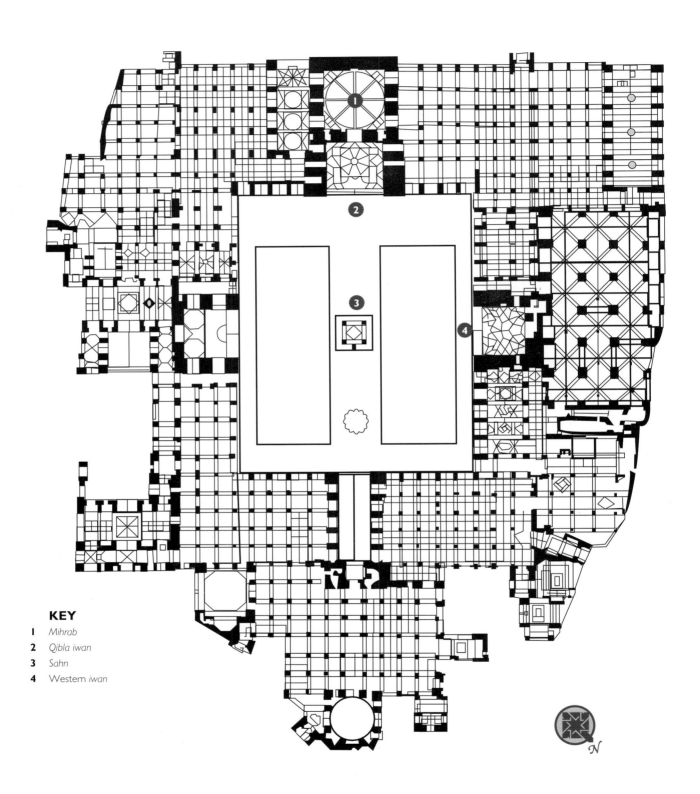

KEY

1 *Mihrab*
2 *Qibla iwan*
3 *Sahn*
4 *Western iwan*

Isfahan, ground plan of the Masjid i Jami. (After Schroeder)

Buwayhids in the tenth century, there are few architectural remains predating the Seljuk conquest. The major building of the Seljuk period, and possibly the most significant monument in Isfahan, is the Friday Mosque, or Masjid i Jami. Built of brick, its plan of four vast *iwans* facing a central *sahn* flanked by low ranges of double arcaded *riwaqs*, became standard in Persian mosque architecture. This arrangement of *iwans* facing a central court is pre-Islamic, and has its origins in Parthian and Sasanian palace architecture – the clearest example being the Parthian palace of Ashur on the Tigris in northern Mesopotamia. In the Masjid i Jami, the *qibla iwan* is surmounted by two minarets and leads into the domed prayer sanctuary containing the *mihrab*. On either side of the sanctuary, and surrounding the central *sahn*, is a multitude of vaulted bays. Access to the mosque is through a portal near a small bazaar, and the perimeter walls are completely obscured by adjoining shops and buildings. Its monumental impact is experienced from within the huge space of the *sahn*. Like the Great Mosque at Qairawan, this is an ancient building that has evolved over centuries, and its irregularities, which point to its organic growth, also determine its character. The crystalline precision of those architectural forms facing the *sahn* is in marked contrast to the amorphous labyrinthine spread of countless interior vaults which casually terminate at the irregular perimeter walls.

A major mosque existed on this site before the Turkish conquest and it was damaged soon after Tughril Beg captured the city in 1051. Further destruction was caused by fire during religious riots, and this prompted Nizam al-Mulk to rebuild the prayer sanctuary, but parts of the older mosque were retained. Some can be seen under the dome of the mosque's main sanctuary built by Nizam al-Mulk. The lighter design of the superstructure in this sanctuary, consisting of a zone of transition and the dome, fails to integrate with the older infrastructure, which has arches of a different curvature and cumbersome supporting double piers. If Nizam al-Mulk's sanctuary is less than perfect, his architect had an opportunity to improve on this when Taj al-Mulk, Nizam's rival, commissioned the smaller sanctuary in the north of the mosque. Here, it is generally agreed, is a domed chamber which from floor to apex is as near mathematical perfection as can be achieved. Eric

Isfahan, the west *iwan* of the Masjid i Jami

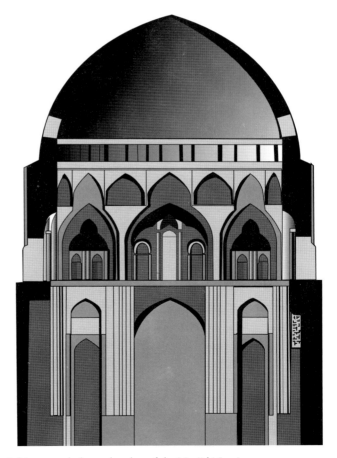

Isfahan, north dome chamber of the Masjid i Jami

Shroeder's analysis shows that its height and horizontal divisions conform to Golden Section proportions determined by the pentagon. It is a structure of great resolution and harmony, and the impact of its noble austerity is greatest from within, where the vertical momentum of its arcuated forms is initiated in the corners by the tall slender lancet arches which carry the eye up to the deep hollows and facets of the squinches. These, with their intermediate arches and niches all sharing the same contour, carry sixteen arches supporting a pointed brick dome lined with a shallow ribbed relief which conclusively assimilates these ascending patterns into one crowning stellar cinquefoil. Robert Byron has given an incomparable analysis of the two sanctuaries, which he maintained 'illustrate the heights of art independently':

> The two dome-chambers of the Friday Mosque point this distinction by their differences. Both were built about the same time, at the end of the XIth century. In the larger, which is the main sanctuary of the mosque, twelve massive piers engage in Promethian struggle with the weight of the dome. The struggle in fact obscures the victory . . . Contrast this with the smaller chamber, which is really a tomb-tower incorporated into the mosque. The inside is roughly thirty feet square and sixty high; its volume is perhaps one third of the other's. But while the larger lacked the experience necessary to its scale, the smaller embodies that precious moment between too little experience and too much, when the elements of construction have been refined of superfluous bulk, yet still withstand the allurement of superfluous grace; so that each element, like the muscles of a trained athlete, performs its function with winged precision, not concealing its effort, as over-refinement will do, but adjusting to the highest degree of intellectual meaning. This is the perfection of architecture, attained not so much by the form of the elements – for this is a matter of convention – but by their chivalry of balance and proportion. And this small interior comes nearer to that perfection than I would have thought possible outside classical Europe.[6]

Other Seljuk work in the mosque features inventiveness and ingenuity, rather than genius. Its interior is characterised by the intriguing irregularity of its multitude of capricious open and closed brick vaults. Open vaults intermittently illuminate the space, and closed vaults display a variety of structural methods, including rib vaults similar to those in the Cordoba Mosque. Brick is arranged in an endless variety of hexagonal, octagonal and decagonal stellar patterns, which according to some sources reveal the mystic mathematics of Sufism.[7] The dates of the monumental iwans, with their bold honeycombed muqarnas, are uncertain. Brickwork behind the western iwan suggests that the basic structure is Seljuk, but the vaulting is later and the decoration is eighteenth century. The base of the southern iwan contains an inscription by Nizam al-Mulk, but roof, minarets and the tiles inside the iwan are the work of Ouzun Hassan Beik (1475) who was also responsible for the tiles on the riwaqs. Inside the vault of the iwan the muqarnas contain tile mosaic of Kufic characters which have been formalised into simple rectilinear icons representing the names of Allah, Muhammad and Ali. The tiles on the outer facing of the iwan are Safavid, and date from the reign of Shah Tahmasp in 1531. The Seljuks handled mass and volume in this mosque admirably; structural integrity took precedence over surface decoration. Much original Seljuk work has been obscured by reconstruction and tilework, and the extensive use of tiles, as opposed to bricks, to enliven exterior surfaces did not begin until the Ilkhanid period in the thirteenth century.

Of the Ilkhanid period, the Masjid i Jami contains Sultan Oljeitu's magnificent stucco mihrab, is signed as the work of Badr and dated 1310. It occupies a small shabastan (winter gallery) near the western iwan. The niche is framed by an arch and colonettes set in a large panel which sits against the qibla wall like a flat stele. The whole panel is animated by deeply chiselled, dense and complex arabesques. The framing Thuluth inscription is set against a background of twisting vine-leaves and lotus flowers, which entwine the script without choking or obscuring it. The cursive movement of this is offset by a small horizontal panel set above the hollowed niche which contains an ingenious geometric pattern that transforms itself, like Escher's Metamorphoses, into a plaited Kufic inscription proclaiming the Shi'ite shahada, '[I bear witness that] There is but one God; Muhammad is his prophet, and Ali is the friend of God'. Similar Ilkhanid stucco work (c.1300) can be seen at the shrine of Pir Bakran in Linjan, fifteen miles from Isfahan. Here the arabesques are complemented by large panels containing the names of the Prophet's descendants through Ali, cryptically written in a maze-like configuration of Kufic.

The townscape of Isfahan is punctuated by minarets, of which the tallest date from Seljuk times. The minaret of the Masjid i Ali is like a tapering factory chimney 54 metres high. It is an elegant two-tiered cylinder in which the separating balcony flares out like the lotus capital of an Egyptian temple. As the column rises, the brick surface reveals various changing stellar and lozenge patterns with bands of turquoise glazed faience gleaming below the balcony. The Saraban Minaret likewise has a richly patterned brick surface, two *muqarnas* balconies and light blue faience inscriptions. These minarets are among the earliest to display the sparing use of tile and

Isfahan, the minaret of Masjid i Ali

glazed brick, and here is the genesis of a tradition of tile decoration that was to flower so brilliantly in the Timurid and Safavid periods. Returning to monochrome brick, perhaps the most austere and formally satisfying monument near Isfahan is the oldest minaret, Chihil Dukhtaran (1107), in which the tapered cylinder is relieved only by the texture of its subtle decoration and the Mecca-facing window which pierces the column two-thirds of the way up. Tall cylindrical minarets of this type were a Seljuk innovation and, like tomb towers, represent its finest architectural achievement. The function of such tall structures has been the cause of some speculation. They were too tall to be of practical use to the *muezzin*, and many were free-standing structures in remote regions far away from any mosque. Hillenbrand suggests that they acted as landmarks affirming the faith, or in a world where politics and religion are frequently indivisible, they can be viewed as victory monuments. On a more practical level they also functioned as watch-towers, beacons and land-locked lighthouses.[8]

One minaret that is clearly a victory monument is in a remote rocky valley at Jam in Afghanistan (1179). The tallest minaret of its type, at nearly 67 metres, it has three shafts separated by *muqarnas* balconies. The decorative scheme is mainly determined by Kufic inscriptions which interweave vertically up the first shaft, or form horizontal girdles in the upper tiers. The first shaft is covered with bands of Kufic containing the 'Mary' *sura* of the Qur'an, above which is placed a crisp Kufic inscription picked out in light turquoise faience which resonates against the biscuit-coloured brick. The rest of the inscriptions are political and boast of Sultan Ghi ad Din's victory over the Ghasnavids. In Ghazna itself (Afghanistan) stand two earlier victory towers, 233 metres apart, of which only the flanged octagonal shafts remain. These brick shafts, with their fine and intricately carved panels of geometry, arabesque and Kufic bands, originally supported cylindrical columns which would have been about 47 metres high. The smaller minaret was believed to have been built by Mahmud, the founder of the Ghaznavid Empire and patron of Firdawsi and Ibn Sina, but has now been attributed to Bahram Shah. The larger, more successful work is by Ma'sud III. As Robert Byron pointed out, the Ghasnavid towers, with their star-like flanges, are formally similar to the Gunbad i Qabus built in the same century, but the austerity of the former is a striking contrast to the elaboration of the latter, suggesting that at that time 'two separate ideas were at work in Persian architecture'.⁹ Other ideas were also evolving in domed mausolea which were becoming monumental in scale, like Sultan Sanjar's mausoleum at Merv, Turkmenistan, or more experimental in the use of octagonal plans, such as the Jabal i Sang at Kirman, Persia. Such forms were to evolve more significantly on a larger scale during the Mongol Ilkhanid and Timurid dynasties in the fourteenth and fifteenth centuries.

The Seljuk sultanate in Anatolia, known as the sultanate of Rum (or East Rome), was established in 1075 and ruled independently of Persia thirty years after the Great Seljuks (Tughril Beg, Alp Arslan and Malik Shah) had established their empire in the east. For many years the Great Seljuks had encouraged Turcoman raids and migration into Byzantine territory, but only after the decisive battle of Manzikert in 1071 did a Muslim state become possible in Anatolia. The sultanate was created by Süleyman, after he had been banished there and gained a following from dissident Turcoman groups. With their support, Süleyman quickly captured Konya, and moved north to Iznik (ancient Nicaea), where he established his capital. By the time of his death he had gained most of Anatolia through diplomacy or conquest and was generally recognised as an independent sovereign.

Süleyman's death was followed by a period of turmoil, but his son, Kılıç Arslan, successfully regained control of Anatolia and brought some stability to the area. Just as he was beginning to consolidate his position and expand eastwards, the first Crusader army arrived by way of Constantinople. Kılıç Arslan had no difficulty in defeating this invasion led by Peter the Hermit's disorganised army, but he underestimated the Crusader threat, returning east and resuming his campaign against his Turkish Danishmend rivals. Iznik was unprotected, and a stronger, regular Crusader force besieged the city. Kılıç Arslan returned but found that his army was powerless. Emperor Alexius arrived from Constaninople during the stand–off and outwitted both Turks and Franks by launching a third force of Byzantine troops which captured the city from the undefended side. Turks and Franks both suffered serious reverses. The early

battles between Muslim and Christian quickly revealed disunity and rivalry within both camps. There was mutual distrust between Byzantines and Franks (Greek versus Latin Christendom), and the Fatimids lost no time in seeking Frankish support against their arch enemies, the Seljuk Turks (Shi'ite versus Sunni Islam). In order to contain the Franks, the Byzantines cultivated a diplomatic understanding with the Turks which tacitly allowed Kılıç Arslan to resume his territorial expansion east from the security of his new capital at Konya.

Konya was to remain the capital and contains some of the finest examples of Seljuk architecture. Anatolian Seljuk architecture represents a synthesis of regional styles which have been adapted in a very distinctive and practical way to suit the climate and needs of the region. Many of its features, including the mausoleum, *iwan* and domed bay, are Persian imports, but there are fundamental differences. Seljuk architecture in Persia is distinguished by its structural and decorative brickwork. Its domes and vaults display virtuosity and plasticity in the use of brick, and its decoration is integrated and constructed rather than applied as surface veneer. Anatolian buildings are made principally of stone, leading to a more solid, compact and enclosed architecture which is generally smaller in scale. However, diminished scale has not reduced its monumental impact; most Anatolian buildings are free-standing masses, clear and precise in their simple geometry, and make an impact externally. This is a reversal of the Persian model, where the architectural form of the mosque and *madrasa* is best experienced from within the *sahn*. In Anatolian mosque architecture the *sahn* is either totally eliminated, or symbolically acknowledged within the sanctuary by opening up a small section to the sky.

The earliest Anatolian mosques are hypostyle in plan and consist of prayer halls with flat, wooden, earth-layered roofs supported by columns. Wood was plentiful, and in some instances rich timber roof construction and slender wooden columns with *muqarnas* capitals can still be observed in mosques dating from the thirteenth and fourteenth centuries (Süleyman Bey Cami, Beyşehir, 1296; Mahmut Bey Cami, Kastomonu, 1366). Among the earliest of the hypostyle type is the Ala'al Din Mosque in Konya, which was begun in 1156 by Sultan Mesud. The central section, *mihrab* bay and *türbe* (mausoleum)

Konya: the interior of the Qarata'i Madrasa

were added by his successor Kılıç Arslan II (1156–92), and the final section was completed by Keykavus I (1210–19) and Keykubad I (1219–21) who employed Muhammad ibn Khawlan from Damascus. The mosque is inside the citadel walls adjacent to the palace but little remains today of the citadel, or palace, except the ruined fragment of the Ala'al Din Kiosk. The broad exterior form of the mosque, pierced by high windows, is typically Seljuk – a rectangular horizontal mass of dressed stone broken by the upward projection of the hexagonal pyramid of the tent-domed *türbe* roof and the slender cylinder of the corner minaret. These elements (cylinder, cone, pyramid and rectangle) provide the repertoire of simple geometric forms that define the character of Seljuk architecture. Nevertheless, Syrian influence can be identified in the design of the framing portal panel, where reticulated bands of grey and white marble inlay artfully transform and twist into the serpentine interlace which embellishes the contour of the central arch.

Inside is a large hypostyle hall of antique columns which carry arcades running in both directions, and in the centre of the mosque are piers supporting a series of vaults. In the *mihrab* bay there is a dome placed on a zone of transition that consists of a twenty-sided figure made up of flat mosaic pendentives, known as Turkish triangles. The use of this flat arrangement of triangles, rather than curved pendentives or *muqarnas*, is a Seljuk innovation. Such a feature is best seen nearby in the Qarata'i Madrasa (1251) where a large dome, more than 12 metres in diameter, is supported in each corner with pendentives made up of five narrow triangles, variously angled, with their apexes pointing down to the corner of the bay. Each triangular panel consists of tile mosaic in which the tesserae are formed into a Kufic maze configuration repeating the names of Muhammad in the centre and those of the first four caliphs on either side. Around the base of the dome is a floriate Kufic inscription with the opening 'Fatiha' *sura* of the Qur'an, and the dome itself is covered with radial patterns representing the stars of the firmament.

Tiling is used extensively in the *iwan* vault and around the central court, with colours limited to turquoise, aubergine, violet and white. The *iwan*, and the rooms of the *madrasa*, providing accommodation for a dozen students, face an inner courtyard containing a fountain, and the whole interior is illuminated by

Konya: the portal of the Qarata'i Madrasa

Konya: gateway of the Ince Minare Madrasa

a lantern in the dome. The plan is irregular, and Hillenbrand comments that this apparent lack of planning, which is a feature of so many Seljuk buildings, may indicate an ambivalence of function.[10] Like the Ala'al Din Mosque, the entrance portal shows Syrian influence in the grey and white interlaced panel that frames the door. The design is enlivened by three deeply drilled hemispherical bosses projecting from the surface. It has been suggested that these may have their origins in Byzantine metalwork, or the heraldic devices carried on the centre of shields. Below the 'Syrian' panel, the door is set in a shallow recess that terminates above with a broken arch filled with *muqarnas* that create a low horizontal relief pattern of chevrons. Imposing decorative portals, pierced by deeply cut conical hoods of *muqarnas*, increasingly become a major point of architectural emphasis, relieving and offsetting the bulk of plain dressed stone in the façade.

One very beautiful and discrete portal in Konya is that of the Sirçali Madrasa (1242). The door is set in a deep recess under which an elliptical portal arch, wreathed with a band of floriate trefoils, springs from two flanking slender colonettes decorated with chevrons. Above are medallions, and the whole portal is framed with borders of delicate lace-like radial patterns carved in low relief, and a moulding punched with stellar motifs. Through the portal is a large *iwan*, flanked by two domed chambers, looking on to an open court on either side of which are two-storeyed cells. Anatolian *madrasas* roughly fall into two types, the open court plan, of which this is one, and domed *madrasas* such as the Qarata'i. This small *madrasa* with its *iwan* facing a court of double arcaded cells, is related to the Persian type, and the Persian connection is established by an inscription that states that one of the architects was Osman ibn Mehmet from Tus. Attributed to him is the *iwan* tile mosaic consisting of radial patterns, like those on the portal, and executed in similar colours to the tiles in the Qarata'i Madrasa. The limited range of colours available at this time were exploited to remarkable effect, as in the *mihrab* of the Sirçali Cami, where depth and resonance is achieved with a subtle low-toned combination of turquoise and deep cobalt blue.

In contrast to the discretion of the Sirçali Madrasa, the portal of the Ince Minare Madrasa (1258) is flamboyant. It represents – to use Tamara Talbot Rice's apt word – the 'baroque' phase of Seljuk architecture.

This particular style, which it shares with a number of other buildings, is unique to Seljuk architecture. It is the work of Abdulla ibn Keluk, also responsible for the Gök Madrasa at Sivas. The sobriety of classic Seljuk architecture, with its straight edges and simple geometry, is replaced in this façade with exuberant convolutions of form. Mouldings tie themselves into Celtic knots, and ribbons of calligraphy festoon and drape the portal, interlacing up the centre as on the minaret of Jam. At the centre of the façade is a scooped-out niche containing the door, and in the rounded corners, where normally there are *muqarnas*, are heavily sculptured vegetal forms reminiscent of art nouveau. This is a domed *madrasa* with similar features to the Qarata'i Madrasa, such as a lanterned dome set on flat triangular pendentives. Here the interior decoration is much simpler, with glazed bricks arranged in angular patterns, and the dome rests on a central court faced by an *iwan*, flanked left and right by small cells. The plan is irregular, and the larger units are roofed with four domes anticipating the increased role the dome was to play in subsequent Turkish architecture. Today only the first shaft of the single minaret survives, but originally there were three tiers, rising to a conical point, divided by two balconies. Each shaft, constructed with diagonal patterns of glazed brick, varied in its disposition of lobed and flanged vertical ribs. While most Anatolian buildings were made of stone, minarets are invariably built of brick, patterned and glazed with an ingenuity that rivals their Persian counterparts.

The Gök Madrasa (1272) at Sivas has an open courtyard plan with three *iwans* facing the court and six cells on either side on two floors. The mosque occupies a small domed chamber to the right of the entrance – a feature it shares with the Çifte Minare Madrasa at Erzurum. The portal of the *madrasa* is its most famous feature, but the façade needs to be considered as a whole, because the richness of the centre is balanced by the heavy ornamentation on the flanking towers, which engage into the corners like round bastions. The lower halves are deeply cut with a dense arabesque of vegetal forms which break out of the surface in a sculptural outgrowth of form. Between these and the central portal the plain dressed stone of the façade is broken by shallow trilobed recesses and small windows which flank the projecting entrance. The broad portal, consisting of a tall framing

Konya: the Ince Minare Madrasa

Sivas: the Gök Madrasa

rectangle pierced by a niche with a conical *muqarnas* hood, exhibits a classic format, which became more or less standard for all portals and *mihrabs* in both Seljuk and Ottoman architecture. What is distinctive about this, and the Çifte Minare Madrasa nearby, is the richness and elaboration of form. The niche is framed by a pointed arch set in a rectilinear panel with numerous borders of arabesque. Flanking this are two broad pilasters containing decorative panels of arabesque and geometry and, characteristic of most Seljuk *madrasas* and mosques, the whole structure is surmounted by two brick minarets with glazed tiles.

Set deep in the portal is the door, over which a segmental arch of joggled voussoirs is flanked by two pieces of relief sculpture depicting serpentine clusters of dragon-like heads. As at Aleppo, dragons frequently fulfil the roles of protecting as well as adorning buildings, and in like manner a similar group of bronze dragons served as door knockers to the Ulu Cami at Cisre, south-east Turkey. Such devices have been traced to Tang China, and they represent one of a number of oriental motifs which were beginning to penetrate Islamic art during the Ilkhanate period.[11] Sivas was then under Mongol control,

TOP
Divriği: the mosque and hospital

ABOVE
Divriği: the portal of the mosque and hospital complex

and while the Seljuk Vizir Sahip Ata was founding the Gök Madrasa, his Mongol counterpart, the vizir to the Il Khan of Persia, was building the Çifte Minare Madrasa nearby. As well as Chinese influences, other cultures also contributed to this invasion of animal forms into Seljuk stone carving in architecture during this 'baroque' period. Heraldic beasts, birds and other symbols became integrated into decorative panels or appeared in sculptural relief. Contemporary tiles from Kashan and Takht i Suleyman, north-west of Tehran, display similar dragon and animal designs, but their architectural use in Persia was limited.

Besides dragons, the Gök Madrasa displays in its façade a heraldic image of the tree of life, which became a frequent symbol in Seljuk architecture. Its origins were in the ancient Near East, but it is likely that many animal forms also have older roots in Hittite, Scythian, Altaic nomad, Armenian and Byzantine sources, rather than in the Far East. They appear in abundance in the most extraordinary of all the 'baroque' Seljuk buildings, the mosque and hospital at Divriği, eastern Turkey (1228). Here the decoration is limited to the four portals of the mosque and hospital, and it has been variously identified as demonstrating Caucasian, Hindu, Chinese, Persian, Byzantine, Armenian and Crusader influences. The plinths of the west portal with their strong horizontal accents, recall Hindu architecture, and Talbot Rice has drawn attention to delicate filigree details in the arabesques and half-moon motifs that resemble Indian jewellery.[12] A finely inscribed relief of a double-headed eagle also suggests the art of the jeweller, enameller or metalworker, although the heraldic image can be found in twelfth-century Persian pottery and Buwayhid and Byzantine silks. Jairazbhoy suggests that Crusader prisoners may have been involved with building the hospital portal; its shape and rounded mouldings resemble a western arch but with eastern trappings.[13] The patron was Ahmad Shah, a Mengushid Turk, the architect Khurramshah, an Armenian from Ahlat, and one of the craftsmen involved was Ahmad ibn Ibrahim from Tiflis. The few facts surrounding this building do little to explain its strange cultural synthesis or its remarkable energy and originality. The mosque and hospital at Divriği form two self-contained units separated by the *qibla* wall of the mosque, but they occupy a single enclosed

rectangular plan. The mosque space is divided by a wide central aisle leading to a domed *mihrab*, flanked on either side by two narrower aisles. The interior is covered by stone vaults, and the dome of the *mihrab* bay is capped by a flanged pyramidal crown which breaks out of the roof-line like a small spire. Vaulted construction is a significant aspect of Seljuk architecture, and at Divriği each vault is different, most of them ribbed and with a variety of stellar patterns and clusters. Besides vaults, there are domes, including a domical lantern lighting the centre of the mosque, the ribbed *mihrab* dome and a dome chamber in the hospital which is similarly capped with a flanged pyramidal tent-dome. As Hillenbrand observes, its interior, like so many Seljuk buildings, is crypt-like in appearance due to the few small windows.[14] The minaret sits on a heavy circular drum engaged in the corner of the mosque like a bastion, reinforcing a monumental air of solidity and mass.

This sense of mass is nowhere more manifest than in Seljuk caravansarais (*hans*), a major genre of Anatolian architecture. With their curtain walls, buttressed towers and narrow windows, they have a fortified aspect that reflects their origin in *ribats* and desert fortresses. Most date from the first half of the thirteenth century; many larger *hans* were established through royal patronage and are known as Sultan Hans. Their principal purpose was to accommodate merchants and travellers, and in the larger *hans* facilities included bedrooms, dormitories, kitchens, stables, storage rooms, workshops, coffee rooms and a mosque. Most consisted of an open court with shared and private facilities, leading to an adjacent covered hall, but smaller *hans* dispensed with the court and all accommodation was contained under one roof. Situated on arterial roads, they also doubled up for military purposes and security was a determining factor in their design. The severity of the curtain walls, with their corner towers, was relieved only by a single entrance portal, which usually had lavish decoration. In the larger *hans* the vaulted entrance porch, flanked by rooms for staff, opened on to a courtyard in which cloisters led to rooms and dormitories on one side and shared facilities on the other. Facing the open courtyard another portal led to a large vaulted hall illuminated by small upper windows and a central lantern. With its stone troughs, this hall was used for stabling and additional shelter

TOP
Kayseri: the Döner Kümbet

ABOVE
Sultan Han near Kayseri

during the winter months. In some *hans*, such as the Sultan Han on the Kayseri–Sivas Road, the courtyard contained a small mosque raised on four axial arches, recalling a structural format going back to ancient Persian fire temples. Unlike Anatolian *madrasas* and mosques, *hans* usually display remarkable symmetry and consistency of plan and form.

With its smooth, dressed stone exterior, the *han* at Tercan, eastern Turkey, is one of the most austere and impressive. Its curtain wall is broken only by the entrance portal and the series of circular towers with conical tops which engage into its walls like minarets. The Sultan Han near Kayseri (1230) is more elaborate, and like the Agzikara Han in Kayseri and the Sultan Han near Aksaray (1229) has a mosque in the centre of the court. This forms a cubic structure pierced by three windows standing above four axial horseshoe arches. Access to this mosque is via two staircases which bestride the supporting arch facing the entrance portal. The decoration on the arch mouldings, windows and corners is restrained and elegant. Wreathing one of the arches is a serpentine pattern which terminates at the apex with two dragons face to face. Other borders have rosettes and punched-out trefoils, while a knotted interlace frames each arch, recalling patterns more associated with metalwork or pavement mosaic. On the other side of the court an imposing portal leads into the hall where the central aisle is tunnel vaulted, and like a church nave it is set higher than the side aisles, which consist of transverse arcades formed by horseshoe arches identical in shape to those that support the mosque. In their harmony of proportion and symmetry, the geometries of the Tercan Han and the Sultan Han near Kayseri express and exemplify a reticent spirit of pure classicism. It is probably true that Seljuk architecture is at its noblest in the *han*, a notable exception to the general rule that the best architecture springs from only religious motives.

The last major category of Seljuk architecture to consider is the mausoleum, *türbe* or *kümbet*. With conical and pyramidal spires, they may occupy a bay, or small courtyard in a mosque, like the *türbes* in the Ala' al-Din Mosque in Konya and Khwand Khatun complex at Kayseri. However, they may be free standing and distinctive landmarks when occasionally they form clusters, like those grouped around the türbe of Sultan Saltuk at Erzurum. Their conception and design owes more to Persia than any of the Seljuk buildings we have considered so far, although Armenian, Georgian and Byzantine influences are apparent in their construction and use of material. In conception they relate closely to the Persian tomb tower, with the chapel placed over a crypt containing the cenotaph. However, the Anatolian mausoleum is a two-storey structure; the transition from square underground crypt to octagonal or cylindrical chapel is articulated by the chamfered base, and the door to the upper chamber is elevated, where it can be reached by external steps.

The other major difference is in the use of stone rather than brick, and it is here that Georgian, Armenian and Byzantine influences play their part. In Georgian and Armenian churches, like those at Mtzskheta and Ani, blind arcading and the pyramidal shapes of the towers and lanterns bear a striking similarity to those in a number of Seljuk mausolea. The Döner Kümbet at Kayseri (1276), the Ulu Kümbet at Ahlat and the Hatuniya Türbe at Erzurum (1253) are articulated and decorated in their elevations and conical roofs with mouldings, blind arcades and niches similar to those in eastern Anatolian churches. Armenian influence also shows in the sculptural decoration of a number of mausolea where animal and figurative elements occur. The Döner Kümbet in Kayseri is one of the most richly carved, with lions, eagles, birds and a palm leaf configuration depicting the tree of life. Byzantine influence can be identified in some buildings, such as the Sultan Saltuk Mausoleum in Erzurum (1170), which is like a domed baptistry built in chequer patterns and horizontal courses of brown and pink stone. The Saltuk Mausoleum is a domed octagon, but Seljuk mausolea, like their Persian cousins, can be cylindrical, polygonal or lobed in plan. The mausoleum of Mama Khatun at Tercan (1192) has a plan of eight lobes and is situated in an unusual circular enclosure, plain on the outside except for the portal and lined inside with arcaded alcoves. The simplicity of the outer enclosure wall and the undulating roof and walls of the mausoleum find visual correspondence in the round, cone-topped towers of the monumental *han* nearby. In Konya, lobed and ribbed formations in shining green faience crown the tomb of the mystic poet Mevlana Celaleddin Rumi (1274). With the sound and image of the reed so vividly evoked in the opening verses of his great work, the *Masnavi*, it is

appropriate that lobed clusters, like bundles of reeds, should form the drum and roof of his mausoleum.

Rumi (1207–73) was a Persian scholar from Balkh, who settled in Konya and taught religious sciences until he met the itinerant dervish Shams al-Din and thereafter devoted his life to mysticism. He wrote two of the greatest works of Persian literature, the *Divan i Shams i Tabriz* and the *Masnavi*, a long religious poem popularly regarded as the Persian Qur'an. He founded the Mevlevi order of whirling dervishes, and he introduced dancing and shamanistic practices into Sufi ritual (*dhikr*). Rumi follows Firdawsi, Ibn Sina, al-Ghazzali and Omar Khayyam as one of the great poets and thinkers of his time. He flourished in an age of political decline when Seljuk rule collapsed in the face of the Mongol advances. Political instability is not usually good for architecture which depends on state patronage, but in the latter part of the thirteenth century architecture flowered in Anatolia. The Mongols offered their patronage, but their vassals, the Seljuk princelings, decided they had nothing left to lose and sought immortality in building projects.

Mongol rule was invested principally in Persia. Its grip on Anatolia was never secure or centralised and much administrative authority was devolved to the Seljuk vassals. Gradually power was wrested from both the Mongols and Seljuks by a new class of Turkish *beys*, who established independent principalities known as *beyliks* as new waves of Turcoman tribes fled before the Mongol advance. Groups began settling initially in Cilicia and on the Black Sea coast, and newly formed *beyliks* were soon able to challenge the Seljuk and Mongol seats of power in central Anatolia. Mehmet Bey captured Konya in 1276 and declared Turkish, rather than Persian, the official language. His hold on power was brief, but after the Mongol collapse in 1335, the Karamanli group, which he represented, re-established the *beylik* in the region. With further migration and settlement across Anatolia, other *beyliks* were established. The most significant Turkoman group to emerge was led by Osman Ghazi, whose territorial ambitions began in the western borderlands, where he established a territory extending from Eskişehir in the south to Iznik and Bursa in the north. When his son, Orhan Ghazi, captured Bursa and made it his capital, a momentum of conquest was created which grew into the Ottoman Empire.

CHAPTER 9

OTTOMAN ARCHITECTURE

Orhan Ghazi captured Bursa in 1326 and it served as the Ottoman capital until the conquest of Constantinople in 1453.[1] The Ottoman *beylik* grew out of one of the *ghazi* states – one of those border territories that had formed a battleground between Muslims and Christians. *Ghaza* means holy war, a concept that became a principle behind subsequent Ottoman conquests, providing an Islamic dimension which both supported and transcended the dynastic ambitions of the Ottomans. In 1345 the Ottomans annexed Karası territory to the west, and ten years later they gained a foothold in Europe by taking Gallipoli. Orhan's successor, Murat I, began his holy war in the west by taking Edirne in 1361, occupying Thrace and establishing suzerainty over the Balkans by defeating the Serbs at the battle of Maritza. To the east he extended Ottoman territory in Anatolia by taking Ankara and Konya, and when the Serbs and Bosnians, with Bulgarian support, rebelled in the west, Murat occupied Bulgaria and crushed the Serbs at Kosova. The process of expansion and consolidation was continued by his successor, Beyazit I, who pushed into southern Hungary, blockaded Constantinople, captured Sivas and made territorial gains in eastern Anatolia until he was held in check by Tamerlane. Beyazit was defeated at the battle of Ankara in 1402. Murat II was a strong leader who centralised power and regained lost territories. The battle of Varna consolidated the Ottoman hold on the Balkans, and Mehmet II (Muhammad the Conqueror), Beyazit's successor, filled the crucial territorial gap that divided and threatened the empire. This he achieved in 1453 when he captured Constantinople.

After the conquest, Mehmet II was very conscious of the fact that he was now heir to the Roman Empire, and it became his ambition and that of his successors to regain it for Islam and create a new world empire. He wasted no time in destroying the last pocket of Byzantine resistance in Trebizond and extending his authority in the Balkans. Halil İnalcik makes the point that the sultan now claimed three titles, Khan, Caesar and *Ghazi*.[2] The title Khan asserted Ottoman claims on all Turkish lands, because their descent from the Kayı clan gave them sovereignty over all the Turkish tribes. *Ghazi* gave him the religious status of holy warrior, and Caesar the authority to extend his rule over the whole of Christendom. His successors added to this the title of caliph after Selim's capture of

Egypt and the Hijaz. Aware of the great tradition he had usurped, Mehmet's first action in Constantinople was to conserve and rebuild. Since the Crusader sack of Constantinople in 1204 the city had been in continuous decline; it was depopulated and most of its buildings were in a ruinous state. On entering the city, Mehmet marched to Justinian's great cathedral, the Haghia Sophia, and ordered his troops to show respect as he converted the church into a mosque. His reconstruction of the city began with its restoration and the construction of his own mosque, which he built over the ruins of the Church of the Holy Apostles. Haghia Sophia remained one of Istanbul's principal mosques until the twentieth century, and this ancient building had a major impact on the development of Ottoman architecture.

Ottoman architecture did not begin with the conquest of Constantinople, and before examining the impact of the Haghia Sophia it is necessary to look at the genesis of Ottoman architecture in Bursa and Edirne, where a distinct architectural language was formed well before 1453. The first Ottoman buildings were established soon after Orhan's conquest of Bursa in 1326.

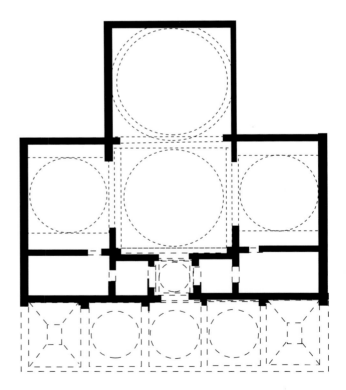

Bursa: plan of the Orhaniya mosque

Bursa: interior detail of the Ulu Cami

His own mosque, Orhaniya, was begun in 1339, and it displays early, uniquely Ottoman features. Access is through an arcaded portico which opens into two domed central cubic halls which form the main axis of the building. The first hall is a domed court flanked on either side by two smaller rooms forming altogether the lateral section of an inverted T-plan, and the further hall, the mosque, is raised on a stepped platform. Two significant features appear here, the T-plan and the use of the dome as the principal means of space enclosure. The T-plan is an Ottoman innovation which was adopted for the early mosques of both Bursa and Istanbul. Domes were built by the Seljuks but in Ottoman architecture they became the major determining factor in its creative growth and development. The hemispherical dome dominates three types of early mosque plan: in addition to the T-plan, there are small mosques consisting of a single domed prayer hall and large hypostyle mosques in which the sanctuary is covered by many domes.

The Ulu Cami, or Great Mosque, in Bursa, is one of the largest hypostyle mosques. Built by Beyazit I in 1395, its interior is divided into bays with square piers supporting twenty domes of equal size. Those along the central aisle leading to the *mihrab* are set higher, and the second dome along this axis is pierced by an oculus which allows light through to the nineteenth-century fountain below. Unlike many Seljuk buildings, this is well lit, with substantial windows in the perimeter walls and small windows grouped around the base of each dome. The interior is whitewashed and covered with bold iconic calligraphic inscriptions. The other hypostyle mosque of this period is the Eski Cami at Edirne, which was constructed soon after Beyazit's defeat by Tamerlane. Building was started in 1404 by Süleyman, but he was ousted by his brother Mehmet I who completed the work in 1414. The Eski Cami was the main congregational mosque of Edirne before the larger Üç Şerefeli Cami was built. Its prayer hall is smaller than that of the Bursa mosque, with only four piers supporting nine domes of equal size. The domes are much larger than those at Bursa, and those occupying the central aisle are supported on pendentives, triangles or *muqarnas*. On either side of the entrance to the mosque are two large inscriptions with the names of Allah and Muhammad, which herald the interior decoration consisting of calligraphic forms of monumental proportions like those at Bursa. From the exterior, both mosques present a simple rectangular mass with a roof-line made up of a flat uniform array of domes. This repetitious format became a common feature of secular buildings, such as *hans* and *bedestans* (markets), but for mosque architecture it soon became redundant, and more inventive, elegant and imaginative possibilities of dome construction were introduced.

The most memorable and best preserved buildings in Bursa are the Yeşil Cami and Yeşil Türbe (green mosque and mausoleum) built by Mehmet I in 1421. The unity and harmony of conception of both anticipates in spirit the classical form of the later Ottoman mosques. The sense of unity is reinforced by the excellent preservation of the interior tilework, which is quite outstanding. The plan of the Yeşil Cami follows the T-plan format established by the Orhan Cami, with two domed cubes, consisting of court and mosque forming the main north-south axis of the building. Before entering the court, there is a lateral space, like a narthex, which leads off left and right to two small corner rooms. Within the walls of this narthex are staircases giving access to the royal loggia and apartments above. The interior is based on the Persian model of an *iwan* court, except that here, as in many Anatolian mosques, the whole is covered and enclosed under two hemispherical domes. The dome over the court has a lantern which admits light and symbolically alludes to its Persian predecessors where the open sky is mirrored in the fountain below. The court with its onyx fountain is flanked by two domed *iwans*, and beyond, just before the raised platform of the prayer hall, doors give access on either side to two domed rooms provided to accommodate dervishes. Instead of pendentives, squinches or *muqarnas* the transitional zone carries the hemispherical domes on a series of folded prismatic triangles. The external façade is symmetrical with harmonious proportions and fine-quality stone carving. The central portal is flanked on each side by paired windows on two storeys, and projecting corbels indicate that it was intended to have a portico. The upper windows are open loggias with finely cut filigree balconies, and the lower windows, separated by external *mihrabs*, are set in beautifully cut decorative recessed panels.

The domes are now sheathed in lead but originally they were covered with green tiles, which remained in place until the seventeenth century. The interior tilework is the best of its period, and inscriptions pinpoint the work of various craftsmen including Mehmet the Eccentric, who worked on the royal loggia, and the 'Masters of Tabriz' who were responsible for the *mihrab*. As Blair and Bloom have pointed out, the epithet 'Tabrizi' is commonplace and could be misleading. It springs up in Egypt, Syria and Central Asia, and may simply be a term to denote a master tile-maker, rather than to identify craftsmen specifically with Tabriz.[3] The man with overall charge was Nakkas Ali, who may have been one of a number of Turkish artists taken to Samarqand in the wake of Tamerlane's conquests. The work is Persian, the style is known as 'international Timurid' and its technique is *cuerda seca*. Developed in Central Asia, *cuerda seca* involved applying different coloured pigments to the tiles, and separating each on firing by using a mixture of wax or oil with manganese. Each colour is outlined by a thin dark line, and many of the tiles in Bursa are enhanced with overglazed gilding. The majority of hexagonal tiles lining the wainscot are turquoise-green in colour, gilded with lace-like medallions and bordered

with *cuerda seca* arabesques and calligraphy. The tiles in the ceilings consist of floriate arabesques, like carpet panels, with circular medallions picked out in white, yellow, turquoise, blue and black. The *mihrab*'s majestic presence dominates the sanctuary of the mosque. It is like a suspended tapestry made of densely patterned tiles in turquoise, gold and white, with blues of cobalt, Prussian and ultramarine. The same concentration of colour and arabesque occurs in the *mihrab* niche with a central panel containing the name of Allah, and its hood is tightly packed with twelve tiers of *muqarnas* inscribed and outlined in golden yellow.

The Yeşil Türbe is a domed octagonal mausoleum situated among cyprus trees near the mosque. In the nineteenth century it was damaged by earthquake, so much of the green tiling on the exterior today is restoration work. It contains an even more splendid *mihrab* than does the Yeşil Cami which is crested with bold floral sprays that fan out like the decorative borders and pendants of a Persian manuscript or court carpet. The gilded green octagonal tiles in the wainscot are enlivened by carpet-like motifs consisting of large arabesque medallions and pendants. Similar motifs, confirming the international language of these patterns, appear in decorative panels in the Blue Mosque at Tabriz (1465). In the centre of the Yeşil Türbe's *mihrab* niche is an elegant arabesque of carnations and roses against which hangs a mosque

Bursa: the *mihrab* of the Yeşil Türbe

lamp flanked by two candlesticks containing the names of Allah and Muhammad. Two symbols are brought together here, the garden of paradise and the lamp symbolising God's divine light as revealed in the Qur'an (*Sura* 24:35). The cenotaph of Mehmet I displays tilework of equal magnificence, with floral motifs set in trefoil panels at the base and bands of Nashki script on the sides and sloping top. Unlike Seljuk tombs the upper chambers of Ottoman *türbes* are not empty, and they display some cenotaph or sarcophagus. Mehmet I's cenotaph is a sparkling memorial which stands over the point where his body is interred in the crypt below.

The twelve *türbes* in the Muradiya Cemetery in Bursa contain the bodies of one sultan and numerous princes, princesses and retainers. These buildings show a marked change from the Seljuk format of conical roof and exterior elaboration in stone. The *türbes* are built in the Byzantine manner with hemispherical domes, courses of alternating brick and ashlar and plain exteriors with no stone dressing or decoration. The only sultan buried here is Murat II, whose grave is set in the centre of a square ambulatory under an open dome exposing the tomb to the elements, and allowing the rain and snow to water the ground below. Goodwin compares the simplicity of Murat's tomb with the splendour of Mehmet's, and attributes Murat's modesty to his unworldliness and devotion to the Sufi orders.[4] Murat ruled for thirty years, in which time he extended and consolidated the empire; but he became world weary, abdicated twice in favour of his son, Mehmet II, and sought the contemplative life. His tomb set a precedent for a whole picturesque genre of Ottoman tombs, which are similarly exposed to the elements in open cages of masonry and ironwork. A number of *türbes*, like Murat's, have a second chamber to accommodate the graves of relatives, and one poignant reminder of the barbarities of Ottoman successions, and the excesses of later sultans, can be seen in a sixteenth-century *türbe* containing the bodies of Murat III's sons. Murat III is interred in a *türbe* next to the Haghia Sophia in Istanbul but when he died in 1595 nineteen of his younger sons were strangled to ensure the undisputed succession of his son Mehmet III.

Murat II was buried in Bursa but his court and the recipients of his patronage were in Edirne. Edirne was established as the capital by Süleyman after the battle of

Edirne: the Üç Şerefeli Cami

Ankara, and after the conquest of Constantinople it also served as a summer capital. The city has a remarkable legacy of Ottoman architecture which reaches a climax in the sixteenth century with Sinan's great Selimiya. Murat's main work was the building of the Üç Şerefeli Mosque (1447), which represents a major transitional phase in Ottoman architecture. The open court here revived a custom that had broadly disappeared in Anatolian architecture, and which became significant in later Ottoman architecture. The lateral axis of the prayer hall, and its relationship with the *sahn*, looks back to the Damascus plan, and Syrian influence should not be ruled out. The Syrian contribution to Anatolian architecture went further than mere decoration, and a number of mosque plans like those at Dunaysir, Mardin and Diyarbakr bear this out. In plan the Üç Şerefeli resembles the İsa Bey mosque (1374) built at Seljuk near the ruins of the Temple of Diana at Ephesus. The İsa Bey's architect came from Damascus, and Syrian interlace patterns crown the windows and adorn the *mihrab*. Its *sahn*, which is slightly larger than the prayer hall, had arcaded *riwaqs*. Similarly in the Üç Şerefeli domed *riwaqs* are a strong feature of the *sahn*, but perhaps more important than the revival of the *sahn* is the scale of the dome that dominates its interior.

The Üç Şerefeli dome is 24 metres in diameter, and its weight is carried on the thick buttressed walls of the prayer hall and two hexagonal piers from which spring four supporting pointed arches braced with tie-beams. The cavernous dome is set relatively low on these huge piers and sturdy arches, making it somewhat cumbersome and oppressive. The flanking domes and side bays are relegated to the wings and subordinated by the

Portrait of Mehmet II by Gentile Bellini

Istanbul, Topkapı Palace: the Çinili Kiosk

centralising power of the main dome, allowing, according to Goodwin, students and dervishes to occupy these spaces without disturbing prayers in the main prayer hall.⁵ The spatial transition between central dome and side bays is abrupt and awkward, but the attempt to distribute space around a central dome, and the scale of the undertaking, indicates a new direction in architectural thinking. Its exterior profile reveals a descending order of domes from prayer hall, to portico, to *riwaq*, thus establishing a keynote in Ottoman architecture whereby a building's visual impact is principally determined by the composition, disposition and rhythm of its domes. Later architects were to find ways of raising the central dome, varying the size and elevation of the others and allowing for greater mediation between one space and another. The Üç Şerefeli Mosque has four minarets and is named after the three balconies that adorn the tallest. They remained the tallest in Turkey until Sinan built the Selimiya in Edirne. The Üç Şerefeli indicates that all the components of Ottoman architecture were well in place before Mehmet's conquest of Constantinople, even if they were in a transitional state.

In Constantinople Mehmet the Conqueror ensured that the fall of Byzantium made possible the rise of Istanbul, and he quickly set about ambitious building projects. These included his own mosque, the grand bazaar and the Topkapı Palace on Seraglio Point. Before taking the city in 1453, he had already constructed, in four months, the massive fortress of Rumeli Hissar. It commands the narrowest point of the Bosphorus and embodies both the spirit of conquest and the conqueror. Mehmet was not just a warrior, but a man of great refinement, as Gentile Bellini's famous portrait suggests. He tended his gardens, patronised the arts and architecture and received distinguished western artists into his court. Bellini arrived as a part of a peace treaty signed with the Venetians, and it is possible that the architects Antonio Filarete and Michelozzo di Bartolomeo may have worked for Mehmet. While building the Topkapı Palace, Mehmet negotiated with Lorenzo de Medici the loan of Florentine craftsmen in exchange for the escaped adventurer Benardo Bandini Baroncelli, one of the Pazzi conspirators responsible for the assassination attempt on Lorenzo and the murder of his brother Guiliano. In his capacity as Caesar, Mehmet regarded it his duty to know and understand Christian culture. He commissioned a history of the Roman Empire and translations of Ptolemy's *Geography* and invited numerous Italian scholars to his court to advise and assist him with his collection of Greek and Latin manuscripts.

The cultivated aspect of Mehmet's personality was expressed in the Çinili Kiosk (1472), the earliest surviving building within the grounds of the Topkapı Palace complex. It is a square two-storeyed pavilion, with *iwans* on three sides and a cruciform centre court leading to three royal rooms which overlook the park. It is built in brick and stone and its form and plan is Persian, although only traces of contemporary Persian palaces survive for comparison. Its plan is similar to the fifteenth-century pavilion of the Shirvinshah's summer palace at Baku, Azerbaijan, and some of the later Safavid palaces of Isfahan. Access to the Çinili Kiosk is by two staircases which lead to a raised portico supported by tall slender stone columns similar to the wooden columns seen in the Ali Qapu Palace and Chihil Sutun Pavilion in Isfahan. Like the Ali Qapu, this raised platform provided a grand-stand view of the polo court, which once stood at the front of this pavilion. The main door is through an *iwan* covered in tiled bricks forming angular patterns and geometricised Kufic in turquoise, Prussian blue, ultramarine and white. The angularity of these patterns is offset by the cursive rhythm of an inscription in *cuerda seca* set in an arabesque band that runs horizontally around three faces of the *iwan*. The letters are picked out in white and yellow, and the inscription consists of Persian verses extolling the beauty of the building. Despite the Persian flavour it is thought that the tiles are from Iznik, the main centre of tile production in Turkey.

Mehmet's own mosque, the Fatih Cami (1470), or Conqueror's Mosque, was built on a choice location over the ruins of the Church of the Holy Apostles, and many of the ancient stones in this building were re-used in the mosque. It was totally destroyed by earthquake in the eighteenth century, and today's building is mainly Mustafa's restoration of 1771. Only the *sahn*, parts of the entrance portal, the *mihrab* and a few other remnants are original. However, Mustafa's reconstruction follows the original foundations and provides some conclusions about its scale and the extent of the whole complex. This was the first *külliya* in Istanbul and it still is enormous in

its scope and impact. It is here, in the Ottoman *külliyas*, that all the functions of the Prophet's Medina mosque were systematically organised and accommodated. It was an urban plan, a university city and an architectural expression of what the Muslim community stood for. The mosque, with its adjoining *sahn* and cemetery, was situated in a large precinct which served as a camping ground for caravans, and to the east and west of this were eight *madrasas*. The eastern *madrasas* were known as the Akdeniz Madrasas (Black Sea) and the western the Karadeniz Madrasas (White Sea – Mediterranean); opposite, separated by a narrow alley, were smaller annexes. A library and primary school stood near the entrance to the precinct, and to the south were a hospital, baths, hospice, soup kitchen and caravansarai. A saddle market also existed in the area, and the rents from this supported the mosque and its charitable institutions.

The *sahn*, with its two monumental entrances and domed *riwaqs*, is slightly larger than the mosque. It forms an open enclosure the inclusion of which became a major feature of Ottoman architecture, complementing the covered space of the prayer hall. The mosque dome measured 26 metres in diameter and was joined by a half dome which extended the space to the *mihrab*. The use of half domes to lengthen space and carry the hyperbolic thrust of the central dome outwards and downwards to buttresses in the load-bearing walls was a Byzantine device. The Haghia Sophia was the supreme model, and the diameter of its dome at 31 metres was to remain a challenge to the Turks. Only Koca Sinan matched this with his Selimiya, and one tradition states that Mehmet executed his architect, Atik Sinan (not to be confused with Koca Sinan), for failing to produce a dome which matched the Haghia Sophia in size. Nevertheless, the Fatih dome was the largest in the Ottoman Empire. It was supported on buttresses within the walls, two huge piers and two antique porphyry columns which had been taken from the Church of the Holy Apostles. It was flanked by three subsidiary domes over the side aisles, and unlike most Ottoman domes, it was set on a drum, pierced with windows and strengthened by buttresses.

Perhaps more significant than the mosque itself is the scope and scale of the ancillary buildings. The eight *madrasas* constituted a major university; it is important to stress that, while Mehmet was opening his court to

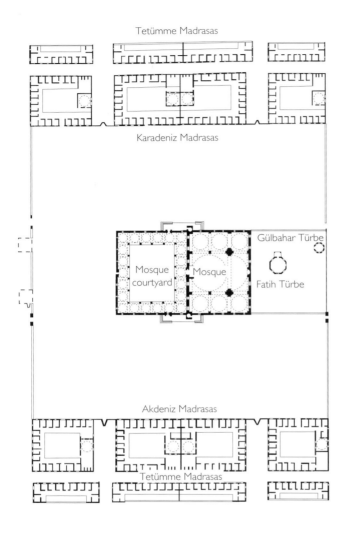

Tetümme Madrasas

Karadeniz Madrasas

Mosque courtyard

Mosque

Gülbahar Türbe

Fatih Türbe

Akdeniz Madrasas

Tetümme Madrasas

Istanbul, plan of Fatih Külliya

one of the largest in Istanbul, was nearby. The *imaret*, or soup kitchen, was destroyed; there is speculation about its size and the number of people it catered for. Goodwin, quoting from contemporary sources, states that cell accommodation for one hundred travellers was provided and they were entitled to three days' free board.[6] The caravansarai provided stabling and storage, and merchants stopped at the hospice, or at one of the hundred and fifty lodgings beyond the mosque precincts. All that we see today is a mere fragment of a complex which was at the hub of a dynamic community.

Mehmet's successor, Beyazit II, established a smaller *külliya* of greater architectural refinement at Edirne. This was less comprehensive in facilities, and the education it offered was medical, not theological. The major buildings to the right of the mosque included a medical school, asylum and hospital. The square plan of the school, with cells and lecture hall facing an arcaded inner court, is much the same as the theological *madrasas* at the Fatih complex. At right angles to the medical school is the hospital, built around two courts and terminating with an unusual domed hexagonal building. The section generally regarded as the asylum, around the first court, contains the kitchen, seven cells and two double rooms flanking the gate. The inner court, with two *iwans* and four domed cells, was perhaps the pharmacy and administrative centre. The court leads into the distinctive hexagonal building, which has a large lanterned dome, 14 metres in diameter, on pointed arches above a central fountain. This central space with its radiating *iwans* is beautifully proportioned and truly monumental. The six arches that support the dome frame six *iwans*, five of which lead into pentagonal rooms; the sixth, opposite the main entrance, is longer and terminates in an apse. This apsidal *iwan* has a raised platform, probably where musicians played their therapeutic music.

The whole complex, including mosque, *imaret*, bakery, hospital and medical school, was staffed by one hundred and sixty-seven people, and the hospital employed doctors, oculists, a dentist and barber surgeons. The mosque is relatively small, with a single domed cubic prayer hall. Seen from the river, it has a classical purity. On either side of the prayer hall are two square *tabhanes* (rooms for itinerant dervishes), cruciform in the centre, with four rooms in each corner. Some sources describe

western culture, he was first and foremost a Muslim intellectual dedicated to the promotion of Muslim scholarship. Each *madrasa* consisted of nineteen cells built around a central court enclosing a lecture hall, with an annex opposite accommodating nine more cells. There were problems of overcrowding, and it is reported that at one stage a thousand students attended the *madrasas*, which suggests that four or five students occupied each cell in all eight *madrasas*. The hospital, which was totally destroyed in the earthquake of 1776, was staffed by Jewish doctors and contained a kitchen and fourteen wards around an inner courtyard. The hospice, which survives, has domed *riwaqs* around an inner court, a kitchen and a small prayer hall. A substantial bath-house,

Edirne, welfare complex of the Beyazit II mosque

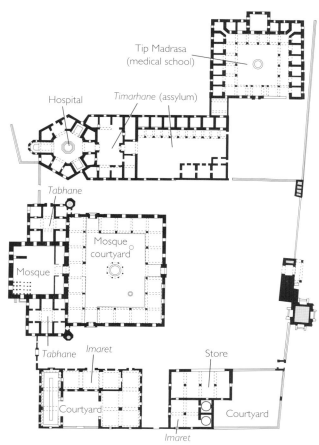

Edirne, plan of the *külliya* of Beyazit II

these wings as *madrasas*, rather than *tabhanes*, and this open-ended ambiguity of function, typical of so many Muslim buildings, recalls the *madrasas* and *khanqahs* of Cairo. They occupy almost as much room as the main prayer hall, which indicates the priority given to the clergy that used them. Beyazit was a stout defender of Sunni Islam, a devout follower of the *sharia*, as well as a mystic, scholar and poet, who cultivated the dervish orders. He rejected the cultural cosmopolitanism of his father and sold off many of the Italian paintings that adorned Mehmet's palace.

Beyazit's *külliya* at Edirne presents a classical Ottoman profile in a flat landscape near the river. Its horizontal wings are articulated by the rhythms of its arcades and saucer-shaped domes of various sizes, broken by the vertical thrust of pyramid-capped chimney stacks,

tall pencil-shaped minarets, pepper-pot lanterns and the cubic mass of the mosque. Its compact organisation and simple geometry of form recall the work of Seljuk predecessors, although the architectural vocabulary is now entirely different. It was followed by a truly classical form of mosque design in Istanbul – Beyazit's *külliya* built near the old forum of Theodosius. Set in a vast square, the mosque can be viewed from some distance. Its plan is symmetrical, consisting of *sahn* and prayer hall occupying two adjacent squares of equal size. The monumental exterior of the *sahn* façade is identical on three sides, with each face divided in the centre by a tall portal flanked by twelve windows set in two storeys. The central aisle of the prayer hall has a dome placed between two half domes, similar to the Haghia Sophia. On either side are four bays making up the side aisles, and the central domes are supported on pendentives springing from four piers, two granite columns and buttresses in the walls. Two wings spreading out laterally from the northern end of the prayer hall form two *tabhanes*.

This was the first time that the dome structure and plan of the Haghia Sophia was adopted. That this great building would be influential was inevitable, but it is clear that Ottoman architecture had already reached a considerable degree of maturity and sophistication. Greater invention and new permutations in the organisation of interior space were developed, but it was not only the Haghia Sophia that made this possible. The interior of the Beyazit mosque is quite dark, and from the outside the dome lacks the presence of those of later Ottoman mosques. This is partly due to its size (only just over 17 metres in diameter) and also to a lateral emphasis created by the *tabhane* wings, which hold the minarets 87 metres apart. Nevertheless, the Beyazit Cami is a seminal work because it establishes with precision and clarity the broad composition and form of the classical Ottoman style. The genius of one man, Koca Sinan, brought this to maturity.

The architect of the Beyazit Cami was Yakup Shah ibn Sultan Shah. As a rule architects can be identified through Ottoman records of the designers and builders on their pay-roll. Sinan ibn Abdulmennan, or Koca Sinan (1491–1588), was a towering figure who transformed Istanbul and made it very much the Ottoman city we see today. He was born a Christian in the Kayseri region of Anatolia and was conscripted into the Janissary army through the *devşirme* system. The *devşirme* (meaning gathering) was a form of Ottoman 'tax' levied on Christian peasants, but instead of raising money the most fit and intelligent boys in the community were rounded up and enslaved into the service of the Sultan. This form of 'taxation' was not quite as barbaric as it may sound; it involved approximately one family in forty, the boys were given the best education and training the state could offer, and like the Mamluks in Egypt they were groomed for the highest offices of state. A form of meritocracy, it guaranteed quality and loyalty in the civil service and army. Sinan rose through the ranks of the Janissary army, the Sultan's *corps d'élite*, serving throughout the empire as an engineer before becoming chief court architect at the age of forty-eight. He served three sultans, Süleyman the Magnificent, Selim II and Murat III before his death at the age of approximately ninety-eight.

Of these sultans, he was closest to Süleyman the Magnificent, and Sinan's architecture achieved supremacy with the age of Süleyman. In the West Süleyman was known as the 'Magnificent', but in the East he was the 'Law Giver'. Both titles are apt, because his court was renowned for its magnificence, but more importantly he was a wise ruler dedicated to law reform and a world leader whose impact on the West was marked by his diplomacy and military campaigns which extended the empire to the gates of Vienna. His reign was the high point of Ottoman power and culture, but his failure to capture Vienna also heralded a turning point in Ottoman fortunes. Like many of his predecessors, he was a scholar and poet able to compose verses in both Turkish and Persian. He brought many scholars into his court and commissioned a history of the House of Osman, numerous biographies and works on theology and philosophy. Süleyman was an accomplished goldsmith – craftsmanship was a significant part of a prince's education up to the end of the sultanate (Abdul Hamid, 1876–1909, was an expert furniture maker). Süleyman's patronage of architecture was placed chiefly in his friend Sinan, and their relationship has been compared with that of Bernini and Urban VIII.[7] Sinan's responsibilities, however, were wider than Bernini's, going far beyond creative and aesthetic matters. He was a wise counsellor and courtier who administered a major government department responsible for building, planning and the whole civic infrastructure, including building maintenance, drains and fire regulations.

In his memoirs Sinan claimed that his three royal mosques, the Şehzade (1548), Süleymaniye (1557) and Selimiye (1575), embodied in turn his apprenticeship, maturity and a work of genius. In his apprenticeship, the Şehzade Cami provided his first opportunity to impress Süleyman. It was commissioned by the grief-stricken sultan following the death of Crown Prince Mehmet from smallpox at the age of twenty-one. Like the Beyazit Cami, the *sahn* and prayer hall are two adjacent squares of identical size forming two boxes of open and closed space. The prayer hall has a centralised cruciform plan made up of a central dome set above four half-domes. Each half-dome is paired by two smaller half-domes (exedra) which fill the corners of the side bays at a lower level. The symmetry of this formation, and the use of half-domed exedra, breaks open the old compartmentalised space and introduces a fluid transition from one domed surface to another, as well as crowning the hall with a coherent quatrefoil pattern. The domes are

Istanbul, the Sehzade Cami

supported on pendentives which spring from piers built into the walls, projecting outwards on the exterior face of the *qibla* wall, leaving a clear wall space inside, and inwards from the north wall where they support the galleries. Further underpinning of the domed superstructure is provided by four free-standing piers which continue up through the roof-line forming domed stabilising turrets. The interior is loftier and lighter than the Beyazit Cami, achieved through the orchestration of windows which pierce every available surface between piers, buttresses and bays, circumscribing the drum and half-domes and surrounding the *mihrab*. The whole prayer hall is like the interior of an oriental lantern breathing in beams of light.

The *sahn* façade has a similar composition to that of the Beyazit Cami, except that the side portals are not centrally placed. The front façade is centrally divided by the portal, which is flanked by four sets of two-storeyed,

paired windows, rectangular with iron grills at the bottom, and latticed with semicircular arches at the top. The exterior profile of the mosque is magnificent, with the lofty central dome at the apex of a pyramid of descending domes, varied in size and accent, which cascade and settle on the tops of the *riwaqs*, crowning and adding grandeur to the monumental entrance façade. This descending rhythm is offset by the vertical push of the stabilising turrets with their ribbed domes, and the thrust of the slender minarets with their light, graceful decoration. On the ground floor Sinan introduced on both sides an arcaded gallery which covers the external buttresses and lightens the whole structure at the base, setting up a beautiful play of solid and void across the whole façade. In the cemetery garden is Şehzade Mehmet's octagonal *türbe* with its distinctive ribbed dome and pink and white exterior. The ornate cresting at the top of the octagon and

Istanbul, the interior of Süleymaniye Külliya

the rich tiles of the interior make this one of Sinan's most elaborate and elegant structures.

The work of Sinan's maturity is the Sülemaniye Külliya (1557), which is his grandest and most impressive work in Istanbul. The *külliya* is enormous, and what is preserved is more extensive than the Fatih complex. The mosque is square in plan, sandwiched between the smaller rectangle of the *sahn* and the larger rectangle of the cemetery, which contains Süleyman's *türbe* and that of his wife, Roxelana. The complex is built on a sloping site, and to the west of the precinct wall is a road with a number of buildings consisting of a small Qur'an school for boys, two law schools and a medical school, all constructed over thirty-six shops. The rents from these shops contributed towards upkeep of the *külliya*. The road turns right and begins to slope down, passing the hospital, *imaret* and *tabhane*. It makes another right hand turn past Sinan's tomb leading steeply down to two

further law schools and the baths. Up on the terrace overlooking this road is the *darül hadis*, a *madrasa* for the study of *hadith*, and the domed chamber of the *darül kurra* for Qur'anic studies. Each of the law schools was devoted to a different *madhhab*.

The interior of the mosque follows the Haghia Sophia plan, with a strong central orientation towards the *mihrab*. This is reinforced by arcades which spring from two pairs of red granite columns placed between the four great piers carrying the superstructure of the central dome, two half-domes and exedra. The side aisle bays each have five domes, three large and two small. Like the Şehzade Mosque, the domes are supported by four piers and buttresses set within the walls, which project outwards from the *qibla* and side walls, forming major structural and design features on the exterior of the building. The plan follows the Haghia Sophia but there the similarities stop. The huge piers of the Haghia Sophia effectively block out a clear view of the side aisles, which become lost in shadow, whereas the Süleymaniye is a much lighter, more open structure and the eye is carried through and across the arcades and bays to the perimeter walls. The Haghia Sophia is an awesome building, which holds its secrets in its rich polychrome, glittering surfaces, dark corners and concealed spaces. The Süleymaniye is a clarified version of the Haghia Sophia, provoking a similar sense of wonder through its rigour, crystalline precision and logical organisation of space.

The same precision and logic determines its exterior, the buttresses forming a bold structural framework from which much of the building appears to hang. From the side elevation, the flying buttresses radiate from the central dome initiating a rhythmic sequence of steps which progress down from the domed stabilising turrets to the paired exterior buttresses which firmly stand out like domed towers. On both sides these buttresses frame two-tiered arcaded galleries over which projects a broad-eaved roof providing shelter for those taking ritual ablutions at the taps below. The fragility of the gallery columns gives lightness and elegance to these arcades, and the flanking entrances with their stone lattice balustrades provide an extended range of open space at ground level. Like the Doge's Palace in Venice, this building contradicts the golden rule that a heavy foundation should support a light superstructure. The framing buttresses hold everything

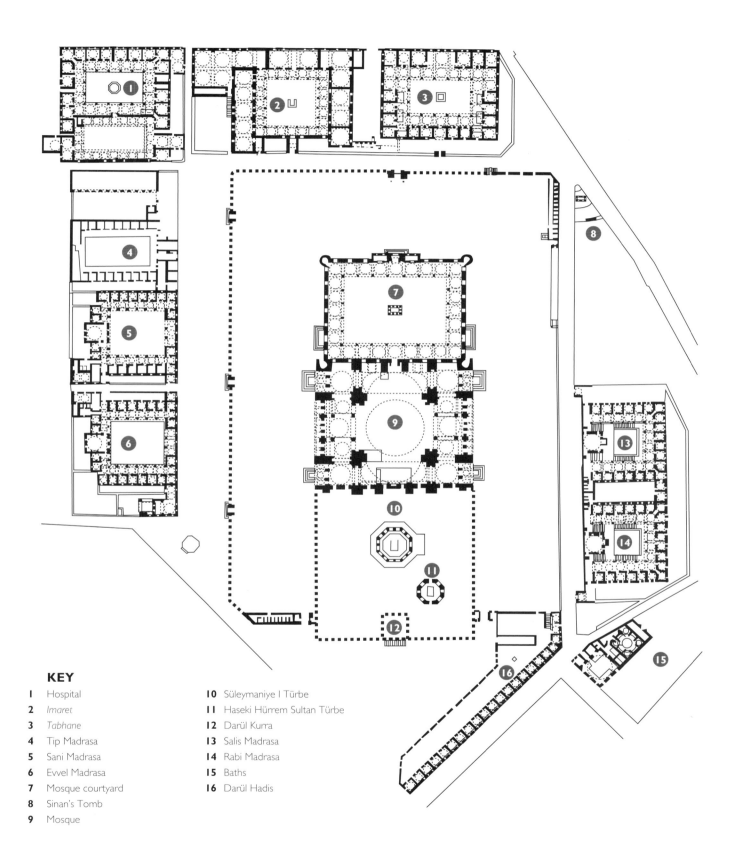

KEY

1   Hospital
2   *Imaret*
3   *Tabhane*
4   Tip Madrasa
5   Sani Madrasa
6   Evvel Madrasa
7   Mosque courtyard
8   Sinan's Tomb
9   Mosque

10   Süleymaniye I Türbe
11   Haseki Hürrem Sultan Türbe
12   Darül Kurra
13   Salis Madrasa
14   Rabi Madrasa
15   Baths
16   Darül Hadis

Istanbul, plan of the Süleymaniye Külliya

together and prevent any sense of crushing weight on the open galleries at the base. The simple grandeur of the massive battered buttresses projecting from the exterior of the *qibla* wall equally contribute to the structural and compositional strength of the building. The whole exterior is set off by minarets at the four corners of the *sahn*. Those flanking the north wall of the prayer hall are the tallest, at 76 metres, and the disposition and proportion of all four minarets recall those of the Üç Şerefeli in Edirne.

The grey marble *mihrab* symbolically echoes the design of the main entrance portal to the mosque, which stands on the same axis leading into the *sahn*. The surrounding panels of Iznik tiles anticipate the more extensive use of tile-work in the *mihrab* area in later Ottoman buildings. Like the rest of the mosque the tile-work here is restrained, but it also reflects a change from earlier Timurid and blue and white styles of decoration. A more naturalistic floral style and a tomato red colour were introduced here. The leaf and flower motifs in the *mihrab* are somewhat measured, but the most striking features in the *mihrab* design are the circular calligraphic inscriptions over the flanking windows. Stained glass makes a brilliant, jewel-like contribution to the *qibla* wall, with some fine examples of the work of Sarhos (the drunkard) Ibrahim. The full force of the new floral style of tile-work can best be seen in the Haseki Hürrem Sultan Türbe (mausoleum of Roxelana) in the cemetery garden: lush floral, paradisiac images of tulips, carnations and trees with white blossoms and turquoise leaves, set in a background of deep ultramarine blue.

The tiles at the Süleymaniye are a prelude to the glories in two of Sinan's smaller mosques built in Istanbul for the grand viziers Rüstem Paşa and Sokollu Mehmet Paşa. The central *mihrab* of the Rüstem Paşa Cami (1561) is a masterpiece of tile decoration, a bountiful floral paradise which raises the question of symbolism in Islamic art. There has been much speculation regarding the symbolism of the *mihrab*, but one enters doubtful territory when ascribing symbolic meaning to the decorative arts of Islam. Few explicit examples of symbolism occur in Islamic art; the mosque lamp, representing the light of God in the *mihrab* of the Yeşil Türbe, represents one occasional manifestation. However, the western habit of seeking symbolic explanations usually leads nowhere when applied to

Istanbul, tiles from the Rüstem Paşa Cami

Islamic art, where meaning is expressed in the totality of experience, rather than in iconic detail. There is general consensus that in appropriate instances the *mihrab* can be viewed as a gate of paradise, and that of Rüstem Paşa Cami, and the tiles in the *qibla* wall of Sokollu Mehmet Paşa Cami (1572) do sumptuously express this idea. In the Rüstem Paşa's *mihrab* there is a repertoire of forms similar to those in Persian weaving, where sickle leaves, forming fragile arabesques, hold and embrace vases, from which spring sprays of blossom contained in crested medallions. The mosque is decorated throughout with the tile collection bequeathed by Rüstem Paşa, who was an enthusiastic collector of Iznik tiles, and for this reason it has been criticised for lacking coherence and consistent quality. It is certainly excessively lavish compared with many of Sinan's other mosques, but after the recent restoration it conveys a clarity, brightness and opulence, which more than compensates for occasional lapses of taste.

The Rüstem Paşa Cami is an oasis of tranquillity and luxury built on a raised platform containing storerooms which serve the surrounding tinsmiths' bazaar. Sokollu Mehmet Paşa's Mosque is on a steep slope beneath the hippodrome on the hill down to the Church of Sts Sergius and Bacchus. The steep incline means that the building cannot be viewed adequately from the outside. It is approached up steps through a courtyard surrounded by a *madrasa* consisting of single cell units and a lecture hall over the entrance staircase. Here Sinan was more in control of the design without the problem of how best to use a bequest of Iznik tiles. The central section of the *qibla* wall surrounding the *mihrab* is tiled

Istanbul, the interior of the Sokollu Mehmet Paşa Cami

Christians say in the realm of Islam no dome can equal that of the Haghia Sophia; they claim that no Islamic architect would be able to build such a large dome. In this mosque, with the help of Allah and the support of Sultan Selim Khan, I erected a dome six cubits higher and four cubits wider than the Haghia Sophia.[8]

Sinan's claim is somewhat exaggerated because it is not larger or higher, but more or less equal in size. It is placed on eight piers, and the central space consists of an octagon within a square. Between the eight piers marking out the octagon alternating half-domed exedra create a quatrefoil distribution of space pushing out to the corners. The *mihrab* is contained in a deeply recessed half-domed apse which marks the orientation of the mosque as it projects out of the centralised space through the centre of the *qibla* wall.

The centralisation of space is affirmed by the tribune (*dikka*), raised on shallow cusped arches, which covers a fountain situated at the hub of the mosque directly under the dome. The accommodation and enclosure of the fountain in this manner is a throwback to Seljuk and Bursa traditions. On the *minbar* drilled and fretted filigree reveals a delicacy of form consistent with the latticed windows, arabesques and light flourishes of calligraphy. In the prayer hall the light and colour are subtle and radiant. The honey-coloured stone, and alternate arch voussoirs picked out in terracotta red, immediately establish a warmth to the interior which is in marked contrast to the colder austerities of the Sülemaniye in Istanbul. The window glass is almost entirely clear, so that maximum illumination falls on the warm buffs, pinks and terracottas of the stone-work, offset by cooler blues, whites and greens in the tiles of the royal loggia and the wainscoting of the *mihrab* apse. Horizontal bands of calligraphy above the galleries provide alternating colour bands, where cursive script is picked out in white on blue, blue on white and white on red. The carpet provides a flat pulsating plane of colour, which is deep orange red, tempered with blue, while the central *dikka* draws the eye to its rich intensity of red and gold. The recently restored dome, the climax of the building, provides an opulent display of painted decoration consisting of a circlet of white calligraphy in the centre, inscriptions in maroon

magnificently with arabesque panels containing palmettes and vine motifs in turquoise and light green, balanced with blue cartouches and roundels filled with lively calligraphy picked out in white. The *minbar*, set with fragments of the black stone from Mecca, is made of marble and its conical top is also richly sheathed in tiles. The lofty interior is remarkably grand for such a small building, demonstrating Sinan's genius for making the best of confined and awkward spaces.

A work of genius and one of the world's greatest buildings, which Sinan claimed as the fulfilment of his ambitions, is the Selimiya at Edirne, designed for Süleyman's successor, Selim II in 1575. The mosque is centralised in plan, with its space harmoniously organised under one huge dome. After all the years of ceaseless invention and virtuosity in dome construction, the supreme achievement of Ottoman architecture was reached on the basis of the simplest plan – the single domed oratory. Sinan achieved a long-term objective by creating a dome rivalling the Haghia Sophia, and he is reported as saying that:

medallions, cloud bands of cream and light arabesques of green and gold which dance over a field dominated by light and dark blue.

Externally the shallow dome is ringed by eight strong buttresses, crowned with pointed domed turrets, radiating from the central octagon. Between these buttresses, projecting half-domed exedra alternate with flat tympana pierced by windows. There are no cascading domes, and the external composition of this building is distinguished by its simplicity, logic and composure. The whole ensemble is enhanced by an elegant space frame created by four tall slender fluted minarets, 70 metres high, made up of four shafts divided by three balconies. These framing minarets elevate the scale of the building and bestow a dramatic silhouette seen from any distance. They provide the first breathtaking experience of Ottoman architecture when entering Turkey by train from the Bulgarian frontier. The mosque is a part of a *külliya*, and its precinct contains a *madrasa* and a *darül kurra* which flank the mosque at the corners of the south side. To the west the mosque is constructed over a covered bazaar (*arasta*), the rents of which, like the shops in the Süleymaniye and Fatih Cami, support the foundation. Access to the mosque

precincts is through the bazaar and up a staircase, and it has been suggested that integration of the bazaar into the fabric of the *külliya* was a way of attracting shoppers from the city centre to the mosque.[9]

Süleyman the Magnificent's heirs lacked his strength of character and purpose. Before the Selimiya was complete, Selim II (the Sot) died in a drunken stupor slipping on the tiles of his bath at the Topkapı Palace. Murat III devoted most of his debauched life to the pleasures of the harem, reputedly siring one hundred and three children. Sinan designed a splendid mosque for Murat at Manisa, but in view of the sultan's predilections it comes as no surprise that his most conspicuous act of architectural patronage should be the Topkapı harem, which he rebuilt following the fire of 1574. It is appropriate that Sinan's most distinguished contribution to this project was Murat's bedroom, but before considering this masterpiece of interior design, it is necessary to look briefly at the evolution and layout of the palace in general.

The Topkapı Saray was begun by Mehmet II on the site of the ancient acropolis on a high promontory, north of the Haghia Sophia, bounded by the Sea of Marmara and the Golden Horn. It stands among extensive parks

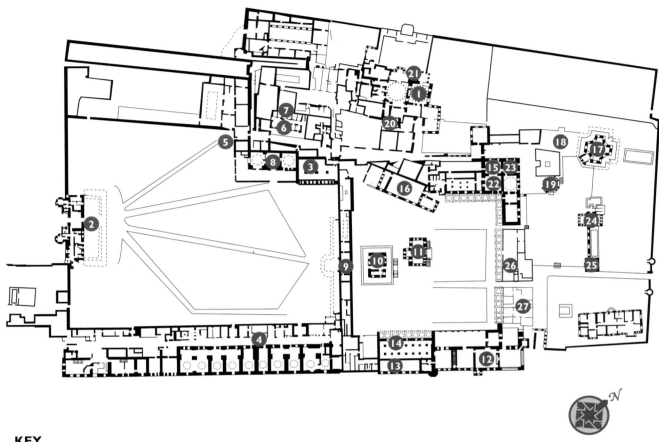

KEY

1	Murat III Bedchamber	10	Throne Room	19	Revan Kiosk
2	Orta Kapı	11	Ahmet III Library	20	Hall of the Hearth
3	Inner Treasury	12	Treasury	21	Ahmet III Fruit Room
4	Kitchens	13	Selim II Baths	22	Court of the Room of the Robe
5	Carriage Gate	14	Hall of the Expeditionary Force	23	Room of the Robe of the Prophet
6	Court of the Black Eunuchs	15	Hirkai-Serif Oda	24	Mustafa Pasha Kiosk
7	Barrack of the Black Eunuchs	16	Mosque of the Agas	25	Physician's Tower
8	Council Chamber, Hall of the Divan	17	Baghdad Kiosk	26	Hall of the Treasury
9	Gate of Felicity	18	Golden Bower of Ibrahim I	27	Hall of the Pantry

Istanbul, plan of the Topkapı Palace

and gardens, and the palace proper consists of a series of detached buildings and pavilions informally arranged around four irregular spacious courts. It was the seat of government, as well as the residence for the sultan's family and household, well into the nineteenth century, when Abdul Mecit finally moved the court to the Italianate Dolmabahçe Palace. Mehmet's early buildings are still partially in evidence, and consist of the Çinili Kiosk, the Gate of Majesty, the Orta Kapı, the inner Treasury, sections of the kitchens and the range of buildings which

served as his pavilion overlooking the Sea of Marmara. Mehmet's palace was exclusively a centre of government and administration, and it was Beyazit II who established the harem. Throughout the reigns of Beyazit and Süleyman the harem consisted of wooden pavilions until Murat rebuilt it with more permanent materials.

Unlike most Muslim palaces, the various functions of the Topkapı buildings are reasonably well documented. The first court encloses the outer grounds and contains little today except the ruins of the Byzantine church of St Irene. The main palace buildings begin in the second court, which includes on the far left the entrance to the harem, the Council Chamber in the Hall of the Divan, the inner Treasury and along the right hand side of the court an extensive range of kitchens, with their distinctive chimneys, added by Sinan after the fire of 1574. At the centre of the north side of the court is the Gate of Felicity, with its rococo decoration, which played an important ceremonial role and beyond which the public had no access. It led directly to the Throne Room in the third court, dating from the time of Selim I, where foreign ambassadors were received. Behind the Throne Room is the eighteenth-century library of Ahmet III, and on the east side are the new Treasury buildings built by Mehmet II, the baths of Selim II and the Hall of the Expeditionary Force. Many of the buildings in this court served as the palace school where the corps of pages, *devşirme* youths, received their rigorous training to serve the empire. The school was founded by Mehmet II, and consisted of six halls for junior and senior students administered by the White Eunuchs who were accommodated in rooms flanking the Gate of Felicity.

Istanbul, Topkapı Palace: the Baghdad Kiosk

The Hall of the Expeditionary Force, now housing the collection of Sultan's costumes, may have served as a dormitory or gymnasium for the pages of the palace school. They also used the adjacent baths where Selim II met his fatal accident. The north-west corner of the court contains the Hırkai-Serif Oda (Pavilion of the Holy Mantle) four domed chambers which house holy relics – including the swords of the first four caliphs, the mantle of the Prophet, his standard, footprint and seal – brought to Istanbul following Selim I's conquest of Egypt and the Hijaz in 1517. After this expedition he became protector of the holy places and claimed the title of caliph. Selim's conquests had enormous impact on the Muslim world, and his historical importance, in this respect, was much greater than that of Süleyman the Magnificent. Süleyman is better known in the West because of his close diplomatic links with Europe and his threat to Vienna. The rooms of the Hırkaı-Serif Oda were established by Mehmet II, but restored and tiled by Murat III, with later additions by Mahmut II. Between the Hırkai-Serif Oda and the Mosque of the Agas are the quarters of the senior officers and students of the household, the most senior hall of the palace school.

The fourth court, with its relaxed air of informality, is essentially a private garden containing a number of loosely arranged pavilions, providing secluded retreats with beautiful views of the city, the Golden Horn and Bosphorus. The most attractive of the pavilions is the Baghdad Kiosk built by the architect Hasan Aga for Murat IV in 1638 following the capture of Baghdad. It has a central dome set on a cruciform arrangement of four *iwans* which project out from the central circle under broad-eaved roofs. Each *iwan* contains four windows illuminating a recess with a low divan sofa. Its interior is rich and intimate, made up of floral patterned Iznik tiles in green, yellow, blue and white, with a continuous frieze of calligraphy above the lower windows. The doors and cupboards are inlaid with shimmering stellar patterns of mother-of-pearl, and flanking corner panels are pierced by shelves forming deep niches shaped like bell-jars. The focal point of the room is the bronze chimney breast (the *ocak*), and the whole interior is crowned by a red dome gilded with arabesques and stars like a richly embroidered palanquin. Sharing the same terrace, and commanding a view of the Golden Horn, is the exotic golden bower of

Ibrahim I, a pool with a fountain, and Murat IV's Revan Kiosk, which served as a religious retreat.

The harem consists of a maze of courts and small rooms, approximately three hundred in total, housing the sultan's family and household. Before the Topkapı became residential, the harem was located in Mehmet's old palace near Beyazit Square. When Süleyman's wife, Roxelana, moved to the Topkapı, she took one hundred ladies in waiting, as well as a large retinue of domestic staff. Murat III installed 1,200 women in the harem, and the palace complex as a whole accommodated 5,000 people most of whom, including children, concubines, slaves, eunuchs and servants, were housed in the harem. In these quarters the Queen Mother (Sultan Valide) was in charge of domestic affairs, and her enormous power frequently extended well into the political sphere. The harem was full of bitter intrigue and rivalry, and its crowded, confined and enclosed world is reflected in the concentrated labyrinthine nature of its architecture. Its unassailable and protected ethos is immediately felt on entering through the Carriage Gate, which opens on to the court and barracks of the harem's formidable guardians, the Black Eunuchs. The entrance to the harem proper leads to the quarters of the women officials and a large two-storeyed court containing apartments belonging to the Sultan Valide. Many of these buildings were built after the fire of 1665, and most, like the Hall of the Hearth, show accretions of refurbishment reflecting subsequent changes in Ottoman taste.

The largest room in the harem is the sixteenth-century Throne Room, probably the work of Sinan, although much altered by the eighteenth-century 'baroque' decorations of Osman III. The room is broadly divided into two, with a gallery for musicians, and the wall spaces are broken by panels banded in red and gold with baroque mirrors and wall fountains. Unlike the public Throne Room which received foreign ambassadors and guests, this Throne Room was strictly private, being reserved for the reception and entertainment of women. Next to this is Murat III's bedroom which retains Sinan's

Istanbul, Topkapı Palace: the Throne Room

original decor. Its harmony of conception undoubtedly makes it the most beautiful room in the Topkapı, but as Hillenbrand observes, its evocation of mosque architecture also endows it with a hint of blasphemy.[10] The room is lined with the finest floral Iznik tiling which is punctuated here and there by deep niched shelving, and the east wall is embellished by a magnificent recessed three-tiered fountain framed by a hipped arch. An elegant calligraphic frieze of white characters on blue ground runs round the room, and at the centre of the west wall, flanked by windows and two gilded canopied beds, stands a bronze *ocak* framed by tiles with pear blossom motifs. The dome is red with richly gilded arabesques containing a circlet of calligraphy in the centre.

The multiplicity of Murat's surviving male offspring posed a problem of succession, with tragic consequences. Murat's eldest son, Mehmet III, claimed the sultanate and was advised by his mother, Baffo, to safeguard his succession by invoking the law of fratricide (*zanan-nameh*) and execute his nineteen brothers. In the absence of a law

Istanbul, Topkapı Palace: the 'Fruit Room' of Ahmet III

of primogenitor (which was not established until the seventeenth century), *zanan-nameh* had been introduced by Mehmet II in order to avoid the greater bloodshed caused by previous wars of succession. The strangulation of Mehmet's brothers was the last brutal application of this law. Future younger princes were incarcerated in a building known as the Kafes, or Cage, in the heart of the harem. Two fine rooms, close to Murat's bedroom, have until recently been identified as the Kafes. They form a kiosk and were built either by Murat III, or Ahmet I, and contain some of the best tilework in the harem, although many of the originals have now been replaced by modern copies. In addition to the tiles, the colour of these sumptuous, claustrophobic rooms is enhanced by the golden bronze of the *ocak* and jewel-like intensity of the stained glass set in delicate gilded window grills. The original dome, painted on canvas, is remarkably well preserved, due to the fact that until recently it was masked by the later addition of a false ceiling.

Similarly, much of the original sixteenth and seventeenth-century decor has been covered and refurbished and reveals changes in style and the onset of European influence. One of the finest and most delightful rooms in the harem is the small eighteenth-century dining room of Ahmet III, known as the 'Fruit Room'. Its interior display of mirrors set in painted panels of pastel coloured flowers and fruit is pure Ottoman rococo.

Michael Levey makes the point that during the eighteenth century, when diplomatic contact between the Ottoman Empire and Europe became more relaxed, there was a happy concordance between French rococo and Ottoman court taste.[11] Turkey, and *turquerie*, had caught the European imagination, and here was an intriguing synthesis between East and West, which was made possible by a state of cultural equality and mutual respect. In the nineteenth century, however, Europe became the dominant partner, and western cultural imperialism gradually corrupted, weakened and in some cases, destroyed the possibility of meaningful continuity, change, or renewal within Islam's great architectural tradition.

Rather than trace the decline of Ottoman architecture, this chapter concludes with a consideration of the last great classical Ottoman mosque, that of Sultan Ahmet I (the Blue Mosque). It exhibits a flowering of Ottoman confidence and splendour, and it is ironic that this ostentation should follow a period of political decline and humiliation. Situated opposite Haghia Sophia, and begging comparison with it, this building became the pre-eminent mosque of Istanbul and the focus of ceremonial, as imperial processions made their way to the Friday prayers from the Topkapı Palace. Its opulence reflects Sultan Ahmet's personality, for he was neither abstemious nor pious, and like his immediate predecessors enjoyed his leisure and the luxury of the harem. It was commissioned at great expense, against much religious opposition, and involved the purchase and demolition of a number of palaces situated beside the ancient hippodrome. The architect was Mehmet Aga, a *devşirme* recruit, who had been a musician and worker of mother-of-pearl before graduating, via Sinan's drawing office, to become imperial architect. The Blue Mosque, begun in 1609, was to be his major work, and he died in 1617 just after its completion.

Architecturally it represents a consolidation on the grand scale of what was already achieved. The most notable exterior features are the six slender minarets, four framing the architectural pile of the prayer hall, like the Selimiye, and two flanking the northern façade of the court. In plan it follows Sinan's Şehzade mosque with the *sahn* and prayer hall forming two equal boxes of open and closed space. Like the Şehzade, the prayer hall has a quatrefoil plan, but the central dome is smaller, and the half-domes and exedra appear constricted and shallow compared to Sinan's amply arranged plan. The main body of the mosque and *sahn* are contained within a wider precinct wall, of which only the north wall remains fronting on to the hippodrome. To the south of this enclosure were the *külliye* buildings consisting of a *madrasa*, *türbe*, kitchens, caravansarai, school, *maristan* and bazaar. The plan, distribution and alignment of the mosque and *külliye* buildings take account of the Haghia Sophia, which is drawn into and plays a crucial monumental role in this grand spatial design.

This mosque has always been a favourite with the general public, and because of its situation it is the best known and most visited by tourists. Its sumptuousness, compared to the disciplined austerity of the Süleymaniye, naturally gives it more immediate and popular appeal. Architectural historians, though, have not been generous in their assessment. Mehmet Aga was not a great

engineer, and the four great piers carrying the superstructure of the dome are cumbersome. The *muqarnas* in the spandrels of the arches overlap the voussoirs in a ragged and unresolved manner. Nevertheless, the building has a splendour and magic that more than compensate for these flaws. It is lightened by the high quality of the extensive tiling in the galleries and its painted decoration. The heaviness of the piers is relieved by fluting, gilded calligraphy and painted flourishes of floral motifs. The recent restoration has produced a rich and radiant colour balance in which the dominant cool blue of the gallery tiles is complemented by the gradual introduction of warmer reds, oranges and gold in the higher reaches of the building. As well as tiled, painted and gilded surfaces, its interior was illuminated with Venetian stained glass, and the doors and shutters provide further embellishment with inlaid ivory, mother-of-pearl and sea-tortoise shell.

Outside the south-east corner of the mosque a ramp leads up to the rooms of the royal kiosk, which in turn lead to the royal loggia occupying a section of the gallery inside the mosque. The royal kiosk and loggia mark the terminus of weekly ceremonial, but the mosque's regal and imperial ethos is elsewhere reinforced at every level by its scale, the splendour of its interior and its prestigious location. Michael Levey draws comparison between this and contemporary works by Shah Abbas I in Isfahan.[12] Both Shah Abbas and Sultan Ahmet cultivated splendid courts and shared an opulent taste and enthusiasm for building and the arts. Their mosques, impressively situated in major public spaces, express courtly magnificence rather than religious piety. They are representative of the spectacular flowering of the arts in a number of lavish courts in the seventeenth-century Muslim world, including the Moghul courts of Jahangir and Shah Jahan. Such extravagance and luxury inevitably lead to decay if the fruits of that art become over-ripe. They did, and the seventeenth century across the eastern Muslim world became a prelude to artistic and political decline. Before examining this state of affairs, it is necessary to look back and consider the evolution and climax of architectural achievement in Persia and Mughal India before decline set in.

OPPOSITE
Istanbul, the Sultan Ahmet Cami (Blue Mosque)

CHAPTER 10

ILKHANID, TIMURID AND SAFAVID ARCHITECTURE

The Mongol invasions of the thirteenth century had a devastating impact on the Muslim world, but it was from the ashes of this destruction that some of Islam's finest architecture emerged. After uniting the Mongol tribes in 1205, Chengiz Khan invaded north-west China, overran the Kin Empire and captured Beijing in 1215. He then turned his attention to Central Asia and sent an exploratory trade mission to Samarqand where his merchants met the Khwarazm Shah, Muhammad II. Suspecting that these merchants were spies, Muhammad ungraciously beheaded them, a diplomatic outrage that gave Chengiz Khan the excuse to attack Persia. Overwhelmed by the onslaught of the Mongol army, Muhammad fled west, and within a few years Chengiz Khan had conquered Transoxiana and northern Persia, reaching as far west as Azerbaijan. The great cities of Transoxiana were completely destroyed: Bukhara in 1220, then Samarqand, Balkh, Merv and Nishapur. Those cities that resisted were burned to the ground and frequently every living person and creature destroyed. Sometimes women and children were taken into captivity, but the male inhabitants were invariably slaughtered, except (significantly) artists, artisans and scholars. Samarqand and Bukhara were eventually rebuilt, but many cities were completely obliterated and the population of that region has never recovered.

Chengiz Khan died in 1227, and his empire was divided among the eldest sons of his senior wife Börte. Ögödae succeeded Chengiz Khan as Great Khan and ruled the khanate of East Asia, which included Mongolia and most of China. He was succeeded by his nephew Mangu Khan, who with his brother, Kublai Khan, completed the conquest of China. Kublai Khan eventually became Great Khan and established the Yuan dynasty in China, ruling from the new capital of Beijing. Kublai's other brother, Hülägu, established the Ilkhanid dynasty in Persia and penetrated farther into the Muslim world, capturing the rest of Persia, Armenia, Georgia and Iraq. Baghdad fell in 1258, and the caliphate was destroyed with it. The death of the caliph was a symbolic blow to the Muslim world, but the office was revived three years later by the Mamluk Sultan Baibars.

The religious identity of the Mongols was complex and varied. As a loose federation of tribes, they had previously embraced Nestorian Christianity, Shamanism and Buddhism. Although he regarded himself as an instrument of God, Chengiz Khan's religious position was equivocal. His grandson, Batu, adhered to Shamanism with its belief in one God, as well as the divinity of the Sun, Moon, Earth and Water. When Güyük was elected Great Khan, Nestorian Christianity flourished under Mongol rule and Christians held high offices of state, though it is doubtful if Güyük himself became a Christian. Under Möngke, religious toleration prevailed, and the Mongol capital, Karakorum, was famous for its churches, mosques and Buddhist temples. Toleration was also exercised under the Buddhist Ilkhanid rulers Abaqa and Arghun, but this inclusive spirit ended with the accession of Ghazan Khan, the first Ilkhanid ruler to convert to Islam. Ghazan Khan was a strong and uncompromising leader who severed his allegiance to the Great Khan and set about the task of strengthening the Muslim identity of Persia. Initially, this encouraged intolerance towards non-Muslims, and many temples, churches and synagogues were destroyed.

Beginning with Hülagü, the Mongols gradually began to rebuild on the devastation they had wrought. Ghazan Khan built a huge complex, now in complete ruins, in the suburb of Shenb near Tabriz in Persia. The focal point was his own tomb, the Ghazaniya, a do-decagonal structure with a dome, possibly 42 metres high. Contemporary accounts also describe the building of two *madrasas* devoted to the Hanafi and Shafi'i schools of law, as well as a *khanqah*, *maristan*, library, academy, observatory and palace. These foundations reflect Ghazan's scholarly personality and his interests in medicine, astronomy, natural history, chemistry and architecture. His equally learned vizir, Rashid ad Din, distinguished for his encyclopaedic world history, the *Jami' at Tavarikh*, continued the cultural embellishment of Tabriz by establishing a university in the eastern suburbs which accommodated over a thousand students. Outside Shenb and Tabriz, Ghazan ordered the building of a mosque and public baths in every city. The baths in particular signalled change in Mongol attitudes, because their slow conversion to Islam was reputedly attributed to a nomadic reluctance to wash.[1] Ghazan encouraged communications and trade between East and West, and Tabriz considerably increased its reputation as a major commercial city with a cosmopolitan population. Its international character was vividly described by Marco Polo some years earlier when he stayed there for several months during the reign of Ghazan's predecessor, Ghaykhatu. He describes a population made up of Armenians, Georgians, Jacobites, Nestorians and Latins.[2] The Latins were mainly Genoese and Venetians, and during Ghazan's rule the Chinese population, consisting of physicians, scholars and engineers, increased considerably.

Ghazan's younger brother, Oljeitu, succeeded him, and his great building enterprise was the creation of a new capital at Sultaniya between Tabriz and Varamin. Little survives of this city today except his mausoleum (1309), which is a seminal masterpiece foreshadowing Sinan's Selimiya in Edirne and the Taj Mahal. It moves on from some of the more ambitious later Seljuk mausolea, such as Sultan Sanjar's at Merv and the Jabal i Sang at Kirman. Like the Jabal i Sang, Oljeitu's mausoleum is a domed octagon 53 metres high, monumental in scale, which raises questions regarding religious propriety. Despite the Prophet's disapproval of funerary ostentation, the mausoleum evolved as a major category of Islamic architecture. Its position in Persia took on an increasingly significant and symbolic role due to the influence of Sufism and the growth of Shi'ism. Tombs of revered Sufi saints became a part of the urban landscape, but the tombs of the Prophet's descendants (known as *imamzadas*), including those of the Shi'ite Imams, and their relatives and descendants, have a high religious and political profile.

Oljeitu converted to Shi'ism and visited the tombs of Ali and Husain at Najaf and Karbala in Iraq. It was claimed that his intention was to move the bodies of Ali and Husain and inter them in his mausoleum, so making Sultaniya a major centre for Shi'a pilgrims. If this were true, it might explain the reason for the additional chamber on the south side of the octagonal core of the mausoleum. Ali's name appears in Kufic inscriptions of brick and faience throughout the mausoleum, and Oljeitu issued a new coinage struck with Ali's name. Further evidence of his conversion to Shi'ism has already been observed in his beautiful stucco *mihrab* (1310) with its Shi'ite *shahada* in the winter gallery of the Masjid i Jami in Isfahan. Oljeitu attempted to impose the Shi'ite faith on all of Persia but there was great resistance, and eventually he was persuaded back to the Sunni fold. It has

Sultaniya: the mausoleum of Sultan Oljeitu

Sultaniya: the mausoleum of Sultan Oljeitu

been suggested that evidence of this change of direction can be seen in the mausoleum itself where a new decorative scheme, consisting of extensive carved and painted stucco, was introduced to overlay much of the original brick and tile work.

The structural core of the mausoleum consists of an octagonal arrangement of tall pointed arches supporting a shallow zone of transition made up of horizontal bands of *muqarnas*. On this stands a light pointed dome 26 metres in diameter, which diminishes in thickness and weight as it reaches its apex. The solid brick piers that make up the supporting arches are varied in size and plan (up to 7 metres thick) and increase in width on the north side to form an expansive façade. The lateral pressure of the dome is contained within these piers, but despite their considerable mass the internal composition of double arcades, recessed and framed by eight principal arches, gives a feeling of dignity and grace. Following the precedent of the Tomb of the Samanids at Bukhara, the exterior design is articulated by an upper gallery with large triple windows piercing each face of the octagon, providing a light, open support for the dome. The gallery is covered with twenty-four vaults decorated with an extraordinary repertoire of geometric ornament, strapwork and arabesque executed in painted stucco. The open form of the upper gallery contrasts with the solidity of the first storey, which is pierced on three sides by tall pointed central entrances surmounted by triple arrangements of small narrow windows. The façade is relieved by panels of blind arcading originally set with tiles of blue faience which also cover the whole of the tapering dome. The dome remarkably is set within a circle of eight minarets at the corners of the octagon. These minarets, which reached the height of the dome's apex, were also covered with blue faience; the beginnings of that extensive use of tilework, characteristic of Persia and Central Asia, to adorn both interior and exterior surfaces. The mausoleum represents a landmark in architectural evolution, because its scale, centralised plan and grand conception, point the way to Mughal India.

Sultaniya never materialised as a Shi'ite centre of pilgrimage, but Mashhad and Qumm did, and there is no shortage elsewhere in Persia of holy shrines and tombs. Mashhad and Qumm respectively contain the tombs of the eighth Imam Riza and his sister, Fatima. Imam Riza

(765–817) lived during the caliphates of Harun al-Rashid and his son, Ma'mum. The latter decided that Imam Riza should be his successor in order to prevent bloodshed and to acknowledge the political aspirations of the Shi'ites. Ma'mum's strategy was probably both to draw the teeth of the Shi'ite opposition and to subvert the Imamate by giving Riza worldly powers. Riza accepted the succession on condition that his role was purely spiritual. The result was a dramatic increase in the number of Shi'ite converts, and Ma'mun had Riza quietly poisoned. He is buried near his old adversary Harun al-Rashid, and his tomb and shrine at Mashhad (meaning martyrium) are part of an extensive complex, including the Timurid masterpiece, the Gawhar Shad mosque.

The tomb of Imam Riza's sister, Fatima, is venerated in the holy city of Qumm. Here there are clusters of Ilkhanid *imamzada* tombs situated, as in many Persian cemeteries, on the outskirts of the town near the city gates. Isolated from the main pack of Ilkhanid tombs is the oldest, the Imamzada Ja'far (1278–79), which is octagonal in plan and crowned by an eight-sided pyramidal tent-dome. The later fourteenth-century tombs

Isfahan, the Imamzada Ja'far

are also octagonal, but the domes, usually of the sixteen-sided type, are set prominently on a drum at some length behind the outer walls. Exterior walls are battered with deep-pointed arched recessed panels, and the octagonal interiors are invariably capped with hemispherical domes. One recently restored Ilkhanid *imamzada* is the Imamzada Ja'fa at Isfahan (1325), built for a descendant of Imam Muhammad ibn Ali Baqir, the fifth Imam. Its form is octagonal with battered walls relieved by tall pointed recessed panels. A projecting cornice slightly masks the hemispherical dome, which has a somewhat shallow appearance from the outside. The tilework is in light blue, dark blue and white and is concentrated in panels above the entrance, on the spandrels of the recessed arches and in horizontal bands of geometry and calligraphy on and below the cornice. Glazed tiles form an elegant geometric trellis in the dome, and there is a fine overall balance between mosaic faience and the textured surfaces of biscuit-coloured brick. The sunlight picks out the horizontal courses of brick in sharp relief and reveals a satisfying contrast of glazed and matt surfaces, warm and cold colours.

Following the Seljuk tradition, there are notable tombs of the flanged type. The tomb tower of 'Ala ad Din at Varamin (1299) is circular with thirty-two right-angled flanges on the outside supporting a conical outer dome. Decoration is restricted to a horizontal band beneath the dome consisting of calligraphy surmounted by strapwork panels executed in light blue faience and terracotta. The interior is circular, capped with a hemispherical inner dome. Another flanged tomb is at Bastam, northern Iran (1308–9), a site developed around the shrine of the mystic Bayazid al-Bistami. The tomb, like that at the Çifte Minare Madrasa at Erzurum, is behind the *qibla* wall of the mosque. The exterior is made up of twenty-five right-angled flanges crowned with two bands of inscription contained in square panels executed in faience. One notable deviation from the flanged type is the tomb tower at Radkan (1280–1300), which is dodecagonal in plan and ribbed with thirty-six engaged round shafts. The patterned ribs extend from a dodecagonal base and terminate in a trefoil niche, above which is a calligraphic frieze in terracotta and light blue faience. The double dome is conical outside and hemispherical inside, covering an octagonal interior.

Despite being the first capital of the dynasty, Tabriz has only one surviving free-standing Ilkhanid monument, the Masjid i Jami of Ali Shah (1310–20). All that remains is the ruin of the massive brick *iwan* and *qibla* wall. The *iwan* spans just over 30 metres and the side wall is 10.5 metres thick. The springing of the arch is 25 metres from the ground and the great *iwan* vault, which collapsed soon after construction, is estimated to have been 45 metres high. It is a colossal structure which was built to exceed in scale the great Sasanian arch at Ctesiphon. This single *iwan* faced an arcaded *sahn*; the interior was quite sumptuous and decorated with mosaic faience and gilded surfaces. Like the mausoleum of Oljeitu, the Masjid i Jami of Ali Shah displays a magnitude of scale that distinguishes Ilkhanid architecture from that of its Seljuk predecessors. Its bulk probably also reflects the ambitious personality of Ali Shah, who ruthlessly eliminated his more cultured rival, Rashid ad Din, to secure his vizirate. On a much lighter scale, the taller proportions typical of Ilkhanid architecture can be seen in the Masjid i Jami in Yazd (1325). The vertical thrust of the attenuated *iwan* entrance portal, surmounted by tall paired minarets,

Yazd: the entrance portal to the Masjid i Jami

seems out of scale with the adjacent building. Its dramatic, ceremonial impact foreshadows the spirit of triumphalism in later Mughal architecture, such as Akbar's victory gate, the Buland Darwaza, forming the main entrance to the Jami Masjid in Fatehpur Sikri. Another distinctive feature of this mosque is the arrangement of two spacious vaulted prayer halls which flank the domed sanctuary.

One of the most beautiful surviving structures of the late Ilkhanid period is the recently restored Masjid i Jami at Varamin (1326), Persia. Constructed within five years, it expresses with remarkable unity of form the classic four-*iwan* plan. Compared to later mosques of this type, the square format of the *sahn* is small in relation to the surrounding *riwaqs*, *iwans* and lofty scale of the sanctuary *iwan* and dome. The square dome chamber is topped by a zone of transition consisting of an octagon of alternating blind arches and brick *muqarnas* squinches, carrying a sixteen-sided structure which forms a lantern supporting the dome. The quality of decoration, made up of brick, plaster and blue faience, is distinguished. Diagonals, squares and herring-bone patterns are formed by bonding, raising, depressing and moulding the brick work. Plaster friezes of fluid arabesque and Naskhi calligraphy complement the geometric designs of light and dark blue glazed faience set in unglazed terracotta.

The development of glazed tiles is one of the glories of the Ilkhanid period. The Kashan potteries, which were pre-eminent during the Seljuk period, survived the destructive Mongol invasions, and produced during the early fourteenth century some remarkable glazed *mihrabs* and cenotaphs distinguished for their lustre, resonance and depth of colour. These *mihrabs*, made up of several tiled panels, were moulded in relief and densely painted in blue, turquoise and white, with a lustre overglaze. Fine examples include the *mihrab* from the Imamzadah Yahya at Varamin (1305) (St Petersburg, Hermitage), the *mihrab* from the Masjid i Maydan at Kashan (1325) (Islamic Museum in Berlin) and the cenotaph of Qadi Jala al-Din Ali (British Museum). They display an extraordinary verve and tension between the symmetry of the high relief and the free brushwork of the background arabesques. A number of these was produced by one distinguished family in Kashan, Abu Tahir and his descendants. The Muzaffarids, immediate successors to the Ilkhanids, used

tile decoration over the whole external surface of discrete sections of buildings (such as portals), and not just on domes, panels and friezes. The entrance portal to the Masjid i Jami in Kirman inaugurated this lavish and opulent use of tile decoration which is seen in later Timurid and Safavid architecture.

The Timurid age, which produced some of Islam's most vivid architecture, was established in the wake of Tamerlane's military campaigns. Born in Kish in 1336, Tamerlane, or Timur, was the Turkish chief of the Barlas tribe. He assembled a considerable army of Turkish and Mongol troops, and like Chengiz Khan before him set out on a series of wars which established an empire covering northern India, Persia, the Caucasus, Armenia, Georgia, Mesopotamia, Anatolia and northern Syria. His death in 1405 thwarted his ultimate ambition to recreate the empire of Chengiz Khan and rule China. Tamerlane was a soldier but unlike Chengiz Khan and Hülägu failed to implement any adequate long-term machinery of government in the conquered territories. His campaigns were brutal, and the atrocities committed worse than those of his Mongol predecessors, although fewer cities were razed to the ground. He was, according to Bertold Spuler, an uneducated but intelligent man, who showed only a utilitarian regard for the arts and learning.[2] Nevertheless, he admired architecture and recognised its contribution to the prestige and glorification of his own capital at Samarqand. In the course of his campaigns conscripted artists and artisans were forcibly sent there, and as we have observed in the Yeşil Cami and *türbe* at Bursa, the ultimate consequence was to create and spread an international Timurid style.

The city of Samarqand had been completely destroyed during the first Mongol invasion of 1220, but rebuilding took place during Tamarshirin Khan's reign in 1326. Tamerlane's first major building project in Samarqand was the Bibi Khanum Mosque, a huge structure of four-*iwan* type with a *sahn* measuring 74 by 64 metres. Inspired by Oljeitu's mosque in Sultaniya in Persia, it was built to impress, with a huge main entrance portal 18 metres wide and 30 metres high, flanked by enormous buttressing minarets. Smaller minarets articulated the corners of the mosque, and the sanctuary *iwan* echoes in scale that of the entrance portal with two tall flanking minarets. The massive brick construction in the

TOP
Samarqand, the mosque of Bibi Khanum from the north-east

ABOVE
Samarqand, the mosque of Bibi Khanum: showing the mosque and left minaret from the entrance

TOP
Samarqand, the mausoleum of Gur i Amir from the south-east

ABOVE
Samarqand, the mausoleum of Gur i Amir: illustrating the portal of the entrance from the north

main entrance *iwan* and sanctuary dome chamber is complemented by the lighter structure of over four hundred domed bays which made up the hypostyle halls behind the *riwaqs*. The sanctuary was crowned with a double dome, hemispherical inside and bulbous outside, which sprang from a tall drum – a feature that became a defining characteristic of Timurid architecture. Bulbous domes set on high drums also appear above the innovative dome chambers set behind the smaller lateral *iwans* facing the *sahn*.

One of the most beautiful domes in the Muslim world is the ribbed, melon-shaped dome that crowns Tamerlane's mausoleum, the Gur i Amir, in Samarqand. Built in 1404 by Muhammad ibn Mahmud of Isfahan for

Tamerlane's grandson, Muhammad Sultan, who died in 1402 fighting Beyazit I at the battle of Ankara, it later became a dynastic tomb for Tamerlane and his line. The tomb faces a *sahn*, which was originally flanked by a *madrasa* and *khanqah*. Cruciform on the inside, and octagonal outside, the tomb chamber supports a double dome. The pointed inner dome is contained within the tall cylindrical drum from which springs the high profile of the ribbed bulbous outer dome. On the outside the tall drum is covered with large elegant Kufic inscriptions surmounted by a cornice of horizontal bands of *muqarnas* from which spring the dome's sixty-four ribs covered with brilliant blue tiles. Timur's male descendants were interred in the tomb, but the women were buried in the nearby cemetery of Shah i Zinda which developed around the sacred mausoleum of Qutham ibn Abbas, a companion of the Prophet. A *madrasa* and a number of early tombs were built near the saint's mausoleum, and during the Timurid period the necropolis was extended along a street which terminates at a monumental gate built by Ulughbeg in 1428. The tomb chambers are mainly square, with domes of varied type, displaying circular and flanged ribs as well as smooth tiled surfaces set on tall attenuated drums. Vivid mosaic tilework, using turquoise, cobalt, black, white and golden buff, is restricted to the

Samarqand, mausoleum of Gur i Amir: mosaic design on a tile arch

domes and drums as well as a number of elaborate portals which face the street. A fine example is the portal of Shirin Bika Aqqa with its beautiful flourishes of flanking Naskhi inscriptions picked out in white against a background of turquoise and cobalt.

Outside Samarqand, Tamerlane created the vast palace of Aqsaray at his birthplace in Kish (which he renamed Shahr i Sabz). Babur, founder of the Mughal dynasty, described its four-*iwan* layout with central arcaded court, pool and imposing audience chamber *iwan* which begged comparison with Ctesiphon. All that remains is the ruin of a gigantic portal, 22 metres wide and 56 metres high, flanked by round bastions, polygonal at the base and richly decorated with tiles executed by craftsmen from Tabriz. His other major work, still in a

Turkestan City, the shrine of Ahmad Yasavi

good state of preservation, is the shrine of Ahmed Yasavi in Turkestan City, formerly Yasi in Kazakhstan. Ahmed Yasavi, who lived in the twelfth century, was the founder of a Sufi order and his tomb became a major centre of pilgrimage. Tamerlane rebuilt the shrine as a funerary *khanqah* combining a number of utilities in a remarkably cohesive form. Set within a rectangular plan, it is a free-standing structure with a sculpturally compact profile. Its high entrance portal marks the apex of a design that falls rhythmically from this point through the central dome to the bulbous mausoleum dome and its flanking subsidiaries at the rear. The side walls are decorated with glazed bricks forming geometric patterns of rectilinear Kufic and a cornice band of Naskhi calligraphy. A large deep *iwan* forms the entrance portal leading to a domed square meeting hall in the centre of the building where the Sufi ceremonies, or *dhikr*, took place. Beyond this is the tomb of the saint under a tall *muqarnas* vault set within a drum, which carries the melon-shaped outer dome. Numerous rooms flank the main axis of the central hall and tomb, including a mosque, library, kitchens, baths and meditation rooms. Throughout the building the vaulting is complex, varied and inventive, and the extensive use of brick *muqarnas* in the central hall and tomb richly contributes to that balance between diversity and unity which characterises the whole structure.

Tamerlane's successor, Shah Rukh, was a more cultivated man, and during his reign Timurid architecture evolved that vibrant vocabulary of colour and form which was to determine the language of Persian architecture

Mashhad: the mosque of Gawhar Shad

well into the Safavid age and beyond. Two of the most beautiful buildings to emerge are named after his wife, Gawhar Shad, who was a formidable personality and a major patron of the arts. The Gawhar Shad Mosque at Mashhad (1418) and the *musalla* and *madrasa* of Gawhar Shad at Herat (1417) are the products of her influence and patronage. The Timurids were Sunni Muslims, but the Gawhar Shad Mosque at Mashhad was built to enhance and extend the shrine of Imam Riza, and as Blair and Bloom suggest was probably intended to appease the Shi'ites.[3] The mosque is of the four-*iwan* type, and the architect, Qavam al-Din of Shiraz, extended the northern side, adding two assembly rooms which connect the mosque to the tomb. There is no external façade or entrance portal, and access is mainly through the tomb complex. The visual impact of the mosque is best experienced from within the *sahn*, which is surrounded by two tiers of *riwaqs* and dominated by the sanctuary *iwan* flanked by tall engaged tower minarets. Every surface is vividly covered with brilliant tile mosaic, and it is probably appropriate here to quote Robert Byron, whose elegant description most matches its lyricism and beauty of form.[4]

> The whole quadrangle was a garden of turquoise, pink, dark red, and dark blue, with touches of purple, green, and yellow, planted among paths of plain buff brick. Huge white arabesques whirled above the *iwan* arches. The *iwans* themselves hid other gardens, shadier, fritillary-coloured. The great minarets beside the sanctuary, rising from bases encircled with Kufic the size of a boy, were bedizened with a network of jewelled lozenges. The swollen

sea-green dome adorned with yellow tendrils appeared between them. At the opposite end glinted the top of a gold minaret. But in all this variety, the principle of union, the life-spark of the whole blazing apparition, was kindled by two great texts: the one, a frieze of white *suls* writing powdered over a field of gentian blue along the skyline of the entire quadrangle; the other, a border of the same alphabet in daisy white and yellow on a sapphire field, interlaced with turquoise Kufic along its inner edge, and enclosing, in the form of a three-sided oblong, the arch of the main *iwan* between the minarets.[5]

The latter inscription, as Robert Byron observes, was designed by Shah Rukh's son, Baisanghor, who became one of the leading calligraphers of his day.

At Herat the same architect, Qavam al-Din, was commissioned to design the Gawhar Shad *musalla* and *madrasa*. Unfortunately only one minaret in the *musalla* survives, and all that remains of the *madrasa* is one minaret and the mausoleum. In anticipation of a siege at Herat by the Russians in 1885, the emir, acting on the advice of British officers, ordered the destruction of what was left of the Gawhar Shad *musalla* and *madrasa* in order to deprive the invading Russians of cover. The tile mosaic in the surviving minaret shows a perfection of design and subtlety of colour, which exceeds, in Robert Byron's opinion, that of the Gawhar Shad in Mashhad.[6] The mausoleum was one of a pair which formed a part of the *qibla* end of the *madrasa*. Like the Gur i Amir in Samarqand, it consists of a ribbed dome over a cruciform inner chamber, but the cross-vaulted interior is far more refined. Four intersecting arches support the dome and divide the structure into various squinches, conches and domelets. The rosette plan of the vault is reminiscent of the dome clusters of Ottoman buildings, and this may account for the gentler concavities of squinch, conch and dome. These sections are not deeply compartmentalised, and the fluid transition from one surface to another is facilitated by the delicate plaster work with its incised shell-like motifs, fans and finely cut *muqarnas*.

Samarqand, the Shirda Madrasa in the Rigistan

Another *madrasa* by Qavam al-Din is the Ghiyathiya Madrasa at Khargird eastern Iran, which is distinguished by its fine proportions and symmetry of design. The square *sahn* is of the four-*iwan* type, with equal sized *iwans* and bevelled corners. Behind the double arcades of the *sahn* are sixteen students' rooms, and flanking the main entrance are two cruciform chambers which display something of the vaulting ingenuity of the Gawhar Shad Madrasa. One chamber has a *mihrab* and served as a mosque, while the other, carrying an octagonal lantern, was probably an assembly hall. Domed cruciform rooms in the corners of *madrasas* became a Timurid feature; they served as tombs, lecture rooms, assembly halls, mosques or oratories. As Hillenbrand observes, this diversity of purpose, masked by the standard four-*iwan* façade, gradually conflates both the visual and functional distinction between mosque and *madrasa*.[7] Another distinguishing feature of the Timurid *madrasa* is its grand scale, and in some instances (as at Bukhara and Samarqand) there is a monumental massing and grouping of a number of *madrasas* together. The Rigistan at Samarqand is a striking architectural ensemble consisting of the royal *madrasa* by Ulughbeg (1417–21) and two seventeenth-century *madrasas*, the Shirdar (1616–36) and the Tilikari (1646–60). In this extraordinary public space Ulughbeg also built a *khanqah*, but this was destroyed in the seventeenth century to make way for the Shirdar Madrasa. The seeds of Mughal architecture can be detected in the horizontal sweep of Ulughbeg's royal *madrasa*, with its imposing central portal and flanking double arcades framed by engaged tower minarets with blue cupolas. The lofty *mihrab* dome marks the position of the mosque which is laterally arranged and three bays deep, along the *qibla* side of the *sahn*. The other three sides of the *sahn* are made up of fifty students' rooms, and within each corner of the *madrasa* are four cruciform chambers which probably carried domes in similar fashion to those flanking the *iwan* portal of the Shirdar Madrasa opposite. As in later Mamluk buildings, in Timurid architecture the changing proportion of mosque *vis-à-vis* student accommodation gradually created a more composite structure which combined both functions.

Women provided the patronage for the finest Timurid buildings, and among the best of the later period is the Blue Mosque (Masjid i Muzaffariya) in Tabriz, commissioned by Saliha Khanum, the daughter of the Qaraqoyunlu ruler, Jahanshah (1465). Its geographical proximity to Anatolia, and the harsher climate of Tabriz, explain why the architecture of this mosque is closer to early Ottoman structures. Instead of the open four-*iwan* plan there is an enclosed, domed structure, surrounded on three sides by a domed ambulatory. Eight piers supported a gallery and central dome, 16 metres in diameter, but this collapsed in an earthquake along with the minarets. The tilework is the best of its period with exceptionally fine tile mosaic in the *iwan* of the entrance portal. The blue cable moulding around the arch is delicately picked out in white, black, gold and lustre, while the side panels display elegant arabesques in buff, cobalt and light turquoise, lightened and punctuated with white Chinese lotus flowers. The same lotus motifs with turquoise stems can be seen in repeat patterns against unglazed brick on the piers of the main dome chamber. Its opulent splendour reflects the courtly patronage that made it possible, and it provides a magnificent conclusion to a period which vividly orchestrated colour and architectural form in a manner that has never been surpassed.

Samarqand, the Rigistan: Shirdar Madrasa

Courtly splendour, with a lighter, more lyrical touch, reached its ultimate climax in the Safavid court of Shah Abbas I in the early seventeenth century. It was he who re-established Isfahan as the capital of Persia, creating a city that one poet described as 'half of the world'. The extravagance of his court belied the pious origins of the Safavid dynasty, which began as a religious movement. The lineage of the Safavid family is obscure, despite their claim to be descendants of the Prophet through the seventh Imam, Musa al-Kasim. Such a claim ensured their Shi'ite pedigree, but their religious authority was rooted in the Safaviyya Sufi order which their founder, Shaikh Safi al-Din, established in Ardabil at the beginning of the fourteenth century. Under the leadership of his successor, Junayd, the spiritual affairs of the order became subordinate to the radical political agenda he spearheaded, and the movement became increasingly Shi'ite in its identity. Junayd and his son, Haydar, were killed in battle. When Ishmail (1499–1524) became head of the Safavid order there was sufficient religious fervour to overthrow rivals and capture Tabriz in 1501. He declared himself Shah Ishmail I, and within ten years he had conquered the whole of Persia and forcibly imposed the Shi'ite faith on the Sunni majority. As R. M. Savory points out, this Shi'ite identity for the first time moulded the country into something approaching a nation state, as well as emphatically reinforcing the territorial and cultural differences between Persia and the Ottoman Empire.[8]

To begin with, it was a theocratic state, and Shah Ishmail's authority was based on the belief that he was 'the Shadow of God upon Earth'. His divine invincibility was shattered by the defeat of the battle of Chaldiran at the hands of the Ottomans who temporarily occupied his capital, Tabriz. This humiliation lost him the respect of his Turcoman followers, the *Qizilbash*, and resulted in conflicts and power struggles. His successor, Shah Tahmasp (1524–76), reigned for fifty years and successfully defended his realm against the constant attacks of the Ottomans in the west, and the Özbegs in the east. After several weak leaders and assassinations, Shah Abbas I (1589–1627) came to the throne.

The long years of dynastic and factional conflict had destroyed the spiritual authority of the Safavid rulers, and power was now exercised entirely in the secular domain. Internal strife had also led to territorial losses in the east,

Tabriz, detail of the Blue Mosque

where much of Khurasan and Sistan had been captured by the Özbegs and Mughals. On accession, Shah Abbas quickly had to prove that he was a strong and decisive monarch, so he took ruthless measures to weaken the *Qizilbash*. They had formed the backbone of the army, but wielded disproportionate power, and their old tribal loyalties were incompatible with the interests of the nation state Shah Abbas was trying to consolidate. So he created a new army, drawn from Georgian, Armenian and Circassian prisoners of war (known as *ghulams*). *Qizilbash* chiefs had also served as governors, raising taxes and holding considerable political and financial power in the provinces. In order to break this monopoly, Shah Abbas began training a new political class of civil servants drawn, like the army, from the ranks of *ghulams*. By these means the *Qizilbash* were gradually ousted and the loyalty of the civil service and military was assured. Shah Abbas now turned his attention to the enemy without, embarking on successful campaigns to regain Khurasan and Sistan. Once his eastern and western borders were stabilised, he decided to rule from the centre, moved the capital from Qasvin to Isfahan and began rebuilding the city.

The vision and scale of this ambitious urban development is only paralleled in the West by cities like St Petersburg, Washington and Paris – also products of similar visionaries, Peter the Great, Pierre l'Enfant and

Louis Napoleon (with Baron Haussmann). The new plan of Isfahan links the old city around the Masjid i Jami to the Ziyanda river, and the focal point is the vast square, the Maydan i Shah. This is the largest square in Asia (512 by 159 metres) surrounded by double-storied arcades of shops, like extended *riwaqs*, broken on each side by four major monuments. The northern and southern arcades are divided in the centre respectively by the portals of the bazaar and the Masjid i Shah (now renamed Masjid i Imam). The arcades on the west side are broken by the Ali Qapu Palace, and directly opposite on the east side by the Masjid i Shaikh Lutfallah. Behind the Ali Qapu and the western side of the Maydan were extensive palace gardens linking the Maydan with the Chahar Bagh, a wide avenue lined with plane trees, which leads down to the Ziyanda river and beyond. The Chahar Bagh (meaning four gardens) is divided into two parts by the Allahverdi bridge, and four gardens were arranged east and west of the two halves of this great promenade. In addition to the Ali Qapu Palace, there are surviving pavilions from other royal palaces, the Chihil Sutun and Hasht Bihisht, off the

Chahar Bagh in what is left of the royal park and Bagh i Bolbol ('the garden of the nightingale').

Shah Abbas lavished his patronage on the royal mosque, the Masjid i Shah (1611–38). It has a bent plan, turning 45 degrees from the pivotal position of the entrance portal on the Maydan. This ensures the correct *qibla* alignment. The deeply recessed entrance portal took four years to complete and the intricate tile mosaic in the *muqarnas* hood is quite stunning in its depth, richness and variety of colour. Two panels of tiles, in the design of prayer rugs, flank the entrance, and before the main *sahn* is an intermediary vestibule. The *sahn* is beautifully proportioned, and the double arcades and *iwans* are mirrored in an expansive water tank. Every surface is covered with tiles and each *iwan* hood differs in its vaulted structure and surface design. In its decoration it is a development of the Gawhar Shad, although the term 'decoration' in this context seems insubstantial and pejorative. The quality of the tilework is inferior to that in the entrance portal because Shah Abbas, fearing the mosque would not be completed in his lifetime, sanctioned the

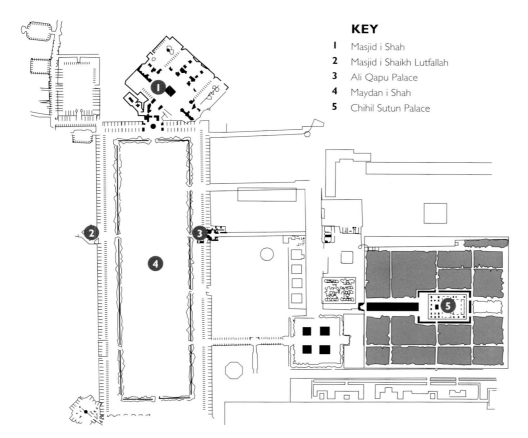

KEY

1   Masjid i Shah
2   Masjid i Shaikh Lutfallah
3   Ali Qapu Palace
4   Maydan i Shah
5   Chihil Sutun Palace

Isfahan, plan of the Maydan i Shah

TOP
Isfahan, the Masjid i Shah (Masjid i Imam)

ABOVE
Isfahan, the Masjid i Shah (Masjid i Imam): detail of the portal

faster process of painted *haft-rang* (seven colours) tiles. Nevertheless, the relationship of colour to form took on a new dimension, and as Arthur Upham Pope observed, the impact of the tilework 'etherealises' the architectural masses with its 'glowing misty blue'.⁹

Blue is the keynote colour, but the floral arabesques also include turquoise, green, yellow, gold and white, which sparkle in the sunlight, producing a shimmering sensation of incorporeality without obscuring the underlying clarity of the building's structure. Its blithe harmony and symmetry of form is animated by patterns of light and shade, solid and void and the fluid interpenetration of space. No section is isolated, with space alternating between open and closed units of dome chambers, open arcades, courts and multi-domed prayer halls. The mosque retains certain Timurid features in its plan, such as the dome chambers situated behind the lateral *iwans*, and winter prayer halls flanking the main sanctuary dome. These halls give access to two rectangular garden courts with pools, fountains and trees, which served as *madrasas*. The *riwaqs* here are single-storeyed cloisters

providing space for instruction, but no lodgings for students. Nothing has been added to or subtracted from this building, and its singular unity of form intensely encapsulates the vision of its creator, putting this on par with Sinan's Selimiya or the Taj Mahal.

For sheer quality, the more modest Masjid i Shaikh Lutfallah (1601–28) in many respects outranks the Masjid i Shah. This private oratory, dedicated to the memory of Shah Abbas's father-in-law, was built earlier, and the tile mosaic is the same quality as that in the portal of the Masjid i Shah. Like the larger mosque, the plan is oblique in order to ensure the correct *qibla* alignment. The façade is set back from the Maydan and covered with blue tiled panels picked out in turquoise and buff. The broad, single-shell dome, festooned with blue and white arabesques, is described as *café-au-lait* in colour. It sits on a turquoise drum with white Kufic inscriptions and a cornice band of white calligraphy set in cobalt blue. The portal is outlined by turquoise cable moulding, and the *muqarnas* hood is set with intricate pieces of tile mosaic which equal the Masjid i Shah portal in their magnificence. Entrance is by an angled passage. The square oratory rises through the intermediary of ample corner squinches to form an octagon carrying the drum and dome. The interior is defined by eight arches outlined with turquoise cable moulding and framed with flourishes of white calligraphy on a blue ground. The interior of the dome is decorated with a central stellar pattern from which cascades glazed lemon-shaped medallions set against a ground of matt unglazed buff brick. Light flickers across gleaming and matt surfaces as it is filtered through the sixteen paired filigreed window grills which pierce the drum.

TOP LEFT
Isfahan, the Masjid i Shah (Masjid i Imam): detail of the portal

TOP RIGHT
Isfahan, the Masjid i Shaikh Lutfallah: detail

ABOVE
Isfahan, the Masjid i Shaikh Lutfallah: detail

Safavid art was essentially courtly in spirit. Secular architecture here, as elsewhere, was constructed with less permanent materials. Few pavilions survive to reveal the splendour of Isfahan's palace architecture. The character of the Persian palace was defined more by the extensive garden settings than the architecture. The layout was symmetrical, and pavilions were strategically placed at significant intersections, or at the end of long flower beds and water channels. The Chihil Sutun Palace (or Pavilion) stands at the end of a pool, 110 metres long and 16 wide, in a garden planned by Shah Abbas I. The pavilion is an open-plan structure built in three different sections, starting with Shah Abbas I's triple-domed reception hall, with tall columned, open-sided porticos, or talars. An *iwan* leads into the central chamber, and in front of this another section, built by Shah Abbas II, provides a central hall with a fountain flanked by open talars. The third

extension, probably built at the beginning of the eighteenth century, is the main talar with a flat wooden roof supported by twenty timber columns fronting the pool. These tall, slender columns, with their stone bases carved in the form of lions, recall their regal origins in the audience halls (*apadana*) of Archaemenid architecture.

The decoration of the palace is varied and reflects changing taste from the earliest murals, dating from 1640, to the mirror mosaic of the eighteenth century. Mirror mosaic became very popular during the Qajar period (1786–1925), but most of the decoration here is probably eighteenth century. The talar columns were sheathed in mirror mosaic as early as the seventeenth century, and mirror mosaic of the same period was observed in the audience hall by Sir John Chardin, a French Huguenot who stayed in Isfahan between 1673 and 1677.[10] Murals on interior and exterior walls reflect

Isfahan, the Chihil Sutun

the style of contemporary manuscript painting, although western influence can be seen in history paintings which have a more official role. A number of paintings recall Omar Khayyam – scenes of wine drinking, picnics and idly amorous couples – expressing luxury, languor and gratification, which this whole pleasure-dome and its setting so vividly celebrates. The lyrical spirit is also sustained in paintings which are inspired more directly from Persian literature. Historical paintings show the Safavid monarchs receiving diplomatic missions and entertaining foreign notables, such as the Mughal Emperor Humayun. Ambassadors appear in western dress, and the sense of volume and chiaroscuro in a number of these paintings suggests western influence. Their function was to advertise the status of Persia as a world power, and they recall paintings fulfilling a similar role in the Doge's Palace. While I am not suggesting Venetian influence here, it is worth noting that some of the mirror glass in the Chihil Sutun was a gift from the Doge.[11]

The most imposing palatial building in Isfahan is the Ali Qapu (meaning 'Lofty Gate' or 'Sublime Porte') which faces the Maydan. An open veranda, or talar, is raised over the second storey, offering a grandstand view of the Maydan with its spacious setting for polo matches, pageants and military parades. Elsewhere the square was used as a market where merchants spread their various wares and pitched their tents and market stalls, mingling with itinerant vendors, water-sellers, story-tellers and street entertainers. The Ali Qapu also formed a ceremonial gate to the palace with accommodation for the palace guards on the ground floor. The upper rooms were used for audience halls, receptions, banquets, concerts, private activities and offices. A notable interior is the 'music room', in which the fragile fabric of the vaults, ceiling and *muqarnas* is pierced and fret-sawed into bottle-shaped recesses used to display the Shah's glass and ceramics. A number of smaller rooms contain paintings, like the Chihil Sutun, which, to quote Della Valle, 'show men and women in lascivious postures'.[12] As Wilfrid Blunt observed, 'they are mildly erotic, but no more so than the paintings of Boucher and Fragonard'.[13]

Two bridges in Isfahan are remarkable, the elegantly arcaded Allahverdi and Khwaju. The Allahverdi Bridge, known as the Si-o-se Pul, or 'thirty-three arched bridge', is 300 metres long and was completed under the

Isfahan, the Ali Qapu

direction of Shah Abbas I's general, Allahverdi Khan, in 1602. The piers and towers are built of stone, the superstructure brick, and above each side of the roadway vaulted arcades provide a shelter for pedestrians. The more complex Khwaju Bridge, built by Shah Abbas II in 1650, functions also as a dam. It is shorter than the Allahverdi Bridge, with two-tiered arcades on either side also providing pathways. Its line is broken at the ends and centre by projecting kiosks, and below the roadway vaulted galleries set over flights of steps (on the downstream side), provide cover for groups of people who frequent this place as a cool and pleasant summer rendezvous.

Outside Isfahan the patronage of Shah Abbas was bestowed on the shrine of Imam Riza at Mashhad. This was considerably extended, creating new courts on the north side, and such notable interiors as the octagonal domed chamber of Allahverdi Khan, which ranks in quality with the Masjid i Shaikh Lutfallah. Of the late Safavid period, possibly the most delightful building in Isfahan is the Madrasa of Madir i Shah (1716), built by the last of the Safavids, Shah Sultan Husain. The *madrasa* is part of a range of buildings, including a caravansarai, stables and bazaar, fronting the Chahar Bagh. Its plan retains certain Timurid features, such as corner dome chambers, in addition to those behind the four main *iwans*, and the bevelled corners of the garden court are reminiscent of the Ghiyathiya Madrasa at Khargid. The tilework in the arcades is mostly geometric, but the sanctuary *iwan* and dome are covered with elegant floral arabesques in limpid blue, turquoise and gold, providing a perfect backdrop at the end of a garden vista framed by trees. The court is divided by pathways and water channels into a miniature *chahar bagh* full of plane trees, flowers and shrubs.

Although in many respects inferior to the Masjid i Shah and Masjid i Shaikh Lutfallah, the Madir i Shah has its own unique charm and magic. The former buildings represent the fulfilment and flowering of a long architectural tradition, but as Arthur Upham Pope points out Safavid art was slow to decline.[14] The Madir i Shah is the last great Safavid building, and like the Alhambra, it synthesises landscape and architecture in a consummate way, enfolding its garden in a shimmering mirage of colour. This setting encapsulates those Persian sensibilities that are so finely expressed in the lyric poetry and quatrains of Hafis, Sa'di and Rumi. It is arguable that it represents, not just the swan-song of Persian architecture, but of Islamic architecture as a whole.

RIGHT
Isfahan, the Madir i Shah
Madrasa: a view through the
entrance into the courtyard

BELOW
Isfahan, the Madir i Shah
Madrasa

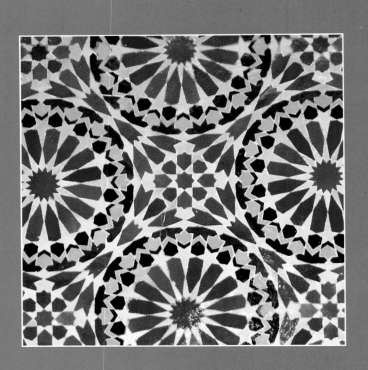

CHAPTER 11

ISLAMIC ARCHITECTURE IN SOUTH ASIA

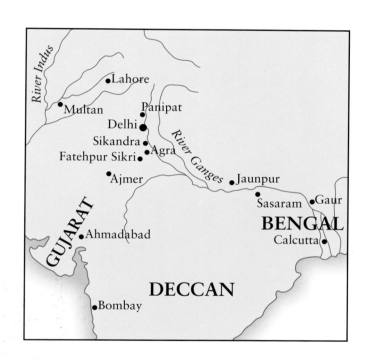

Islam gained a foothold on the Indian sub-continent as early as Umayyad times, when Arab trade missions were established on the Malabar coast. In 711 Muhammad ibn Qasim, a governor from Basra, invaded Sind with 15,000 men and occupied an area from Karachi to Multan. Islam sustained a fragile hold here, but more significant were the eleventh-century raids into India from Afghanistan initiated by the Ghaznavid dynasty. Mahmud of Ghazna, the patron of Firdawsi and Ibn Sina, began his numerous raids on India in 1001 with a major victory near Peshawar. Acting in the name of Sunni Islam, he created a significant empire which stretched from the Punjab to Khurasan. Nothing of any architectural note has survived in India from this period, but Mahmud made his capital at Ghazna (Afghanistan) a centre of architectural distinction. The city was later sacked and burnt by the Ghurid sultan Ala ud Din Hassan, and all that survives are the flanged shafts of the richly carved minarets, or victory towers, of Masud and Bahram Shah. Like the Ghurid minaret of Jam, the towers of Ghazna need to be borne in mind when considering the early Muslim architecture of Delhi.

The Ghaznavids were replaced by their former vassals, the Ghurids, who originated from a region east of Herat. Led by Muhammad of Ghur, they invaded India, taking Sind in 1176 and Peshawar in 1181, but in 1191 they suffered a major defeat at the battle of Tairin against the prince of Ajmer, Prithwiraj III. Despite this setback, Muhammad of Ghur went on the offensive a year later and challenged a Rajput army of 300,000 horsemen and 3,000 elephants with an army less than half that size. His light and mobile cavalry won the battle, and he captured

Delhi, the Quwwat al-Islam mosque: showing the *riwaqs*

Ajmer but failed to take Delhi. In 1193 his brilliant slave and deputy, General Qutb ud Din Aibak, captured Delhi on the sultan's behalf. Muhammad of Ghur went on to gain lands as far as Bengal, but he was assassinated in 1206, and Qutb ud Din seized power. He was a Turk who had risen to power up the meritocratic ladder available to the slave troops of the Ghurid army. He founded the Slave King sultanate of Delhi and assumed control of all the Ghurid territories in India, but not of Afghanistan.

In 1193 Qutb ud Din established the first mosque within the former fortifications of the Chauhan Rajputs. The area is known as Fort Rai Pithora (named after Prince Prithwiraj) and the inner citadel where the mosque is located is called Lal Kot, one of the cities of Delhi. The complex, built between 1193 and 1198, is situated 17 kilometres south of Delhi. The mosque, known as the

and prayer hall are placed one on top of the other, and the structure is trabeated (column and beam construction). The only arcades to be seen are those in the screen; these were not constructed in the usual manner with voussoirs but corbelled with projecting horizontal stone courses.

These arches are Islamic in design, but the building method is Hindu. The masons who built here lacked the knowledge of arch and vault construction and therefore they must have been built by local Hindu craftsmen. Hindu, Jain and Buddhist architecture was essentially trabeated, and did not employ the arch, vault, or dome in a structural or load-bearing sense. Arches and domes are used in a very limited capacity, and they are invariably carved and sculpted rather than constructed. As Martin Briggs observed, the genius of Hindu, Jain and Buddhist art is sculpture, and sculptural thinking determines archi-

Delhi, detail of the *sahn* of the Quwwat al-Islam

Delhi, the Quwwat al-Islam: illustrating the *sahn*

Quwwat al-Islam ('Might of Islam') was built over the site of a Hindu temple, and columns from this and other temples, Hindu and Jain, were used in the mosque's construction. Another pre-Islamic feature that stands in the *sahn* is an iron column of the Gupta period (fourth century AD) which came from a temple of Vishnu and probably originated in Bihar. Qutb ud Din's mosque stands discretely among two incomplete extensions made by his successors, Iltutmish and Ala ud Din (the second sultan of the Khalji dynasty). The *sahn* of the Quwwat al-Islam is surrounded by *riwaqs* on three sides and the prayer hall is separated from the *sahn* by an imposing screen of five arches. The recycled columns in the *riwaqs*

tectural mass and form as well as its dense iconography and decoration.[1] Hindu craftsmanship is evident in the carved arabesques and calligraphy around the screen, where the design is animated in a serpentine fashion and lacks the tension and discipline that normally regulate such work.[2] Fragments of Hindu carving, including figures, have been retained in the recycled masonry. These Hindu elements are cited as early examples of syncretism in Indo-Muslim architecture, but probably they were included because they were at hand.

Indo-Muslim architecture later absorbed some of the vocabulary of Hindu, Jain and Buddhist architecture, such as the bracketed column, *chattri* (domed kiosk), *chajja* (sloping eave) and *jarokha* (balcony), into the framework of an imported architectural style which had matured in Persia and Central Asia. The syncretism of later Mughal architecture reflects India's great capacity for absorbing and reconciling the pluralism that defines, shapes and nourishes its culture. India comfortably accommodated Islam, but it was the common spiritual currency of mysticism that brought Islam and the older religious traditions together. Sufism's belief in the transcendence of mystical truth and experience over the particulars of orthodoxy had a strong ecumenical appeal. The Muslim rulers of India were Sunni, but Islam's success in converting so many was due to the missionary role of the Sufi orders during the twelfth century, as well as the appeal of Islam to low-caste Hindus. A number of Sufi orders, like the Shuhrawardi, were associated closely with the ruling classes, and they attracted many converts because they were seen to have enormous political influence and patronage. Another important Sufi order was the Chishti, founded by Shaikh Muin al-Din, who settled in Ajmer during the reign of Prithwiraj. His successors founded *khanqahs* all over India, and their

lifestyle, yogic practices, forms of meditation and use of *sama* (music, poetry and song) to induce ecstasy had much in common with existing Hindu and Buddhist religious practice.

If the hand of Hindu craftsmanship created cultural ambiguities in the main body of the Quwwat al-Islam, this is less so in the case of the minaret, the Qutb Minar. This is a detached, tapering, sandstone tower, and its considerable height of 72.5 metres recalls its antecedents in Afghanistan. Both sultans of Ghur, Ghi ad-Din and his brother, Muhammad of Ghur, have their names inscribed on this and the Jam minaret and both are victory towers. The Qutb Minar is five storeys high, with four *muqarnas* balconies. In its use of angular flanges and semicircular ribs, it resembles the tomb towers of Persia and Afghanistan, but here they are stacked on top of each other, creating different permutations of pattern and relief on each storey. The first storey, built by Qutb ud Din, has alternating flanges and ribs. The next three storeys are by Iltutmish, the second

LEFT
Delhi, the Qutb Minar

ABOVE
Delhi, Ala'i Darwaza

ribbed and the third flanged. In the fourteenth century Firuz Shah Tughlaq faced the fourth storey with white marble and added a fifth with a cupola. The fourth is a smooth white cylinder, and the fifth is banded with ribs and blind arches. The bands of carved inscriptions are possibly the finest in India.

The size of the Qutb Minar is impressive, but it would have been completely dwarfed if Ala ud Din Khalji's plans for a second minaret had been completed. The Alai Minar was designed to be twice the height of the Qutb Minar, but thankfully all that remains is the stump, 29 metres high. The Alai Minar was to be another victory monument because Ala ud Din's conquests extended Muslim control as far as the Deccan, where the rulers became vassals of the Khalji dynasty. Qutb ud Din's successor, Iltutmish, extended the arcades of the Quwwat al-Islam to the north and south and began an enlargement of the *sahn* which would have brought the Qutb Minar

Delhi, Alai Minar

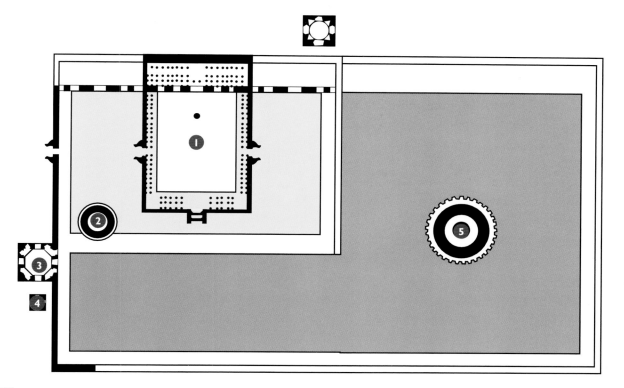

KEY

I   Original mosque of Qutb ud Din
2   Qutb Minar
3   Ala'i Darwaza
4   Tomb of Iman Zamin
5   Alai Minar

Iltutmish's Extension

Ala ud Din's Extension

Plan of the Quwwat al-Islam

into the main mosque precinct. This project was never completed, but he got as far as creating a new southern *riwaq* and his successor, Ala ud din, added an entrance gate known as the Ala'i Darwaza in 1311. This is a domed sandstone cube pierced by four archways inlaid with white bands of marble inscriptions which frame the arches and flanking windows. Fine inscriptions and arabesques are cut into the sandstone, and the tall arches, which are lined with sharp spearhead cusps, are the first true Islamic arches constructed in India. Red sandstone was also used in the nearby tomb of Iltutmish (1235), the oldest surviving Muslim tomb in India. It follows Persian precedent, because tomb building was a distinct Muslim innovation in a country with a tradition of cremation among its non-Muslim population. It is a domed tomb with the main entrance on the east, two openings on the north and south and a solid *qibla* wall containing three *mihrabs*. The central *mihrab* was decorated in white marble and the tomb interior is covered with calligraphy and arabesques containing decorative Hindu motifs. The design follows the Seljuk model with the cenotaph functioning as a memorial in the oratory and the tomb proper in the crypt below. The dome has now collapsed, but it was constructed in the Hindu manner, corbelled, with projecting horizontal courses of stone.

Outside Delhi the formative phase of Indo-Islamic architecture can be seen in the congregational mosque at Ajmer (1200–29). Built exclusively of sandstone, it displays many similarities to the Quwwat al-Islam. Its prayer hall and *riwaqs* are likewise trabeated and constructed from recycled Hindu columns. Only those in the prayer hall are now standing, but they are three rather than two columns high. Following the tradition of Hindu temple building, the mosque is on a raised platform, which is reached by a flight of steps, and Hindu building methods can be seen in the corbelled domes over the prayer hall and in the arcades of the prayer hall screen built by Iltumish. These arcades have cusped arches, and the central arch, which is larger than the others, is set in a *pishtaq* supporting the stumps of paired minarets in the Seljuk style. The carved Kufic and Naskhi inscriptions on the arcades of the screen are much more disciplined than those in the Quwwat al-Islam, and John Hoag has suggested a close relationship between these and the Ghurid brickwork on the minaret of Jam and the *madrasa* of Shai i Mashhad in Afghanistan.[3]

The use of sandstone and white marble in these early buildings is critical, because it was these materials that shaped and defined the subsequent character of many great Mughal buildings. Sandstone and marble became the inimitable properties of much Indo-Islamic architecture, just as brick and tile expressed the essence of Timurid and Safavid architecture. Islamic architecture in the sub-continent was initially a cultural import from Persia, Central Asia and Afghanistan, but its forms were gradually recomposed, adapted to new circumstances and enriched by indigenous Hindu and Buddhist elements. Its proportion, rhythmic organisation and composition may at times recall the architecture of Isfahan and Samarqand, but these formal components were completely transformed by the nature of the building material. Sandstone has a monochrome density, opacity, warmth and weight, which calls for the compensatory relief of white marble. Marble articulates rather than lightens the monumentality of form, and despite certain compositional similarities Indo-Islamic architecture is the antithesis of Timurid and Safavid architecture, with its shimmering, incorporeal and polychrome surfaces.

Delhi is an accumulation of eight cities and with the rise of the Tughluq dynasty five separate developments had already been built by the middle of the fourteenth century. The Quwwat al-Islam complex at Lal Kot was followed by Siri to the north, and the Tughluq dynasty added Tughlaqabad, Jahanpanah and Firuzabad. Ghiyas al-Din Tughluq, the first of that dynasty, built the fortified citadel and palace of Tughlaqabad 7 kilometres east of Lal Kot for defence purposes. India was spared much of the devastation wrought by the Mongols in the rest of Asia. Nevertheless, the Mongol conquests did have a major impact on India, isolating her from much of the Muslim world and forcing her to accept numerous refugees from Persia, Central Asia and Afghanistan. Among this influx were scholars and artists who contributed to the cultural and political life of Delhi and strengthened its sense of Muslim identity. Two buildings that strongly affirm this identity are the tombs of Tughluq at Tughlaqabad and of Rukn i Alam at Multan. The tomb of Ghiyas al-Din Tughluq (1325) is a domed cube with three portals resembling the Ala'i Darwaza and the tomb of Iltumish, but like those buildings its ancestry goes back to the 'Tomb of the Samanids' and pre-Islamic *chahar taqs*. It is a squat, ground-hugging building, with thick inward-sloping walls in keeping with the fortified ethos of its setting. It is built of sandstone over a rubble core, and the dome is faced with white marble and crowned with a pot finial. There is a notable lack of decoration, and its sturdy sandstone bulk is relieved by panelling and white marble bands which divide the structure horizontally and outline the portal arches. Lighter touches appear in the tympani grills, and crisper accents are provided by trilobed merlons above the cornice, and spearhead cusps lining the portal arches, but these features fail to mitigate its underlying severity of form. It is a building that sums up the spartan character of Ghiyas al-Din Tughluq's short reign.

More in tune with the lighter spirit of contemporary Persian architecture is the tomb of Rukn i Alam at Multan (1320). Built soon after Oljeitu's mausoleum at Sultaniya, the tomb of Rukn i Alam, with domed octagon and ring of towers, begs comparison with the great Ilkhanid monument. Set on high ground, this impressive tomb, 35 metres high, was originally built by Ghiyas al-Din Tughluq for himself when he was governor of Multan. After his accession to the Delhi sultanate and premature death, his son, Muhammad Tughluq, gave the tomb to Rukn i Alam, the head of the Shuhrawardi Sufi order, evidence of the power and influence the orders enjoyed. The first Shuhrawardi *khanqah* was established in Multan by Shaikh Baha al-Din Zakariyya, and from the outset the Sufis were courted by the ruling classes who needed their political and spiritual support. Baha al-Din Zakariyya had sided with Iltutmish in a power struggle against Nasirud Din Qabacha, and for this support Iltutmish rewarded him with the title 'Leader of Islam'.[4] In turn his grandson, Shaikh Rukn i Alam, enjoyed the favour of the ruling sultans, and as a token of their esteem he was given the mausoleum. The tomb of Rukn i Alam was built in the Persian manner, with brick, and selected areas are decorated in white, blue and azure tiles, set against moulded and glazed brick. It consists of two octagons, one above the other. The lower is pierced by three entrances and has battered walls with tapered circular towers engaged in the angles. The upper octagon is smaller with perpendicular walls set back to allow a narrow passage for the *muezzin*. The upper octagon is pierced with windows which form a gallery supporting a

Delhi, the tomb of Ghiyas al-Din Tughluq

Multan, the tomb of Rukn i Alam

narrow zone of transition carrying the white hemispherical dome. Buttress-turrets with cupolas and finials extend the vertical thrust of the corner towers on the lower octagon, and similar turrets above the cornice crown the angles of the upper octagon. They call to mind the circlet of minarets at Sultaniya, and the manner in which they enliven the roof-line anticipates the distinctive use of *chattris* in Mughal architecture.

In the reign of Muhammad Tughluq Delhi was abandoned in 1317, and a new capital established at Dawlatabad in the Deccan. His successor, Firuz Shah, restored Delhi as the capital, and in 1354 he created Firuzabad, Delhi's fifth city, 10 kilometres north-east of the old settlements. The citadel of Firuzabad (now known as Kotla Firuz Shah) once contained eighteen palaces and eight mosques, but little has survived except the ruins of the Lat Pyramid. This stepped pyramid, described as a 'marker' for the main mosque, displayed some of the earliest examples of *chattri* pavilions, and a stone Asokan column (third century BC) formed a centrepiece on the upper colonnaded terrace.[5] Like the wrought iron Gupta column in the Quwwat al-Islam, here is another example of a pre-Islamic 'trophy' taking pride of place in a mosque context. Its antiquity and sanctity was obviously respected, and here it assumed a new meaning as a marker for a place of worship for the Muslim faithful, but how it functioned is open to question. In the Quwwat al-Islam deviation from normal religious practice can be observed when individuals wait in turn to clasp their hands behind their backs around the iron column, in the belief that such action will bring good luck. It is no doubt a harmless example of misdirected reverence, but the columns raise the possibility of syncretism and heterodoxy at a popular level of worship. Whatever the answer, the Lat Pyramid, in both its form and function, as Blair and Bloom have stated, departs 'from the normal canons of Islamic architecture'.[6] Nevertheless, Firuz Shah himself was a pious and puritanical Muslim who strictly banned any form of pictorial representation in his palace. His orthodoxy is clearly manifest in his tomb and *madrasa*, which were constructed alongside a tank built by Ala ud Din Khalji, known as the Hawz Kass. This large *madrasa* complex, made up largely of two double-storeyed wings joined together by Firuz Shah's tomb, became one of India's major centres of Sunni learning.

Firuz Shah died in 1388, and ten years later Tamerlane invaded India and sacked Delhi. The sultanate was destroyed, many artists and artisans were abducted to Samarqand, and the city, declining into anarchy, ceased to be Islam's cultural centre. Other cities rose in importance and for the best part of a century the most interesting architectural developments occurred in the provinces. Jaunpur, founded by Firuz Shah, began to flourish under the Sharqi Sultanate. Two mosques here, the Atala Mosque (1408) and Jami Masjid (1470), display a very distinct regional style in their use of monumental gates and towering sanctuary *iwans*. Both have unusually tall sanctuary *iwans* with battered walls, like Egyptian pylons. The sanctuary *iwan* of the Atala Mosque is flanked by sturdy piers displaying blind arches and horizontal mouldings. Its recessed centre pierced at ground level by three openings and punctuated by numerous ranks of windows above. It is only through the upper windows that the tall sanctuary dome situated behind can be glimpsed; otherwise it is blocked from view by the *iwan*. The shallow prayer halls are located laterally along the *qibla* wall, and the *sahns* are surrounded on three sides by *riwaqs*, each of which is broken in the centre by a monumental gate. These plans confirm what had been evolving earlier in Indo-Islamic architecture and what was to be a common format.

Another interesting regional development can be seen in Gujurat, which became independent of Delhi in 1396. Muzzafar Shah established a new sultanate in 1407, and his grandson, Ahmad Shah, founded the city of Ahmadabad in 1411, initiating an ambitious building programme which included numerous mosques and a citadel. Ahmadabad was created out of an existing Hindu town, and indigenous craft traditions are manifest in the distinct fusion of Hindu and Islamic elements in the Jami Masjid (1423). Here the most notable feature is the sanctuary screen, which is pierced in the centre by a lofty central arch, with smaller arches on either side stepping down to the arcaded wings which line the rest of the façade. The engaged columns flanking the central arch display an enormous richness of Hindu stone carving,

Delhi, the Qala i Kuhna Masjid in the Purana Qila

with a variety of latticed and fluted patterns, as well as mouldings, brackets, rosettes and intricate motifs which resemble balconies, pavilions and decorative niches. Only in Seljuk Anatolia are there similar displays of sculptural virtuosity in a Muslim building. Hindu influence is not just confined to surface decoration but can be seen in the hypostyle prayer hall in the ingenious structural union of column, beam and dome.

After Tamerlane's sack of Delhi a degree of stability was established when the Sayyid dynasty took over and ruled as viceroys on behalf of Tamerlane and Shah Rukh. However, Delhi's fortunes did not revive until the middle of the fifteenth century, when the last of the Sayyid rulers abdicated in favour of Bahlul Khan, the leader of the Afghan Lodi tribe. Of the architectural contribution of the Sayyid and Lodi periods all that remains is a number of tombs in the Delhi suburbs. Among the Lodi sultans, only Sikandar Lodi left much in the way of substantial building. In Delhi he created the Bara Gumbad Mosque and Tomb, but more significant was his decision to establish a second residence and court at Agra, creating what became for a time a *de facto* alternative capital to

Delhi. His tomb (1495) is 8 kilometres outside the city at Sikandra. With *chattris* prominent at each corner, this unusual single-storeyed sandstone building has a complex square plan accommodating forty vaulted chambers. It was later restored by the Mughals when Akbar's Hindu wife, Mariam uz Zamani (who converted to Christianity), was interred here. The Sayyid and Lodi tombs are noted for their octagonal plans, and from these modest beginnings such structures as Humayun's Tomb and the Taj Mahal grew. The tomb of Isa Niyazi (1540–47) represents a maturation of this form during the Sur dynasty. It is a domed octagonal structure pierced by openings on seven sides and surrounded by an arcaded ambulatory with projecting eaves. (See page 210.) These slanting eaves derive from Hindu *chajjas*, which formed pillared porches in Hindu temples. Above the eaves, and clustered around the dome, eight *chattris* create a lively cyclic rhythm above the cornice and echo in diminutive form the shape of the whole. Dominating the centre of its spacious octagonal enclosure, it is reminiscent of the Haram al-Sharif with the Dome of the Rock and its various subsidiaries. It is a building that looks forward as well as back, because its kiosk form, projecting eaves and outward display of major and minor domes foreshadow Ottoman structures like the Baghdad Kiosk.

The Lodi dynasty, consisting of three rulers, Bahlul, Sikandar and Ibrahim, came to an end with Babur's victory over Ibrahim at Panipat in 1526. Babur was the first of the Mughal rulers, but he established only a fragile hold on India during the last four years of his life. *Mughal* is a Persian word for Mongol, and although Babur had some Mongol blood from his mother he was descended on his father's side from Tamerlane and took pride in his Turkish identity. He came from Farghana and spent most of his early life trying to restore his territorial rights to that district. After exile in Afghanistan and briefly capturing Samarqand, he gave up his claims to Farghana and turned his attention to conquering Tamerlane's former Indian territories. After four incursions into the Punjab, he pushed farther east and successfully captured Delhi and Agra. The four years he spent in India produced no architecture, and his memoirs show that he found little in India that satisfied his taste. He was, however, a keen gardener and botanist and established a number of gardens in the Persian style. In this respect his contribution was more useful than bricks and mortar, because he established in India the *chahar bagh*, which provided the spatial context for the glories of later Mughal architecture.

Babur died in 1530, and his successor, Humayun, faced a turbulent decade trying to retain the empire and contain the power of the recalcitrant Afghans. The Afghans regarded the Mughals as usurpers and were unwilling to yield their control of regional power or compromise their tribal loyalties to the ousted Lodis. Humayun's hold on the eastern provinces was weak, and it was from Bihar that the powerful Afghan leader, Sher Shah, emerged to lead two attacks against Humayun which culminated in his defeat in 1540. In his five-year reign, Sher Shah became one of India's most effective rulers, setting up a machinery of government which, according to Gavin Hambly, laid the foundations for subsequent Mughal and British rule.[7] Under his administration, Delhi's self-confidence returned and building activity resumed on a large scale. In 1540 Sher Shah continued work on the foundations laid by Humayun at Delhi's sixth city, Purana Qila. This fortified enclosure is 1.5 kilometres long with three gates containing two significant buildings, the Qala i Kuhna

Masjid and the Sher Mandal. Features of Hindu origin now became firmly established within the architectural vocabulary of Indo-Islamic architecture and are manifest in the western entrance gate. The right hand flanking tower of the gate is surmounted by a *chattri*, and above the entrance are projecting balconies known as *jarokhas*. Inside the citadel, the Qala i Kuhna Masjid faces a garden which has replaced the original *sahn*, and its façade in sandstone and white marble confidently asserts a form and plan which became more or less standard in Indo-Islamic mosque architecture. Five entrances, framed in taller recessed arches, pierce a prayer hall made up of a single aisle arranged laterally along the *qibla* wall. The larger central recess is framed by a *pishtaq*, and the tympanum over the doorway is decorated in white marble mosaic and pierced by a window with a bracketed *jarokha*. Projecting *jarokhas* also appear at the sides and back of the mosque, and Hindu building methods can be seen in the corbelled arches in the octagonal towers set in the rear corners.

The citadel once contained numerous palace buildings, but all that survives is the Sher Mandal. This garden pavilion is a two-tiered arcaded octagonal structure

Purana Qila, Sher Mandal

crowned with a *chattri*. It follows in spirit the tradition of Timurid and Safavid pavilions, like the Hasht Bihisht in Isfahan, but the sandstone creates a much greater sense of architectural presence and permanence – something that later distinguished Indo-Islamic palace architecture from the rest of the Muslim world. Another octagonal building, the most striking to emerge during his reign, is Sher Shah's own tomb at Sasaram in the capital of his former sultanate at Bihar. G. H. R. Tillotson suggests that Sher Shah may

have built it before he captured Delhi in 1540.[8] Its octagonal plan and style echo that of the tomb of Isa Niyazi in
Delhi, except that this is much grander, with two tiers of
chattris encircling the dome. Standing on a high walled
podium flanked by corner pavilions, it is set majestically
on an island reached by a causeway in the centre of a large
tank. It recalls the pavilion in the centre of the great cistern
at Qairawan, Tunisia, but this is a tomb and not a pleasure
dome, and the water here provides an appropriate feeling
of space, serenity and isolation.

Sher Shah was succeeded by Islam Shah, an able
ruler, who nevertheless failed to pacify the country and resolve the tribal divisions of the Afghans. For this reason the
Sur regime quickly collapsed after his death in 1554, and
Humayun, after fifteen years in exile, took the opportunity
of recapturing his Indian territories. Humayun lost not
only India to Sher Shah in 1540 but also Afghanistan. He
became a fugitive and like his father before him found
sanctuary in Persia, where Shah Tahmasp gave him asylum
and provided him with the military means to regain his
Afghan territories. After some years he took Kabul and
consolidated his position, ruling for ten years. When the
Sur regime fell apart, he had no difficulty in marching on
Delhi and restoring his fortune. Humayun's volatile career
ended prematurely by his accidental death in 1556 just a
few months after the conquest of Delhi, and the throne
went to his thirteen-year-old son Akbar.

Akbar the Great (1542–1605) ruled for nearly fifty
years. During his extraordinary reign the Mughal empire
expanded to cover more than half of the sub-continent,
and there evolved a distinctive imperial style of architecture over which Akbar presided. It was Akbar's reign that
saw the creation of the Mughal style, but its emergence
has to be understood against his cultural background and
that of his immediate predecessors. Akbar had a Persian
mother and Turkish father; Persian and Turkish were the
languages of the court, and he was culturally steeped in
the literature of Persia and encouraged a school of painting based on the Safavid style. Babur and Humayun were
highly cultivated men with roots in Central Asia, and
both spent time in the Persian court absorbing Safavid
culture at its blossoming. During their brief time in India,
Babur introduced the *chahar bagh* and Humayun a
number of distinguished Persian painters, but they also
brought with them not just their Persian taste but a

TOP
Delhi, Isa Niyazi tomb

ABOVE
Delhi, the tomb of Humayun

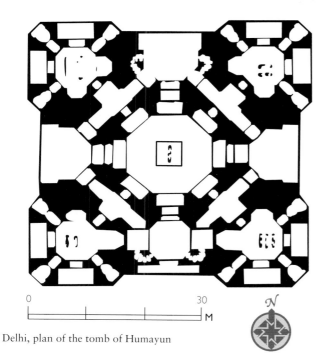

0   30
                                                  M

Delhi, plan of the tomb of Humayun

longer, deeper cultural association with Timurid Central Asia. These Timurid and Persian elements contributed to the shaping and periodical reinvigoration of the character and spirit of Mughal architecture.

These influences can clearly be seen in the first major example of Mughal architecture, Humayun's Tomb (1562–71) in Delhi, but they mingle with elements already well established during the earlier Delhi sultanates. The Timurid and Persian connection came through the two architects linked with this building, Sayyid Muhammad and Mirak Sayyid Ghiyath, who had previously worked extensively in Herat and Bukhara.[9] The tomb was commissioned by Humayun's widow, Haji Beggam, and it is the first of those great mausolea, culminating in the Taj Mahal, that came to epitomise the imperial style of Mughal India. It is also the first building to occupy the centre of a spacious *chahar bagh*. The garden is divided by water channels and axial paths which terminate at four gate-houses set in the walled enclosure. The monument rests on an imposing arcaded podium, made up of one hundred and twenty-four vaulted units, the scale and grand horizontal sweep of which represent a distinct Mughal innovation. At first glance the plan appears to be a square with chamfered corners, but it is essentially a cluster of four octagons around a central core. In this respect it represents a regrouping in plan of octagonal elements already well established in buildings like the Sher

Mandal and the Timurid-style tombs built during Humayun's first reign. As Ebba Koch observed, it is an elaboration of a ninefold plan, with domed chamber in the centre, four chambers at the corners and four open halls, or *iwans*, in the centre of each side. Its cue comes from the garden pavilion, *hasht bihisht*, and there is an intriguing overlap between tomb and palace architecture.[10]

It is built of red sandstone, and its double dome is faced with white marble; strips, borders and panels articulate the varied planes that make up its elevation. It is a two-storeyed building, and its deeply shaded windows, *iwans* and arcades, in both superstructure and podium, create a satisfying contrast of light, dark, solid and void. The façade is broken by major and minor *iwans*, and variations of plane and surface are achieved by the chamfered corners and angled recesses which push back the *pishtaqs*. The angles of the building are punctuated at the top by an array of small 'minarets', which are decorative descendants of those that encircle the domes of the Sultaniya and the tomb of Rukn i Alam. The roof-line is also lightened by an elegant display of *chattris*; four are placed over each corner section with smaller pairs above the *pishtaqs*. Inside the tomb the central octagon contains Humayun's white marble cenotaph, and in the Seljuk tradition this chamber functions as an oratory with the grave proper in the crypt below. There is no *qibla* wall here, but one of the latticed *jali* screens on the western side contains a *mihrab*. According to John Hoag, the arrangement of passages around the oratory forms an ambulatory allowing for the circumambulation of those wishing to pay their respects to a man whom many regarded as a saint. He has suggested that this practice may have been a prelude to the divine kingship which later Mughal emperors bestowed upon themselves.[11]

This belief in divine kingship was fostered to some extent by Akbar who believed that his conquests were God given and his rule divinely guided. An orthodox Sunni Muslim, as his empire expanded he came to appreciate the pluralism of his country and made every effort to give non-Muslims a greater opportunity to participate in the affairs of state. He believed that good government should promote harmony among all his subjects, and he made it his duty to understand and appreciate religious diversity. Religious debate was encouraged across all creeds, and religious literature was

Fatehpur Sikri, the tomb of Salim Chishti

disseminated through numerous translations in Persian, Turkish, Arabic, Hindi and Sanskrit. It is possible that he inherited this religious tolerance from his Mongol predecessors, but Akbar went a stage further and in later life broke away from Muslim orthodoxy to cultivate a faith known as Din Ilahi ('Divine Faith'). This faith was inclusive in its scope and has been described as syncretic, prompting the charge of heresy in more orthodox quarters. It was probably no more than the expression of an ecumenical attitude, and as such it was in line with much Sufi doctrine. From his youth Akbar had been influenced by the Sufis and paid regular homage at the shrine of Khwaja Muin al-Din Chishti at Ajmer. His veneration for the Chishti saints increased when Shaikh Salim of Sikri prophesied the birth of three sons for him. This prophecy came true, and Akbar insisted that two of his pregnant wives spend their confinements near the shaikh's cell at Sikri. It was these events that determined him to honour the holy ground where the saint lived by building the new capital of Fatehpur Sikri.

Situated 40 kilometres from Agra, Fatehpur Sikri (1571–85) is noted for the unity of its architectural style and its superb state of preservation; the city was inhabited by the court for only fourteen years and then gradually abandoned. The reasons for its abandonment are not clear, and they have variously been put down to the inadequate water supply, Akbar's campaigns in the north or sheer waste and prodigality.[12] It consists mainly of a mosque and palace, and the buildings express a remarkable degree of cultural synthesis in keeping with Akbar's inclusive religious philosophy. This synthesis is also explained by the participation of Hindu craftsmen from Gujarat, where a regional style of assimilated Hindu and Islamic forms had already been well established. According to Ebba Koch, Fatehpur Sikri was an architectural expression of Gujarat's absorption into the Mughal empire.[13] This event was celebrated in the building of a victory gate in the side of the mosque, the Buland Darwaza (1575–76), but ironically, except for the *chattris*, this gate is uncompromisingly Islamic. With this exception, however, Hindu influence is manifest elsewhere in the mosque and most emphatically in the architecture of the palace.

At the time of building, the congregational mosque, the Jami Masjid (1571), was the largest in India, and it is entered on the south side through the Buland Darwaza.

The lofty scale of this gate, 54 metres high, is amplified by the steep approach up a commanding flight of steps. Its plan forms a half octagon, and its two-storeyed elevation, with a grand *iwan* entrance, recalls Humayun's Tomb. The spacious *sahn* has low arcaded *riwaqs* around three sides, and the prayer hall, five aisles deep, supports three domes and is laterally arranged along the *qibla* side. The arcaded façade of the prayer hall has a large central *iwan* which completely obscures the main dome behind, like those tower *iwans* at Jaunpur. The slender columns in the trabeate prayer hall recall the Jami Masjid at Ahmadabad, and the corbelled supports for the domes are further evidence of Hindu construction techniques. The *sahn* contains two tombs, those of Salim Chishti and Islam Khan. Salim Chishti's Tomb is the more arresting, due to its lively fusion of Hindu and Muslim elements and the vivid contrast of its white marble against the uniform sandstone of the rest of the mosque. The slanting canopy which surrounds the tomb is an adaptation of a Hindu *chajja*, and the serpentine brackets appear to be a flamboyant derivation of dragon struts. A veranda around the tomb forms an ambulatory, and its walls are made up of latticed screens (*jali*) perforated with the most delicate geometric patterns.

So far the story of Indo-Islamic architecture has shown a gradual assimilation of Hindu forms into Islamic structures. But as Tillotson has observed, in the case of Fatehpur Sikri's palace architecture the reverse is true – Islamic forms are grafted on to Hindu structures.[14] The plan of the palace, with its various patios and pavilions and division between the public and private domain, is Islamic, but the buildings are essentially Hindu in form. For example, projecting from the colonnades of a spacious court is the public audience hall (the Diwan i Am), a trabeated box with bracketed columns supporting a flat roof with wide *chajja* eaves. All the architectural elements are Hindu except a low screen made up of stone *jalis*, but functionally it is thoroughly Islamic, serving as a loggia for the emperor. The private audience hall, the Diwan i Khas, is one of the most puzzling buildings in the palace complex. Externally it is a two-storeyed building with four *chattris* at each corner, wide *chajja* eaves and a balcony on the first storey supported by prominent serpentine brackets. The inside is dominated at the centre by the famous column with its huge capital made up of a

Fatehpur Sikri, the Diwan i Khas

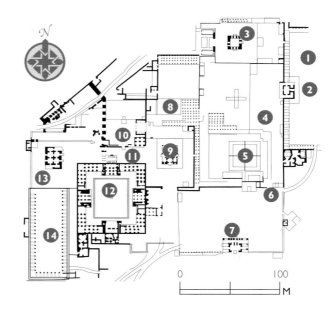

Plan of Fatehpur Sikri

KEY

1 Court of the Diwan i Am	8 Panch Mahal
2 Pavilion of the Diwan i Am	9 Sunahra Makan
3 Diwan i Khas	10 Garden
4 Turkish Sultana's House	11 Hawa Mahal
5 Anup Talao	12 Jodh Bai's Palace
6 Khwabgah	13 Birbal's House
7 Daftar Khana	14 Stables

writhing cluster of serpentine brackets surmounted by a low latticed balustrade. Radiating from this 'throne', like the spokes of a wheel, are four bridges connected at the corners to a gallery which encircles the room at first-storey level. There are numerous interpretations regarding the symbolism of the elevated throne and the function of this hall, but all is speculation. What is reasonably certain is the Gujurati influence, and a precedent for the serpentine brackets on Akbar's column can be seen on the minarets of the Sidi Bashir Mosque in Ahmadabad.[15]

The Diwan i Khas is to the north of a huge open court, the *mardana*, which was reserved for the emperor and his court. The space is broken by pavilions and articulated by a square pool, the Anup Talao, which conceptually echoes the internal plan of the Diwan i Khas with a centrally located island reached by four bridges. Nearby is the Turkish Sultana's House, which almost certainly did not house a Turkish sultana in the *mardana* – the men's domain. Like the Alhambra, many of these buildings are identified with popular names which reflect local tradition rather than historical fact. The purpose of

the pavilion is unknown, and like so many Muslim palace buildings we can assume that its use was open ended and multifarious. Women were allowed to impinge on the men's domain in the five-storeyed Panch Mahal, which overlooks the *mardana*. This trabeate structure consists of a stack of columned halls which decrease in size, pyramidal fashion, above the first two storeys. It is crowned with a *chattri*, and the broad *chajja* eaves contribute to its distinct Hindu character. *Jali* screens were originally placed between the columns to conceal the women who used this building to observe the events in the *mardana* below.

The *zanana* complex is the harem, where the buildings are more enclosed. A number of free-standing pavilions include the Sunahra Makan, named after the gold of its murals, and Birbal's House, two-storeyed and symmetrical with *chajja* eaves. The dominant building is the palace of Jodh Bai, a two-storeyed quadrangular structure enclosed by high walls, broken by entrance gates, and corner *jarokhas*. Projecting from the wall on the north side is a two-storeyed wind tower with walls of latticed stone, providing another airy vantage point for the women to see

Fatehpur Sikri, the Panch Mahal

Agra, detail of the Jahangiri Mahal within the fort

Sikandra, the entrance to tomb of Akbar

the garden opposite. Inside the palace is a range of apartments looking out on the courtyard, with four projecting, two-storeyed pavilions which recall the four-*iwan* plan. It also follows the Hindu tradition and has been compared with such Rajput palaces as the Gujari Mahal at Gwalior and the Raj Mandir at Orchha.[16] The Jodh Bai Palace did not belong to Jodh Bai, the wife of Jahangir. It was probably built for the wives of Akbar, but some scholars suggest that it was Akbar's palace and that the women were accommodated in an adjacent court which until recently was identified as the stable block.[17] This is a long deep arcaded court with domed cell units and an ambulatory corridor running along its inside wall. Tillotson thinks its close proximity to the harem makes it unlikely that it was the stables, and he suggests it probably was quarters for the women servants.[18] On the other hand, Koch argues that its design and recent archaeological evidence support the traditional view.[19] There is no doubt that the size of the units and lack of privacy make them more suitable for horses than the emperor's wives; the degree of speculation indicates the recurring problem of functional ambiguity in Islamic architecture.

In 1585 Akbar left Fatehpur Sikri and settled in Lahore to attend to problems on the north-west frontier. He spent thirteen years there and then moved back to the centre, preferring Agra to Fatehpur Sikri. Earlier, in 1564, work had commenced on the rebuilding of the fort in Agra, and two magnificent gates (1566–69), the Hathi Pol and Akbari Darwaza, bear witness to the emergence of an unprecedented grandeur in Indo-Islamic military architecture. Inside the fort the Jahangiri Mahal is the only substantial building dating from Akbar's reign (1570).

Here again there is a mixture of Islamic and Hindu elements. The exterior façade on the west has a broad horizontal sweep broken by a projecting central *iwan* with a deep arch. Polygonal towers crowned by prominent *chattris* are set in the corners, and the upper storey consists of a bracketed gallery with *chajja* eaves projecting below the cornice. The sandstone surface of the lower storey is relieved by blind arches and panels picked out in white marble. In the upper storey *jarokhas* are set in the front and angled sides of the *iwan*, and the windows of the gallery with their *jali* screens provided a look-out for the women of the harem. The inner court and flanking halls are trabeate in structure, and the proliferation of Hindu brackets are in the Rajput style of Gwalior. However, the eastern façade returns to more traditional Islamic forms; here the recessed arches and tall veranda columns have a distinct Persian and Central Asian flavour.

Akbar died in 1605 and was succeeded by Jahangir, an aesthete, who lacked the political energy of his father and showed less interest in military matters or the affairs of state. Despite this the empire expanded, and the wheels of government, delegated to an able civil service, worked efficiently during his twenty-two year reign. The success was partly due to the political skills of his cultivated wife, Nur Jahan, who came from a distinguished Persian family and did much to promote Persian taste and literature in the court. Jahangir was a connoisseur of painting rather than of architecture. He also had a love of nature, and like his great-grandfather, Babur, he was a keen gardener and played a major role in the creation of the Shalimar Gardens at Srinagar in Kashmir. His involvement with architecture began with the completion of Akbar's tomb at Sikandra. This was begun in the year of Akbar's death (1605), but the design had been in place well before Jahangir took responsibility for operations in 1608. The tomb is set in a vast *chahar bagh* enclosure and entered by an imposing Persian style *iwan* gate richly inlaid with marble mosaic and surmounted by four prominent white marble cylindrical minarets. The tomb is on an arcaded podium with tall *iwans* in the centre of each side and octagonal towers surmounted with *chattris* at the corners. The superstructure does not relate to the character and scale of the enormous podium, confirming the change of direction that Jahangir initiated when he visited the site in 1608.[20] The superstructure is like the Panch Mahal at

Agra, detail of the tomb of Itimad ud Daulah

Fatehpur Sikri, a three-storeyed stack of trabeated halls, surmounted by a white marble court screened with *jalis*. It is enlivened by a rich and varied display of *chattris*, but as Tillotson observed, the pyramidal ensemble lacks a sense of climax and calls out for a central dome.[21]

The unresolved elements in the design of the tomb of Akbar are partly due to the abrupt change of direction in the building programme and partly due to the hybrid mixture of Hindu and Islamic elements. In so many instances, as Tillotson rightly argued, Akbar's architecture is an 'elaborate medley' of form, rather than a true synthesis.[22] The latter involves an integration of form which is unselfconscious and unforced, which grows and matures into a new order organically and harmoniously. Akbar's pick-and-mix architectural vocabulary produced vigorous and intriguing metaphors, but it was frequently ungrammatical and often confused. The process of true synthesis began in the reign of Jahangir and reached its maturation in the Taj Mahal. The first building to express a new direction, as well as the opulence and refinement of Jahangir's reign, is the tomb commissioned by Nur Jahan for her father, Itimad ud Daulah. From the Agra Fort it stands, like an ivory casket, on the opposite side of the Jumna river one mile

Agra, the tomb of Itimad ud Daulah

upstream. It was the first building to be built entirely with white marble and *pietra dura* inlay. Situated in a *chahar bagh*, it is a low rectangular building with a domed pavilion on its flat roof and four minarets crowned with *chattris* engaged in each corner. The minarets are divided horizontally by bracketed balconies and their octagonal shafts become cylinders three-quarters of the way up and terminate with circular *chattris*. This building is distinguished by its colour and fine surface decoration. The arabesques and geometry have a lightness of touch, suggesting Persian influence, and the *pietra dura* inlay, with its hard and precious stones, adds delicacy of detail. This surface decoration is applied uniformly over the whole building, and the fragility of form is enhanced by the *jalis*, which fill all the window apertures. It is more like an *objet d'art* than monumental architecture, and its jewel-like nature and intricate Persian elegance reflect the taste of both patrons – Jahangir, the connoisseur, and Nur Jahan, the poet.

Jahangir's tomb at Shadera, near Lahore, was commissioned by Nur Jahan in 1627. Like Itimad ud Daulah's tomb, it consists of a broad cloistered podium framed by four tall, tapered, corner minarets with *chattris* crowning their octagonal shafts. The *pietra dura* detailing is of the highest quality, and the combination of pink sandstone and white marble reinforces a shift of emphasis in the use of materials. It now lacks the open screened pavilion which once stood on the podium, but its low-slung composition expresses a spacious elegance and light touch which make it an appropriate prelude to the age of Shah Jahan. It inaugurated a golden age in which Mughal architecture reached its peak of refinement, and like Süleyman the Magnificent or Lorenzo de Medici, Shah Jahan stands as a personification of its cultural splendour. He was a self-indulgent man and a lavish patron of the arts, but unlike his father he was a more energetic ruler and an active participant in military campaigns. He came to the throne in 1627 at the age of thirty-five and resumed Akbar's policy of securing control over the Muslim sultanates in the Deccan. He also tried, and failed, to recapture lost territories in Farghana and Kandahar. While he was on one of his arduous campaigns his wife, Mumtaz Mahal, died in childbirth at Burhanpur in 1631. She was the granddaughter of Itimad ud Daulah and niece of Nur Jahan, and during their nineteen years

of marriage she bore him fourteen children. She always accompanied Shah Jahan on his military campaigns, and it was a tribute to her fortitude, loyalty and love that he built her tomb, the Taj Mahal (1632–48).

It is necessary, for a moment, to suspend our picture postcard image of the Taj Mahal and try to understand and appreciate it within the wider context of its site and plan. Like Itimad ud Daulah's tomb it has a riverside location and among the most impressive views are those from the Jumna, or at a distance from the Agra Fort. It is set in a grand *chahar bagh*, with water channels forming the usual

Agra, the Taj Mahal

quadripartite division. They intersect at the centre to form a tank, and pathways further subdivide the gardens to form sixteen in total. The mausoleum breaks from tradition by being situated, not in the centre of the *chahar bagh* but to one side, where it majestically takes up its riverside position on a raised terrace. It stands on a podium framed by four tapering cylindrical minarets which act as graceful space markers. Two flanking buildings on the lower terrace are a triple-domed mosque and an identical building opposite, known as a *jawab*, an assembly hall. Facing the mausoleum at the end of a water channel running along the north-south axis is the main gate piercing the enclosure wall. The plan is governed by absolute symmetry in both its broader measure and detail. The symmetries seem multidimensional as they are inverted and mirrored in the water or repeated in the rhythmic intervals staked out by shrubs and cypresses, echoing less formally the vertical alignments of the minarets.

Agra, the Taj Mahal

Agra, the triple-domed mosque flanking the Taj Mahal

Agra, plan of the Taj Mahal

In plan the mausoleum is basically a square with chamfered corners forming an irregular octagon, but this deceptive simplicity conceals a ninefold plan similar to that of Humayun's Tomb. Octagonal regularities are embedded more deeply in the structure, consisting of a cluster of four solid masonry octagons enclosing an octagonal void in the centre (a simpler variation of this plan is echoed in the gate-house). This octagonal centre is surrounded by a square ambulatory which locks the plan together with a harmony and resolution that make the diagonal arrangement at the centre of Humayun's tomb seem restless in comparison. The square of the plan is repeated in the elevation, where the height to the top of the dome (excluding the finial) equals the width. There is uniformity in the vertical divisions of the elevation, with each angled facet being of equal width, except for the *iwans* which count as double units. The bulbous dome is flanked by *chattris* and set on a tall drum so that from a distance it is prominent above the *pishtaqs*.

It has a two-storeyed elevation, and the harmony of its proportions suggests a renewal of the Safavid tradition. It is within the perfection and resolution of its proportions that the various hybrid elements become subsumed into the whole, allowing genuine synthesis to take place. Some writers emphasise the Persian influence, and Hermann Goetz went so far as to claim it as 'a work of the finest Safavid taste'.[23] They exaggerate the Persian dimension, but it was probably necessary at the time for the master-builders to reconsider the compositional

Agra, the entrance to the Taj Mahal complex

genius of Persian architecture in order to devise a scheme that would make a new synthesis possible. There was no master-architect as such, but the names of Nadir al-Asar, Mamur Khan and Mukarrimat Khan appear in contemporary documents, and it is significant that the first two were principally mathematicians and had a family background in Herat.[24] As well as the grace and subtlety of its proportions, the use of white marble and *pietra dura* on such a scale makes it unique. All the accompanying buildings are of sandstone, and marble is restricted to sheathing the domes and framing the *pishtaqs*. The density of sandstone ensures that the flanking mosque and *jawab* recede, so that the white mausoleum is revealed in all its pristine glory.

The *pietra dura* detail is exquisite and used here much more selectively than in the tomb of Itimad ud Daulah. It is restricted to the arabesques in the spandrels of the arches, and the *iwans* are framed with bands of Naskhi, which are sharply and elegantly inscribed, as if written with a quill. Contemporary documents list the semi-precious stones as jasper, topaz, agate, cornelian, onyx, lapis, turquoise and blood-stone. In the wainscot panels plant motifs in *pietra dura* and carved relief display a realism which has prompted suggestions of western influence. *Pietra dura* motifs also appear on the cenotaphs and the surrounding *jali* screens, where individual flowers display remarkable *trompe-l'oeil* virtuosity. Blair and Bloom suggest that the western influence may have come from European herbal engravings, which began to influence Mughal manuscript painting in the early seventeenth century.[25] The realism of these motifs contradicts the whole tradition of Islamic arabesque, where stylised floral and vegetal motifs are locked into a ground supported by an underframe of geometry. Where these motifs appear in carved relief, they are rendered with individuality and naturalism, floating in a space that takes little account of the ground.

While the Taj Mahal was being built, Shah Jahan began to add new palace buildings next to Akbar's Jahangiri Mahal in the Agra Fort. The garden layout of the Taj Mahal is echoed in the fort by a similar *chahar bagh*, the Anghuri Bagh, which was being planted at the same time on a much smaller scale. This is divided in the quadripartite manner with a marble tank at the centre, and three pavilions are symmetrically arranged on a raised terrace on

Agra, the Taj Mahal

the eastern side of the garden. The central pavilion, the Khas Mahal, is a colonnaded hall of white marble flanked by two buildings with curved gilded copper-plate roofs, the Bangla i Darshan and Bangla of Jahanara. The Anghuri Bagh and its surrounding buildings are the private quarters of the palace, and tradition has ascribed these gilded pavilions to the women's sleeping quarters, but it is now thought these rooms were more open and flexible in their use.[26] On the north-eastern side of the Anghuri Bagh is the Sheesh Mahal, or Glass Palace, named after its decor of mirror-glass, and nearby is an octagonal pavilion, the Mussaman Burj. This copper-domed pavilion looks out on the river and is richly decorated with *pietra dura*, *jalis* and marble reliefs. Sprays of flowers on the marble wainscot are similar to those in the Taj Mahal, and the walls are pierced with belljar-shaped niches similar to those in Ottoman architecture. The whole ensemble recalls seventeenth-century palace architecture elsewhere, such as the Ali Qapu Palace and the Baghdad Kiosk, and the western derivation of the floral motifs in the wainscot anticipates those rococo accents in the 'Fruit Room' of the Topkapı.

To the north of the Mussaman Burj is the private audience hall, the Diwan i Khas, on a high terrace overlooking the river on one side and the cloistered Machchi Bhawan square on the other. The Diwan i Khas consists of a white marble hall, enclosed at the back, with an open arcaded portico in front. Its simple interior is relieved by arched recesses, and the decorative detail consists of delicate relief carving with inlaid flowers made up of red cornelian and white marble. The use of cusped arches in the portico and elsewhere in the palace is a distinctive

TOP LEFT
Agra, the Fort: detail of the Mussaman Burj

TOP RIGHT
Agra: Khas Mahal and Bangla i Jahanara

ABOVE
Agra, the Fort: the Diwan i Am

feature of the age of Shah Jahan. The Machchi Bhawan, or 'Fish Square', is so named because it once contained a garden with a fish tank. It is surrounded by a two-storeyed arcaded cloister with a royal loggia, framed by baluster columns, projecting from the south wing. Below this is the public audience hall, the Diwan i Am, which is a large hypostyle hall, three bays deep and nine in width, with a flat roof supported on arcades of cusped arches. Its design is identical to a prayer hall, except that the emperor's throne stands in place of the *mihrab*, and according to Koch this signifies the union of political and spiritual authority.[27]

The only formal difference between this, and the prayer hall of the fort's principal mosque, the Moti Masjid, is the presence of three domes on the roof of the latter. The façade of the Moti Masjid prayer hall has no centralising feature, such as a *pishtaq*, but a continuous arcade with a *chajja* eave below the cornice. The same format can be seen in the design of the private and public audience halls in the Red Fort at Delhi, and what we see here is another exchange of ideas between hitherto separate architectural domains. In the case of funerary and palace architecture we have already seen how the secular and sacred spheres reciprocated in their use of the ninefold plan and *chahar bagh*. As well as this kind of interchange, the age of Shah Jahan produced stylistic innovations which extended the absorption of Hindu and other elements. New forms were added, existing ones modified and western influence was not just confined to decorative detail, but also extended to the introduction of baluster columns. The curved *banglar* roof is an innovation based on Bengali vernacular architecture, and, in company with cusped arches, baluster columns and bulbous domes, gives rise to those florid 'baroque' rhythms that became the *leitmotif* of later Mughal architecture.

In 1638 Shah Jahan moved the capital back to Delhi and began work on Shahjahanabad, the seventh city. Today this forms the core of Old Delhi, and Shah Jahan's surviving monuments consist principally of the Jami Masjid and the Red Fort. The Jami Masjid is one of the largest and most imposing mosques in India (1644–58). It is set on an elevated site at the heart of the commercial area of the city, and its steps are thronged with activity. The life and energy of the bazaars and market stalls spill over into the mosque, and more than most this building exemplifies the living faith of Islam. It is raised on a lofty podium approached by three steep flights of steps surmounted by gates which lead into a vast *sahn*. The *riwaqs* form a cloister around the *sahn* with arcades open on both sides, so that from the outside there is the unusual feature of an open arcade above the podium. The arcade sweeps majestically around the perimeter walls, broken only by the imposing gates and corner *chattri* towers. The prayer hall is of the three-domed type, and the lower half of the façade is pierced with an arcade which is broken at the centre by a commanding *iwan*. The high *pishtaq* is flanked by slender engaged columns crowned with pinnacles, which are echoed on a larger scale by the octagonal shafts of the tall minarets on either side of the prayer hall façade. The materials are sandstone decorated with white marble, and the bulbous white domes are crowned with lotus finials and articulated with fine vertical lines of black marble. It lacks the sophistication and grace of the Taj Mahal, but it has a nobility, breadth and monumentality of scale, that sets the tone for later Mughal buildings, such as the Badshahi Mosque at Lahore (1673–74).

Work commenced on the Red Fort in 1638 and Shah Jahan employed a number of architects who had worked with him on the Taj Mahal. In building the Red Fort he was able to plan with the kind of symmetrical rigour he had exercised at the Taj Mahal. The Red Fort was not just a residential palace, but it functioned as the centre of government, housing administrative buildings, the treasury, a garrison, the arsenal, shops and factories. Its red sandstone walls are pierced by two magnificent gates, the Lahore Gate and the Delhi Gate, which lead

Delhi, the Jami Masjid

into the two main axes of the palace. The Lahore Gate marks the beginning of the east-west axis leading ceremoniously to the public buildings. The Delhi Gate opened on to the main north-south axis, a public thoroughfare lined in part with bazaar stalls. From the Lahore Gate a high vaulted bazaar extends to an open space with a pavilion gate, known as the Naqqar Khana, or Drum House, which contained a gallery for musicians. It marked the transition between the public and private domains, where members of the public would dismount before proceeding towards the Diwan i Am. In style the Diwan i Am follows its counterpart at Agra, with cusped arches and paired columns around the perimeter. The back wall is solid and in the centre is an extraordinary throne with a baldachin formed by a *bangla* roof supported on baluster columns. It is covered with intricate *pietra dura* work depicting plants, birds and beasts and includes a rare figurative image of Orpheus playing to the animals. Some of these panels were Italian imports, and according to Koch this throne was a symbol of Solomon's throne, and the image of Orpheus represented Shah Jahan's rule in an idealised state of justice and peace.[28]

Beyond the Diwan i Am, on the same east-west axis, is the Rang Mahal, one of a number of private buildings

Delhi, Red Fort: Diwan i Khas

Delhi, Red Fort: the Moti Masjid

arranged along the eastern edge of the palace overlooking the river. The Rang Mahal was the principal pavilion for the women's quarters and consisted of five pavilions extending south to the Mumtaz Mahal, now housing a museum. To the north of this is the Khas Mahal, the emperor's private domain, containing his sleeping quarters and an open veranda facing the Rang Mahal. An octagonal tower, the Mussaman Burj, provides a breezy vantage point for viewing the river or watching blood sports, which took place on the ground below. Adjacent to this is the Diwan i Khas which follows the architectural precedent of Agra. Unlike at Agra, however, the structure is free standing and sports four instead of two *chattris* on its roof. The florid interior consists of cusped arches set on piers, and *pietra dura* decoration adorns the lower registers. The ceilings and arches are festooned with elegant arabesques picked out in silver and gold, providing a sumptuous setting for the Peacock Throne.

To the north of the Diwan i Khas is the Moti Masjid, or Pearl Mosque, built by Aurangzib for his private use in 1659. Enclosed by a sandstone wall, the mosque and inner court are constructed and faced with white marble. The prayer hall is three bays by two, with a wider central nave. The arches are cusped, and the central arch in the façade rises above its neighbours to form a shallow curved *bangla* roof. The domes are bulbous, with heavy lotus finials, and the whole building is compact, dense and florid – almost *art nouveau* in the linearity of its detail. Those 'baroque' rhythms that emerged in Shah Jahan's architecture are here taken a stage further, and a number of elements become exaggerated to the point of caricature. The form is modelled rather than constructed, gravitating towards that Indian sculptural tradition which is not always at ease with the structural rigour of Islamic architecture. The Moti Masjid signals the decline of Mughal architecture, and this decline is highlighted in other buildings commissioned by Aurangzib. The tomb he built at Aurangabad for his wife, Rabia Daurani, conspicuously begs comparison with the Taj Mahal, and the fact that it falls so short of the mark makes it an embarrassing failure. Other buildings, such as the Badshahsi Mosque in Lahore, retain something of the grandeur and dignity of the Shah Jahan period, but there is a lack of invention which reflects the conservatism of his reign.

Unlike his father, Aurangzib was not a great patron of the arts and architecture – his abstemious puritanism guaranteed that. Religious orthodoxy drew him closer to the *mullahs* with their desire for a more Islamic form of government. Because of this he reversed those policies of his predecessors which encouraged religious, political and cultural inclusiveness. He reimposed the poll tax on non-Muslims, enforced moral censorship, closed Hindu schools and destroyed a number of temples. All these measures alienated his Rajput subjects and sowed the seeds of the empire's ultimate decline. Aurangzib made considerable territorial advances in the south, but his conquests only weakened and bankrupted the empire, and when he died in 1707 there was political turmoil, social unrest and struggles for succession. It was not until Muhammad Shah came to the throne in 1720 that stability was restored. The position of the emperor remained significantly weak, and the days of divinely guided kingship were over. Muhammad Shah's reign inaugurated a more

tolerant era, but his fragile hold on the empire was shattered when Nadir Shah, arriving from Persia in 1739, invaded India and sacked Delhi.

The Mughal dynasty never recovered, and thereafter the emperors became mere puppet rulers. Their empire fragmented, with power devolving to the regions where Shi'ite, Sunni, Hindu and Sikh rulers established their own independent principalities. The spirit of Mughal architecture survived in a number of distinguished buildings, such as Safdarjang's mausoleum in Delhi (1754), but elsewhere the Mughal style was transformed into something else. A number of Rajput rulers, closely allied to the Mughal court, had already absorbed Mughal elements into their palace architecture. The palace at Amber makes free use of Mughal forms in the central chamber of the Jai Mandir apartments, a building that has an interior like a mother-of-pearl jewel-box studded with glass mosaic, *pietra dura* arabesque, cusped niches, marble relief and arched panels punched with poly-

Jaipur, Palace of the Winds

chrome bottle shapes. The pleasure pavilion of the palace at Udaipur has cusped arches, baluster columns and latticed windows, and its audience chamber is like a *sheesh mahal* with niches covered with mirror-glass. In the newly created city of Jaipur, there is an extraordinary ensemble of *bangla* roofs and *chattris* incorporated into the multitude of oriel windows which make up the six-storeyed façade of the Palace of the Winds. These hybrid forms are symptomatic of regional independence and Hinduism's enduring capacity to absorb and assimilate other traditions. A similar situation can be observed among the Sikhs, where Mughal forms enter their architectural vocabulary in the Punjab with such buildings as the Hazuri Bagh Baradari in Lahore.

Finally the British, gifted with a knack for architectural revivalism, had no difficulty in adapting Indo-Islamic architecture to the sub-continent's new public buildings. Railway stations, hotels, law courts and government buildings provided imaginative scope for new hybrid

Amber Palace

forms of Indo-Islamic architecture (or Indo-Saracenic as it became known). Notable examples are the palace at Baroda (1878) by Charles Mant and Robert Fellowes Chisolm, and the palace at Mysore by Henry Irwin (1900). The story of Indo-Islamic architecture did not end there, because it was imported into great Britain. Sir Charles Cockerell's work at Sezincote House in Gloucestershire is an early example (1805), and John Nash's Royal Pavilion at Brighton represents its most extravagant expression (1822). Emigration into Britain

produced the first mosque at Woking in 1889, and today there is a remarkable change in the urban landscape as bulbous domes with lotus finials now form a part of the pluralist language of Post-Modernist British architecture.

At best, this latest manifestation of Post-Modernism goes no further than playful and clichéd juxtapositions of Indo-Islamic symbols and surfaces in an intriguing and entertaining manner. However, the future of Islamic architecture must lie in a deeper restatement of its universal values and meanings. Post-Modernism as an expression of pluralism has to be welcomed, but not if it means pastiche and historicism. Up to the beginning of the eighteenth century the story of Islamic architecture had been one of remarkable invention, continuity and adaptation. It organically evolved a language of form based on the manipulation of open-ended geometries, creating an architecture that is distinguished by its adaptability and functional diversity. At the heart of Islamic architecture there is a formal continuum which accounts for its unity, flexibility and transferability. A deeper analysis of the internal structures, processes and traditions that made this continuum possible is now taking place, and a new Islamic architecture is emerging which is addressing the needs of today without sacrificing continuity and tradition. Now that the tyranny of international modernism has receded, leading architects and designers are reassessing and reinterpreting the Islamic tradition in a truly fresh and creative way. Promising developments have already taken place, and such projects as the King Fahd and Agha Khan awards for architecture are concentrating attention on new ways of thinking and research. In Great Britain, the Prince of Wales Institute of Architecture is engaged in researching and regenerating the Islamic tradition, and the creative example of such diverse people as Hassan Fathy, Rasem Badren, Jahangir Mazlum and Abdel Wahed El-Wakil, demonstrates emphatically that the story of Islamic architecture is taking on a new meaning and lease of life.

Notes and References

Introduction: The Prophet's Ministry and the Muslim Faith

1. The most lucid and readable accounts of the Prophet's ministry can be found in the writings of W. Montgomery Watt. See his chapter in *The Cambridge History of Islam*, Holt, Lambton and Lewis (eds), volume 1A (Cambridge University Press, Cambridge, 1970). For a fuller account read his book, *Muhammad, Statesman and Prophet* (Oxford University Press, Oxford, 1961).
2. See the relevant chapter in *Approaches to Islam* by Richard Tames (John Murray, London, 1982).
3. There are many collections of *hadith* but possibly the most important is Bukhari. Many of the extracts I use are taken from this source. See also Muhammad Ali, M., *A Manual of Hadith* (Curzon Press, London, 1977); Rahman I. Doi, A., *Introduction to the Hadith* (Arewa Books, Ibadan, 1981).
4. One of the best books which reveal the faith through sacred literature is *Islam* by John A. Williams (Prentice Hall, New Jersey, 1961).
5. See Coulson, N.J., *A History of Islamic Law* (Edinburgh University Press, Edinburgh, 1964).
6. See Nicholson, R.A., *The Mystics of Islam* (Routledge & Kegan Paul, London, 1963).
7. The writings of Titus Burckhardt, listed in the Selected Bibliography, reveal the mystical dimension of Islamic art and architecture.

Chapter 1: The Religious Basis of Form and Function in Islamic Architecture

1. Blunt, A. *Artistic Theory in Italy 1450–1600* (Oxford University Press, Oxford, 1964), p. 108.
2. Burckhardt, T. *Sacred Art in East and West* (Perennial Books Ltd, 1967), p. 106.
3. Grabar, O., *The Formation of Islamic Art* (Yale University Press, New Haven, 1973), p. 76.
4. Arnold, T., *Painting in Islam* (Dover, New York, 1965), p. 6.
5. Arnold, T., op cit., p.6.
6. Arnold, T., op cit., p. 9.
7. Arnold, T., op cit. p. 9.
8. Grabar, O., 'Islam and Iconoclasm', in Brier, A., and Herrin, J. (eds), *Iconoclasm* (Centre for Byzantine Studies, Birmingham, 1977).
9. Arnold, T., op cit., p. 2.
10. Sordo, E., *Moorish Spain* (Elek, London, 1963), p. 51.
11. Hillenbrand, R., *Islamic Architecture: Form, Function and Meaning* (Edinburgh University Press, Edinburgh, 1994), pp. 254–255.

Chapter 2: Umayyad Architecture

1. Lewis, B., *The Arabs in History* (London, 1958), p. 55.
2. Grabar, O., op cit. (1973). See chapter 3, 'The Symbolic Appropriation of the Land'.
3. Grabar, O., op cit. (1973), p. 59.
4. Creswell, K.A.C., *A Short Account of Early Muslim Architecture* (Penguin, London, 1958), p. 37.
5. Grabar, O., op cit. (1973), p. 64.
6. Creswell, K.A.C., op cit., pp. 67–73.
7. Creswell, K.A.C., op cit., p. 73.
8. Ettinghausen, R., *Arab Painting* (Skira, New York, 1977), p. 24.
9. Ettinghausen, R., op cit., p. 28.
10. Beckwith, J., *Early Christian and Byzantine Art* (Yale University Press, New Haven, 1979), p. 167.
11. Grabar, O., op cit. (1973), p. 141.
12. Hillenbrand, R., op cit., p. 331.
13. Hillenbrand, R., op cit., p. 162.
14. Grabar, O., op cit. (1973), p. 161.
15. Grabar, O., op cit. (1973), p. 162.
16. Ettinghausen, R., op cit., p. 34.
17. Creswell, K.A.C., op cit., p. 150.
18. Grabar, O., op cit. (1973), p. 162.
19. Stierlin, H., *Islam Volume 1: Early Architecture from Baghdad to Cordoba* (Taschen, Cologne, 1996), p. 75.
20. Ettinghausen, R., op cit., p. 38.
21. Grabar, O., op cit. (1973), p. 156.
22. Creswell, K.A.C., op cit., p. 88.
23. Ettinghausen, R., op cit., p. 32.
24. Grabar, O., op cit. (1973), p. 47.
25. Grabar, O., ibid.

Chapter 3: An Emerging Islamic Identity

1. Lewis, B., op cit., p. 71.
2. Lewis, B., op cit., p. 81.
3. Creswell, K.A.C., op cit., pp. 170–173.
4. Creswell, K.A.C., op cit., pp. 201–202.
5. Hillenbrand, R. op cit., p. 396.
6. Hillenbrand, R., op cit., p. 76.
7. Creswell, K.A.C., op cit., p. 279.
8. Hillenbrand, R., op cit., p. 298.
9. Creswell, K.A.C., op cit., p. 297–298.
10. Burckhardt, T., *Art of Islam* (World of Islam Festival Publishing Co., London, 1976), p. 91.
11. Hillenbrand, R., op cit., p. 46.
12. Grabar, O., op cit. (1973), p. 120.
13. Michell, G. (ed.), *Architecture of the Islamic World* (Thames & Hudson, London, 1978), p. 221.

Chapter 4: TULUNID AND FATIMID EGYPT

1. Behrens-Abouseif, D., *Islamic Architecture in Cairo: An Introduction* (American University in Cairo Press, Cairo, 1989) p. 49.
2. Creswell, K.A.C., op cit., p. 294.
3. Jones, O., *The Grammar of Ornament* (Studio Editions, London, reprinted, 1988), p. 57.
4. According to Nikolaus Pevsner, the earliest European universities evolved independently of the ecclesiastical schools in order to develop a more secular curriculum. The first universities were in Italy, where Bologna and Salerno established secular and practical subjects like medicine and civil law. In England the universities of Oxford and Cambridge developed their collegiate structure during the thirteenth century in response to the need for more administrators. Pevsner, N. and Sherwood, J., *The Buildings of England: Oxfordshire* (Penguin, London, 1974), p. 21.
5. Hillenbrand, R., op cit., p. 167.
6. Hillenbrand, R., op cit., p. 126.
7. Behrens-Abouseif, D., op cit., p. 72.
8. See 'A Preliminary' in Lawrence, T.E., *Crusader Castles* (Immel Publishing, London, 1992).

Chapter 5: UMAYYAD, ALMORAVID AND ALMOHAD ARCHITECTURE IN SPAIN AND MOROCCO

1. Watt, M. W., *A History of Islamic Spain* (Edinburgh University Press, Edinburgh, 1965), p. 3.
2. See Watt, M. W., op cit. (1965), pp. 31–32; Sordo, E., op cit., pp. 18–19; Burckhardt, T., *Moorish Culture in Spain* (Allen & Unwin, London, 1972), chapter 2.
3. Castejon, R., *The Mosque of Cordoba* (Editorial Everest-Leon, Castejon-Leon, 1973), p. 16.
4. Burckhardt, T., op cit. (1972), p. 11.
5. Burckhardt, T., op cit. (1972), pp. 12–13.
6. Hillenbrand, R., op cit., p. 443.
7. Burckhardt, T., op cit. (1972), pp. 34–35.
8. Hillenbrand, R., op cit., p. 382.
9. Hillenbrand, R., op cit., p. 140.

Chapter 6: NASRID, MUDEJAR, MARINID AND SA'DIAN ARCHITECTURE IN SPAIN AND NORTH AFRICA

1. Grabar, O., *The Alhambra* (Allen Lane, London, 1978), p. 33.
2. Bargeburh, F., *The Alhambra: A Cycle of Studies on the Eleventh Century in Moorish Spain* (Walter de Gruyter & Co, Berlin, 1968). Solomonic symbolism and association is one of the major themes presented in this remarkable book.
3. Sordo, E., op cit., p. 165.
4. Charles Jencks, *Post-Modern Architecture* (Academy Editions, London, 1991). Charles Jencks quotes the phrase in his summary of Klotz's notions on narrative content in Post-Modern Architecture, p. 15.
5. Bargeburh, F., op cit., p. 135.
6. Bargeburh, F., op cit., p. 98.

7. Godrey Goodwin states with some certainty that they were fourteenth century and not from Nagrallah's Palace as Bargeburh suggests. However, more recent publications by Robert Hillenbrand broadly suggest that they were probably from the eleventh-century palace. See Godfrey Goodwin, *Islamic Spain* (Penguin, London, 1990), p. 75; Sheila Blair and Jonathan Bloom, *The Art and Architecture of Islam 1250–1800* (Yale University Press, New Haven & London, 1995), p. 126; Robert Hillenbrand, *Islamic Architecture* (Edinburgh University Press, Edinburgh, 1994), p. 453.
8. Bargeburh, F., op cit., p. 99.
9. Grabar, O., op cit. (1978), pp. 128–129.
10. Grabar, O., op cit. (1978), p. 103.
11. Bargeburh, F., op cit., p. 105.
12. Jones, O., op cit., p. 71.
13. Grabar, O., op cit. (1978), p. 57.
14. Bargeburh, F., op cit., ?
15. Grabar, O., op cit. (1978), p. 124–127.
16. In the case of Gabo, I have in mind his fountain situated on the south bank of the River Thames in London opposite the Palace of Westminster. Duchamp refers to a sculpture of drops in his notes for *The Bride Stripped Bare by Her Bachelors, Even* (the Green Box).
17. Burckhardt, T., op cit. (1976), p. 80.
18. Bargeburh, F., op cit., p. 98.
19. Goodwin, G., op cit., p. 77.
20. Goodwin, G., op cit., p. 79.
21. Goodwin, G., op cit., p. 113.
22. Lisa Jardine, *Worldly Goods* (Macmillan, London, 1996), p. 88.

Chapter 7: AYYUBID AND MAMLUK ARCHITECTURE

1. Rogers, M., *The Making of the Past: The Spread of Islam* (Elsevier/Phaidon, Oxford, 1975), p. 46.
2. Burns, R., *Monuments of Syria: An Historical Guide* (I.B. Tauris, London & New York, 1992), p. 188.
3. Behrens-Abouseif, D., op cit., p. 97.
4. Behrens-Abouseif, D., op cit., p. 109.
5. This palace built by Shapur I in the third century AD has an *iwan* 25 metres in span and 35 metres high. It always held a special place in the Muslim imagination and provided a challenge to generations of Muslim builders.
6. Behrens-Abouseif, D., op cit., p. 125; see also Lings, M., *The Quranic Art of Calligraphy and Illumination* (World of Islam Festival Publishing Co., 1976), p. 119.
7. Rogers, M., op cit., pp. 97–99.
8. Behrens-Abouseif, D., op cit., p. 22.
9. Hillenbrand, R., op cit., p. 197.

Chapter 8: SAMANID AND SELJUK ARCHITECTURE IN PERSIA AND ANATOLIA

1. Hillenbrand, R., op cit., p. 289.
2. Pope, A., *Persian Architecture* (George Braziller, New York, 1965), p. 44.
3. Byron, R., *The Road to Oxiana* (Jonathan Cape, London, 1937), p. 231.

4. Hillenbrand, R., op cit., p. 275.
5. Nasr, S.H., *Islamic Science: An Illustrated Study* (World of Islam Festival Publishing Co. Ltd, 1976), p. 200.
6. Byron, R., op cit., p. 196.
7. Ardelan, N. and Bahktiar, L., *The Sense of Unity: The Sufi Tradition in Persian Architecture* (Chicago, 1971), p. 108.
8. Hillenbrand, R., op cit., p. 155.
9. Byron, R., op cit., p. 324.
10. Hillenbrand, R., op cit., p. 210.
11. Jairazbhoy, R., *An Outline of Islamic Architecture* (Asia Publishing House, Bombay, 1972), p. 199.
12. Talbot Rice, T., *The Seljuks* (Thames & Hudson, London, 1961), p. 161.
13. Jairazbhoy, R., op cit., p. 194.
14. Hillenbrand, R., op cit., p. 95.

Chapter 9: OTTOMAN ARCHITECTURE

1. Periodically Edirne became the capital.
2. İnalcik. H., 'The Emergence of the Ottomans' in *Volume 1A: The Cambridge History of Islam*, Holt, Lambton and Lewis (eds.) (Cambridge University Press, Cambridge, 1970), p. 296.
3. Blair, S. and Bloom, J., op cit., p. 144.
4. Goodwin, G., *A History of Ottoman Architecture* (Thames & Hudson, London, 1987), p. 71.
5. Goodwin, G. op cit. (1987), p. 97.
6. Goodwin, G. op cit. (1987), p. 125.
7. Levey, M., *The World of Ottoman Art* (Thames & Hudson, London, 1975), p. 61.
8. Kuran, A., *Sinan: The Grand Old Master of Ottoman Architecture* (ADA Press Publishers, Istanbul, 1987), pp. 168–169.
9. Goodwin, G. op cit. (1987), p. 270.
10. Hillenbrand, R., op cit., p. 461.
11. Levey, M., op cit., pp. 113–114.
12. Levey, M., op cit., p. 102.

Chapter 10: ILKHANID, TIMURID AND SAFAVID ARCHITECTURE

1. This observation was made by Professor Charles Beckingham in a lecture on 'Islamic Fundamentalism' delivered 3 March 1991 at the University of Warwick.
2. Spuler, B., *The Mongols in History* (Pall Mall Press, London, 1971), p. 80.
3. Blair, S. and Bloom, J., op cit., p. 41.
4. Entry to the mosque is forbidden to non-Muslims and in 1934 Robert Byron entered the mosque in disguise.
5. Byron, R., op cit., p. 243.
6. Byron, R., op cit., p. 245.
7. Hillenbrand, R., op cit., p. 227.
8. Savory, R.M., 'Safavid Persia' in *The Cambridge History of Islam*, Holt, Lambton and Lewis (eds.) (Cambridge University Press, Cambridge, 1970), p. 398.
9. Pope, A.U., op cit., p. 85.
10. Blunt, W., *Isfahan: Pearl of Persia* (Elek, London,

1966), p. 134. Sir John Chardin was a Huguenot jeweller who purchased jewels for Shah Süleyman. Fleeing French persecution in 1681, he settled in England and became court jeweller to Charles II.
11. Blair, S. and Bloom, J., op cit., p. 195.
12. Blunt, W., op cit., p. 72.
13. Blunt, W., op cit., p. 71.
14. Pope, A.U., op cit., p. 99.

Chapter 11: ISLAMIC ARCHITECTURE IN SOUTH ASIA

1. Briggs, M., 'Muslim Architecture in India' in *A Cultural History of India*, Basham, A.L. (ed.) (Clarendon Press, Oxford, 1975), p. 314.
2. Tillotson, G.H.R., *Mughal India* (Penguin, London, 1990), p. 30.
3. Hoag, J., *Islamic Architecture* (Faber & Faber/Electra, London and New York, 1975), p. 147.
4. Rizvi, S.A.A., 'Islam in Medieval India' in *A Cultural History of India*, Basham, A.L. (ed.) (Clarendon Press, Oxford, 1975), p. 284.
5. During the third century BC the Mauryan Emperor Asoka converted to Buddhism (262 BC) and set up stone pillars (*lats*) throughout the empire on which were inscribed edicts of the Dharma. These pillars were Archaemenid in style and were up to 17 metres high and crowned with sculptured animals.
6. Blair, S. and Bloom, J., op cit., p. 154.
7. Hambly, G., *Cities of Mughal India* (Elek, London, 1968), p. 39.
8. Tillotson, G., op cit., p. 139.
9. Koch, E., *Mughal Architecture* (Prestel, Munich, 1991), p. 44.
10. Koch, E., op cit., pp. 44–46.
11. Hoag, J., op cit., p. 177.
12. Tillotson, G.H.R., op cit., p. 106.
13. Koch, E., op cit., p. 56.
14. Tillotson, G.H.R., op cit., p. 108.
15. Koch, E., op cit., p. 60.
16. Tillotson, G.H.R., op cit., p. 117.
17. Blair, S. and Bloom, J., op cit., p. 274.
18. Tillotson, G.H.R., op cit., p. 119.
19. Koch, E., op cit., p. 68.
20. Tillotson, G.H.R., op cit., p. 87.
21. Ibid.
22. Tillotson, G.H.R., op cit., p. 118.
23. Goetz, H., 'Persia and India after the Conquest of Mahmud' in *The Legacy of Persia*, A.J. Arberry (ed.), (Oxford, 1953), pp. 112–113.
24. Hoag, J., op cit., p. 185.
25. Blair, S. and Bloom, J., op cit., p. 281.
26. Tillotson, G.H.R., op cit., p. 78.
27. Koch, E., op cit., p. 109.
28. Koch, E., op cit., p. 111.

GLOSSARY

Islamic and oriental terms

ablaq — two-toned masonry usually arranged in horizontal courses

adhan — call to prayer

apadana — an ancient Persian columned hall

banglar — a curved roof derived from Bengali houses used in Mughal pavilions

baraka — blessing

bayat — self-contained living apartment

bayt — a house or apartment forming a self-contained unit in a palace

bedestan — a market

caravansarai — accommodation for travellers, merchants and animals

chahar bagh — a Persian garden divided into quadrants

chahar taq — a pre-Islamic (Zoroastrian) fire temple

chajja — wide sloping eaves

chattri — a domed kiosk in Indo-Islamic architecture

dakhmas — Persian towers of silence used by the Zoroastrians to expose the dead

darül-hadis — Ottoman theological college

darül-kurra — Ottoman Qur'an school

dershane — lecture hall

dhimi — Christians and Jews under Muslim rule

dikka — a raised platform used by prayer leaders

diwan-i-am — public audience hall

diwan-i-khas — private audience hall

hadith — traditions, sayings and accounts of the Prophet

hajj — pilgrimage to Mecca

hakim — a physician, sage and philosopher

hammam — baths

harem — the women's quarters of a house or palace

hijra — the migration from Mecca

ihram — purity

ijma — consensus

ijtihad — free reasoning

iman — belief

imaret — a soup kitchen

iwan — an open vaulted hall or portal

jali — a latticed screen

jarokha — a balcony

khan or han — a form of inn or urban caravansarai

khanqah — a residence for Sufis

khutba — a sermon delivered at the Friday noon prayers

külliya — an Ottoman mosque complex

kümbet — a tomb

madhab — one of the schools of law

madrasa — theological college or law school

maqsura — an enclosure placed in a mosque for the privacy and protection of the caliph or sultan

mardana — in Indo-Islamic architecture, the men's quarters of a house or palace

maristan — a hospital

mashhad — shrine

mashrabiya — screens made up of small pieces of Egyptian turned wood

mawali — non-Arab converts to Islam

mihrab — prayer niche

minbar — pulpit

miraj — The Prophet's 'night journey'

Moriscos — Spanish Muslims who converted to Christianity

Mozarab — Christians under Muslim rule in Spain

Mudejar — Arab minorities who retained their religion and law within Christian society and rule

mudejar — the style of architecture given to Muslims working for Christian patrons in Spain

muqarnas — stalactite sections which form a vault, niche or frieze

ocak — an Ottoman fireplace

pir — mentor

pishtaq — a lofty screen framing an arch, or a portal

qasr — palace or fort

qibla — the direction of prayer facing Mecca

qiyas — analogical reasoning

rak'ah — prayer movements and postures performed facing Mecca

razzia — raid on a Meccan caravan

ribat — fortified accommodation for soldiers – another name for a caravansarai

riwaq — a cloister arranged around a courtyard

sabil — a public fountain

sabil kuttab — a Qur'an school combined with public fountain

sahn — the courtyard of a mosque

salat — prayer

shahada — profession of faith in God and his Prophet Muhammad

sharia	religious law
sheesh mahal	room decorated in mirror work
sufi	mystic
sura	chapter (relating to the Qur'an)
tabhane	a part of an Ottoman mosque or külliya providing accommodation for travellers and dervishes
talar	columned hall or veranda
türbe	Seljuk and Ottoman mausoleum
ulama	learned authorities
umma	the Muslim community
zakat	alms-giving
zenana	in Indo-Islamic architecture, the women's quarters of a house or palace
ziyada	outer perimeter wall of a mosque

English architectural terms

arcuate	form of structure based on the arch
battered	inward sloping
chevron	v-shaped
corbel	a bracket, projecting stone, or series of projecting stones
drum	a circular wall supporting a dome
foil	a leaf shaped curve
exedra	a semicircular recess, niche or apse
hypostyle hall	hall of columns
impost	a block of stone usually with angled sides placed on top of a column under the capital
lambrequin arch	an arch with a soffit lined with pendants or muqarnas
loggia	an open gallery or balcony
lozenge	diamond-shaped pattern
oculus	circular window or opening
pendentive	a curved triangular section which fits a dome to a square bay
pier	square sectioned column or solid masonry support
soffit	the underside of an arch
spandrel	the triangular space formed by the springing of the arches
squinch	a triangular arch or niche placed diagonally or in corners in order to fit a dome or polygon to a square bay
trabeate	form of structure based on the column and beam
voussoirs	wedge-shaped stones which lock together to form an arch

TABLE OF DYNASTIES

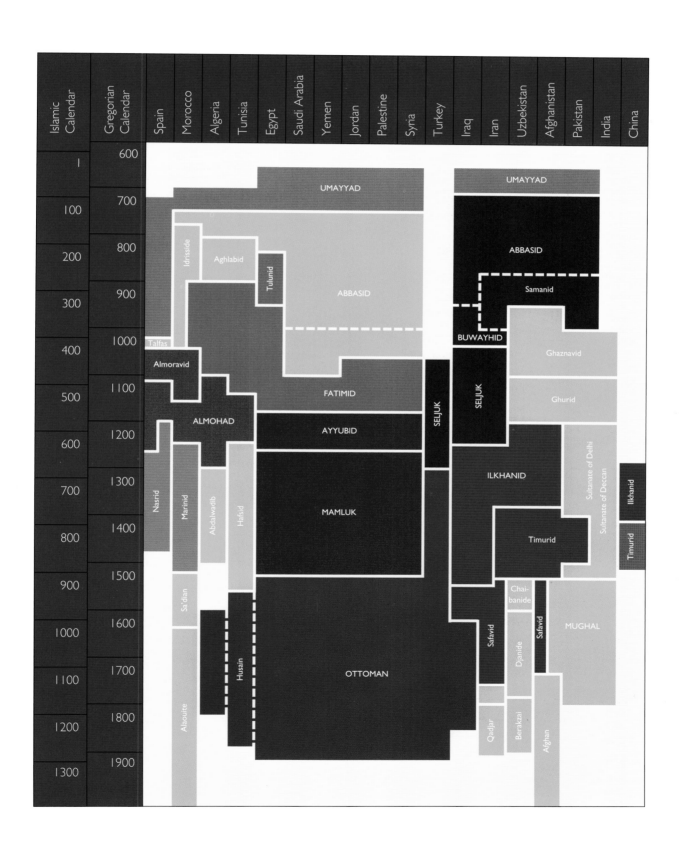

Islamic Calendar	Gregorian Calendar	Spain	Morocco	Algeria	Tunisia	Egypt	Saudi Arabia	Yemen	Jordan	Palestine	Syria	Turkey	Iraq	Iran	Uzbekistan	Afghanistan	Pakistan	India	China

SELECTED BIBLIOGRAPHY

Art and Architecture

ARDELAN, N., and Bahktiar, L. *The Sense of Unity: The Sufi Tradition in Persian Architecture* (University of Chicago Press, Chicago, 1971)

ARNOLD, T., *Painting in Islam* (Dover, New York, 1965)

BAHKTIAR, L., *Sufi Expressions of the Mystic Quest* (Thames & Hudson, London, 1976)

BARGEBUHR, F., *The Alhambra: A Cycle of Studies on the Eleventh Century in Moorish Spain* (Walter de Gruyter & Co., Berlin, 1968)

BASHAM, A.L. (ed.), *A Cultural History of India* (Clarendon Press, Oxford, 1975)

BEHRENS-ABOUSEIF, D., *Islamic Architecture in Cairo: An Introduction* (American University in Cairo Press, Cairo, 1989)

BLAIR, S., and Bloom, J., *The Art and Architecture of Islam 1250–1800* (Yale University Press, Pelican, New York and Harmondsworth, 1995)

BLUNT, W., *Isfahan: Pearl of Persia* (Elek, London, 1966)

BRYER, A., and Herrin, J. (eds), *Iconoclasm* (Centre for Byzantine Studies, Birmingham, 1977)

BURCKHARDT, T., *Art of Islam* (World of Islam Festival Publishing Co., London, 1976)

—*Moorish Culture in Spain* (Allen & Unwin, London, 1972)

BURNS, R., *Monuments of Syria: An Historical Guide* (I.B. Tauris, London & New York, 1992)

BYRON, R., *Road to Oxiana* (Jonathan Cape, London, 1937)

CASTEJON, R., *The Mosque of Cordoba* (Editorial Everest-Leon, Castejon-Leon, 1973)

CRESWELL, K.A.C., *A Short Account of Early Muslim Architecture* (Penguin, London, 1958)

DALRYMPLE, W., *From the Holy Mountain* (HarperCollins, London, 1987)

DANBY, MILES, *The Fires of Excellence: Spanish and Portuguese Oriental Architecture* (Garnet Publishing, Reading, 1996)

DAVIDSON, C.C., *Architecture Beyond Architecture: Creativity and Social Transformation in Islamic Cultures*; The Aga Khan Award for Architecture (Academy Editions, London, 1995)

DUNCAN, A., *The Noble Sanctuary* (Longman, London, 1972)

EL-SAID, I., and Parman, A., *Geometric Concepts in Islamic Art* (World of Islam Festival Publishing Co., London, 1976)

ETTINGHAUSEN, R., *Arab Painting* (Skira, New York, 1977)

ETTINGHAUSEN, R., and Grabar, O., *The Art and Architecture of Islam, 650–1250* (Yale University Press, New Haven, 1987)

FRISHMAN, M., and Hasan-Uddin Khan, *The Mosque: History, Architectural Development and Regional Diversity* (Thames & Hudson, London, 1994)

GIRAULT DE PRANGEY, P.J., *Impressions of Granada and the Alhambra* (Garnet Publishing, Reading, 1996)

GOODWIN, G., *A History of Ottoman Architecture* (Thames & Hudson, London, 1987)

GRABAR, O., *The Alhambra* (Allen Lane, London, 1978)

—*The Formation of Islamic Art* (Yale University Press, New Haven, 1973)

—*The Shape of the Holy: Early Islamic Jerusalem* (Princeton University Press, Princeton, 1996)

HAMBLY, G., *Cities of Mughal India* (Elek, London, 1968)

HAYES, J.R. (ed), *The Genius of Arab Civilisation: Source of Renaissance* (Phaidon, Oxford, 1978)

HILL, D., and Graber, O., *Islamic Architecture and its Decoration* (Faber & Faber, London, 1967)

HILLENBRAND, R., *Islamic Architecture: Form, Function and Meaning* (Edinburgh University Press, Edinburgh, 1994)

HOAG, J.D., *Islamic Architecture* (Faber & Faber/Electra, London and New York, 1975)

—*Western Islamic Architecture* (Studio Vista, London, 1968)

HOLOD, R., and Hasan-Uddin Khan, *The Mosque and the Modern World* (Thames & Hudson, London, 1997)

HUTT, A., *Iran 2* (Scorpion Publications, London, 1978)

—*North Africa* (Scorpion Publications, London, 1977)

IRWIN, R., *Islamic Art in Context* (Abrams, New York, 1997)

JAIRAZBHOY, R., *An Outline of Islamic Architecture* (Asia Publishing House, Bombay, 1972)

JONES, O., *The Grammar of Ornament* (Studio Editions, London, reprinted 1988), p. 57.

KOCH, E., *Mughal Architecture* (Prestel, Munich, 1991)

KURAN, A., *Sinan: The Grand Old Master of Ottoman Architecture* (ADA Press Publishers, Istanbul, 1987)

LAWRENCE, T.E., *Crusader Castles* (Immel Publishing, London, 1992)

LEHRMAN, J., *Earthly Paradise: Garden and Courtyard in Islam* (Thames & Hudson, London, 1980)

LEVEY, M., *The World of Ottoman Art* (Thames & Hudson, London, 1975)

LINGS, M., *The Quranic Art of Calligraphy and Illumination* (World of Islam Festival Publishing Co., London, 1976)

MICHELL, G. (ed.) *Architecture of the Islamic World* (Thames & Hudson, London, 1978)

MICHELL, G., and Martinelli, A., *The Royal Palaces of India* (Thames & Hudson, London, 1994)

OKASHA, S., *The Muslim Painter and the Divine* (Park Lane, London, 1981)

ONEY, G., *Ceramic Tiles in Islamic Architecture* (Ada Press, Istanbul, 1987)

PARKER, R., and Sabin, S., *A Practical Guide to the Islamic Monuments in Cairo* (American University in Cairo Press, Cairo, 1973)

POPE, A., *Persian Architecture* (George Braziller, New York, 1965)

PORTER, V., *Islamic Tiles* (British Museum Press, London, 1995)

ROGERS, M., *The Making of the Past: The Spread of Islam* (Elsevier/Phaidon, Oxford, 1975)

SORDO, E., *Moorish Spain* (Elek, London, 1963)

STIERLIN, H., *Islam Volume 1: Early Architecture from Baghdad to Cordoba* (Taschen, Cologne, 1996)

STRATTON, A., *Sinan* (Macmillan, London, 1972)

TALBOT RICE, D., *Constantinople* (Elek, London, 1965)

—*Islamic Art* (Thames & Hudson, London, 1965)

TALBOT RICE, T., *The Seljuks* (Thames & Hudson, London, 1961)

TILLOTSON, G.H.R., *Mughal India* (Penguin, London, 1990)

UNSAL.B., *Turkish Islamic Architecture* (Alec Tiranti, London, 1959)

VOGT-GOKLIN, U., *Living Architecture: Ottoman* (Osbourne, London, 1966)

WILBER, D., *The Architecture of Islamic Iran: The Il Khanid Period* (Greenwood Press, Connecticut, 1969)

History, Culture and Religion

COULSON, N.J., *A History of Islamic Law* (Edinburgh University Press, Edinburgh, 1964)

GUILLAUME, A., *Islam* (Pelican, London, 1964)

KRITZEK, J., *Anthology of Islamic Literature* (Pelican, London, 1964)

LEWIS, B., *The Arabs in History* (London, 1958)

NASR, S.H., *Ideals and Realities of Islam* (Unwin, London, 1979)

—*Islamic Science: An Illustrated Study* (World of Islam Festival Publishing Co., London, 1976)

NICHOLSON, R.A., *The Mystics of Islam* (Routledge & Kegan Paul, London, 1963)

RODINSON, M., *Mohammed* (Pelican, London, 1973)

SHAH, I., *The Sufis* (Jonathan Cape, London, 1971)

SPULER, B., *The Mongols in History* (Pall Mall Press, London, 1971)

TAMES, R., *Approaches to Islam* (John Murray, London, 1982)

WATT, M.W., *A History of Islamic Spain* (Edinburgh University Press, Edinburgh, 1965)

—*Islamic Philosophy and Theology* (Edinburgh University Press, Edinburgh, 1962)

—*The Majesty of Islamic Spain* (Sidgwick & Jackson, London, 1974)

—*Muhammad, Statesman and Prophet* (Oxford University Press, Oxford, 1961)

WILLIAMS, J.A., *Islam* (Prentice Hall, New Jersey, 1961)

ACKNOWLEDGEMENTS

The Publishers would like to thank the many people and picture libraries whose assistance and co-operation made this book possible.

ANDES PRESS AGENCY: © C. & D. Hill / Andes Press Agency p. 150 top and bottom; p. 168; p. 170; p. 171 left and right.

ANCIENT ART AND ARCHITECTURE COLLECTION: © Ronald Sheridan / Ancient Art and Architecture Collection p. 36 top; p. 57; p. 58 left; p. 59; p. 143 top; p. 192 top and bottom; p. 193 left; p. 194. © B. Norman / Ancient Art and Architecture Collection p. 130; p. 131; p. 201 right. © Chris Hellier / Ancient Art and Architecture Collection p. 149 top and bottom; p. 157; p. 169; p. 173; p. 175. © G. Tortoli / Ancient Art and Architecture Collection p. 158. © John King / Ancient Art and Architecture Collection p. 186 right. © Stephen Coyne / Ancient Art and Architecture Collection p. 223 top.

AXIOM: © Eitan Simanor / Axiom p. 28. © Chris Bradley / Axiom p. 29 top left and bottom left; p. 31. © Chris Coe / Axiom p. 51; p. 56. © James Morris / Axiom p. 62 top; p. 64; p. 66 left; p. 70 left and right; p. 72 bottom; p. 74 top and bottom; p. 76; p. 77; p. 116; p. 122 top; p. 124 right; p. 125 top and bottom; p. 126; p. 127; p. 132; p. 133; p. 134; p. 135. © Fredrik Arvidsson / Axiom p. 205 top; p. 207; p. 208; p. 210 bottom; p. 212; p. 214 left; p. 215; p. 216 top and bottom; p. 217; p. 221 left and bottom left; p. 223 bottom.

CHRIS BARTON: p. 3; p. 4; p. 35; p. 38; p. 62 bottom left; p. 93 bottom; p. 112 right; p. 118 top; p. 119 top; p. 120; p. 129; p. 147; p. 148 top and bottom; p. 174; p. 177.

THE BRIDGEMAN ART LIBRARY: p. 72 top.

THE BRITISH LIBRARY: © Oriental and India Office Collections p. 19.

CORBIS: © Angelo Hornak / Corbis p. 39; p. 71 bottom; p. 124 left; p. 214 right. © Nik Wheeler / Corbis p. 46; p. 47; p. 58 right. © Vanni Archive / Corbis p. 81. © K. M. Westermann / Corbis p. 71 top. © Christine Osborne / Corbis p. 117. © Wolfgang Kaehler / Corbis p. 138. © Roger Wood / Corbis p. 128; p. 181 top; p. 183; p. 187; p. 190; p. 196; p. 197; p. 205 bottom. © Adam Woolfitt / Corbis p. 152 bottom. © José F. Poblete / Corbis p. 159. © Michael Nicholson / Corbis p. 160 bottom. © Chris Hellier / Corbis p. 163 left. © David Samuel Robbins / Corbis p. 186 left; p. 189. © Brian Vikander / Corbis p. 188; p. 210 top.

SYLVIA CORDAIY PHOTO LIBRARY: © Chris North / Sylvia Cordaiy Photo Library p. 48.

SALMA SAMAR DAMLUJI: p. 91 left; p. 111 left and right; p. 112 left; p. 113 left.

EDIFICE: © Edifice / Darley p. 108 bottom right.

EGYPT: CAUGHT IN TIME, Colin Osman (Garnet Publishing 1997): p. 118 bottom.

NICK HOLROYD: p. 200; p. 201 left; p. 202 left and right; p. 203 top; p. 209; p. 213 top; p. 218 bottom left; p. 219; p. 220; p. 224; p. 225.

IMPRESSIONS OF GRANADA AND THE ALHAMBRA, Girault de Prangey (Garnet Publishing 1996): p. 101 top middle; p. 104 bottom left.

METROPOLITAN MUSEUM OF ART: p. 139.

JOHN MILES: p. 193 top right and bottom right.

THE NATIONAL GALLERY: © National Gallery Picture Library p. 160 top.

SAMARKAND: CAUGHT IN TIME, Sabir Kurbanov (Garnet Publishing 1993): p. 185.

PETER SANDERS: p. 33 top and bottom; p. 62 bottom right; p. 69; p. 82; p. 84 bottom left; p. 85 left; p. 86 right; p. 88; p. 96; p. 100 top left and top right; p. 103 bottom right; p. 110; p. 113 right.

SAUDI ARABIA: CAUGHT IN TIME 1861-1939, Badr El-Hage (Garnet Publishing 1997): p. 9.

TRAVEL INK: © Travel Ink / Brenda Kean p. 98 bottom. © Travel Ink / Ronald Badkin p. 103 top right; p. 222. © Travel Ink / Ian MacFadyen p. 218 top.

THE TRAVEL LIBRARY: © The Travel Library / R. Richardson p. 52; p. 102 bottom; p. 103 top left. © The Travel Library / Steve Outram p. 68. © The Travel Library / Peter Terry p. 93. © The Travel Library / Alan Bedding p. 165. © The Travel Library / Stuart Black p. 166.

MATTHEW WEINREB: p. 84 top; p. 87; p. 89 top and bottom; p. 100 bottom left; p. 101 bottom; p. 102 top; p. 104 top left and right; p. 106 left and right; p. 107; p. 108 top and bottom right.

WERNER FORUM ARCHIVE: p. 2; p. 53 left; p. 85 right; p. 91 right.

RICHARD YEOMANS: endpapers; p. 30; p. 36 bottom; p. 49; p. 53 right; p. 55; p. 65 top and bottom; p. 66 right; p. 119 bottom; p. 122 bottom; p. 145; p. 152 top; p. 182; p. 195; p. 221 right.

ALL PLANS AND ELEVATIONS © Garnet Publishing.

ALL MAPS © GEOprojects (UK) Ltd.

INDEX

Page numbers in *italics* refer to illustrations.